DYNAMICS OF SPIRITUAL LIFE

AN EVANGELICAL THEOLOGY OF RENEWAL

RICHARD F. LOVELACE

INTER-VARSITY PRESS
DOWNERS GROVE
ILLINOIS 60515

© 1979 by Inter-Varsity Christian Fellowship of the United States of America

InterVarsity Press is the book-publishing division of Inter-Varsity Christian Fellowship, a student movement active on campus at hundreds of universities, colleges and schools of nursing. For information about local and regional activities, write IVCF, 233 Langdon St., Madison, WI 53703.

Distributed in Canada through InterVarsity Press, 1875 Leslie St., Unit 10, Don Mills, Ontario M3B 2M5, Canada.

ISBN 0-87784-626-X
Library of Congress Catalog Card Number: 78-24757

Printed in the United States of America

Acknowledgment is made to the following for permission to reprint copyrighted material:
From the Revised Standard Version of the Bible, copyrighted 1946, 1952, © 1971, 1973. All quotations from the Scripture are from the Revised Standard Version unless otherwise noted.
From the New American Standard Bible, © The Lockman Foundation 1960, 1962, 1963, 1968, 1971, 1972, 1973, 1975.
The poem "Gratitude to the Unknown Instructors." Reprinted with permission of Macmillan Publishing Co., Inc. from Collected Poems by William Butler Yeats. Copyright 1933 by Macmillan Publishing Co., Inc., renewed 1961 by Bertha Georgie Yeats.
From Things to Come by Herman Kahn and B. Bruce-Briggs. Reprinted with permission of Macmillan Publishing Co., Inc. Copyright © 1972 by the Hudson Institute, Inc.
From "Stars, I have seen them fall" from The Collected Poems of A. E. Housman. Copyright 1936 by Barclays Bank Ltd. Copyright © 1964 by Robert E. Symons. Reprinted by permission of Holt, Rinehart and Winston, Publishers, The Society of Authors as the literary representative of the Estate of A. E. Housman, and Jonathan Cape Ltd., publishers of A. E. Housman's Collected Poems.
From the lyrics to "Why Don't You Look into Jesus," from the album, Only Visiting This Planet, Street Level Records. Reprinted with permission of Solid Rock Records—A Division of Solid Rock, Inc.
The chart on the Dynamics of Spiritual Life is adapted from Homosexuality and the Church. Copyright © 1978 by Richard F. Lovelace. Published by Fleming H. Revell Company. Used by permission.
Chapter seven is a revised version of "The Sanctification Gap," which first appeared in Theology Today (January 1973) and is used with permission.
Chapter nine is a revised version of "Live Orthodoxy," which first appeared in Encounter (Autumn 1974) and is used with permission.

19	18	17	16	15	14	13	12	11	10	9	8	7	6	5	4	3
95	94	93	92	91	90	89	88	87	86	85	84	83	82	81		

PREFACE

THIS WORK IS A MANUAL OF spiritual theology, a discipline combining the history and the theology of Christian experience.
Catholic Christians have long recognized the existence and
central importance of this study, and it is time that Protestants realized that they share with Catholics a deep interest
and a rich heritage in Christian spirituality.[1]

The practical occasion for the writing of this work is the
emergence of a general spiritual awakening in America
during the 1970s, closely associated with the Evangelical and
Charismatic movements but ranging far beyond these in
its overall impact. For several decades I have studied the
history and theology of religious awakenings against the
background of the general history of Christian experience.
In doing so I have sought to isolate the main streams of
spiritual vitality which have flowed through the church's
history and to determine the principles which govern the

force of these. Gradually I have come to formulate a general theory of individual and corporate spiritual health. Part of my intention in publishing this manual through a channel specializing in college ministry is to help orient the large numbers of young converts who are now emerging from our campuses, as I did in the 1950s, with no religious background to help them understand the spiritual movement of which they are a part. These new Christians have few theologically complete and balanced guides to instruct them in how to grow and maintain their fellowship with God.

At another level, this work offers a general plan for reformation and renewal in the Christian church. It is in many respects an updating of Philipp Spener's *Pia Desideria* (1675), which articulated Spener's longing for reformation in the supposedly reformed Lutheran church.[2] I believe, however, that reformation and renewal are already in motion, as they were when Jonathan Edwards began his written efforts to sift and tune the Great Awakening, to interpret its meaning to its enemies and to correct the weaknesses among its friends. Edwards's theology of revival is thus another important prototype for this book and a source of wisdom on which I have constantly drawn in its composition.[3]

Spirituality is in many ways treated as the neglected stepchild of the Christian movement. It is often reduced to an emotional frosting spread over the surface of other parts of Christianity which are considered more substantial and important, such as the maintenance of sound doctrine, correct social engagement or institutional policy. But it is seldom recognized to be the indispensable foundation without which all of these are powerless and fall into decay. In parts of the church a fairly shallow spirituality is the bread and butter of daily experience, but it is almost invisible as a matter of serious concern among church leaders because it is either taken for granted or unconsciously held in contempt. Other parts of the church have developed an intricate machinery for spiritual perfection which intimidates the laity and most of the leaders. Other sectors have neglected a program of spiritual development because they have concluded that it is either too hard or not worth doing. In many of these circles spiritual theology, if its existence is recognized at all, is likely to be dismissed as "mere pietism."

This reveals a profound misunderstanding of the historic identity of Pietism and Puritanism, the two theological siblings which energized Protestant development in evangelistic mission and social action in the seventeenth and eighteenth centuries. Both of these movements had come to recognize that reforming doctrines and institutions in the church was futile unless people's lives were reformed and revitalized. In this sense it is clear that the Bible is a "pietist" manifesto, although it condemns the emotional introversion of some later forms of Pietism. Its message constantly insists that we must watch over our hearts with all diligence, for out of them flow the springs of life (Prov. 4:23). It tells us that the greatest eloquence, theological knowledge and dedication to social charity are nothing without love (1 Cor. 13:1-3). Agape is not a mere emotional by-product of action but a supernatural outpouring of the grace of God infusing all our behavior with the life of Christ. It is the love of God which "has been poured out within our hearts through the Holy Spirit who was given to us" (Rom. 5:5 NASB). This kind of love, as Augustine never tired of insisting, is the pivotal factor in the church's life.

The goal toward which many Christians in both the Catholic and Protestant communions are striving today is ecclesia reformata semper reformanda, a reformed church always reforming. The Puritans and Pietists rediscovered a truth which is clear in the Augustinian tradition: the precondition of perpetual reformation is the spiritual revitalization of the church. Luther had understood this; he traced many of the distortions arising in the church's life during its long history to the loss of the doctrine of justification by faith, and he warned that if this were lost again all those distortions would reappear.[4] What he may not have fully realized was that the understanding of justification was one of a complex of factors determining spiritual vitality, and that if others of these were missing or unarticulated in the church's experience—such as the deep conviction of God's holiness and human need which drove Luther himself toward sanctification—then, even while the church held to justification by faith alone, it would suffer distortion in other dimensions.

The German Pietists balanced Luther's stress on justification with a stronger development of his teaching on sanctification and reasserted his conviction that the life of the church was critically dependent on the spiritual condition of its people. A. W. Boehm, the ecumenical agent of Halle Pietism in London, stated this with great clarity. He dismissed much activity in the church as a lifeless product of human conditioning:

> Faith, as it is now in Vogue, signifieth no more than a stiff adhering to a certain Sect or Denomination of Men, and a zealous Defence of such particular Tenets as have been received and approved of by that Party. All the Ingredients of such a Faith, are nothing but humane Education, Custom, Tradition, Perswasion, Conversation and the like. The Zeal which goeth along with it, is the Product of Self-love, and of corrupt Reason, the two great Framers of Sects and Party-Notions.[5]

Boehm saw most of the church evading the issues of personal reformation and renewal, the purging of self-love and the purifying of the mind, which were paramount in the New Testament:

> True Christianity, according to its intrinsick Constitution, is an active, lively, strong, vigorous Principle, seated in the inmost Center of the Soul, and swaying by its Dictates all the Actions that proceed from it: But the Chris-

tianity now in Vogue, hardly toucheth the Heart at all. . . . *True Christianity* is a Creation of God. But the Advocates of false Christianity, do not rise *above themselves*, but spin all their religious Duties, as it were, out of their own Bowels. There is nothing of Heaven in it; nothing of Grace; nothing of the divine Nature.[6]

The emphasis in much of the church's life was therefore *eccentric*, peripheral to the central concern of the gospel:

Another Character of *True Christianity* is, to be principally concerned with the *Essentials* and *Substantials* of Religion: Such as is the great Work of *Faith* and of the *New Birth*, with the Rest of Christian Virtues that freely accompany it. . . . But the *False Christian* is chiefly, if not only busie about the ceremonious Part, and some *accessory* and *circumstantial* Points. He bringeth forth every Age, if not every Year, new Schemes, new Models, new Projects of Religion. He mouldeth it one Time into this, and again at other Times into another Form, according as the Humor of the Age, and the Interest of Men worketh, which with him hath the greatest Influence in Affairs of Religion. And at this rate, alas! the *Substance* of Christianity lieth neglected, in the midst of so many *Schemes*, framed under Pretence to support it![7]

Boehm, like his mentors Spener and August Hermann Francke, predicted that the church would eventually be freed from being blown out of shape by these winds of doctrine when it would center its concern on the practice and principles of godliness:

There will be a Time, when the Church of Christ will come up from the Wilderness of various Sects, Parties, Nations, Languages, Forms, and Ways of Worship, nay of Crosses and Afflictions, *leaning upon her Beloved*, and in his Power bidding Defiance to all her Enemies. Then shall that Church which now doth but look forth as the Morning in its Dawn, after a continual Growth in Strength and Beauty, appear *Terrible as an Army with Banners*; but terrible to those only that despised her whilst she was in her Minority, and would not have her Beloved to reign over them.[8]

The great prophets and pioneers of evangelical renewal who looked forward to this ultimate unveiling of the church's grandeur constantly stressed that this goal could only be attained through a strategy of spiritual revitalization combined with doctrinal and structural reformation. I hold this conviction also. The instruments through which God works in the church are human beings. If our hearts and minds are not properly transformed, we are like musicians playing untuned instruments, or engineers working with broken and ill-programmed computers. The attunement of the heart is essential to the outflow of grace. This is not to emphasize faith and experience over works, thought and social action. We must aim at building the structures of God's kingdom but recognize that we will only create these through the transformation of our experience. Concentration on reformation without revival leads to skins without wine; concentration on revival without reformation soon loses the wine for want of skins.

A number of problems which have troubled the church in this century are only solvable if we return to the vital core of biblical teaching dealing with Christian experience, just as the uneasy struggles in the late medieval church could only be resolved when Luther struck through to their spiritual root in his doctrine of justification. There are many lines of estrangement in the modern church which are readily dissolved by the application of a balanced understanding of spiritual dynamics. For one thing, different groups within the church are at odds with one another because their models of the Christian life, its beginnings and its fullness, are so diverse. One group of genuine believers can never remember a conscious conversion to faith in Christ; another insists that a datable experience of being "born again" is essential; a third says that a second distinct experience of "the baptism of the Holy Spirit" is necessary for Christian maturity. When we "test the spirits" in the lives of representatives among these groups, we often find an equal level of spiritual vitality—or deadness!—in each sector. The Christian life is being offered in diverse packages, but what is inside is the same—newness of life in Christ. Nonetheless, the different groups enjoying this life are readily offended by one another's packages. One man's piety is often another man's poison.

What is needed to reconcile these models with one another is a "unified field theory" of spirituality. As Newtonian physics is a valid special case within Einsteinian relativity, so each of these models expresses valid and genuine experience, but only a broader theory of spirituality can show why each model works, or fails to work in some instances.

Several other divisions in the church are soluble on this basis: the uneasiness between relational theologians and those who stress adherence to orthodox conceptual truth, and particularly the estrangement between social activists and those concerned for evangelism and spiritual nurture. Some popular and fruitful Protestant models of spirituality have made little effort to include bridges between interior spiritual development and responsible engagement with society and culture. (I am thinking here of some components in the Keswick stream and Watchman Nee.) But I have earnestly tried in what follows to sketch a model of integral spirituality which moves easily between these poles of Christian consciousness. I might add that I was initially converted to Christianity from atheism through reading Thomas Merton's Seven Storey Mountain and that my effort here (which in so many other ways parallels Merton's) strives in the same direction he was traveling in his later years.

One of the greatest handicaps this book must fight is the reader's conviction that he or she already knows what it says because it touches on familiar territory (although for many Christians there are parts of it which will be as strange as the wind from other planets, however commonplace in classical spiritual theology). I would ask you to keep in mind that it is as important to understand the relations between the various dynamics as it is to understand the dynamics themselves. Also keep in mind that the analysis in this work of the negative factors in Christian experience—the familiar triad of the world, the flesh and the devil—attempts to break new ground, and that every other element in the analysis shows up in a new light through its relationship to them. Although part of the church pays lip service to the reality of sin and worldliness and even demonic agents, it seems to me that much of the church's warfare today is fought by blindfolded soldiers who cannot see the forces ranged against them, who are buffeted by invisible opponents and respond by striking one another.

This work also tries to begin constructing a bridge between classical pastoral theology and the new forms of pastoral psychology. A number of Christian psychologists today are searching eagerly for ways to integrate biblical pastoral counseling and the new insights of psychology without reducing either to the other. It is my observation that most psychologists begin to build their bridge aiming broadside at the whole of systematic theology, instead of focusing on the dynamics of spiritual life which must be the main point of contact on the theological side of the stream. In chapter six, "The Renewal of the Local Congregation," I have tried to help psychologists in the integration process.

The structure of the book is important. Part I, comprising the first five chapters, surveys the history of awakenings since the Reformation and analyzes the elements of vitality within them that seem to have been particularly marked by the Spirit's tongues of flame. Part II re-examines some of these elements in greater depth and enlarges on their significance for reformation and renewal in the church of the future. The reason this work is both a manual for individual spiritual growth and also a program for reformation and renewal in the church will become increasingly apparent as the book goes on. Individual and corporate spiritual vitality are coinherent; it is impossible to grow to full stature as an individual while separated from smaller and larger groups in the church, nor can the body grow without the renewing of its members.

Some readers will be surprised that I have not devoted more time to techniques and regimens of spiritual development: programs of meditation, fasting, vocal and mental prayer, the use of diaries, spiritual directors and the intricate ladders by which the believer is assumed to climb from acquired to infused contemplation. I have no bias against these aids, and I deeply respect the great saints of the church who have found them helpful. But they can intimidate those who are young in the faith, and my intention here has been to construct "a little Rule for beginners," as Benedict would say.[9]

Ladders are always intimidating, and it is my suspicion that Christians should always assume that they start each day at the top of the ladder in contact with God and renew this assumption whenever they appear to have slipped a rung. The Triple Way of classical mysticism, which moves from the stage of cleansing one's life through illumination toward union with God, seems to reverse the biblical order, which starts from union with Christ claimed by faith, leading to the illumination of the Holy Spirit and consequent cleansing through the process of sanctification. Doubtless there is a valid place for both models in promoting Christian experience—some Christians need to work at one end of the series, some at the other—but it is my assumption that growth in *faith* is the root of all spiritual growth and is prior to all disciplines of works. True spirituality is not a superhuman religiosity; it is simply true humanity released from bondage to sin and renewed by the Holy Spirit. This is given to us as we grasp by faith the full content of Christ's redemptive work: freedom from the guilt and power of sin, and newness of life through the indwelling and outpouring of his Spirit. Readers who move through this book appropriating by faith all of the provisions of redemption which it describes will have a better perspective on their need for the additional help of techniques and disciplines.

Already it must be apparent to the reader that this is spiritual theology written by a Protestant, and an Evangelical Protestant at that. I must be candid in admitting that this is the particular tribe in Israel which has nurtured my understanding. On the other hand, my constant effort has been to grow more and more into a mere biblical catholic Christian —that is only good strategy, for when one is persecuted under one label, one can always flee to another—and I have made a deliberate effort to write this work with a universal audience in mind. Research in spiritual theology has taken me in and out of many other tribes in Catholic, Protestant and Jewish spirituality, and I have tried to remember the knack of speaking to these. It is my hope that this book can be picked up by a Roman Catholic in the Third World, or a Palestinian Jew who is intrigued by what is going on among Christians, without generating the feeling of being a stranger at a party. Some of the later chapters (ten and eleven) are more deliberately written with Evangelicals in mind, mostly because they address themselves to reforms which must be made in that sector of the church. If you have a clearly formed view in another theological tradition, please be patient with the mobile sculpture I have built from parts borrowed from Augustine, Luther, Calvin, Wesley and Edwards. Not every part of it is going to satisfy everyone. But you must feel free to detach pieces which annoy you and to try substituting analogous structures from your own tradition. Remember that genuine experience of Christ has generated several different theological languages during the church's history. Because of human limitations and the grandeur of the subject, no single language has been adequate to convey this. Reporters on Christian experience who describe it in a language strange to us may only be viewing the same thing from another perspective. We need to listen with care and sensitivity for the distinctive notes of true Christianity expressed in unfamiliar patterns.

Since Evangelical Protestantism has been so intimately involved in the historical track of spiritual awakenings, I have had to talk about this movement often enough to make Christians in other traditions uncomfortable. For the sake of clarity, politeness and truth, I have capitalized the word *Evangelical* when it refers to a particular subculture, the twentieth-century descendants of American revivalism and Fundamentalism; it is an obvious injustice to deny the adjective *evangelical* to Christians in other sectors of the church who are embracing and teaching the heart of the evangel although differing in their understanding of Scripture. ("Charismatic" Christians probably need to adopt some such maneuver also.) When *evangelical* is used to refer to Christians during the period from the Reformation through the nineteenth century, it designates those who stand in the tradition of Protestant live orthodoxy defined in what follows. There is surely an evangelical impulse behind many spiritual currents within the Catholic tradition which flow from Teresa of Avila, John of the Cross, Berulle, Condren and many others in more recent years; but this is material for another book. The adjective in the subtitle of this one should be read as uncapitalized.

It may be helpful for me to clarify the meaning of several other important terms as they have been used in this work. *Spiritual* (as in *spiritual life, spiritual gifts*) usually means *deriving from the Holy Spirit*, which is its normal significance in Scripture. *Renewal, revival* and *awakening* trace back to biblical metaphors for the infusion of spiritual life in Christian experience by the Holy Spirit (see Rom. 6:4; 8:2-11; Eph. 1:17-23; 3:14-19; 5:14). Usually they are used synonymously for broad-scale movements of the Holy Spirit's work in renewing spiritual vitality in the church and in fostering its expansion in mission and evangelism. Reformation refers to the purifying of doctrine and structures in the church, but implies also a component of spiritual revitalization. Renewal is sometimes used to encompass revival and reformation, and also to denote aggiornamento, the updating of the church leading to new engagement with the surrounding world. Mysticism, wherever it is viewed positively in this work, is a nontechnical term denoting movements stressing Christian experience and encounter with God, particularly within the central Puritan stream and the practical tradition of Bernard of Clairvaux, John Tauler and the Friends of God, The Imitation of Christ, Teresa and John of the Cross.[10] The speculative mysticism which derives from Plotinus and the Pseudo-Dionysius, and which perhaps culminates in Meister Eckhardt, is not, in my view, a positive Christian development. In no case does my positive response to any exemplar of Catholic practical mysticism imply blanket theological approval; it simply recognizes the apparent reality of genuine experience of the Holy Spirit.

DYNAMICS OF RENEWAL

PART I

JONATHAN EDWARDS AND THE JESUS MOVEMENT

1

THE UNITED STATES HAS JUST celebrated its two hundredth anniversary. This is an appropriate time for a book on the reviving of the Christian church in this country and in the Western world, but it does not seem at first to be an auspicious one. America and the rest of Western culture now seem to be more on the edge of dissolution than on the point of renewal. A cloud of irony hangs over our festivities. The situation in this country seems to call for a jeremiad, not a celebration. The worst scandal in our government's history still lingers in our memories. Race prejudice, latent under the surface of political campaigns, seems intensified by our very efforts to correct it. The crime rate is outstripping police restraint and turning private surveillance into a growth sector. Pornography and violence fill the media, and a host of other social problems run in counterpoint with an uncertain economy.

In the rest of Western culture the situation is no less grave. Economic problems which are only painful in America are critical elsewhere. The open market of ideas which has sometimes accompanied free enterprise is yielding to closed totalitarian systems of the right and left in country after country. The Western civilization rooted in Christianity is increasingly faced with Arnold Toynbee's rephrasing of Nicodemus's question, "Can a man be born again when he is old?"

Of course, as Augustine pointed out, a civilization can decline and fall without implicating or affecting the Christian church. The City of Man cannot blame the City of God for its own decay, and the church may well prosper at the same time that other powers fail. But Toynbee and other historians have argued that the fate of civilizations reflects the strength of the religious ethos around which they are built, and observers during this century both within and outside the church have expressed doubts about the savor of its salt.

And yet there have been stirrings of new life within the church since the middle of this century. The Second Vatican Council's search for *aggiornamento*, the updating and renewing of the church's witness in the modern world, struck a note that was already being sounded in other parts of professing Christendom. That note has continued to echo in a variety of movements, books and programs dealing with church renewal that have emerged during the last decade. Some of these contradict one another. One person's updating of the gospel is another's heresy. But many of these currents complement and reinforce one another. The whole work of renewing the Christian church, if it is accomplished in any measure in this century, will be the product of many of these forces acting and interacting.[1]

This book originates in reflection on one of these renewal sectors, the Evangelical movement. This movement has a unique theological contribution to bring to the whole of Christ's body. But before it can release its gift most fully to the rest of the church it needs conceptual development.

Roots of the Evangelical Movement

The Evangelical movement has the deepest historical roots of any contemporary renewal movement. Its theological origins begin with the Protestant Reformation of the sixteenth century, but its spiritual lineage traces back even further into the mystical and ascetic countercultures of the medieval and early church through Bernard, Anselm, Augustine, Athanasius and Irenaeus. Since the Reformation it has enjoyed periodic seasons of growth and influence within Protestantism, striving to conserve and propagate the theology of grace in periods when legalism and secularism have surrounded and invaded the church. In the Great Awakening of the eighteenth century it united Protestants of all denominations into an international, ecumenical renewal movement centered on the experiential application of live Reformation orthodoxy. In the Second Awakening at the beginning of the nineteenth century, it consolidated and augmented the efforts of earlier evangelicals toward an expanding world missionary witness and launched many impressive programs of social reform including the abolition of slavery. In the latter half of the nineteenth century "revivalism" was still a dominant voice in the leadership of most American churches.

It was at this point that American evangelicalism began to suffer one of those periods of attenuation and loss of identity which afflict every part of the church from time to time. Revivalism, redefined now as a movement centered on mass evangelism rather than as a comprehensive renewal movement affecting the whole church and the surrounding culture, became Fundamentalism, a desperate attempt to hold on to the consensus of Reformation orthodoxy and to enforce it politically within the major denominations. This effort failed. The evangelical stream divided, and the components involved in its original wholeness were distributed in varying combinations among "liberals," "moderates" and "conservatives." For almost a generation conservative Fundamentalism became a minority protest movement, viewed by the rest of the church as a vestigial remnant of folk religion destined to die out as the century progressed.

But it did not die out. Instead, it went into enclaves of pastoral and educational resistance and sought to consolidate its position. It developed scholars who began to make tentative efforts toward the recovery of the original evangelical synthesis. In midcentury it developed an ecumenical council, the National Association of Evangelicals, and rallied its troops around a popular leader, the mass evangelist Billy Graham. A wave of growth followed in the next several decades which was readily dismissed by the surrounding culture and much of the church as a resurgence of civil religion but which added converts, leaders and new organizations with a vigorous outreach. The church and the surrounding culture learned new ways to adjust to the growing movement, to file it under older categories, to tolerate it and perhaps to immunize themselves against it. And then in the early 1970s popular Evangelicalism seemed to make another quantum leap which brought it under new surveillance in the media in what was called the Jesus movement, an explosion of Christianity in the midst of a new societal frontier formed by the mutating youth culture of America.

The Jesus Movement and Contemporary Signs of Renewal
From the perspective of the late seventies it is easy to dismiss the Jesus movement as a creation of the media, another ephemeral surge of piety magnified out of proportion. Newspaper and periodical coverage of the movement, which first enlarged to the point of national visibility in the spring of 1971, has considerably diminished. Much of the remaining commentary has been particularly concerned with problematic features of the movement, such as the ideological programming of converts and the subsequent efforts of their dis-

tressed parents to have them kidnaped and deprogrammed.

Critics of the Jesus people have included not only "liberals" upset by Neo-Fundamentalism but also Evangelical spokesmen who have attacked the shallow theology and sensational tactics of the movement's leaders and vigorously repudiated its claims to be the onset of a major spiritual awakening.[2] Critics of the movement on the college scene have complained of emotional "crashing" on the part of converts unable to maintain the spiritual "high" promised them by evangelists. At the same time these critics have observed other students successfully shielding themselves from Christianity by dismissing it as a preoccupation of "Jesus freaks." The dampening of social activism by premillennial pessimism and absorption in charismatic phenomena has been another target for criticism. It might appear that the Jesus movement was just another fad among the youth culture, whose fashions in drugs and lifestyles are notoriously migratory, and that the movement has lost its energy or mutated into new forms.

This kind of analysis, however, is partially a function of the way the onlooker defines terms. If "Jesus movement" means the fundamentalist missionary effort to reach the counterculture, then by definition it must have dissipated. The counterculture itself has dissolved into the hills and farmlands of America. Those who go searching for it in local concentrations within the cities find that it has vanished like a school of sounding fish. Since so many street people have left the urban centers in search of agrarian utopias, it is naturally hard to go on producing street Christians. Among those already converted, the countercultural lifestyle may be undergoing transformation: the three-hundred-odd communes which used to exist on the West Coast have been considerably reduced in number as young converts get organized and move toward integration with ordinary society.

But the mission to the counterculture may be only one component of the phenomenon which surfaced in the early seventies. One of the initial journalistic surveys of the movement divided it into three sectors: converted street people, college students reached by several ministries of campus evangelism and the Catholic pentecostals.[3] This analysis reduces the movement to two major sectors: a revival among the youth culture in general, embracing both the "straights" and the "freaks," and another area of renewal involving the Charismatic movement both within the major Protestant denominations and in the Catholic Church.

Even this typology, however, is not ample enough to include all the segments of the body of Christ which are showing signs of new life. Several kinds of cross-denominational small group meetings among lay people are proliferating rapidly: ecumenical Bible-study groups among neighborhood women and prayer support-groups among businessmen and government leaders. On the ministerial level, there is a new openness toward personal spirituality among many non-Evangelical scholars and intense interest among mainline seminary leaders in the spiritual formation of students.[4] Leaders of American Christianity who have been indifferent or negative toward Evangelicalism in the past are now approaching it with new respect, and Evangelicals are making new efforts to interpret their position and tradition to the rest of the church.

It seems at times that some measure of evangelical renewal is occurring everywhere in American Christianity—except perhaps in the comfortable pews of the Middle-American church. The resulting tableau is like Elijah's altar before the fire had fully taken hold: there are burning areas in the tinder all around the drenched logs, but those have not yet ignited. This underlines the fact that the Jesus movement was so named, not primarily because it involved a renewed emphasis on Christ or Christology, but because it has ostensibly directed attention away from the Christianity of the institutional church—a rather dubious asset for the missionary—and toward the person and teaching of Christ, which constitute an indestructible trump card.

And yet there are signs that the central mass of institutional Christianity is also on the verge of igniting. Objective observers and church administrators have come to agree that denominations and local congregations which are "conservative"—a problematic word, but one which in most instances seems to have some reference to Evangelical beliefs —are growing.[5] A recent Lilly Foundation study on readiness for ministry indicates that the kind of minister that local churches are most eager to hire is the candidate with the most Evangelical profile, and ministerial dossiers are growing more "conservative" as a result.[6] The emergence of the "God-issue" in the 1976 presidential campaign in connection with candidates Carter and Ford, both of whom can be classified as Evangelical Christians, is another straw in the wind. There seems to be a growing mood among the American people of revulsion at the corruption which has been exposed at every level of national life and increasing resistance to the comparatively small elite of secular humanist leaders who have been our cultural bellwethers.

It is just at this point, however, that critics can argue that what is taking shape is fundamentally a nonreligious cultural backlash, a massive reactionary movement which is the product of a "future shock" generated by too much rapid social change. A similar line of argument has already been applied to the Jesus movement, interpreting it simply as another manifestation of the antirational mysticism at the heart of the counterculture's reaction against technology, somewhat akin to the occult revival. Undoubtedly there are elements of truth in this analysis. Many of those in Middle America who are moving in a conservative direction are reacting against liberal social activism. Driven by nostalgia for less complicated days, they are seeking a haven of private spirituality. Large-scale social movements are never easily reduced to simple spiritual explanations. On the other hand, large-scale religious movements such as the Reformation have often involved socioeconomic causes as part of their internal workings. This does not invalidate or explain away their components of genuine spiritual motivation.

In order to discern whether or not the present situation is moving toward the status and dimensions of a religious awakening, it will be helpful at this point to review the connection of Evangelicalism with previous cycles of spiritual awakening in the church. As I have already intimated, the Evangelical movement today can be closely correlated with such phenomena in the past.

Earlier Renewal Movements

As early as the Montanist movement of the second century, the concept of decline and renewal in the church appears. The followers of Montanus were convinced that the Christian movement of their time had lost the spirituality and the supernatural gifts of the first-century church, but their sectarian rigor and their erroneous prophecy of the imminent return of Christ probably helped to polarize the rest of the church toward the assumption that it was immune to decline. Augustine's treatment of history tended to confirm this position, since it contrasted the stability of the City of God with the cyclical, Sisyphean careers of human empires. Augustine himself, however, was part of an ascetic reformation movement which sought to challenge the post-Constantinian church to shed its conformity to the world. Monastic revival movements continued to protest decline in the church—and to exemplify that decline once their prime was past—into the High Middle Ages.

In the twelfth century, Joachim of Fiore proposed a typology of history which articulated the deep popular longing for spiritual renewal in the church. The people of God, he said, have experienced the imperfect life of the Age of the Father (the Old Testament era), and they have endured a less than perfect existence in the Age of the Son (the era of the Catholic Church). But now they can look forward to the imminent Age of the Spirit in which the declining church will be transformed and revived, the Holy Spirit will be poured out upon her people, and the everlasting gospel will be proclaimed to the ends of the earth. The Joachimite theology of history was rapidly condemned by the church as heretical, but the hope which it expressed continued to flow in half-hidden streams of popular expectation until the Reformation of the sixteenth century.[7]

Most of the forces which prepared for the Reformation were already latent in the Western historical situation in the century after Joachim taught. The nobility in the rising nation-states had become restless under the financial and political power claimed for the church under a sort of papal colonialism, so that there were increasing local incentives to rebel against the Catholic system. The southern renaissance was declaring intellectual independence from the control of Catholic doctrine, and its northern counterpart was producing Christian humanists with a critical approach to history and a desire to clear away the rubble produced by the decay of learning. These humanists wanted to penetrate to the original sources of truth, including the text of Scripture.

By the late fourteenth century popular mystical movements were denouncing indulgences and intimating that the pope was Antichrist, and Wyclif was asserting the supreme authority of Scripture and attacking the cult of saints, relics, pilgrimages, indulgences and the treasury of merit. A century later, on the eve of the Reformation, most of these emphases had become common assumptions of Catholic humanists like Erasmus and Thomas More, and yet their criticism did very little to alter the abuses in the system.[8]

The spiritual, political and economic situation in Europe was like a carefully built bonfire waiting to be lit, but the torch that set it burning was the spiritual crisis of Martin Luther. His struggle led eventually to the rediscovery of the doctrine of justification by faith. It can be argued that the nontheological forces which supported Luther's reformation simply reached a critical level of strength at the same time Luther made his discovery. But what made the Reformation catch fire as an international movement of new life within the church was the reduplication of Luther's experience and insight among a number of Christian humanists who found this doctrine the key to their spiritual release and to their conceptual understanding of the needs in Western Christendom. Luther himself felt that the perceptions of the radical depth of sin and the sovereignty of grace which were inherent in the doctrine were the essential key to reforming the problems which earlier critics had only been able to uncover. The inability of conservative reformers like Erasmus to perceive this occasioned Luther's break with them.[9]

Few modern Christians can read the works of the Reformers and doubt that what was happening in the Reformation was a genuine work of spiritual renewal, as well as a traumatic adjustment of doctrines, practices and systems of political control within Western Christianity. New spiritual life broke out in the church wherever Luther's doctrine penetrated. There were, however, limits to its penetration. It captured intellectual and spiritual leaders and their territories, but it did not always revive the great masses of the laity in any depth and number.

Subsequent generations of Protestants were capable of turning Luther's teaching into dead orthodoxy, and this seems to have happened especially in the Lutheran sector. Here a one-sided emphasis on justification, along with the resulting neglect of sanctification and the uses of the law, often produced what Bonhoeffer has bitingly called "cheap grace." Luther had warned against this abuse of his doctrine, and Calvin had included in his *Institutes* a carefully balanced treatment of sanctification. But by the end of the sixteenth century, Protestants in both the Lutheran and Reformed spheres were referring to the "half-reformation" which had reformed their doctrines but not their lives, and were seeking for a new revitalization of the church.

The pre-Pietism of Johann Arndt and the early Puritanism which took hold in England, Holland and America retained the Reformation emphasis on justification but added to it a strong emphasis on sanctification and particularly regeneration, the spiritual rebirth of the converted Christian. These two movements, Puritanism and Pietism, were undoubtedly powerful religious awakenings which penetrated the church extensively, reaching both leaders and lay people. Cotton Mather looked upon the late seventeenth-century Pietism of Philipp Spener and A. H. Francke as a revival powerful enough to inaugurate the millennium, and Jonathan Edwards mentions a number of previous examples of awakenings among the Puritans.[10] While the Puritan attempt to ward off cheap grace led to an admixture of legalism which has darkened the movement's image among later generations, recent historians have defended the spiritual vitality at the heart of Puritanism and have recognized its first flowering as a renewal of the Protestant impulse.

The First Great Awakening
Most church historians, however, have preferred to speak only of two major evangelical awakenings after the Reformation. The first of these is usually designated the "Great Awakening" in its American phase, and the "Evangelical Revival" in the English context, while the remarkable revival of continental Pietism under Count Ludwig von Zinzendorf during the same period is often neglected except for its effect on John Wesley. Actually all three of these concurrent renewal movements should be viewed as parts of one major evangelical revival which can be termed the "First Great Awakening," since they were linked together both by common emphases and by many instances of intercommunication and reciprocal causation.

The beginnings of this awakening can be traced to the decade of the 1720s, a time when the interests of Puritanism had reached a low point both in England and America after decades of steady decline, and when even the Pietism of Halle seemed to have the wind out of its sails. In America Christians had been praying since the late seventeenth century for an effusion of the Holy Spirit on the rising generations of their listless and unconverted children. In 1727 Theodore Frelinghuysen's Dutch Reformed church in New Jersey seemed to experience a new surge of vitality as the pastor "fenced the table" in administering communion, insisting on evidence that his parishioners had experienced the regenerating power of godliness and were not merely going through a form in their church life.

That same year, in Germany, another phase of the awakening was getting under way. One of the graduates of A. H. Francke's university at Halle, Count Ludwig von Zinzendorf, had established on his estate a community of refugees including Moravians, Reformed and Catholics, and was seeking to forge this heterogeneous group into an instrument for promoting renewal in the church. He had given the community the name Herrnhut, "the Lord's watch," after a passage in Isaiah which seemed to sum up the Puritan and Pietist longing for continuing renewal and reformation in the Christian movement:

For Zion's sake I will not keep silent,
And for Jerusalem's sake I will not keep quiet,
Until her righteousness goes forth like brightness,
And her salvation like a torch that is burning....
On your walls, O Jerusalem, I have appointed watchmen;
All day and all night they will never keep silent.
You who remind the LORD, take no rest for yourselves;
And give Him no rest until He establishes
And makes Jerusalem a praise in the earth.
(Is. 62:1, 6-7 NASB)

Following the thrust of this passage, Zinzendorf placed a strong emphasis on a continuous watch of corporate prayer on behalf of Herrnhut and the rest of the body of Christ. This was partially a matter of desperate necessity. For three years after its founding in 1724 the different factions among the settlers quarreled as constantly as their parent denominations in the church at large, putting the community periodically on the brink of disruption. Zinzendorf's response was to set up the famous round-the-clock prayer watch in which Moravians prayed for the revival of the church for one hundred years. In August 1727, the community experienced a "baptism of the Holy Spirit" climaxing in a communion service. From this point on unity prevailed. Within the larger community Zinzendorf organized smaller cells, the prayer bands, in which lay people were encouraged to confess their faults to one another, counsel together and support each other in prayer.

Using the experience of Herrnhut as a paradigm for the whole church, Zinzendorf soon began to send out of the community missionary teams of two different types, one kind to take the gospel initially to the tribes outside Christendom who had never heard it and the other to visit established churches and convey the message of regeneration and renewal. His ultimate goal was the unification of the revived segments of the body of Christ. Although his work fell short of this union, it did consolidate the foundation for the evangelical movement as an international, ecumenical coalition for the reforming and reviving of the churches on the basis of Reformation theology. In the twentieth century both the Evangelicalism of Lausanne and the ecumenism of the World Council of Churches can trace their historical origins to the work of Zinzendorf.[11]

While Herrnhut was expanding and spreading abroad its arms of witness, another awakening was occurring independently in America, in Jonathan Edwards's church at Northampton. When Edwards inherited his grandfather Stoddard's congregation in 1727, he tells us, they were "dry bones," possessing the form of godliness but denying its power. As Edwards saw them, they were respectable, and they had a kind of rote orthodoxy which shuffled doctrines aimlessly like faded packs of cards. But their ultimate concerns were not God and his kingdom, but land and the pursuit of affluence. Their children, Edwards says, were given to night walking and tavern haunting; no doubt if they had had drugs, they would have used them.

But the generation gap between a powerless orthodoxy and its apostate children was reversed in 1734, as the outpouring of the Holy Spirit began to "turn the hearts of fathers to their children and the hearts of children to their fathers" (Mal. 4:6). Edwards describes the ensuing revival in his *Faithful Narrative of the Surprising Work of God.* A stirring of interest began in the young people as they suddenly seemed to come in direct touch with the realities behind the God-talk of the minister, and this interest spread to their parents. As the Holy Spirit opened the eyes of their hearts and illuminated theological concepts, the opaque orthodoxy of the laity suddenly became a transparent medium for vision through which they saw the glory of God. The gravity of covetousness which had drawn their hearts to earthly concerns was reversed, and merchants began to neglect their business to talk about God and their souls. The Word of God suddenly had free course in congregational worship since the laity were now in touch with the regions described in the minister's sermons. Hymns were now a delight rather than a habit and a duty. The lay people's passivity in witness gave way to a new concern for others.

The illumination of the heart which brought converts in touch with the reality of God simultaneously revealed to them how deeply sin gripped their own lives. They suddenly became aware that their problem was not isolated acts of conscious disobedience to God, but a deep aversion to God at the root of their personalities, an aversion which left them in unconscious bondage to unbelief, selfishness, jealousy and other underlying complexes of sin. Some were in agony —even convicted because they were not more sensibly convicted—until they broke through to the realization that the only righteousness that could reconcile such depravity to a holy God was that of Jesus Christ, who offered himself for them on the cross. The new lives which they began to live issued out of hearts thoroughly broken because of sin.[12]

While Edwards was observing and documenting the revival in Northampton, another awakening was occurring in the Middle Colonies, led by graduates of William Tennent's Log College who were taking the Puritan message from house to house and keenly applying the law and the gospel to the varying conditions of their parishioners.[13] Still another phase of the awakening was developing in England. In 1738 three years of Moravian influence culminated in John Wesley's insight into the meaning of justification by faith as he heard Luther's *Commentary on Romans* read at one of the Herrnhuter cell groups. It was not long after this that George Whitefield and he, barred from Anglican congregations because the Reformation doctrine they preached had become so strange to the contemporary church, began preaching outdoors to thousands of hearers in the coal-mining districts. When Whitefield brought the new instrument of mass evangelism to America in the late 1730s, he found a country already experiencing a powerful wave of spiritual renewal. The awakening was not particularly centered around any leaders, not even the Log College men or Edwards. It almost seemed that the local ministries in every village were developing tide pools of spiritual interest, reinforced and augmented by news of spiritual activity elsewhere.[14] What Whitefield did was to dig a trench between the pools, unifying these isolated stirrings into a coherent evangelical party in the American church.

Edwards's writings on revival, which interpreted the awakening in this country and abroad, performed this same unifying function. These works comprise the foundational theology of spiritual renewal in English, and perhaps in any language. I shall be referring to Edwards's conclusions re-

peatedly in the rest of this work, but it will be helpful here
to summarize briefly the main structure of his teaching. Revival, in his understanding, is not a special season of extraordinary religious excitement, as in many forms of later
American revivalism. Rather it is an outpouring of the Holy
Spirit which restores the people of God to normal spiritual
life after a period of corporate declension. Periods of spiritual decline occur in history because the gravity of indwelling sin keeps pulling believers first into formal religion and
then into open apostasy. Periods of awakening alternate with
these as God graciously breathes new life into his people.
Every major advance of the kingdom of God on earth is signaled and brought about by a general outpouring of the Holy
Spirit. Edwards finds biblical evidence of such outpourings
in the days of Enoch when men first began to call upon the
name of God; in the second generation of Israelites after the
exodus who conquered Palestine; in the returned exiles under Ezra who resettled the land; and in the establishment of
the new Israel of God on the day of Pentecost.

In postbiblical history, Edwards's postmillennial expectations led him to chart four subsequent stages in the sub-
duing of the earth, each accompanied by a redemptive judgment on God's enemies and an outpouring of the Spirit on
his people: (1) the calling of the Gentiles at the time of the
destruction of Jerusalem; (2) the overthrowing of Roman
persecution and the Christianizing of the empire in the Constantinian revolution; (3) the destruction of Antichrist (Roman Catholicism and all other pseudo-Christianity) and the
establishment of a revived church in a new state of purity
and glory to rule among the nations for a thousand years;
and (4) the destruction of a final rebellion against God
effected by the return of Christ and leading to the last judgment and to the establishment of the eternal state. Edwards
suspected that the Great Awakening was the beginning of
the third stage, the church's millennial glory. Earlier generations of Puritans had felt that England and the New Eng-

lish colony in America would have a special role in establishing the kingdom of God among the other nations, and Edwards adapted this concept of America to his postmillennial vision. A revived American church would serve as a base for the missionary expansion of the gospel until all the earth was filled with the knowledge of the Lord as the waters cover the sea.[15]

As the Great Awakening unfolded in America after Whitefield's arrival in 1739, Edwards became aware that the revival involved a spiritual struggle in which every advance of renewal would involve severe conflict with fallen human nature and the powers of darkness. Since the work of revival involves the displacement of the world, the flesh and the devil, periods of renewal are times of great spiritual agitation in which troop movements on both sides are dimly visible in the background. As the sun shining on a swamp produces mist, the rising of the countenance of God among his people may result initially in disorders and confusion.

The devil, who is losing ground as the revival progresses, fights back in a number of ways. His main strategies are those of accusation and infiltration. He may attack the subjects of revival directly and internally with despair and discouragement; Edwards saw this happen at the close of the first Northampton revival in 1734. He may plant lies, caricatures or stereotypes in the minds of unbelievers or unrevived Christians so that they will reject the work of God and attack its progress. If possible, he will set the leaders of the revival against one another in this way in order to divide and conquer. To create evidence to corroborate accusations he will overbalance the zeal of converts and cause them to run to extremes. Finally, he will sow tares among the wheat in the form of counterfeit revivals, leading people to confound these with the real work which is in progress and to discredit it.[16]

Edwards's initial writings on the awakening were designed to defend the reality of the work of God from those who attacked it because of its incidental defects. Increasingly, however, he shifted the focus of his criticism from the opponents of the revival to the problems within the awakening movement itself. Under pressure from Charles Chauncy's valid criticism of the shallow emotionalism and self-righteous divisiveness of some converts, Edwards increasingly stressed that the core of the awakening was not an emotional experience but a Spirit-given apprehension of the reality of God which purged the heart and led inevitably to a meek and lamblike spirit and to an outflow of good works.

The Distinguishing Marks of a Work of the Spirit of God (1741) defended the revival because it possessed five marks of genuineness: it exalted Jesus Christ, attacked the kingdom of darkness, honored the Scriptures, promoted sound doctrine and involved an outpouring of love toward God and man. In Thoughts on the Revival in New England (1742) and A Treatise Concerning Religious Affections (1746), however, Edwards was especially concerned to make clear that fallen human nature is fertile ground for a fleshly religiosity which is impressively "spiritual" but ultimately rooted in self-love. High emotional experiences, effusive religious talk, and even praising God and experiencing love for God and man can be self-centered and self-motivated. In contrast to this, experiences of renewal which are genuinely from the Holy Spirit are God-centered in character, based on worship, an appreciation of God's worth and grandeur divorced from self-interest. Such experiences create humility in the convert rather than pride and issue in the creation of a new spirit of meekness, gentleness, forgiveness and mercy. They leave the believer hungering and thirsting after righteousness instead of satiated with self-congratulation. Most important, their end result is the performance of works of mercy and justice.

In the extensive section on good works which closes Religious Affections, Edwards establishes the principle that a full-fledged revival will involve a balance between personal concern for individuals and social concern. A revival is therefore not something exclusively "spiritual" and "religious." Edwards insists that the proliferation of religiosity in the form of meetings, prayer, singing and religious talk will not promote or sustain revival without works of love and mercy, which will "bring the God of love down from heaven to earth . . . to set up his tabernacle with men on the earth, and dwell with them."[17]

It is sometimes suggested that the American phase of the awakening was short-lived, nipped in the bud by its excesses. But the renewing impulse actually continued to deepen and expand for decades. It is possible that the real awakening in America came, not in the firestorm of 1739-42, but in later years as the church responded to Edwards's critique of the revival. The initial flare-up of enthusiasm was like the ignition of a bed of charcoal which must subside before the coals are usable.

What were the essential elements of the First Awakening, the components which signaled or effected the work of the Spirit in this movement? Three different theologies were catalysts in the revival: Pietistic Lutheranism, Puritan Calvinism and Wesleyan Arminianism. Despite their ideological and personal differences, the major leaders and commentators in the awakening admitted that the blessing of the Spirit rested upon all three of these strains of teaching, and this laid the basis for evangelical consensus in the future. Each of these theologies centered on the experience of grace in the lives of believers. Each sought to balance carefully the two thrusts of the Puritan and Pietist synthesis of "live orthodoxy": (1) the Lutheran doctrine of justification by faith and (2) the experience of regeneration and progressive sanctification.

This balance varied in its application according to the needs of the church in the different sectors of the awakening. Among American Puritans, where Calvinist doctrine was fairly well known—often in the form of a conceptual "dead orthodoxy"—there was considerable stress on the illuminating and assuring work of the Spirit in transforming head knowledge into heart experience, and sanctification was more emphasized than justification. In the English situation, however, where a works-oriented legalism was ascendent and justification by faith was virtually an unknown doctrine, the Wesleys found spiritual release in the rediscovery of Luther's teaching and later went on to teach that higher levels of sanctification are also the fruit of faith, not moral striving. The Lutheran Pietism of Herrnhut concentrated on rebirth and on the liberating message of justification and was so free in its approach to sanctification that it often appeared antinomian to Wesleyans and Puritans. In all these situations, however, the essential theological tool was *experientialized* Reformation theology applied to the particular kind of deadness and darkness afflicting parishioners in a given area.

There were, however, new dimensions of concern and strategy preceding and accompanying the First Awakening. In the extensive corporate prayer which antedated and supported the revival there was a movement away from the Old Testament pattern of fasting and humiliation common among seventeenth-century American Puritans and an abandonment of theocratic efforts to enforce pure religion in America. Pentecost became the model for revival prayer, and a new strategy of leavening the surrounding culture with the free witness of the gospel was adopted. Puritans and Pietists alike recognized that something beyond the pure experiential orthodoxies they had built was needed to revive the church: an effusion of the power of the Holy Spirit. Cotton Mather, who designed the posttheocratic strategy for America, articulated this most clearly:

We can do very little. Our Encumbrances are insuperable; our Difficulties are infinite. If He would please, to fulfill the ancient Prophecy, of *pouring out the Spirit on all Flesh*, and revive the extraordinary and supernatural Operations with which He planted His Religion in the primitive Times of Christianity.... His Kingdome would make those Advances in a Day, which under our present and fruitless Labours, are scarce made in an Age.[18] Other emphases in the First Awakening had already appeared in Puritan and Pietist evangelicalism but were expanded and reinforced in the revival. The fellowship of believers, both on the larger ecumenical level and in the breakdown of local congregational life in small group meetings, had been a recurrent theme since the Reformation, but the work of Zinzendorf and the Wesleys brought this to particular prominence during the First Awakening. The band meetings had an inevitable tendency to develop the ministry of the laity and narrow the gap between them and professional clergy, but this laicizing occurred even in areas with greater clerical control, often with disruptive force.

Protestant foreign missions, which had been pioneered by Puritans and Pietists in the late seventeenth and early eighteenth centuries, flowered extraordinarily in the ministry of Herrnhut, and Edwards's vision of the prevailing of the church among the nations prepared the foundation for nineteenth-century missionary expansion. Above all, Protestants began to grapple with the fact that the destruction of the Roman Catholic antichrist would not necessarily clear the way for the expansion of an unreformed and unrevived Protestantism. Zinzendorf treated Rome as just another denomination of Christians in need of renewal, and Edwards turned his sharpest critical tools finally upon the evangelical movement which was seeking to be the leaven of revival among the churches.

Despite the overall brightness of Edwards's picture of the church's future, the lively sense of spiritual conflict which was part of his Puritan heritage forewarned him that further periods of decline and satanic counterattack were possible before the ultimate prevailing of the revived church.[19] This indeed proved to be the church's experience in the late eighteenth century. It was not merely that deism and more radical forms of humanism assailed the church at its borders; the church's own momentum slackened. The impetus of the awakening which began in 1727 continued to pulsate for decades in the churches, most notably on the American frontier, but by the end of the century the evangelicals sensed an inner loss of power along with the challenge from the growing antichristian force of Enlightenment humanism.

The American church was traumatized by economic and political problems in the wake of the Revolutionary War, and deeply apprehensive about the subversive religious and political implications of the French Revolution. The growing frontier threatened the possibility of degeneration into unchurched barbarism. In the civilized East, the rising generation seemed extraordinarily susceptible to infection from foreign currents of atheism, deism and Unitarianism.

In England the Methodist awakening had been contained by its ejection from the Church of England, and evangelical churchmen were rare, surrounded by bishops, prelates and lay people involved in a pattern of formal, moralistic, worldly "churchianity" that was steadily accommodating itself to the process of secularization. Manners and morals seemed to be declining in both countries, and the Industrial Revolution was intensifying existing social problems and creating new ones.[20]

The Second Great Awakening
The church's experience this time constituted a brief recession, not a prolonged decline as before the First Awakening, but the challenge was severe enough to set the evangelicals praying with exceptional urgency. Having experienced such a remarkable advance earlier in the century in response to prayer, they were encouraged to hope for something similar, and what ensued has been generally recognized by scholars as a Second Great Awakening.

In America, circuit-riding Baptist and Methodist ministers took the gospel to the frontier in the great camp meetings beginning in 1800. They were not always well educated; their theology and practice were often open to question. But they had the courage and calling to go where the frontier was developing, and they spoke the people's language.[21] On a very different mission field President Timothy Dwight of Yale, Edwards's grandson, confronted an almost uniformly non-Christian student body and steadily destroyed the arguments of the Enlightenment, inducing a series of revival harvests through his apologetic mastery. Yale and other colleges began to pump new leadership into the churches and the burgeoning foreign missions movement.[22] Meanwhile Lyman Beecher and other evangelists began attacking social and cultural evils in a two-pronged strategy which included crusades against dueling, slavery, alcoholism, war and prostitution, as well as more conventional forms of mission such as evangelism and the distribution of tracts and Bibles.[23]

The same double strategy was pursued in the English sector of the awakening where the evangelicals motivated the abolition of slavery by 1822 and played a main part in a revolution in values which transformed a rather dissolute nation into Victorian England. The instruments effecting these changes were various: the "Eclectic Society" of former slave trader John Newton which rallied the evangelical forces within Anglicanism; the influence of the Venns' church at Clapham which included William Wilberforce and other political and social leaders; and the labors of Charles Simeon at Cambridge, training young ministerial candidates and then securing for them spheres of influence within the Anglican Church. But in order to bring about such widespread and costly changes in their culture, these leaders had to be riding the crest of a powerful grassroots revival. And this was not merely a revival of home mission. By mid-century the trade routes of the British Empire had been turned into a railway system for the delivery of the gospel to other nations.[24]

Most of the elements in the Second Evangelical Awakening were extensions of components already present in the First. Reformational theologies balancing justification and sanctification and applying these vigorously to the lives of believers were still at the center of the work, and there was still a profound sense of prayerful dependence on the Holy Spirit. The community life of Herrnhut was echoed in the parish at Clapham, and the network connecting leaders in different Protestant denominations became not only ecumenical but international. But the Second Awakening reached a new level of organization among evangelicals for the transformation of the church and the confrontation and leavening of the surrounding culture. Social ministries, which had been initiated by the Puritans and especially by the early Pietists, were developed to a degree which has never been equaled by later Evangelicals. Home and foreign missions prospered as well.

Later Awakenings and Orr's Concept of Revival

The momentum of the Second Awakening in the church seems to have extended at least through the first three decades of the nineteenth century, after which a general recession for the evangelical interest began to appear. There is no scholarly consensus on the timing or numbering of subsequent general awakenings in the church. J. Edwin Orr, who has devoted a great deal of painstaking research to this question, has established that there have been at least two subsequent, general surges of religious interest with an evangelical core: the Prayer Revival of 1858-59, which was a spontaneous, lay-directed movement of daily prayer meetings for the outpouring of the Holy Spirit, and the so-called Welsh Revival of 1904-05, which was actually part of a more general surge of religious interest affecting many parts of the world. Orr has also documented many less extensive local awakenings during the nineteenth and twentieth centuries under the ministries of evangelists like Billy Sunday.[25]

Orr's concept of religious revival focuses sharply on the

phenomena described in Acts 1 and 2: corporate prayer of dependence on the Holy Spirit, followed by the spiritual reenergizing of the church and the empowering of preaching and teaching ministries reaching out in evangelism and healing social ministry, leading to the conversion of large numbers both within and outside the church. In Orr's view a period of awakening such as this may be of short duration but may result in decades of progress and consolidation in the church as God raises up new leadership in response to prayer. Orr considers the entire evangelistic and missionary impetus of the late nineteenth century, embracing the ministry of D. L. Moody, to be a result of the Prayer Revival of 1858-59.

Orr's use of the pattern in the early chapters of Acts in understanding church renewal is consistent with the central events of the First and Second Awakenings. The theological objection that the pentecostal experience of Acts 2 is a single, unrepeatable event equipping the church for ministry is answered by the fact that the early Christians experienced a substantial repetition of the pattern of crisis/prayer/empowering, documented in Acts 4:23-37. Nevertheless, compared to earlier awakenings, there are substantial differences in the theological and spiritual depth, and in the social and cultural consequences of the later instances of revival which Orr documents. Evangelicals continued to show evidences of spiritual empowering, it is true; but the substance of the evangelical movement and the tasks to which it addressed itself changed.

The leaders and shapers of the Reformation, the Puritan and Pietist movements, and the first two awakenings included trained theologians who combined spiritual urgency with profound learning, men who had mastered the culture of their time and were in command of the instruments needed to destroy its idols and subdue its innovations: Luther and Calvin, Owen and Francke, Edwards and Wesley, Dwight and Simeon. Evangelicals in the nineteenth and early twentieth centuries to a remarkable extent depended on the leadership of lay evangelists without formal theological training, men like Charles Finney, D. L. Moody and Billy Sunday. This was not without positive effects. It continued the gradual laicization of Protestantism visible in earlier awakenings, and it freed evangelists of inherited formalism which might interfere with their practical outreach. But it led also to a progressively shallower spirituality among evangelicals and to a loss of intellectual command. This loss of intellectual mastery proved to be a critical weakness, since the secular humanist world view which had been in the process of construction since the Enlightenment was receiving powerful reinforcement from the contributions of Darwin, Marx and Freud.

In the early twentieth century the consistent contrabiblical system forged by the secularists struck Western society with the destructive force of a nuclear bomb. The "Fourth Awakening" of 1904-05 was a pulse-beat of evangelistic outreach, but it lacked the theological strength to meet and master secularism, which was both around the church and within it through the intrusion of new, non-Reformational theologies and erosive forms of biblical criticism. Meanwhile a different kind of secularism was infecting the laity. While guarding themselves against "worldliness" in the form of external taboos, they had gradually moved into the kind of worldliness which Edwards had attacked: a covetous immersion in affluence. The dynamic of prayerful concern for God's kingdom which had characterized the earlier evangelicals was replaced by religious forms and legalistic moralism, camouflaging the laity's ultimate concern for the feathering of their own nests rather than for the enjoyment of God and the advancement of his glory.

It is no wonder that the wind went out of the sails of the evangelicals and that they lost control of the seminaries and the larger denominations during the Fundamentalist-Modernist controversy. The Fundamentalists sought to eject the mutating leadership of the church through disciplinary trials, but this was ineffective. Evangelicals had not reproduced themselves in sufficient strength, their children were deserting them for seemingly more plausible theologies, and many of their own number were unconvinced that heresy trials and forced subscription were the answer. The forces which had been united within the old evangelicalism began to come apart. Christians like Walter Rauschenbusch who were concerned for the expression of social compassion were both forced and seduced into theological rationales which undermined the church's redemptive mission to individuals, while those concerned for personal salvation squared off against them in pious individualism. Mass evangelists and orthodox theologians became more and more estranged from one another's worlds, and both often lacked the dynamic of concern for sanctification and dependence on the Holy Spirit found in earlier evangelicals. At the beginning of the twentieth century, even the root of evangelical concern for revival split into two branches which grew separately for most of the rest of the century: the Deeper Life emphasis, represented by Keswick and similar conferences, and the Pentecostal movement. By the 1930s the forces which had been in command of the church during the expanding progress of the Great Century were shattered with virtually all of the pieces marred by unconscious conformity to differing aspects of the surrounding culture.

There is no single and simple explanation of this transformation. It was the product of many subtle changes, some of which will be analyzed in what follows. But perhaps the root cause of the decay of evangelicalism in America was the replacement of the old comprehensive concept of *revival* with the post-Finneyan machinery of *revivalism.* "Holding a revival" became synonymous with "using new methods to do mass evangelism." It is no accident that news media so frequently misprint *evangelism* for *evangelicalism,* for the Evangelical understanding of church renewal has all too often been restricted to church growth. Evangelicals have frequently directed most of their critical faculties not at their own needs but at their liberal neighbors' equally strange reduction of renewal to social action, and they have been content to concentrate their energies on exporting the gospel and enlarging their membership. This approach would never have satisfied the Puritans and Pietists, who were convinced that their primary responsibility was to be *ecclesia reformata semper reformanda*, a reformed church always reforming. As they prayed for the destruction of the papal antichrist, they were increasingly aware of the anti-christian remnants still clinging to them and deforming the church's witness. At their highest moments of insight they recognized that Rome was not the only stumbling block diverting multitudes from belief in the gospel, and that not until the whole organism of the church including Protestant-ism is reformed and revived will the fullness of the nations believe its witness and enter.

An Alternate Concept of Revival

This suggests that the model of renewal in Acts 1—2 and 4 is not the only viable pattern of revival. Another pattern is provided by the Old Testament instances of return to God's law under Josiah and Hezekiah. The interrelationship be-tween *reformation* of doctrine and structures and *spiritual revitalization* in the church is important and complex. While these two factors can at times occur separately, they are most often closely linked together, advancing together in alternate moves like the footsteps of a walking man. Refor-mation grows out of awakened spiritual interest, and spiri-tual renewal seldom persists long without continuing refor-mation. This suggests that God has chosen to bless his church with the fullness of the Holy Spirit on the condition of its moving toward certain vital norms of health and witness.

In our brief survey of the history of awakenings we have

seen glimpses of these norms incarnated in persons and movements on whose activity the blessing of God has rested like visible tongues of fire italicizing these qualities for our instruction. Future awakenings may incorporate other biblical norms as yet undiscovered, but they are unlikely to occur without the full consolidation and realization in the church of those elements which have appeared in the past. The object of this book is to seek the fullest possible current understanding of these principles of revitalization, using biblical and historical resources, in order to restore the Evangelical movement and the whole church of Christ to a level of reformation appropriate to a new and continuing empowering of the Spirit.

In the last several decades in America, we have already begun to see the alternate steps of reformation and revival moving again in the church. For renewal is God's sovereign work and not conditional on comprehensive understanding of any set of principles. A movement to unite and reform Evangelical sectors of the church came in the 1940s after a harrowing economic depression and a war ended by weapons which seemed like a foretaste of the end of the world. Perhaps these providences turned the hearts of men to cry out to God in prayer. In any case, there appeared to be a small-scale outpouring of the Spirit at the midcentury mark resulting in a harvest of new converts and new leadership. The New Evangelicalism cleaned up some of the excesses which had made mass evangelism a religious underworld, pursued scholarship and theological deepening, sought for an elusive balance between ecumenical charity and critical discernment, and tried to shed its graveclothes of cultic folk religion.

Paralleling this development, a new charismatic movement began to appear in mainline denominations and on campuses. While the response of the laity was often superficial and formalistic during the 1950s, there were stirrings of renewal among young Christians all during the 1960s, even while the outward face of the youth culture seemed to be wasting away. It is possible to argue that the Jesus movement of the 1970s is simply the cumulative effect of reform movements antedating it by decades, which have gradually been increasing in strength until they have peaked into visibility in the news media. The mission to the counterculture, for instance, may really have begun with the calling of David Wilkerson to work with the teenage drug problem in the late 1950s.

On the other hand, it is possible to argue that somewhere in the late 1960s another anguished cry of prayer went up from Middle-American Christianity to be answered by a fresh effusion of the Holy Spirit. This outpouring has lifted the results of the previous decades' gradual increase to a new level of significance. In the 1960s, as in the period just before the Second Awakening, Americans felt themselves threatened by foreign currents of revolution lapping at their doors and also by the barbarous frontier of a wildly mutating youth culture. Christian families everywhere agonized as they saw their children ripped away by the gravitational field of a subversive Sodom developing within American culture. When voices within the church announced in the late 1960s that God was dead, many Christians must have duplicated the reaction of Hezekiah to the Assyrian challenge in 2 Kings 18, laying the matter before the Lord and doing the modern equivalent of rending their garments.

There are many respects, of course, in which the development of the counterculture could function as an aid to reformation as well as a challenge toward revival. There are overtones of common grace interwoven with its demonic elements. Human depravity, like the mule, is reluctant to move even when it is given a hard shove; but it will sometimes at least shift its weight from one foot to another. In the 1960s the American straight culture, with its characteristic pattern of sin—pride, ambition, avarice, envy, self-righteousness, conformity, respectability—was confronted by the Dionysian youth culture with another distribution of sin centering around uncontrolled lust, riotous indulgence in sensory experience and resistance to authority. But the differing centers of gravity in the sin of the two cultures permitted a complementary distribution of virtues so that the two could be prophetic toward one another. When straight Americans began to upbraid the hippies for their disorder and licentiousness, they found themselves confronted by prophets from Gomorrah who lashed out at their materialism and their subservience to the child-devouring Moloch of the capitalist success system. When the elders commended the so-called Protestant work ethic, the young people advised detachment from wealth, attention to persons, openness to beauty and the cultivation of diversity. Perhaps this was a false ethic of love, but it was opposing a false ethic of righteousness.

At the same time the youth culture was disenchanted with religion as a formal ritual obligation—"the church service makes me nervous," as Paul Simon says—but very open to religion as experience, as illuminated contact with the divine and the supernatural. Of course this religion was idolatrous in that it sought for contact with false gods, but straight Christianity was often idolatrous also in giving lip service to the true God while its concerns lay elsewhere. Still the thirst for religion as experience in the counterculture was closer to the essence of revival as defined by Edwards than was the formalism of the comfortable pew. It is not surprising then that so many young people turned to the apparent depth of Eastern mysticism in preference to the dried-up cisterns of Western Christendom. The religious quest of the counterculture was ideally suited to convict the Middle-American church of heart apostasy and the loss of the power of godliness.

This is probably the crux of the issue of whether or not the Jesus movement will prove to be the overture to another

major awakening: will it awaken enough of the sleeping
congregations in America to displace the occupying powers
and get the church on the offensive again in its redemptive
mission to individuals and society? Currently the prospects
for this are equivocal. Critics of the Evangelical resurgence
are not wrong in suggesting that some of the movement
is a conservative backlash into Aquarian religiosity among
the young and a pilgrimage from future shock to nostalgia
among their elders. The stresses of the 1960s may have
moved Middle America more toward Archie Bunker than
toward revival. There are signs that the pendulum of the
popular mood has overshot the median of repentance toward
a Neo-Victorian reaction as happened after the Second
Awakening in Britain. From the direction of the counterculture the pressure is off. Certain countercultural norms
may have infiltrated our society, but the youth movement
as a whole has been largely institutionalized and domesticated. The underground newspapers which once sold drugs
and revolution wrapped in a single package have almost
disappeared. Even the campuses are dominated by a mood
which has been described as "eerie tranquility" and "gal-
loping ennui" as the work ethic has come back into style.
It is not surprising that some observers are pessimistic
about the continuing potential for revival in this atmosphere
of reaction, complacency and absense of stress. Religious
and secular forms of piety seem dominated by a pervasive
self-centeredness. Perhaps the Jesus movement was just a
summer shower and not the inundation which the beached
ark of the church needs to get it afloat.

Hopes for the Present
If revival is defined always as a punctiliar outpouring of
the Spirit which converts huge percentages of a population,
as some theorists hold, then we may not yet have experienced a major awakening. The 1977-78 Gallup Poll report,
for example, indicating that 34% of Americans claim to have

experienced regeneration, may not be conclusive, since it probably includes many converts to cults and non-Christian mysticism.[26]

But there are elements in the situation today that indicate that a steadily increasing displacement of the works of darkness is taking place, and this definition of revival is also biblical. In a movement of steadily increasing exponential growth, such as the increment of scientific information in the last hundred years, the increase can go on quietly for a long period and then suddenly appear to peak in an out-pouring of expansion. It is reported that among the applicants to one major secular university recently, nearly a third answered an inquiry about their most significant experience by pointing to a transforming encounter with Christ. This implies that something rather remarkable has been going on in the high schools. That it has also been going on in colleges, despite the general resurgence of apathy, is indicated by the fact that both Evangelical and mainline seminaries continue to receive an enlarging supply of ministerial candidates who are uniquely alive and open to growth. It must be significant that even at a time when the institutional church is shrinking, the number of young people with a sense of call to the pastorate has taken a rapid upturn. Many of these young leaders are concerned to express a distinctly fresh and firsthand Christian faith through literature, art, music and the modern media. We should remember that past revivals have traveled along the channels of communication, and that Edwards predicated that the increase in communication would ultimately lead to worldwide revival if the Christianity being broadcast could itself be revived.[27] The mission to the counterculture has reminded the church that its home mission needs to sit loose toward cultural addenda which interfere with the cross-cultural transmission of the gospel.

Meanwhile the communication between denominational groups and theological parties among professing Christians has been steadily improving, perhaps for similar reasons. Although there is still plenty of distance between ecclesiastical bureaucracies, and also between ministerial leaders where theological polarization has been especially severe, the scholars and teachers who will train tomorrow's pastors and church statesmen are showing a new interest in the theology of the Christian life. Since virtually all of the problems in the church including bad theology issue from defective spirituality, the attention given to spiritual theology —that is, to the question of how to keep all the cells in the body of Christ in optimum health and running order— should culminate in a new vitality in the church.

The German Pietists Spener and Zinzendorf felt that unity among the denominations would come only when all the segments of the church were revived.[28] They understood, however, that this involved a revival of theology as well as a transitory wave of conversions and enthusiasm, and that sound theology would be a decidedly major instrument in reviving the church. This speaks directly to our situation. The Evangelical movement has been losing ground theologically since the Second Great Awakening, and this trend has to be reversed unless we want to go on seeing shallow and short-lived results. Whatever degree of awakening we are experiencing now is not united around any single theology or leader, and perhaps this is a sign that the awakening is genuinely from God and not a human contrivance. But if the separated segments which are being revived are not united by some theological bridge, we will ultimately be left with estrangements between the component organs in the body of Christ—and broken bodies are never very healthy. We need a theological "unified field theory" which conserves and consolidates all the values in the different groups and parties while avoiding their errors and imbalances, which enables the pentecostal and nonpentecostal to affirm one another as Spirit-filled Christians with valid but differing spiritual gifts, and which unites socially concerned Christians with those burdened for the destinies of individuals on a common basis in the redemptive work of Christ.

The intellectual and spiritual hunger of campus Christians today, and especially their interest in apologetics, seems to indicate that such a theological renewal may be in the offing. There are many respects in which the shape of the Jesus movement recalls that of the Second Awakening. One phase of that revival involved practical leaders whose theology and character were often imperfect but whose courage and zeal to reach the lost were exemplary, like the popular leaders in the Jesus movement; but the parallel phase on college campuses obtained some of its driving force from the apologetic theology of men like Timothy Dwight. The leadership which poured out of the colleges and seminaries revived the home church for at least a generation and ignited the great foreign missionary explosion of the nineteenth century.

Can we expect a similar impact to be made on the institutional church by the young leaders emerging everywhere? Much depends on the armor-piercing strength of their theological equipment, which must penetrate the masks of respectability to get at the underlying apathy toward God and lay bare its rootage in sin. But perhaps Linda Meissner's vision of a great army of young people bringing the world to Christ, with the accompanying text from Joel 2 which has so often been a keynote of revival, may prove to be true of this generation: "I will pour out my spirit on all flesh; your sons and your daughters shall prophesy, your old men shall dream dreams and your young men shall see visions" (Joel 2:28).

Much also depends on the openness to repentance within the institutional church, for no leadership can revive that which is not called forth and supported by its own inquiring prayer. But the church may still be in that condition of insecurity which encourages repentance. Although the revolutionary subculture has quieted down, we have been shaken in the heart of our own government and our economy. The condition of Middle-American churchgoers is remarkably similar to that of the Israelites in Haggai's prophecy:

> Consider how you have fared. You have sown much, and harvested little; you eat, but you never have enough; you drink, but you never have your fill; you clothe yourselves, but no one is warm; and he who earns wages earns wages to put them into a bag with holes. . . . You have looked for much, and, lo, it came to little; and when you brought it home, I blew it away. Why? says the LORD of hosts. Because of my house that lies in ruins, while you busy yourselves each with his own house. (Hag. 1:5-6, 9)

But when the people turned from their preoccupation with their own houses to build the temple, they were given a remarkable prophetic encouragement:

> My Spirit abides among you; fear not. For thus says the LORD of hosts: Once again, in a little while, I will shake the heavens and the earth and the sea and the dry land; and I will shake all nations, so that the treasures of all nations shall come in, and I will fill this house with splendor, says the LORD of hosts. The silver is mine, and the gold is mine, says the LORD of hosts. The latter splendor of this house shall be greater than the former, says the LORD of hosts; and in this place I will give prosperity, says the LORD of hosts. (Hag. 2:5-9)

The prophecy of Haggai brings a penetrating challenge to our society. But it offers also a remarkable hope for the church's future.

BIBLICAL MODELS
OF CYCLICAL
AND
CONTINUOUS
RENEWAL

2

WHEN WE TURN TO THE BIBLE TO search out theological explanations for the phenomenon of decline and revival in the
church's history, we are confronted with what seems at first
glance to be a contrast between the Old and New Testaments.
Under the Old Covenant the cyclical pattern of apostasy and
spiritual renewal is one of the most obvious characteristics
of the people of God. The faith of the masses and their leaders
perpetually waxed and waned, while the vitality of the godly
remnant ran through biblical history like a burning fuse,
periodically igniting the surrounding mass in brief periods
of reformation.

In the New Testament, on the other hand, there seems
initially to be no philosophy of history presented which involves such oscillations. The framework of the book of Acts
presents a pattern of almost continuous success for the infant

Christian movement, responding effectively to problems and challenges until its first objective is achieved, the planting of the gospel in the heart of Roman civilization. The church is expected to encounter increasing decay and hostility in the surrounding culture of "the last days," and to be in danger of apostasy. But the New Testament seems to imply that the ups and downs of Israelite history are a thing of the past.

Further reflection, however, will reveal that both the cyclical experience of Israel and the experience of continuous renewal in Acts are coherent with one another, and that both patterns are latent in the entire biblical witness. A careful examination of the bases for these patterns will uncover the elements of renewal which sustain the church during its periods of constant growth and which help restore it when it has fallen into decline.

Models of Cyclical Renewal

The revival theory of Joachim of Fiore, and to some extent that of Jonathan Edwards, linked the hope for renewal in the church with an eschatological program: the Age of the Spirit, or the dawn of the millennium after which Christ would return. But two other factors in the Bible can account for the cyclical pattern of decline and renewal, and it is rather surprising that Edwards did not seize upon these more definitely in his understanding of church history.

The Generation Gap. One of these factors is exposed in the book of Judges. Here we find a series of cycles of decline and renewal among the people of God connected with a gap between generations:

> And the people served the LORD all the days of Joshua, and all the days of the elders who outlived Joshua, who had seen all the great work which the LORD had done for Israel. ... And all that generation also were gathered to their fathers; and there arose another generation after them, who did not know the LORD or the work which he had done for Israel. (Judg. 2:7, 10)

Because the hearts and memories of the succeeding generation were emptied of the experience of the Lord and his
mighty acts, they became filled with the idolatry of the surrounding culture like an empty sponge which has been
dropped in filthy water (Judg. 2:11-12). God's judgment upon
the Baal worship of the Israelites is expressed in their impotence in warfare:

> So the anger of the LORD was kindled against Israel, and he
> gave them over to plunderers . . . and he sold them into the
> power of their enemies round about, so that they could no
> longer withstand their enemies. Whenever they marched
> out, the hand of the LORD was against them for evil, as the
> LORD had warned. (Judg. 2:14-15)

Nevertheless, God acts to turn the cycle of decline upward
again toward one of renewal and raises up judges (shophetim, governors and military leaders) under whose direction Israel is able to repel the invading enemies and secure
rest for the land for the duration of each judge's rulership—
around forty years or about the length of one generation's
dominance in leadership.

The cycle of renewal can be interpreted both as an act of
sovereign mercy and as a divine response to the inarticulate
heart cry of defeated Israel: "For the LORD was moved to pity
by their groaning because of those who afflicted and oppressed them" (Judg. 2:18).

The cyclical pattern thus established —(1) appearance of a
new generation, (2) popular apostasy and enculturation, (3)
national affliction, (4) popular repentance and agonized
prayer and (5) the raising up of new leadership and restoration—is repeated again and again during the rest of the book
of Judges. This pattern embraces the tenures of Othniel (Judg.
3:7-11); Ehud and Shamgar (Judg. 3:12-31, a sequence of two
leaders involving eighty years of deliverance); Deborah
(Judg. 4:1—5:31); Gideon (Judg. 6:1—8:32); Abimelech, Tola
and Jair (Judg. 8:33—10:5, a rather troubled cycle of forty-
eight years under multiple leadership); Jephthah, Ibzan, Elon

and Abdon (Judg. 10:6—12:15, another cycle of several leaders lasting thirty-one years); and finally Samson (Judg. 13:1—16:31, ruling twenty years).

It is apparent that the plot structure of the book of Judges is intended to emphasize the necessity of charismatic leadership for the spiritual and temporal well-being of Israel and God's response to the prayer of his people in raising up the needed leadership. The people pray in response to God's chastening of their apostasy. In the first cycle of decline this prayer is barely more than a wordless groan of misery, but it is real agony and not formal religiosity. In subsequent cycles it becomes a repeated cry to the Lord for help (Judg. 3:9, 15; 4:3; 6:6). Before the troubled leadership of Abimelech, Tola and Jair there is no record of the people's turning to God in prayer; but after this sequence the Israelites are represented as conducting an extensive dialog with the Lord in prayer and abolishing their idols, after which God becomes "indignant over the misery of Israel" (Judg. 10:10-16). This particular instance of deliverance is similar to the church's experience in the Reformation. We have already noted the repetition of the pattern of apostasy, crisis, prayer and deliverance in the major awakenings after the Reformation and in our own experience in the last decade. The book of Judges closes with several anecdotes which are outside the cyclical structure of chapters 1—16 and which are included to make the point that without a central dynastic leadership in Israel the tribes were prone to decadence, violence and division (chapters 17—21; see especially 18:1; 19:1; 21:25).

Since the political function of the *shophetim* ceases with the inauguration of kingship in Israel, we might be tempted to assume that the cyclical pattern of the book of Judges would have no further application to the history of redemption. Two lines of argument contest this, however. First, at the very beginning of God's dealings with Israel as a corporate body, when the tribes have begun to multiply in Egypt, God anticipates the Judges cycle by raising up Moses in answer to the groaning of the covenant people:

> Then the LORD said, "I have seen the affliction of my people who are in Egypt, and have heard their cry because of their taskmasters; I know their sufferings, and I have come down to deliver them out of the hand of the Egyptians. . . . And now, behold, the cry of the people of Israel has come to me, and I have seen the oppression with which the Egyptians oppress them." (Ex. 3:7-9)

It appears that a general principle concerning the deliverance of God's people is being hinted at here: redemption comes under the direction of leaders whom God raises up in his sovereign mercy in response to the deep longing and intercession of the laity generated under the pressure of defeat or suffering.

The second argument against limiting the cyclical pattern of decline and renewal to the book of Judges is the continuance of these cycles even after the monarchy is established in Israel, ostensibly to end the disorder of the premonarchic period. Certainly it is clear that kingship does not cure the pattern of spiritual decline and defeat. Such decline and defeat recurs repeatedly under unfaithful leaders in the southern kingdom such as Jehoram, Ahaz, Manasseh, Jehoiakim and Zedekiah. At first glance it seems that under the monarchy the disposition of the king rather than the heart attitude of the people is the main determinant in the upward or downward movement of the cycles. In the northern kingdom the uniformly bad leadership is described repeatedly as causing the people to sin through idolatry. In the southern kingdom the reviving of the national interest is ascribed to the spiritual fidelity of such kings as Jehoshaphat, Hezekiah and Josiah.[1] Sometimes response and renewal among the people was present at the same time that good kings sought reform (2 Kings 23:1-3). At other times when kings sought for a return to God, the people failed to respond (2 Kings 12:1-21). Indeed, although the divine initiative raised up voices calling for revival, not only among kings and prophets, but

also among priests like Jehoiada, a persistent recurrent gravity toward rebellion and apostasy is constantly noted
among the people, as Stephen's speech before the Sanhedrin
indicates (Acts 7:2-53; see 1 Kings 14:22-24).

The picture is somewhat more complex than the pattern
in Judges, in that the responsibility for decline and the credit
for renewal is shared both by leaders and followers. Behind
the initiative of both, however, is the sovereign will of God,
turning the hearts of kings and peoples to himself or letting
them fall in the natural gravity of sin according to his own
redemptive purposes. He is bound by his own covenants and
promises to the fathers and especially to David, and he is
responsive to the remnant of faithful Israelites which remains even during the darkest periods of decline. But the
overarching cause of the ebb and flow of spiritual life and
temporal prosperity among the people lies in the building of
his redemptive purpose for mankind. Even the prayers for
revival of leaders and people are stirred up by God's Spirit
and reflect a pervasive sense of dependence on God: "Restore
(turn) us again, O God of our salvation. . . . Wilt thou not revive us again, that thy people may rejoice in thee?" (Ps. 85:
4, 6).[2]

Thus far there appear to be two factors associated with the
recurrent gaps between believing elders and the rising generations who fall into apostasy, perhaps after an intervening
generation which is formally religious but has no interior
heart for God. First, there is the gravity inherent in human
sin, a kind of entropy in human nature which guarantees
that the vigor of spiritual life will constantly run down unless it is renewed through the channel of dependent prayer.
Second, in response to prayer God pours out his Spirit and
revives the declining life of his people, raising up new leaders and turning the hearts of the laity to himself. In the leader-
less situation described in Judges, and in some subsequent
revivals in the history of the church, the prayer originates
among the people and God responds by raising up leader-

ship. In the era after the judges when there is an established leadership ruling Israel, the prayer initiative frequently originates among these leaders, though it is often answered in a spiritual response among the laity. Since the kings are types of the messianic leader who is to come at last, it is appropriate that spiritual renewal and material prosperity should accompany their rule in proportion to the conformity with which their own lives foreshadow the graces of the coming King. Many instances of revivals beginning with the prayer of leaders can be found in the church since the apostolic age, when God's people are no longer ruled by monarchs but have all been called as priests and kings.

This is not to say, however, that the ultimate causative factor in the cycles of revival is spontaneous human initiative. Left to itself, sinful human nature would run downward forever, even among the elect of God, because of the disease of indwelling sin. As Paul intimates in Romans 8:26-27, even prayer itself, the pivotal admission of dependence through which decline begins to turn toward renewal, results from the hidden inspiration of the Spirit.

The fact that God's initiative is primary in the renewal of his kingdom is clearly indicated in the conclusion of 2 Chronicles. After noting that the exile is a punishment upon the apostasy of the kings, the author adds:

> All the leading priests and the people likewise were exceedingly unfaithful, following all the abominations of the nations.... The LORD sent persistently to them by his messengers, because he had compassion on his people and on his dwelling place; but they kept mocking the messengers of God, despising his words, and scoffing at his prophets, till the wrath of the LORD rose against his people, till there was no remedy. (2 Chron. 36:14-16)

The passage goes on to describe the total destruction of the house of God and the laying waste of the city of Jerusalem at the decree of God. But when a new cycle of renewal begins after the seventy years allotted by the Lord for the land to enjoy its neglected sabbaths, the human initiative comes neither from the people nor the leaders of Israel, but from a heathen king!

> Now in the first year of Cyrus king of Persia, that the word of the LORD by the mouth of Jeremiah might be accomplished, the LORD stirred up the spirit of Cyrus king of Persia so that he made a proclamation throughout all his kingdom and also put it in writing: "Thus says Cyrus king of Persia, 'The LORD, the God of heaven, has given me all the kingdoms of the earth, and he has charged me to build him a house at Jerusalem, which is in Judah. Whoever is among you of all his people, may the LORD his God be with him. Let him go up.' " (2 Chron. 36:22-23)

Nothing could more effectively emphasize the primacy of God's initiative in revival.

The Powers of Darkness. The generation gap is not the only factor accounting for the cyclical ebb and flow of spiritual life among God's people. A second but related biblical datum is the spiritual conflict with the powers of darkness uncovered in the book of Revelation. This conflict is touched upon at many other points in the Old and New Testaments. As Edwards indicates in his *History of Redemption,* God's kingdom is like an expanding circle of light in the world's darkness, alternately drawing inward in periods of decline and pulsing outward in an increasing circumference. Each of the successively larger outward pulses is accompanied by a new outpouring of the Holy Spirit. The surrounding darkness is not simply fallen human nature. There is another agency battling the light, and spiritual warfare is part of the ebb and flow of the church's experience. The earth is blinded by an occupying army of fallen angelic powers, and the kingdom of God is a liberation army advancing the frontiers of light until all the earth is full of the knowledge of God.

Just as in any battle, the boundary lines shift constantly as territory is won and lost. When the forces of God lose ground or retreat, a spiritual decline results. Outpourings of the

Spirit supernaturally reinforce the armies of the Lord with grace and equip them to recover ground and liberate new territory. Thus spiritual awakenings comprise both punctiliar moments in history in which the Spirit is outpoured and also succeeding periods, often decades long, in which the spiritual advantage so gained is implemented in the destruction of the works of darkness, the purification of the church and the ingathering of the elect. Military defeat and oppression, persecution, and even the personal enmities of which the psalmists speak so often are only visible analogs and evidences of the invisible warfare with the powers of darkness.

Often the real enemy to be fought is not the visible oppressing powers but the idolatry and apostasy by which the powers of darkness have reoccupied the hearts of God's people, as was the case with Gideon, whose most dangerous assignment was not to defeat the Amalekites but to risk the anger of the Israelites by destroying his father's idol. While this may seem to be a slightly different model of decline and renewal than the one proposed in Judges, where the apostasy of successive generations is the point of focus, we should recognize that apostasy is merely a human expression of the invasion of demonic powers. The two models of revival are in reality only one: the expanding of God's kingdom in a liberating warfare against the forces of darkness in which the most important battleground is the hearts of men.

I am aware that at this point my argument has lost credibility for some of my readers. Christians since the Enlightenment have become nervous about acknowledging the reality and agency of demonic powers. Eighteenth-century rationalism offered Western culture a plausible bargain: it would dispose of ghosts, vampires and other troublesome creatures of superstition at the cost of ridding the universe of all created beings in the interval between man and God. In this process both good and evil angels were eliminated in the assumption that they were as trivial and contemptible as their images in popular folk religion.

But the death of Satan was not only a tragedy for the imagination, as Wallace Stevens says,[3] it was the result of a rather amazing *failure* of imagination. It was also, in the Age of Reason, a remarkably unreasonable assumption. That the God who is called "the Lord of hosts" should not include among those hosts some creatures above the estate of man, and that the human conflict between the Cities of God and of Man should have no analog among fallen and unfallen angels, is irrational and unlikely, particularly in the light of the terse but clear biblical evidence to the contrary.

The employment of this dimension of the biblical view of history is frequently attacked as an effort to shift the blame for evil from human beings to devils. But there is no more contradiction between the combination of the world, the flesh and the devil in the production of decline than there is in the conjunction of environmental stress, physical strain and bacteria as causes of illness.

The Bible is extremely restrained in its treatment of angelic beings in contrast to the luxuriant overgrowth of pagan superstition in this area, but it clearly teaches that behind the human power structures of evil there are malignant forces of superhuman power and intelligence directed by "the prince of the power of the air, the spirit that is now at work in the sons of disobedience" (Eph. 2:2). Evidently the evil that emerges naturally from the human can be prompted, shaped and governed by these forces to accomplish their own larger purposes in opposing redemption. Every expansion of the kingdom of God involves combat with and displacement of these occupying powers.

Daniel is told by the angel of the Lord that his prayers have received a delayed answer because of a struggle involving "the prince of the kingdom of Persia," "the kings of Persia" and "the prince of Greece." The fact that he is aided in this combat by the archangel Michael indicates that his opponents are not earthly rulers but governing spirits behind the scenes (Dan. 10:13, 20-21). Paul plainly teaches that the Christian warfare is not "against flesh and blood, but against the principalities, against the powers, against the world rulers of this present darkness, against the spiritual hosts of wickedness in the heavenly places" (Eph. 6:12). Responsible exegesis cannot limit this to hostile earthly power structures or dehumanizing systems and ideologies. The demythologizers are not wrong in pointing to these as superhuman earthly sources of evil, but there is a demonic presence behind them.

The writer of the Revelation, seeking to explain the severity of the opposition to the Christian movement, locates the ultimate cause beyond human society: "Now war arose in heaven, Michael and his angels fighting against the dragon" (Rev. 12:7). When the dragon ("that ancient serpent, who is called the Devil and Satan," Rev. 12:9) is cast down to earth together with his angels, he deceives the nations and makes war upon the Christian movement, but his efforts are not successful: "They have conquered him by the blood of the Lamb and by the word of their testimony; for they loved not their lives even unto death" (Rev. 12:11). The awesome reality behind these symbols is fairly simple to imagine credibly, although it is impossible to comprehend in detail. But there is a strange inability among modern Christians to take this information seriously and an uneasiness even among Evangelicals about paying very much attention to it. I suggest that this reluctance is not because the subject is trivial, morbid or dangerous, but because these forces have access to our minds, and they are just as adept at blinding us to their presence as they are at concealing the gospel from the world (2 Cor. 4:4). Hell is a conspiracy, and the first requirement of a conspiracy is that it remain underground.

These two biblical models explaining cyclical renewal, the pattern of spiritual ebb and flow across the generations and the concept of fluctuations in an expanding warfare against the powers of darkness, are ultimately one and the same. Both in the Judges cycle and in the biblical portrayal of spiritual warfare, popular apostasy is accompanied by enemy encroachment and loss of ground. The defeat of Israel at the hands of its neighbors is simply the visible emblem in history of the internal spiritual losses suffered by the people of God: withdrawal of the Holy Spirit, ascendance of the flesh, conformity to the world, increasing domination by the devil. In both cases deliverance from these forces is only possible by the coming of a leader: in Judges and the rest of the Old Testament, a political leader whose influence lasts a generation; in the hidden spiritual warfare, by the Messiah. Jesus constantly represents his ministry as an attack upon the realm of darkness in order to establish the kingdom of God, and he is presented as battling the occupying spiritual forces, breaking their power, destroying their control and releasing those whom they have held captive.[4] Under messianic rule, visible prevailing of the people of God in history and inner spiritual freedom ought to accompany one another as correlative benefits of the victory of Christ.

A Model of Continuous Renewal

A crucial question arises in light of the New Testament and its revelation of the victory of Christ. If the final leader typified by the judges and kings of Israel has come, why is the advance of the Christian church not continuous? Why is it subject to periods of decline and recovery which so closely resemble the cyclical pattern of the Old Testament? It is understandable that the renewal periods in Judges usually spanned forty years, the lifetime of the human leader. But Christians are under the leadership of a king who is immortal as well as invincible. According to Paul, God "in Christ always leads us in triumph, and through us spreads the fragrance of the knowledge of him everywhere" (2 Cor. 2:14). Why are we so often defeated if he always leads us in triumph? Here is one who fulfills all the leadership roles under the Old Covenant—who is prophet, priest, and king—and

who continually intercedes for us at the right hand of the
Majesty on high (Rom. 8:34; Heb. 8:1). Why don't the cycles
end now, as God's people are led into a steady conquest of the
occupying powers? After all, "the reason the Son of God
appeared was to destroy the works of the devil" (1 Jn. 3:8).
Jesus had told the disciples, "Behold, I have given you
authority to tread upon serpents and scorpions, and over all
the power of the enemy; and nothing shall hurt you" (Lk. 10:
19). In the atonement "he disarmed the principalities and
powers and made a public example of them, triumphing over
them" (Col. 2:15). Paul assured the Romans that "the God of
peace will soon crush Satan under your feet" (Rom. 16:20).
So it seems at first that this victory ought to be constant and
that the cyclical model of spiritual renewal under the Old
Covenant should be replaced by a model of continuous renewal under the lordship of Christ. But even under the New
Covenant, with an eternal and infinitely perfect leader, the
people of God cannot expect to prevail unless they follow
that leader.

The situation in the church has often been analogous to
that of Israel under Joash, Amaziah and Hezekiah, when the
larger mass of the people refused to repent and cooperate
fully with their godly leaders in reformation. The concept of
the believing remnant has a disturbingly constant application to the era of the church. Thus far in time vital Christianity has been a thin stream that sometimes goes underground, only to emerge again to spread abroad like a river
that has been dammed, expanding during awakenings to
form a reservoir that refreshes and transforms a culture for a
generation.

What is involved in the church's periods of recession is
something deeper, however, than simple refusal to follow or
obey its divine leader. The redemptive work of Christ did
not consist in a magnified regent issuing a clearer set of laws
to follow. Redemption is participatory, not imitative. It is
grounded on grace appropriated through faith, not merely on

obedience. Spiritual life flows out of union with Christ, not merely imitation of Christ. When the full dimensions of God's gracious provision in Christ are not clearly articulated in the church, faith cannot apprehend them, and the life of the church will suffer distortion and attenuation. The individual Christian and the church as a whole are alive *in Christ,* and when any essential dimensions of what it means to be in Christ are obscured in the church's understanding, there is no guarantee that the people of God will strive toward and experience fullness of life.

But what are the essential elements of life in Christ? What are the dimensions of experience which issue from our union with him and which can be appropriated by faith and sought for in the life of the church? The answer to this question seems at first to transcend analysis. It is like a blaze of white light which contains an almost numberless succession of colors and wavelengths, "the unsearchable riches of Christ, ... the manifold wisdom of God" (Eph. 3:8, 10). I am seeking to analyze this splendor into a manageable number of definite elements by refracting it through a series of prisms: the experience of the church in periods of renewal, the experience of the revived church in Acts and the New Testament theology of Christian experience (see Figure 1).

Essential Elements of Renewal. There are two redemptive benefits of the atonement, results of our union with Christ in his death and resurrection, which stand out immediately as critically important elements in the history of church renewal: *justification* and *sanctification.* We have seen that most of the major awakenings have involved among their central catalysts a balanced proclamation of justification by faith and the necessity of progressive sanctification. The first evangelistic message of the church in Acts involved at least an embryonic emphasis on these two elements, since it called both for repentance and justifying faith in Jesus Christ (Acts 2:38). When the infant church had received its first

I. Preconditions of Renewal: Preparation for the Gospel

A. Awareness of the holiness of God
$\left\{\begin{array}{l}\text{his justice} \\ \text{his love}\end{array}\right.$

B. Awareness of the depth of sin
$\left\{\begin{array}{l}\text{in your own life} \\ \text{in your community}\end{array}\right.$

II. Primary Elements of Renewal: Depth Presentation of the Gospel

A. Justification: You are accepted

B. Sanctification: You are free from bondage to sin

C. The indwelling Spirit: You are not alone

D. Authority in spiritual conflict: You have authority

$\left.\right\}$ in Christ

III. Secondary Elements of Renewal: Outworking of the Gospel in the Church's Life

A. Mission: following Christ into the world, presenting his gospel
$\left\{\begin{array}{l}\text{in proclamation} \\ \text{in social demonstration}\end{array}\right.$

B. Prayer: expressing dependence on the power of his Spirit
$\left\{\begin{array}{l}\text{individually} \\ \text{corporately}\end{array}\right.$

C. Community: being in union with his body
$\left\{\begin{array}{l}\text{in microcommunities} \\ \text{in macrocommunities}\end{array}\right.$

D. Disenculturation: being freed from cultural binds
$\left\{\begin{array}{l}\text{destructive} \\ \text{protective}\end{array}\right.$

E. Theological Integration: having the mind of Christ
$\left\{\begin{array}{l}\text{toward revealed truth} \\ \text{toward your culture}\end{array}\right.$

Figure 1. Dynamics of Spiritual Life

theologian, the apostle Paul, he went on to establish this balance very carefully in his teaching. In Colossians, for example, he weaves these benefits together closely in delineating what is needed to go on growing up in union with Christ:

As you therefore have received Christ Jesus the Lord, so walk in Him, having been firmly rooted and now being built up in Him and established in your faith, just as you were instructed, and overflowing with gratitude. . . . In Him you have been made complete, and He is the head over all rule and authority; and in Him you were also circumcised with a circumcision made without hands, in the removal of the body of the flesh by the circumcision of Christ; having been buried with Him in baptism, in which you were also raised up with Him through faith in the working of God, who raised Him from the dead. And when you were dead in your transgressions and the uncircumcision of your flesh, He made you alive together with Him, having forgiven us all our transgressions, having cancelled out the certificate of debt consisting of decrees against us and which was hostile to us; and He has taken it out of the way, having nailed it to the cross. When He had disarmed the rulers and authorities, He made a public display of them, having triumphed over them through Him. (Col. 2: 6-7, 10-15 NASB)

This passage speaks on the one hand of justification and the forgiveness of sins under the figure of nailing the certificate of our debt to the cross, and on the other hand of regeneration and progressive sanctification in the metaphor of circumcision linked with that of death and resurrection.

Two additional benefits of the atonement are immediately suggested by the historical and biblical contexts associated with these first elements: the indwelling of the Holy Spirit and the authority of the believer over the powers of darkness. Justification makes possible the most intimate relationship of Christ with the believer, his personal residence in the wellsprings of our existence in the person of the Holy Spirit.

The same Spirit is vitally active in the transformation process of sanctification. Peter's first sermon and its historical context emphasize the importance of the ministry of the Spirit, and Paul mentions his role in administering the benefits of redemption in two major passages dealing with sanctification—Romans 8 and Galatians 5.

Colossians 2:15 includes the triumph of Christ over the powers of darkness among the fruits of redemption, and the New Testament makes clear that our union with Christ gives us authority to execute the judgment he accomplished by displacing the powers of darkness from our lives and from the field of our ministry, just as justification, sanctification and the indwelling Spirit help us to displace sin. Believers are therefore covered by the perfect righteousness of Christ reckoned to them in justification; strengthened by the power of Christ's life in sanctification; given immediate access to the mind and heart of Christ by the indwelling of the Spirit; and equipped with the authority of Christ in resisting, exposing and expelling the forces of darkness. A more thoroughgoing identification with the leadership of Christ himself is impossible to imagine. It is not surprising that Paul, in one of his most famous utterances, is moved to say, "I have been crucified with Christ; it is no longer I who live, but Christ who lives in me" (Gal. 2:20).

These four benefits of redemption—justification, sanctification, the indwelling of the Spirit and authority in spiritual conflict—are normally encompassed in theological treatments of the atonement, and they might be called *primary elements* in the dynamics of spiritual life. In addition to these there are at least five dimensions of our existence in Christ which seem to be distinct and separable as seen in Scripture and revival history, although they in part derive from primary factors, as secondary colors derive from mixtures of the primaries. These are *orientation toward mission, dependent prayer, the community of believers, disenculturation* and *theological integration.*

The first three of these factors are immediately obvious when the early chapters of Acts are correlated with the history of church renewal. We have found that awakenings in church history have involved not only the purification of the existing church but the expansion of its missionary witness. The disciples in Acts 1 were expecting the first of these effects, the transformation of the people of God and the reign of the saints in his kingdom. But they were confronted by Christ with a challenge to wait until later for the external manifestations of the kingdom while realizing those which were internal. At the same time, they were to help initiate the kingdom through the proclamation of Christ's reign throughout the earth. In effect, they could not remain fully in *Christ* without following him in his conquest of the surrounding darkness. And since the "acts of the apostles" were not really their acts alone but those of the risen Lord, they could not plunge into this conflict in their own strength, but had to acknowledge explicitly their weakness and dependence in corporate prayer until they were endued with the power and direction of the Holy Spirit.

Both the preparation for mission in prayer and the ingathering of believers when mission had been launched are enveloped in a context of unity and community, since the disciples and their converts were not isolated spiritual units but members of a supernatural organism, the body of Christ. We have already noted the persistent reappearance of small intentional communities in the history of church renewal and the thematic commitment to the larger ecumenical community characteristic of revival leaders. In order to experience normal spirituality Christians must go with Jesus Christ into mission, must depend on him to direct and empower in this, and must give and take sustenance in community with the members of his body.

The last two secondary factors mentioned are perhaps less obvious. The revived church in the early chapters of Acts was operating only with the experiential core of the gospel message, not with a fully developed theology, and it was still unconsciously wedded to Jewish culture. In subsequent church history some awakenings have taken place in a context of deficient theology and innocent enculturation. The conquest of Roman civilization by the postapostolic church exhibits the first characteristic, while revivals since the Reformation exhibit the second. Nevertheless, the thrust of the church's development in Acts seems to prove that the Christian movement cannot go on to achieve its full maturity unless its mind is fully articulated by theologians like Paul (Acts 9—28) and its cultural limitations transcended by a clear separation of the absolute Christian message from its relative cultural incarnations (Acts 10—15).

Revival and Christian Understanding. Church history shows that the fullness of spiritual life in the church is not *necessarily* conditional on the possession of any of these elements. *Spiritual life is produced by the presence and empowering of the Holy Spirit, not simply by the comprehension of doctrinal propositions or strategies of renewal.* Under the Old Covenant, prior to the conceptual knowledge of any of these elements, there was still a substantial level of spiritual vitality among the people of God. That is why the experience of Pentecost is in some respects a revival, a revitalization and expansion of a life previously existing among God's people.

In a sense Israel possessed some knowledge of justification through the sacrifices and an awareness of the need for sanctification through the law. But many fairly substantial awakenings have taken place in the context of very deficient awareness of the dynamics of spiritual life. The expansion of the church in the first three centuries occurred while justification was still imperfectly understood, for example. But since spiritual life is rooted in faith and missing elements are usually replaced by misapprehensions which amount to unbelief, failure to understand rightly any of the primary or secondary dimensions affected by our union with Christ inevitably produces distortions and deficiencies in the church's experience. The church during awakenings is often like an infant, vigorously alive but with many areas of its future development still embryonic. Its continuance in vitality is not always dependent on perfect comprehension of the provisions of redemption, but it does require *movement toward the experience of those provisions.* Enjoyment of full spiritual vitality by individuals or churches is not an automatic result of comprehending all the facets of redemption; it depends on the *relationship* of believers to the sovereign Lord. Movement toward grace is accepted and blessed by the presence of God, while retreat from growth yields increasing spiritual barrenness.

PRECONDITIONS
OF
CONTINUOUS
RENEWAL

3

BEFORE WE MOVE ON TO A MORE DETAILED examination of the primary and secondary elements of renewal summarized in the last chapter, we need to consider two other factors affecting spiritual life which are so closely linked together that they are like the two sides of a coin. The various elements of renewal are dimensions of our union with Christ. But our first coming to Christ and the strength of our expression of new life in him are dependent on our accurate apprehension of our own need and of the character of the true God.

Acceptance of Christ and appropriation of every element in redemption is conditional on awareness of God's holiness and conviction of the depth of our sin. As Calvin states in the great opening chapter of his *Institutes*, these two factors are essential to that degree of self-knowledge which drives a man to inquire after Christ, and they are deeply interrelated.[1]

Men and women cannot know themselves until they know
the reality of the God who made them, and once they know
the holy God, their own sin appears so grievous that they
cannot rest until they have fully appropriated Christ.

The Old Testament precedes the New for an important
spiritual reason. As Luther said, "Hunger is the best cook";
and the "law-work" of the Old Testament, as the Puritans
would call it, was designed to awaken hunger for every
dimension of redemption. The experience of the people of
God under the Old Covenant was "a tutor unto Christ," and
the degree of spiritual vitality present among the Israelites
was directly proportionate to their progress in "the fear of
the Lord" and in repentance: "For thus says the high and
lofty One who inhabits eternity, whose name is Holy: 'I
dwell in the high and holy place, and also with him who is
of a contrite and humble spirit, to revive the spirit of the
humble, and to revive the heart of the contrite' " (Is. 57:15).
The Israelites whose hearts were thus prepared by the application of the law were especially attuned to the importance
of the sacrifices. Thus they were able to recognize the Lamb
of God when he came and were revived by his ministry.

Knowing God and Knowing Ourselves
Knowledge of God and knowledge of self are preconditions
of spiritual life because revival involves awakening; the connection is so strong that the terms are used as synonyms in
this book. What men wake up to in the light of a revival is
their own condition and the nature of the true God. This was
the experience of Isaiah, whose revitalizing vision of the
holiness and power of God struck at the root of his own self-
understanding: "Woe is me! For I am lost; for I am a man of
unclean lips, and I dwell in the midst of a people of unclean
lips; for my eyes have seen the King, the LORD of hosts!" (Is.
6:5). It was also the experience of Job, who awakened fully
when the voice of God spoke to him out of the whirlwind,
moving him to confess: "I had heard of thee by the hearing of

the ear, but now my eye sees thee; therefore I despise myself, and repent in dust and ashes" (Job 42:5-6).

The Protestant Reformers were fully aware of this factor. It was Luther's perception of the depth of his own sin *coram deo* (measured by the holiness of God, not by common human estimation) that opened his heart to the need for justification by faith.[2] The "Copernican revolution" of the Reformation, which placed the grace of God in Christ in the center of the Christian mental universe, dislodging works and the church from that position, resulted from the same awareness.[3] The Puritans and Pietists and the leaders of the First Awakening carried over these insights into God's holiness and human depravity and articulated them in vigorous preaching. This undoubtedly accounts for the almost devastating impact of their sermons and the depth of the resulting conversions.

Subsequent generations, however, gradually moved away from the Reformation in these areas. Rationalist religion, reacting against exaggerated and overexplicit portrayals of human wickedness and divine wrath among many Puritans, began to stress the goodness of man and the benevolence of the Deity. By the time of the Second Awakening, many leaders of the revival were adjusting to this critique by presenting an increasingly kindly, fatherly and thoroughly comprehensible God. In the late nineteenth century, D. L. Moody determined to center his message around the truth that "God is Love" and to tone down the mention of hell and the wrath of God to the point of inaudibility.[4] But this was only one example of the sentimentalizing of God in every sector of the church, among evangelicals and the rising Liberal movement alike.

The whole church was drifting quietly toward Marcionism, avoiding the biblical portrait of the sovereign and holy God who is angry with the wicked every day and whose anger remains upon those who will not receive his Son. Walling off this image into an unvisited corner of its consciousness, the church substituted a new god who was the projection of grandmotherly kindness mixed with the gentleness and winsomeness of a Jesus who hardly needed to die for our sins.[5] Many American congregations were in effect paying their ministers to protect them from the real God. The decay of spirituality resulting from this deception can already be traced in the latter half of the nineteenth century. It is partially responsible not only for the general spiritual collapse of the church in this century but also for a great deal of apologetic weakness; for in a world in which the sovereign and holy God regularly employs plagues, famines, wars, disease and death as instruments to punish sin and bring mankind to repentance, the idolatrous image of God as pure benevolence cannot really be believed, let alone feared and worshiped in the manner prescribed by both the Old and New Testaments.

It is important that the point made here not be misunderstood. There is no doubt that American Puritans did overstress "hellfire and damnation." At the same time they injected the mysteries of God's sovereignty into the foreground of their preaching in a way that was not only paralyzingly inappropriate but without precedent in Augustine, Luther and Calvin. I am not calling for a return to this. It is only in the light of the revelation through the cross of God's overwhelming love for his creation that we can understand his anger against the distortion or destruction of that creation. The cross, in fact, is the perfect statement both of God's wrath against sin and of the depth of his love and mercy in the recovery of the damaged creation and its damagers. God's mercy, patience and love must be fully preached in the church. But they are not *credible* unless they are presented in tension with God's infinite power, complete and sovereign control of the universe, holiness, and righteousness. And where God's righteousness is clearly presented, compassionate warnings of his holy anger against sin must be given, and warnings also of the certainty of divine judgment in endless alienation from God which will be unimaginably worse than the literal descriptions of hell. It is no wonder that the world and the church are not awakened when our leadership is either singing a lullaby concerning these matters or presenting them in a caricature which is so grotesque that it is unbelievable.

The tension between God's holy righteousness and his compassionate mercy cannot be legitimately resolved by remolding his character into an image of pure benevolence as the church did in the nineteenth century. There is only one way that this contradiction can be removed: through the cross of Christ which reveals the severity of God's anger against sin and the depth of his compassion in paying its penalty through the vicarious sacrifice of his Son. In systems which resolve this tension by softening the character of God, Christ and his work become an addendum, and spiritual darkness becomes complete because the true God has been abandoned for the worship of a magnified image of human tolerance.

The apprehension of God's presence is the ultimate core of genuine Christian experience, and the touchstone of its authenticity is the believer's vision of the character of God. Edwards felt that every experience of God could be counterfeited except those which involved an insight into his holiness. It is significant that during the Great Awakening a sense of the infinite excellence of the divine nature was common among those undergoing conversion. In our own time so many forms of Christianity have become man-centered that this experience is seldom generated by our preaching. In the advanced stages of our anthropocentric religion, God the Father becomes as unnecessary as God the Son, as can be seen in some forms of the Death of God theology of the late 1960s. One of the most hopeful contributions of the Charismatic renewal movement has been its divergence from this trend and its insistence on the experience of God's presence in a context of worship and prayer. But unless the God who is worshiped is the awesome, holy, sovereign Lord of Scripture, even this approach cannot continue to serve as a catalyst for spiritual life.

The Depth of Sin
During the last two centuries the understanding of sin has suffered a correlative decline in the church along with the apprehension of God. The Reformers perceived that fallen human nature was touched in every area by the deforming presence of original sin, the compulsive force operating behind individual acts of transgression. They believed that man has freedom of will to do as he pleases but that without the renewing work of the Spirit he is incurably averse to seeking and serving God. Apart from grace his best actions are still built upon the foundation of unbelief, and even his virtues are organized as weapons against the rule of God.

Edwards summed up the Reformation's critique of humanity's pretense of goodness in a sermon called "Men Naturally God's Enemies," based on Paul's statement in Romans that the unregenerate mind is hostile toward God. Although most human beings give the appearance at times of being confused seekers for truth with a naive respect for God, says Edwards, the reality is that unless they are moved by the Spirit they have a natural distaste for the real God, an uncontrollable desire to break his laws and a constant tendency to sit in judgment on him when they notice him at all. They are at moral enmity with the God revealed in the Bible. Since his purposes cross theirs at every juncture, they really hate him more than any finite object, and this is clearly displayed in their treatment of his Son. They are largely unconscious of this enmity. It is usually repressed through their unbelief, their creation of agreeable false portraits of God, their sense of his distance from us, their fear of punishment or their lack of awareness of the magnitude of their guilt. They are conditioned to pay their respects to some vague image of the Deity, and this is reinforced by fear and self-interest.

Fortunately God's common grace reaches down through un-regenerate humanity like a hand through a glove, relieving us of the full burden of our own evil through constant acts of love and mercy that seem to originate in man. But only in Christian believers is man's willful ignorance disarmed and his goodness rooted in worship and love of God rather than covert self-interest or the service of idols such as the human race. When the Scripture says that "God is angry with the wicked every day" (Ps. 7:11 AV), it is because the unre-generate are constantly (if unconsciously) angry at God and are daily expressing this anger and contempt toward those who represent him on earth, toward one another, and even toward inanimate nature because God has made it. Every day the crucifixion is re-enacted in innumerable attacks upon the purposes of Christ. Even creation, suggests Edwards in an-other famous sermon,[6] groans under its subjection to human misrule and would spew us out if it were not restrained by God.

In the light of this analysis, what is remarkable is not the intensity of God's wrath against sin but the magnitude of his patience and compassion in sparing and redeeming those who are his enemies. If this picture seems excessively dark, it should be remembered that God's grace is constantly and secretly at work in the world to lighten what would be pure darkness if left to itself. It should also be remembered that this estimate of human nature is clearly derived from Scrip-ture, no matter how distant it seems from our common way of thinking about ourselves. When the apostle Paul was being realistic about his own life, he admitted, "I know that noth-ing good dwells within me, that is, in my flesh" (Rom. 7:18). By *flesh* Paul means human nature apart from the renewing work of the Holy Spirit.

In the eighteenth and nineteenth centuries this depth analysis of sin was abandoned by the growing rationalist movement, which because of its dim apprehension of God began to define *virtue* in ways unrelated to worship and faith in him, and thus to affirm the essential goodness of human nature. During the same period the church's consciousness of sin began to erode along with its awareness of God. Gradually sin began to be defined in a way which seemed more rationally defensible: sins are conscious, voluntary acts of transgression against known laws. The depth awareness of sin discovered by Augustine, Luther, Calvin and Edwards was exchanged by most Christians for a concept of sin which was virtually Pelagian.[7]

During the late nineteenth century, while the church's understanding of the unconscious motivation behind surface actions was vanishing, Sigmund Freud rediscovered this factor and recast it in an elaborate and profound secular mythology. One of the consequences of this remarkable shift is that in the twentieth century pastors have often been reduced to the status of legalistic moralists, while the deeper aspects of the cure of souls are generally relegated to psychotherapy, even among Evangelical Christians.

But the structure of sin in the human personality is something far more complicated than the isolated acts and thoughts of deliberate disobedience commonly designated by the word. In its biblical definition, sin cannot be limited to isolated instances or patterns of wrongdoing; it is something much more akin to the psychological term *complex*: an organic network of compulsive attitudes, beliefs and behavior deeply rooted in our alienation from God. Sin originated in the darkening of the human mind and heart as man turned from the truth about God to embrace a lie about him and consequently a whole universe of lies about his creation. Sinful thoughts, words and deeds flow forth from this darkened heart automatically and compulsively, as water from a polluted fountain. "The LORD saw that the wickedness of man was great in the earth, and that every imagination of the thoughts of his heart was only evil continually" (Gen. 6:5). This is echoed in Jesus' words: "Either make the tree good, and its fruit good; or make the tree bad, and its fruit bad; for the tree is known by its fruit. You brood of vipers! how can you speak good, when you are evil? For out of the abundance of the heart the mouth speaks. The good man out of his good treasure brings forth good, and the evil man out of his evil treasure brings forth evil" (Mt. 12:33-35).

The human heart is now a reservoir of unconscious disordered motivation and response, of which unrenewed persons are unaware if left to themselves, for "the heart is deceitful above all things, and desperately corrupt; who can understand it?" (Jer. 17:9). It is as if they were without mirrors and suffering from tunnel vision: they can see neither themselves clearly nor the great peripheral area around their immediate experience (God and supernatural reality). At the two most crucial loci of their understanding, their awareness of God and of themselves, they are almost in total darkness, although they may attempt to remedy this by framing false images of themselves and God. Paul describes this darkness of the unregenerate mind: "Now this I affirm and testify in the Lord, that you must no longer live as the Gentiles do, in the futility of their minds; they are darkened in their understanding, alienated from the life of God because of the ignorance that is in them, due to their hardness of heart" (Eph. 4: 17-18). The mechanism by which this unconscious reservoir of darkness is formed is identified in Rom. 1:18-23 as repression of traumatic material, chiefly the truth about God and our condition, which the unregenerate constantly and dynamically "hold down." Their darkness is always a voluntary darkness, though they are unaware that they are repressing the truth.

The Flesh

The New Testament designates the total organism of sin by the term *sarx* (flesh), referring to the fallen human personality apart from the renewing influence and control of the Holy Spirit. The flesh is always somewhat mysterious to us, particularly in its effect on our minds and in its operation in the redeemed personality. The New Testament constantly describes it as something much deeper than the isolated moments of sin which it generates. The lists of the works of the flesh in Galatians 5:19-21 and Colossians 3:5-9 point mostly to heart conditions rather than discrete actions: sensuality, idolatry, sorcery, hatred, jealousy, party spirit, envy.

Augustine divided the trunk of the flesh into two main branches, *pride* (self-aggrandizement) and *sensuality* (self-indulgence), which in their interaction together might be held to generate most other forms of sin. Luther, however, perceived that the main root of the flesh behind pride and sensuality was *unbelief;* and his analysis takes in some forms of sin which are apparently "selfless" and altruistic, like the ethical behavior of atheistic humanists. In any case, the characteristic bent of the flesh is toward independence from God, his truth and his will, as if man himself were God. Therefore the flesh might be called a "God complex." Kierkegaard, Reinhold Niebuhr and Tillich are not wrong, however, in suggesting that *anxiety* is at the root of much sinful behavior, since the unconscious awareness of our independence from God and an unrelieved consciousness of guilt create a profound insecurity in the unbeliever or the Christian who is not walking in light. This insecurity generates a kind of compensatory egoism, self-oriented but somewhat different from serious pride. Thus much of what is called pride is actually not godlike self-admiration, but masked inferiority, insecurity and deep self-loathing.

Luther was right: the root behind all other manifestations of sin is compulsive unbelief—our voluntary darkness concerning God, ourselves, his relationship to the fallen world and his redemptive purpose. For this reason the entrance and growth of new spiritual life involves the shattering of our sphere of darkness by repentant faith in redemptive truth. If the Fall occurred through the embracing of lies, the recovery process of salvation must center on faith in truth, reversing this condition. Therefore Jesus says to those who are trapped in unconscious slavery to sin, "If you continue in my word, you are truly my disciples, and you will know the truth, and the truth will make you free" (Jn. 8:31-32).[8] The deliverance which brings us into spiritual life in communion with God is summed up in John's description of redeemed behavior as withdrawing from darkness and walking in the light of truth and holiness:

> God is light and in him is no darkness at all. If we say we have fellowship with him while we walk in darkness, we lie and do not live according to the truth; but if we walk in the light, as he is in the light, we have fellowship with one another, and the blood of Jesus his Son cleanses us from all sin. (1 Jn. 1:5-7, compare Ps. 32 and 51)

The truth used by the Holy Spirit to bring about this deliverance is the biblical teaching which reveals to us our need, God's character and the elements of redemptive truth concerning Jesus Christ. This truth is the central core of the dynamics of continuous renewal.

Since unbelief is the heart of sin, and "whatever is not from faith is sin," every thought and action of believers is tinged with some sinful admixture. Sinless behavior requires perfect control and direction by the Holy Spirit, and this implies an enlightening and enlivening work of the Spirit which is never complete in this existence, for none of us walks completely in the light. "If we say we have no sin, we deceive ourselves, and the truth is not in us. If we confess our sins, he is faithful and just, and will forgive our sins and cleanse us from all unrighteousness" (1 Jn. 1:8-9). A sinless man would love God with all his heart, and soul, and mind, and his neighbor as himself, constantly and with full vigor. The most advanced saint on earth has neither the faith nor the Spirit-empowered love to do this, and therefore a continual cleansing of our experience through the blood of Christ is necessary for us to be righteous in the sight of God, and this cleansing involves the awareness and admission of our falling short.

Like the truth about the real nature of God, the truth about the depth of sin has an important apologetic application today. The bulk of mankind in the twentieth century has arrived at the belief that it has "come of age," that it can function in every department of experience without the hypothesis of God. Involved in this belief is the conviction that men can be ethically righteous and respectable without reference to God. A biblical analysis of the nature of sin makes clear that such "goodness" rests on bad faith and on a fearful unconscious resistance to the true God and his claims over the totality of our lives. The proclamation of this analysis will awaken conviction of sin and hunger for Christ in a way that positive exposition of grace alone might not accomplish. Modern man is not immune to the impact of traditional Christian terminology; he is simply inert in the presence of answers to questions he has not yet been induced to ask.

Kierkegaard complained that the New Testament as usually understood is an inadequate instrument for converting respectable people because it was designed for sinners. "Owing to this it is almost impossible by the aid of the New Testament to punch a blow at real life, at the actual world in which we live, where for one certified hypocrite there are 100,000 twaddlers, for one certified heretic, 100,000 nincompoops."[9] But when both sin and righteousness are presented in the depth with which they are actually viewed in the New Testament, this difficulty disappears.

A depth understanding of sin has other important implications for the awakening of the church. Most congregations of professing Christians today are saturated with a kind of *dead goodness*, an ethical respectability which has its motivational roots in the flesh rather than in the illuminating and enlivening control of the Holy Spirit. In 2 Timothy 3 Paul describes this surface righteousness which does not spring from faith and the Spirit's renewing action, but from religious pride and conditioned conformity to tradition, as a form of godliness which denies its power. It goes without saying that many congregations which are built upon such counterfeit piety are Evangelical in name, descendants of the great awakening movements—and yet they themselves are today in desperate need of new awakening! Observers in the Charismatic movement would say that such churches are in need of "the baptism of the Spirit," and they would not be far from truth in this analysis; but what may be instrumental in obtaining such a baptism is an exposure of the subtlety of the flesh.

At the opposite extreme from religious formalism, there is a great deal of active religiosity in the world and in the Christian church which is also energized by the flesh, and sometimes by the devil as well. This "religious flesh" or "fleshly religiosity" will be discussed in some detail in a later chapter dealing with aberrations of revival, but it should be noted here as one of the forms of sin which stifle the church's real vitality and detract from its witness. Paul confesses that all the vigor of his religious life prior to conversion was rubbish, that his zeal only led him to attempt to destroy the purposes of God. And this is God's assessment of religious flesh. At its best it is an ugly disfigurement of the church's face; at its worst it sprays death and deadness on everything it touches (Phil. 3).

The World

For individuals and churches to be infused with spiritual life, not only the flesh as an agent of death but also the world and the devil must be displaced. We discussed the powers of darkness in chapter two. Now we must focus on the world.

When *world* is used in a negative sense in Scripture, what is meant is the total system of corporate flesh operating on earth under satanic control, with all its incentives of reward and restraints of loss, its characteristic patterns of behavior, and its antichristian structures, methods, goals and ideologies.[10] It is substantially identical with the biblical symbol of the harlot Babylon and with Augustine's City of Man. It involves many forms and agencies of evil which are hard to discern and to contend against on the basis of an individualistic view of sin. Included are dehumanizing social, economic and political systems; business operations and foreign policy based on local interest at the expense of general human welfare; and culturally pervasive institutionalized sin such as racism. Like the many-headed beast of Revelation 13, the world is secretly compatible with and operative within systems which are antithetical on the surface, such as capitalism and communism.

Since we are inextricably bound up with corporate sin through our participation in nations and institutions, there is no way that we can avoid implication in the guilt of the fallen world, and therefore biblical saints confess the sins of their community along with those they have personally committed.[11] But we are required to separate ourselves as much as possible from the unholy force field of this planet's corporate flesh; to break our conformity to its characteristic ideologies, methods and motives; and to speak and act prophetically against its injustice and restraint of full human liberation.

Much of the Christian community today is deeply penetrated by worldly patterns of thinking, motivation and behavior, and thus its spiritual life is deadened and its witness rendered ineffectual. Individuals, churches, schools and ministries must become sensitive to the areas of unholy conformity to the world in their behavior if the Spirit of holiness is really to possess them in fullness. But this is an awesome task, requiring an experience of the revelation of God's holiness and the depth of human sin like that which gripped Isaiah, who in his vision of God saw clearly not only his own sin but also the unclean lips of the people among whom he lived. Only this vision will motivate the world—and the church—to appropriate all the dimensions of life available in the fullness of Jesus Christ.

PRIMARY ELEMENTS OF CONTINUOUS RENEWAL

4

I HAVE ALREADY INDICATED THAT THE conditions of spiritual life in Christ are divisible into *primary* and *secondary factors.* The primary factors are those involved in traditional theories of the atonement, which answer most immediately the urgent hunger and thirst for righteousness awakened in the individual who has come into the light concerning the nature of the true God and his or her own sinful condition. They are the heart of the gospel, the good news of the reconciliation Christ accomplished through his death and resurrection.

It is true that a simple exposition of the *person* of Jesus Christ the God-man and an exhortation to encounter him personally and thus experience God's love is often used by the Holy Spirit as the catalyst of conversion. At the outset of their ministry, before the theological mind of Paul had spread out the full spectrum of meaning in the work of Christ, the apostles preached only the messianic identity of Christ, his earthly ministry, death and resurrection, and yet thousands were converted. Indeed the church had no settled consensus of understanding about the person of Christ until response to the rise of Arian unitarianism and other conflicting Christologies brought the church to an agreement at Nicaea in A.D. 325, and even the Nicene formula guarding the full divinity and humanity of Christ was contested in the church until the Council of Constantinople in 381.

The modern Christian who begins to search the New Testament for evidence of the deity of Christ may be surprised to find that it was not an element of the gospel which was pushed to the forefront of the apostolic witness; as B. B. Warfield says, it is a doctrine which is not so much heard as overheard in the scripture. Of course it is clearly taught—in John's repeated references to the Trinity, in Paul's delineation of "the cosmic Christ" and most eloquently in the repentant cry of doubting Thomas, "My Lord and my God!" (Jn. 20:28). But Jesus and the apostles may have moved this essential component of the gospel into the background of their proclamation, knowing that it would scandalize Jewish hearers who had some understanding of the awesome holiness of the true God and would mean little to Gentiles who might all too readily accept the idea of a man who was also a god. This strategy would probably have aided the evangelistic task. It would assume that those who responded to the portrayal of Jesus as the unique Messiah would readily come to acknowledge his deity after subsequent teaching, like the disciples whose first acquaintance with him deepened into later understanding. This may suggest something to us about our own approach to Jewish believers. At the same time the situation of the Gentiles may suggest why many Christian converts who are taught to accept Christ as God, without being taught the nature of God, are shallow and sometimes not even genuine.

In the same way, the full meaning of Christ as the Lamb of

God—that is, of his dying in our place as a sacrifice sufficient to satisfy the requirements of God's holiness and justice in the face of our sins—was not fully stated in the church until Anselm's *Cur Deus Homo* in the eleventh century, although it is clearly part of the apostolic witness.[1] At times in the church's history this understanding of Christ's death as a substitutionary sacrifice has been eclipsed by other aspects of the atonement: in the Eastern church and some more recent theologies by the Incarnation and the idea of participation in the divine life; in some early theologians by the idea of ransom and the defeat of the powers of darkness through the cross; in midnineteenth-century American revivalism by the notion of Christ's death as a public exhibition of divine justice; and in some modern liberalism by Abelard's theory of the exhibition of God's love moving mankind toward repentant faith.

It is too much to say that the church's life is utterly absent or destroyed where the substitutionary penal view of the atonement is not taught. Nevertheless, as the father of American liberalism, Horace Bushnell, commented late in his life, there is something in the sacrificial view of Christ's death which speaks to needs deep within the human heart as nothing else does.[2] There is an essential connection between this doctrine and the perception of God's holiness, as the centrality of the sacrifices in the Old Testament shows. Bushnell also commented that a non-Trinitarian view of Christ greatly impoverishes our vision of the wonder and complexity of the character of God, and it is certainly empirically true in history that a failure to assert the Trinity and the sacrificial death of Christ has involved a waning of spiritual life in the church, and eventually its extinction.[3]

The substitutionary atonement is the heart of the gospel, and it is so because it gives the answer to the problem of guilt, bondage and alienation from God. The earlier this answer can be spelled out in the process of evangelism and nurture, the better. Persons come to Christ initially for a variety of reasons, some of which are eccentric to their principal need for redemption: loneliness, a sense of meaninglessness in the godless life, suffering, fear and so on. Only those are lastingly converted, however, whose eventual motivation is to turn from their sin to God and receive the answer to sin in the work of Jesus Christ: "For everyone who does evil hates the light, and does not come to the light, lest his deeds should be exposed. But he who does what is true comes to the light, that it may be clearly seen that his deeds have been wrought in God" (Jn. 3:20-21). Spiritual life results from fellowship with God. But walking in light is essential to fellowship with the Father and the Son. Believers who are truly established in Christ have experienced the shattering of their spheres of ignorance and darkness by a growing understanding of the nature of God, their sin and God's provision of grace in Jesus Christ. This darkness can only be destroyed by the presentation of the preconditions of renewal and by the proclamation of the heart of the gospel in depth.

Justification
In the New Testament portrayal of the application of redemption, *justification* (the acceptance of believers as righteous in the sight of God through the righteousness of Jesus Christ accounted to them) and *sanctification* (progress in actual holiness expressed in their lives) are often closely intertwined, as if there two concepts were identical.[4] In reality, however, they are quite distinct: justification is the perfect righteousness of Christ *reckoned* to us, covering the remaining imperfections in our lives like a robe of stainless holiness; sanctification is the process of *removing* those imperfections as we are enabled more and more to put off the bondages of sin and put on new life in Christ. The biblical writers closely conjoined these two elements not because they were identical but because they are inseparable in our experience and rooted in our union with Christ. Paul's attack on the legalism of the Galatian Christians indicates, however, that

he rejected unequivocally any attempt to suspend our justification on our actual righteousness according to the law instead of on Christ's righteousness apprehended by faith.[5]

Paul's frequent attacks on the problem of legalism in other epistles indicates that the first-century church was often oblivious of the distinction between justification and sanctification. This problem is even more sharply visible in Christian writings of the second century, which almost uniformly assume that our justification is based on our sanctification and that we are made acceptable to God by our works. This concept reached its highest refinement in the work of Augustine, who taught that along with the gift of faith God infuses into believers' actual experience the righteousness of Christ, placing them in a "state of grace" which makes them acceptable to God. Augustine's teaching on salvation avoided some of the pitfalls of the calculus-of-merit theology common in later Catholicism, since it ultimately grounded justification on final perseverance in dependent faith in Christ, not on our contribution of a percentage of works.

But both the theology of merit and Augustine's teaching on infused grace ultimately place an unbearable burden on the conscience which comes fully into the light. The fully enlightened conscience cannot be pacified by any amount of grace inherent in our lives, since that grace always falls short of the perfection demanded by God's law for our justification (Gal. 3:10; Jas. 2:10). Such a conscience is forced to draw back into the relative darkness of self-deception. Either it manufactures a fictitious righteousness in heroic works of ascetic piety, or it redefines sin in shallow terms so that it can lose the consciousness of its presence.

Western Catholicism had been availing itself of both these remedies for centuries when Luther's struggles as an Augustinian monk convinced him that Augustine's solution to the problem of justification was an unworkable foundation for the Christian life. Wrestling with the meaning of "the righteousness of God" in Romans 1:17, Luther saw that the phrase actually designated the kind of righteousness which God can accept, a righteousness which springs only from faith relying upon the wholly alien righteousness of Christ. At the same time faith itself is a gift of grace. This insight brought immense relief to the Reformer's conscience and released his gifts in an explosive ministry of liberation to the rest of the church. It is providentially fitting that Luther's name resembles the Greek word for *freedom*, for the power of his central insight blows through all his writings like a great wind of joyful liberation.

Viewed from one perspective, the Protestant Reformation was an effort to remake every sector of the church according to biblical direction. In another sense, however, the spiritual heart of the Reformation was more simply an effort to rebuild the understanding of the Christian life, incorporating Luther's insight on justification. The full success of this venture has been repeatedly thwarted by the ease with which sinful people can twist the essential truth of Luther's insight. On the one hand, justification by faith can be transformed into the wholly unbiblical teaching of justification without sanctification, which Bonhoeffer has called "cheap grace."[6] On the other hand, Puritan and Pietist efforts to guard against this abuse often led to an admixture of ascetic legalism in the realm of spiritual discipline. An unbalanced stress on auxiliary methods of assurance—testing one's life by the inspection of works and searching for the internal witness of the Spirit—obscured Luther's teaching on assurance of salvation through naked reliance on the work of Christ. Later the shift toward rationalism in parts of the church began to obscure the holiness of God and the depth of sin, introducing a moralism which found no use at all for the doctrine of justification. These three aberrations from the biblical teaching on justification—cheap grace, legalism, and moralism—still dominate the church today.

A large part of institutional Protestantism assumes that all professing Christians (and perhaps all men) are justified,

whether or not they show evidence of conversion and sanctification. This is simply the modern form of cheap grace. Another sector of Protestantism and much of the Catholic tradition overlooks both the problems of propitiation for sin and
deliverance from its grip, and presents the essence of Christianity as simply doing good on a social or individual basis.
This is the contemporary expression of Enlightenment
moralism. The Evangelical sector of the church, descending
from the Puritan and Pietist traditions through a number of
religious awakenings, has retained a vestigial awareness of
the holiness of God, the depth of sin, the substitutionary aspect of the atoning work of Christ and the doctrine of justification by faith. All too often, however, it retains a legal admixture where it is most deeply serious in its piety, and falls
into either cheap grace or individualistic moralism where it
is inconsistent with its theology.

Only a fraction of the present body of professing Christians
are solidly appropriating the justifying work of Christ in their
lives. Many have so light an apprehension of God's holiness
and of the extent and guilt of their sin that consciously they
see little need for justification, although below the surface of
their lives they are deeply guilt-ridden and insecure. Many
others have a theoretical commitment to this doctrine, but in
their day-to-day existence they rely on their sanctification
for justification, in the Augustinian manner, drawing their
assurance of acceptance with God from their sincerity, their
past experience of conversion, their recent religious performance or the relative infrequency of their conscious, willful disobedience. Few know enough to start each day with a
thoroughgoing stand upon Luther's platform: *you are accepted,* looking outward in faith and claiming the wholly
alien righteousness of Christ as the only ground for acceptance, relaxing in that quality of trust which will produce increasing sanctification as faith is active in love and gratitude.

In order for a pure and lasting work of spiritual renewal
to take place within the church, multitudes within it must be

led to build their lives on this foundation. This means that they must be conducted into the light of a full conscious awareness of God's holiness, the depth of their sin and the sufficiency of the atoning work of Christ for their acceptance with God, not just at the outset of their Christian lives but in every succeeding day. It is only the blood of Jesus Christ which is able "to purify your conscience from dead works to serve the living God" (Heb. 9:14). A conscience which is not fully enlightened both to the seriousness of its condition before God, and to the grandeur of God's merciful provision of redemption, will inevitably fall prey to anxiety, pride, sensuality and all the other expressions of that unconscious despair which Kierkegaard called "the sickness unto death."

Sanctification

On several occasions the New Testament makes clear that cheap grace, the attempt to be justified through faith in Christ without commitment to sanctification, is illegitimate and impossible. The thrust of these passages is not really that we should *add* works to our faith, as if it were possible to advance one step forward into faith but to hesitate before adding a second step into holiness. Faith and repentance are not separable quantities. To have faith is to receive God's Word as truth and rest upon it in dependent trust; to repent is to have a new mind toward God, oneself, Christ and the world, commiting one's heart to new obedience to God. Obviously these two factors are so interwoven that they are experienced as one, so that the condition of justification is not faith plus repentance, but repentant faith. In the famous antiphony to Paul's teaching in James, it is clear that works and merit are not being added to the means of justification, but that the root of living faith which produces works is being distinguished from a dead and sterile conceptual orthodoxy: "So faith by itself, if it has no works, is dead. . . . For as the body apart from the spirit is dead, so faith apart from works is dead" (Jas. 2:17, 26).

An unrepentant faith is a theoretical belief which originates outside the sphere of the Spirit's illumination in a heart
which is still in darkness concerning its own need and the
grace and grandeur of God. Paul points to incomplete realization of truth as the cause of the abuse of grace:

> Are we to continue in sin that grace may abound? By no
> means! How can we who died to sin still live in it? Do you
> not know that all of us who have been baptized into Christ
> Jesus were baptized into his death? . . . We know that our
> old self was crucified with him so that the sinful body
> might be destroyed, and we might no longer be enslaved
> to sin. For he who has died is freed from sin. (Rom. 6:1-3,
> 6-7)

It is true that justification can only be appropriated on the
ground of our union with Christ. But we cannot be in the light
about our union with the perfect righteousness which covers
our sin without simultaneously being in the light about the
power available to transform our lives and displace our sin.
We cannot be in union with half a Christ, as the Puritans
would say. We must appropriate a whole Christ if we are to
remain in light and thus in spiritual life.

There is a deep and indissoluble connection between our
appropriation of justification and our experience of sanctification. On the one hand, the conscience cannot accept justification without sanctification. Assurance of justification
which penetrates and cleanses our consciousness of guilt is
impossible to obtain without an awareness that we are in
some measure committed to progress in spiritual growth.
This assurance increases as we move forward in sanctification and weakens or vanishes as we move away from the light
of holiness (2 Pet. 1:2-11). Though the attempt to claim justification without a clear commitment to sanctification out-
rages our conscience, we usually repress this from conscious
awareness, and the resulting anxiety and insecurity create
compulsive egocentric drives which aggravate the flesh instead of mortifying it. Thus the Protestant disease of cheap

grace can produce some of the most selfish and contentious leaders and lay people on earth, more difficult to bear in a state of grace than they would be in a state of nature.

On the other hand, the conscience cannot accept sanctification unless it is based on a foundation in justification. When this is attempted the resulting insecurity creates a luxuriant overgrowth of religious flesh as believers seek to build a holiness formidable enough to pacify their consciences and quiet their sense of alienation from God. Theoretically this should be a disorder limited to Catholics—medieval asceticism is the largest monument in history to the uneasy conscience which results when justification is misconstrued—but the large number of serious Protestants who are essentially insecure about their own justification makes it common in the rest of the church also.

As Romans 6 makes clear, the ground of sanctification is our union with Christ in his death and resurrection, in which the old nature was destroyed and a new nature created with the power to grow in newness of life. The Holy Spirit begins to apply this completed work in the believer's life at regeneration and continues it in a progressively enlarging sphere of renewal in the personality. This renewal will be complete only in the final resurrection.

Regeneration. The beachhead of sanctification in the soul, regeneration or rebirth, has long been a center of dispute in the church's teaching. Non-Evangelical Protestants are suspicious that this concept is only another device to foster cheap grace, since the experience is so often professed by Christians who are not moving forward in progressive sanctification, who are lacking in social compassion and gripped by conformity to undiscerned corporate sins such as racism. The older Evangelicalism, in turn, doubted the regeneration of "liberal" Protestants because of theological differences and lifestyles conforming to another kind of "worldliness." Each of these sectors in the church must be encouraged to exercise a judgment of charity toward the other's Christianity without excusing its faults. Persons may have a very shallow awareness of sin and still be repentent; and they may have a very confused grasp of redemptive truth and still once have responded in faith toward God in Christ. The stagnant orthodoxy of twice-born bigots and the confused proclamation of social activists whose minds have gone through the blender of secular humanistic education are both chargeable to the church's theological weakness, but this cannot frustrate the sovereign grace of God in regenerating his chosen instruments.

There is another critical area of difference among Christians concerning regeneration: how does it occur? Augustine's doctrine of salvation connected rebirth to the administration of the water of baptism, and this is still assumed in many parts of the church. Some areas within Protestantism, on the other hand, have taught that regeneration does not occur until repentant faith has been exercised. Each of these options has some apparent biblical support but is vulnerable to biblical and practical objections. While water is mentioned in connection with rebirth in John 3:5 and Titus 3:5, the invariable connection of this symbol with the work signified can be questioned on the same basis that causes Paul to contrast physical circumcision with the circumcision of the heart:

> For he is not a real Jew who is one outwardly, nor is true circumcision something external and physical. He is a Jew who is one inwardly, and real circumcision is a matter of the heart, spiritual and not literal. His praise is not from men but from God. (Rom. 2:28-29)

The objection that baptized infants are always regenerated but simply fall away from this grace subsequently, which could explain those congregations which are full of baptized spiritual deadness, does violence to the power and finality of the biblical image of the second birth, which does not suggest the possibility of being born again, and again, and again.

The approach which makes regeneration a consequence of

the exercise of repentant faith is also inconsistent with this image. Birth is a passive experience and not the effect of action initiated by the one born. In the best-known text dealing with regeneration, John 3, this work is said to be the effect of the Holy Spirit's moving, as the trees are moved by the wind: "The wind blows where it wills and you hear the sound of it, but you do not know whence it comes or whither it goes; so it is with every one who is born of the Spirit" (Jn. 3: 8). The listener cannot force the wind to blow by any action, and certainly the trees will not do so. The style of Evangelical Christianity which is constantly pushing and forcing people toward conversion in order to get them regenerated, manipulating them with music, repeated invitations or a sort of sales routine, is an ugly deformity of Christian practice resulting from bad doctrine. It is uncomfortable both for those who feel responsible to do it and for those who are the objects of concern. This kind of pressure is better than hiding the gospel, and it continues to be blessed by genuine conversions through the grace of God, but we should move away from it without lessening our efforts to proclaim the gospel in a more gracious way to those who do not believe.

The practice of Jesus in this matter is instructive. If anyone had the concern and the personal charisma to push persons into the kingdom, he did, and yet his manner reflected the prophecy in Isaiah 42:2: "He will not cry or lift up his voice, or make it heard in the street." Jesus' whole ministry reveals a controlled dignity which did not force persons beyond the moving of the Holy Spirit detectable in their words and actions, so that in bringing them to commitment even the Son of God waited upon the Spirit. Jesus said to one group who doubted him, "No one can come to me unless the Father who sent me draws him" (Jn. 6:44). To another group who opposed him, he said, "You do not belong to my sheep. My sheep hear my voice, and I know them, and they follow me; and I give them eternal life, and they shall never perish, and no one shall snatch them out of my hand" (Jn. 10:26-28).

These passages clearly teach the priority of sovereign grace in the whole process of redemption. Regeneration, continuance in faith and eternal salvation are not an accident of human response but a result of divine control. We would be inclined to reverse Jesus' statement and say, "You are not of my sheep, because you do not believe"; but Jesus does not hesitate to pierce through appearances to the issue of the prior choice and calling of God.

We are dealing here with one of the most problematic and controversial points of theology, the doctrine of election, and we cannot begin to handle this question here in the depth it deserves, except to make two statements. First, the Bible teaches that salvation is completely a matter of God's grace and power, so that none of us can take credit for our own wisdom or initiative in receiving it, but also that we are fully responsible if we refuse it. It is not prudent to take either side of this paradox in isolation and build a rational system around it, since we are dealing with matters vastly beyond the comprehension of human reason. Second, the biblical teaching on election is not a point of arcane theory which can be set aside because it has no relevance to practical Christianity; it affects the shape of the Christian life in many crucial areas. One of these is the dignity of our evangelistic posture. Much of the church is hesitant to accept Evangelicalism's concern for evangelism in part because they are deeply uneasy about the *style* with which evangelistic work is commonly done. When there is a proper understanding of spiritual dynamics, many of these stylistic problems are rather easily transcended.

Luther and Calvin held that regeneration is ordinarily associated with the ministry of the Word and may occur in the process of baptism, but they also believed that it is a sovereign act of the Holy Spirit which cannot be forced by human action or·limited by human assumptions. Calvin comments that John the Baptist was filled with the Holy Spirit even in his mother's womb and that the timing of regeneration in the lives of believers is therefore mysterious, especially in the children of believers.

Regeneration is the re-creation of spiritual life in those who are dead in trespasses and sins (Eph. 2:1). It occurs in the depths of the human heart, at the roots of consciousness, infusing new life which is capable of spiritual awareness, perception and response, and is no longer "alienated from the life of God" (Eph. 4:18). The conscious effects of regeneration are summed up in *conversion*, the response of turning toward God in repentant faith which accompanies the hearing of the gospel. Our task as evangelists is therefore that of midwives, and not that of parents. It is not our responsibility to get people regenerated but simply to present a consistent witness in life and word, and to appeal for commitment to Christ secure in the inward recognition that his sheep will hear his voice and follow him because his Spirit will open their hearts to do so.

In many Evangelical circles it is assumed that repentance ("accepting Jesus as Lord") may come as a second stage occurring considerably later than initial conversion ("accepting Jesus as Savior"). In practice this may occur frequently, largely because some evangelists do not take very clear aim at the target of sin, do not present the meaning of the cross and do not call for repentant faith. Instead, they invite unbelievers to "invite Jesus into their hearts" in order to cure the emptiness of the godless life, a procedure based on Jesus' words to the church at Laodicea in Revelation 3: 20. Perhaps the assumption is that "Your life can be improved by the addition of Christ" is a more palatable message than "Repent and believe in the crucified and resurrected Lord," and that repentance can be added later once the convert has made a sort of commitment, has invited the Spirit into his heart and can understand salvation better. But Revelation 3 is addressed to a *church*, not to unbelievers, and seems to be an invitation to full fellowship with Christ, not a key to regeneration. Persons who invite Christ to enter their lives may be unaware that he has already entered. A passage which gives an indication of the relationship between regeneration, faith and repentance more reliable than Revelation 3:20 is John 3:3-8, 14-15, which connects regeneration with an understanding of Christ's work on the cross.

Because of our muted emphasis on sin, many persons experience a two-stage conversion, but we should recognize that no conversion is complete that does not deal with the problem of sin. If all of our preaching were properly centered around this problem and its answer in the cross, the number of two-stage conversions would probably decrease sharply. It is instructive that Peter's first sermon in Acts 2 includes an appeal for repentance and left its hearers "cut to the heart" with conviction of sin (Acts 2:37-38), and every subsequent apostolic sermon follows this pattern, including Paul's message on Mars Hill to the Greeks, who might be expected to be unfamiliar with the notions of sin and repentance (Acts 17:29-31).

Repentance and Mortification of Sin. Regeneration and conversion are only the first stages of the sanctification process. Frequently in the church it is not followed up with very searching instruction on the depth of the problem of residual indwelling sin, the subtlety of involvement in corporate patterns of sin and the grace of God available for the conquest of the flesh. It is therefore not surprising that many congregations which are full of regenerate people are nevertheless not very alive spiritually, since spiritual life demands *metanoia,* a new mind of repentance, and this requires more than an initial setting of the heart against the shallow expressions of sin which the believer is aware of at the time of his conversion. The full development of *metanoia* in the process of sanctification involves the breaking up of every area of conformity to the world's patterns of corporate flesh and the increasing transformation of our lives by the Holy Spirit's renewing work in our minds (Rom. 12:2). As John Owen says,

"the vigor and power of spiritual life is dependent on mortification of sin."[7]

The lifelong process of mortifying sin involves a gradual
detection process by which the particular forms in which sin
expresses itself in our lives, our characteristic flesh, are uncovered to our view. Some of this discovery of sin occurs
early in our Christian lives, but the subtlety of indwelling sin
is such that many of its deeper roots remain under the surface of consciousness, where they will continue to distort
our lives if they are not uncovered later. New departments of
the flesh open up in our lives as we mature. The child who
has been converted at eight faces a new crisis of repentance at
puberty; the leader who has spent his life learning to use
power constructively must face his own unwillingness to
relinquish it in his later years. Even conversion itself opens
up the possibilities for new developments of "spiritual
flesh": pride in spiritual gifts and achievements, envy of the
spirituality of others, a gluttonous dependence on spiritual
experience which cannot reconcile itself to an obedient walk
of faith independent of sight. The gravity of self-interest
which naturally operates in our lives whenever we move out
of the light and walk in the flesh is able to shape even religious intentions into carnal patterns.

The detection process by which old roots of sin and new
developments of the flesh are discovered is described by
Paul in Romans 7. Before detection every region of the flesh
is latent, present in our lives but working unconsciously. The
probe which causes our independence from God to flare up
into consciousness, expressing itself in overt acts of sin, is
the law—biblical principles of righteousness, ethical truths
written on men's hearts and enacted in their laws, the com-
plaining accusations of others harmed by our sin, every restraint which impinges on our independence and forces it
into open rebellion. "Apart from the law sin lies dead. I was
once alive apart from the law, but when the commandment
came, sin revived and I died" (Rom. 7:8-9). The law is like a

"tracer chemical" which makes the invisible course of a disease evident or a medicine which aggravates a hidden illness until it breaks out in surface symptoms. Particular expressions of our characteristic flesh cannot be detected and put away, releasing a given area of our lives in newness of life, unless this process takes place: "Yet, if it had not been for the law, I should not have known sin. I should not have known what it is to covet if the law had not said, 'You shall not covet' "(Rom. 7:7). A church with a weak understanding of sin will thus inevitably be a church in which the flesh is alive and spiritual vitality is dampened.

But this statement is subject to several important reservations. First, spiritual vigor, either in an individual or in a sector of the church, is not absolutely and automatically dependent on the degree of progress in sanctification, so that only those who are mature in growth and deeply searched out by the detection process of the law will be filled with vitality. It is God's prerogative to bestow the fullness of the Holy Spirit wherever he wills to do so. We often find younger Christians full of spiritual vitality although they will require years of tempering to produce maturity, stability and wisdom. Repentance toward known sin and openness toward further sanctification are evidently more important than actual progress in the mortification of sin.

Second, the rate and depth at which progress in sanctification takes place is determined by the Holy Spirit, the resident counselor in every believer. The process cannot be rushed by overloading the conscience with the administration of the law. God will proceed at a rate and follow a course which are ideally suited to the individual, raising successive issues over the years and making a point of the need for growth in one area after another. He seldom shows us all of our needs at once; we would be overwhelmed at the sight.

Of course, every person on earth, including the proverbial islanders of the South Seas who are supposed to have lived with such placid consciences until the missionaries came

with the law, has a large measure of the flesh exposed simply
through societal restraints and constant friction against the
flesh of others. In this case, the *autonomy* of the flesh, its
existence as a law unto itself, is only shifted over into a state
of *heteronomy* (to use Kant's term for encounter with a law
not willingly accepted from the depths of the heart, but re-
sisted like a straitjacket or outwardly adopted like a mask).
This kind of detection does not lead to spiritual life, however, but to lifeless, conditioned conformity to "dead goodness," or else to open rebellion. In order for the flesh to be
effectively displaced to make room for newness of life, our
response must be *theonomous;* the restraining law must be
perceived as God's will and accepted from the heart because
of repentant submission to him.

Many in the church today have been made aware of large
areas of their characteristic flesh at the level of heteronomy,
but have not broken through to a theonomous perception of
their needs, and thus are trapped in patterns of dead conformity or angry resistance. Thus some Evangelicals are encased in a Spiritless orthodoxy while resisting conviction of
their social apathy, and some non-Evangelicals are engaged
in Spiritless expressions of social activism while avoiding
the sanctification of their minds in theonomous perception
of biblical truth.

The dawning of theonomous awareness of sin is described
in Romans 7:

> We know that the law is spiritual; but I am carnal, sold
> under sin. I do not understand my own actions. For I do
> not do what I want, but I do the very thing I hate. Now if I
> do what I do not want, I agree that the law is good.... For
> I delight in the law of God, in my inmost self, but I see in
> my members another law at war with the law of my mind
> and making me a captive to the law of sin which dwells in
> my members. (Rom. 7:14-16, 22-23)

For the Evangelical a breakthrough into theonomous perception of the flesh would involve a Spirit-illuminated insight

into the biblical grounding and divine reality of orthodox doctrines previously received only by tradition and advocated out of party spirit. There would also be a humbled recognition that many non-Evangelical thrusts against social injustice and Pharisaism are not meaningless heresy but a prophetic expression of the mind of God. For the non-Evangelical a theonomous perception of the flesh would involve a quickened awareness of the extent to which the theory and motivation behind many initiatives of the social gospel have been graceless echoes of the self-righteous and guilt-motivated concerns of secular humanism, a regrounding of social compassion in God-centered concern for Christ's redemptive mission and an awakening to the fact that the Evangelical call for consistently biblical thinking is also a prophetic voice of God to the church. If a widespread mutual movement toward sanctification in these two sectors would occur, the result would be an immense release of spiritual power within Western Christianity and the recovery of the stature and initiative lost by the church in the division of its forces in the late nineteenth century.

Another reservation concerning the use of the law in discerning sin and advancing sanctification is this: without concurrent light on the provisions of grace, the law will not cure sin but only aggravate it, as Paul says in Romans 7:8-9. Because Luther had seen that it is virtually impossible to respond theonomously to the law without the vision of the grace of Christ, Lutheran ministers became suspicious of too much Puritan "law-work" without preceding and accompanying declarations of grace. And rightly so: human beings cannot bear very much reality, as T. S. Eliot said. The anesthetic of grace is constantly needed in the healing process of sanctification along with the surgical ministry of the law. For this reason, many areas of the church which contain a great deal of legal thunder and lightning, exposing at least the surfaces of sin, are full of desperately anxious and bitterly contentious people. Law without grace provokes sin along with exposing it and aggravates it into some of its ugliest expressions.

The counselor who is attempting to move people further in sanctification should therefore begin with a strong emphasis on justification and reiterate this often in the course of his work. Psychoanalysts speak of the "resistance" patients have toward the discovery of traumatic material hidden in the unconscious. The same automatic fear of having repressed problems uncovered will grip and bind Christian believers unless they are very deeply assured that they are "accepted in the beloved," received by God as if they were perfectly righteous because their guilt is canceled by the righteousness of Christ laid to their account. The human conscience is very deeply disoriented in its conviction that we must have works and sanctification to recommend ourselves to God. We must carry out a very deliberate replacement of this misunderstanding with the awareness that God simply wants honesty, openness and a trusting reliance on Christ our Savior. We cannot bear the light on our needs unless we are also in the light concerning God's grace to meet those needs.

Sanctification and Grace. God's gracious provision for our needs includes God's grace for sanctification as well as for justification. It is not enough to tell believers, "*You are accepted* through your faith in Christ." We must tell them also, "*You are delivered* from the bondages of sin through the power of the indwelling Christ." For our consciences are also deeply deluded with respect to the possibility of overcoming the flesh once its dimensions are known. Even if we are assured that our sin is covered, we do not want to face the despair of having to live in conscious helpless awareness of its tyranny, abusing the grace and forgiveness of Christ. If we have to go on running further and further into spiritual debt, we would rather do this in the dark without realizing what is happening.

In order to combat this sense of helplessness before the

binding power of indwelling sin, believers should first be assured that sanctification, like justification, is grounded in union with Christ. The power of sin to rule their lives has been *destroyed* in the cross of Christ; we have died with Christ, and have been raised up together with him in newness of life. Therefore we are not to set the estimates of our power to conquer sin according to past experiences of our will power, but are to fix our attention on Christ and the power of his risen life in which we participate: for we have died, and our life is hidden with Christ in God.

This power is accessible in our experience through *faith*, not through simple striving of the will. Many aspects of the flesh are disarmed and eliminated by a deep apprehension of our justification by faith. Faith in Christ cures unbelief, anxiety and insecurity, and in so doing it cuts the roots of envy, jealousy and a host of related egocentric fleshly patterns.

But *sanctification* is also attained by faith; it involves working but it is not wholly a matter of works. This is the significance of John Wesley's great discovery of the doctrine of Christian perfection. Wesley found that many Christians were willing to advance into the light concerning God's grace and a deep admission of the problem of sin in their lives, but he also discovered that they were content to remain at a substandard level of Christian living because of the magnitude of the problem. Wesley found this out of alignment with biblical teaching on our victory over sin, which commands us to exercise faith that we can overcome it through Christ: "So you also must consider yourselves dead to sin and alive to God in Christ Jesus. . . . For sin will have no dominion over you, since you are not under law but under grace" (Rom. 6: 11, 14). Wesley sought for this level of deliverance from sin in a second work of grace following conversion, the gift of "perfect love" through the indwelling of the Spirit. This second work of grace would release believers from conscious acts of voluntary sin and permit them to walk in unclouded love and obedience toward God.

But the real importance of Wesley's doctrine was not its emphasis on a second stage of sanctification following initial regeneration (which when it occurs is better explained as a large forward leap in progressive sanctification), but its insistence that sanctification, like justification, is based on faith. This understanding was picked up in the nineteenth century by the Deeper Life and Keswick movements and became an important part of non-Pentecostal Evangelical teaching on sanctification in the present century.[8] Where this emphasis is seriously taught and heeded, growth in grace is securely guarded from becoming a matter of works and pride in achievement, and is grounded in a relationship of believing dependence on the risen Christ.

But this doctrine of sanctification through faith must be conditioned by several reservations. First, it must be detached from any assumption that the sin which is to be overcome by faith is limited to conscious voluntary acts of disobedience. Without a depth understanding of sin, "the victorious life" becomes an exercise in futility. The world does not need more "victorious Christians" who drive their neighbors to distraction by their cheerful indulgence in undiscerned carnality.

Second, it must be dissociated from quietism, which can manifest itself in two forms: one which assumes that major problems of sin are easily conquered by a simple moment of believing prayer and do not involve hard work in mortifying sin; and another which suspects that all efforts of the will against sin are "fleshly striving" and must not be undertaken until the Spirit gives inspiration in response to faith. It is true that any contest against sin in our lives must be a dependent striving, but it must be a full and continuous engagement of the will nevertheless.

The paradoxical balance of grace and effort is effectively stated by Paul: "Work out your own salvation with fear and trembling; for God is at work in you, both to will and to work for his good pleasure" (Phil. 2:12-13). Thus Paul's emphasis on the reckoning of faith in Romans 6:11 is followed by vigorous encouragement to disengage our lives from sin and submit them to God:

> Let not sin therefore reign in your mortal bodies, to make you obey their passions. Do not yield your members to sin as instruments of wickedness, but yield yourselves to God as men who have been brought from death to life, and your members to God as instruments of righteousness. (Rom. 6: 12-13)

Here sin is presented as a tyrannical slavemaster to whom we must not yield; later in Romans it is portrayed as an organism seeking control over our lives which must be "put to death."

In other epistles Paul compares the flesh to inappropriate clothing which must be laid aside in order to reclothe ourselves with qualities which match the beauty of our essential union with Christ: "Put off your old nature which belongs to your former manner of life and is corrupt through deceitful lusts, and be renewed in the spirit of your minds, and put on the new nature, created after the likeness of God in true righteousness and holiness" (Eph. 4:22-24). Something much deeper is contemplated here than replacing bad habits with good habits through sheer willpower. We are to detach ourselves from the compulsive organism of sin rooted in unregenerate human nature and to put ourselves in gear with the living power of Christ's resurrection which will then express his character through our lives. But choice and will enter in along with faith and understanding, and neither is spiritually alive without the other.

The process of sanctification is broader and more subtle than our conscious efforts to mortify known patterns of sin in our lives. Much of our growth in grace is quietly effected by events and conditions God brings into our lives to perfect his work in us. We are faced by sacrificial choices, like Abram's call to leave Ur and the later command to offer up Isaac, and our positive response to such choices deepens the purity of our intention to follow Christ. We undergo painful losses and illness, or attack and persecution, and our trust and obedience in these circumstances enlarge our character and conform us to the image of Christ.

If we do not suffer outwardly, God may conduct us through what John of the Cross calls the "night of the senses" (a total suspension of enjoyment and awareness of God in the Christian life, so that we must walk entirely by the obedience of faith) or the "dark night of the soul" (a period in which we seem to be wholly abandoned by God and are conscious only of the wrath our sins deserve).[9] If we interrupt the process of sanctification by procrastinating in meeting an issue that God has set before us or by reverting to a posture of backsliding unbelief, God in his love will inevitably bring our lives into circumstances of failure, frustration or suffering which will drive us back to sobriety.

The progress of our spiritual growth is not a matter of our own initiative and designing; it is under the control and direction of God who has begun a good work in us and will work patiently to perfect it until the day of Christ. To borrow a metaphor from Mahayana Buddhism, we are not like the infant monkey which must cling to its mother with all its strength if it is to avoid falling; we are like the kitten which is carried from place to place in its mother's mouth.

This image raises a final question about the process of sanctification. What if it is interrupted by a plunge into apparently total unbelief? Has regeneration been lost, and must it be regained? What about those passages in Scripture (such as Hebrews 6:6 and 1 John 5:16) which seem to speak about the total loss of spiritual life through sin?

Augustinianism, Lutheran orthodoxy and Wesleyanism seek to remain faithful to the apparent literal meaning of certain texts of Scripture in assuming that salvation may be lost and that a failure to recognize this fosters presumption and cheap grace. The principal Reformers and the Puritans, however, felt that this went against the grain of other passages (such as 1 Peter 1:23 and John 10:28) teaching that regenerate Christians must inevitably persevere to the end as believers in Christ. They also held that such teaching once again made justification conditional on sanctification. This in turn would lead to despair in those who were realistic and spiritually sensitive, or at least to a level of hope which was a tentative guess about our ability to keep believing, rather than a confident assurance of God's power to keep us from falling and bring us faultless before the throne of grace.

The Puritans held that presumption could be avoided if assurance of salvation was denied to those not walking in light. Professing Christians who fell away from faith permanently were understood as temporary believers in whom the roots of sin were never fully broken up by initial regeneration. The biblical model for this view is Christ's parable of the four types of soil: the person whose heart is compared to rocky ground bears fruit for a while but ultimately withers because the root is too shallow, while others with a proper depth of root remain fruitful, or at least alive.

This model of the believer's security is ultimately the one most consistent with spiritual equilibrium and growth. The heart of faith is an absolute trust in God's grace and a comparable distrust toward one's own stamina and faithfulness. Anything less than this generates insecurity, and anxiety short-circuits the sanctification process, for fear and love are incompatible, as John says. If our theology of sin is vigorous and if we insist that walking in light is a condition of assurance, we will not encourage presumption and cheap grace by encouraging believers to hope that the life they have received in Christ is indeed eternal.

The Indwelling Holy Spirit

The statement is frequently made that the ministry of the Holy Spirit is the most neglected topic in the doctrine and practice of the church. Historically this is only partially true.

There have been some remarkable high-water marks of

progress in the church's teaching and experience of the Holy
Spirit. The medieval church left us a magnificently comprehensive hymn describing the manifold work of the Spirit,
the *Veni Creator Spiritus* ("Come, Holy Spirit"); and the
practical mystical tradition accumulated a considerable
store of wisdom concerning his ministry. Among the Reformers, John Calvin has been called the theologian of the
Holy Spirit because his doctrinal work so carefully honors
the sovereign agency of the Spirit in regeneration and sanctification. This emphasis continued in the Reformed tradition,
for the English Puritans (particularly John Owen and Richard
Sibbes) have given us the most profound and extensive bib-
lical-theological studies of the ministry of the Holy Spirit
which exist in any language.[10]

We have already seen that the Great Awakening involved
a renewed emphasis on the Holy Spirit's work of reviving
and empowering the church for mission, and the theology of
Edwards synthesized this new dimension of understanding
with the older Puritan teaching on the Spirit. In the aftermath
of the Second Awakening, Charles Finney's ministry attributed to human initiative much of what had previously been
reserved for the Spirit's operation, but Finney's *Revival Lectures* continued to place a strong emphasis on prayer for the
outpouring of the Holy Spirit. Finney also introduced a new
emphasis on "the baptism of the Holy Spirit" as a second
work of grace after regeneration empowering the Christian
for service, based on his own two-stage experience of conversion and spiritual infilling.

This insistence on a subsequent individual baptism of the
Spirit caught on in English and American Christianity in
the late nineteenth century, combining with the older teaching on the need for repeated outpourings of the Spirit upon
the whole church. In the ministries of D. L. Moody and R. A.
Torrey, and in the so-called Welsh Revival of 1904-05, it became as central an emphasis as the doctrine of Christian perfection in Wesleyanism, which it resembles and to which it

is probably related. It was perhaps inevitable that in the midst of all this instruction on individual and corporate baptisms of the Spirit, a new concern for the supernatural gifts of the Spirit should arise, and thus in the early years of the twentieth century the Pentecostal movement was conceived.

On the other hand, reaction against abuses connected with "extraordinary operations of the Holy Spirit"—that is, the gifts present in the New Testament church, particularly miraculous healings and prophecy—has been a persistent factor in dampening interest in the Holy Spirit among serious theological minds during the church's history. The Reformers, harassed on the one side by Romanists who claimed that the miracles of the saints guaranteed the truth of their doctrine and on the other side by disruptive enthusiasts who claimed to be inspired by the Spirit, adopted as a theological convenience the notion that extraordinary gifts of the Spirit were attestations of new revelation and therefore limited to the final period of revelation, the New Testament era. The Puritans and the leaders of the First and Second Awakenings continued to discourage any emphasis on extraordinary gifts. Sporadic outbreaks of tongues and other gifts did occur in some local awakenings during the nineteenth century, however.

In 1900 the American Bible teacher Charles Parham concluded from study of the book of Acts that the initial evidence of an individual's reception of "the baptism of the Holy Spirit" should be the exercise of the gift of tongues. Shortly after this the gift began to be experienced among his students, and the Azusa Street Revival in Los Angeles in 1906 launched the twentieth-century Pentecostal movement.[11]

An almost immediate reaction set in against the Pentecostal teaching on the Holy Spirit because of the divisive impact on the church of the doctrine of initial evidence. In England, the later Keswick tradition began to emphasize that the fullness of the Spirit was obtained principally through growth in sanctification and not through a second experience of grace involving empowering for service.

Meanwhile other Evangelical leaders began to teach that any movement which spoke too much of the Holy Spirit was dangerous and unbiblical, since the whole work of the Spirit was simply to point to Jesus Christ. This convenient weapon against Pentecostalism was drawn from an incorrect exegesis of John 16:13-14, in which the King James translation reads "He shall not speak of himself.... He shall glorify me." As later translations make clear, this passage must mean "He will not speak on His own initiative" (NASB) or "He will not speak on his own authority" (RSV), which in fact was the original meaning of the Elizabethan translation; otherwise Jesus is disclaiming any discourse about himself in the parallel instances in John 7:17 and 14:10! But twentieth-century non-Pentecostal Evangelicalism has not hesitated to develop a whole mythology concerning "the modesty of the Holy Spirit" out of this transparent error. In many areas it has been considered heresy even to pray to the Holy Spirit, despite the fact that our hymnals are filled with such prayers. This teaching has inevitably had a withering effect on the personal relationship between Evangelical believers and their Counselor, since it introduces an unnatural subordinationism and imperils the equality in power and glory of the persons within the Trinity.

But reaction against "enthusiasm" is not the only dampening factor which has hindered the proper development of the church's understanding of the Holy Spirit. Charles Simeon points out that technical theologians often have a certain uneasiness in dealing with the work of the Spirit because his ministry is so closely involved in the vital issues of Christian living and thinking that the theologian must be carefully tuned in his own sanctification in order to deal with it adequately.[12]

During the last two centuries increasing numbers of "liberal" scholars have consequently neglected this dimension of concern, but so have many "orthodox" theologians. At the grassroots level of the church there are remnants of the old teaching on the Spirit common among the Puritans and the awakeners, but often the seminaries have failed to reinforce and strengthen this popular concern. When this situation among liberal and confessional leaders is added to the Fundamentalist warning against giving too much emphasis to the Holy Spirit, it is not surprising that there are multitudes of churchpeople who "have not so much as heard whether there be any Holy Ghost."

During this century it is mainly among Pentecostal and Charismatic Christians that there has been a full recognition of the Holy Spirit's place in the church. The rapid growth of Charismatic ministries and the spiritual openness and sensitivity of young Charismatic leaders testifies very clearly to the church that the Pentecostal tradition has something that it needs, despite admixtures of extremes and errors. We need to look closely to the Scriptures to determine what the essence of this contribution is, underneath the theological packaging of the old Pentecostal position.

The extensive treatment of the ministry of the Holy Spirit at several key points in the New Testament indicates the strategic importance of this subject for the church's life and mission. The first of these passages is John 14—16, the account of Jesus' last session of teaching the disciples on the night before the crucifixion. These chapters are filled with instruction designed to fortify the Christian community for effective ministry without the physical presence of Christ. One of the most important facts presented is that Jesus will still be spiritually present with his followers in the person of the Holy Spirit, whose indwelling will make real among them the presence of the members of the Trinity, provide continued teaching and guidance, equip them for witness and move the world to accept their testimony. Jesus says that it is actually to their advantage for him to be physically absent, since this will make possible his pervasive spiritual presence through the indwelling of the Spirit. What is involved here is an intermediate fulfillment of the essential core of redemption ultimately consummated in the heavenly city: "I will make my abode among you. . . . And I will walk among you, and will be your God, and you shall be my people" (Lev. 26: 11-12; compare Rev. 21:3).

These chapters clearly show that to de-emphasize the work of the Holy Spirit in order to give prominence to the work of Christ is self-contradictory: to do so ignores the present ministry of Christ and cripples the church in its effort to live out the extension of his rule on earth. The many references to the work of the Spirit in Luke-Acts indicate that the prominence of his ministry prefigured in John was fully realized in the life of the early church which had no restraint in speaking of the Spirit's falling upon believers, filling them for ministry, instructing them and directing their missionary labors, and comforting them.

Even when this has been admitted, there are still many critical questions to be resolved concerning the Spirit's present ministry in the church. In any effort to develop a unified field theory of the Holy Spirit's work, in any attempt to explain the apparent diversity of the Spirit's work in Charismatic and non-Charismatic circles alike, at least three questions must be addressed.

1. *Is the filling of the Holy Spirit an enduement of power for service or a result of growth in sanctification?* Clearly the biblical answer is *both.* In the context of his final teaching about the advent of the Comforter, Jesus says, in the parable of the vine, "Every branch that does bear fruit he prunes, that it may bear more fruit" (Jn. 15:2). In the words that follow he goes on to speak of "abiding in me" in order to bear fruit. Being emptied of sin is joined intimately with being filled with the Spirit. Paul likewise links the putting to death of sin with spiritual vitality: "If by the Spirit you put to death the deeds of the body you will live" (Rom. 8:13). In what is perhaps the principal text of the New Testament on the filling of the

Spirit, Paul embeds his exhortation to "be filled with the Spirit" (Eph. 5:18) in an extensive passage on the necessity of sanctification.

These texts and others like them lead us to one conclusion: any model of the fullness of the Spirit which attempts to make empowering for service relatively separate from growth in holiness inevitably collides with the truth represented in the very title *Holy Spirit*. The principal work of the Spirit in applying redemption lies in making us holy, and being filled with the Spirit simply means having all our faculties under his control rather than under the control of sin.

On the other hand, those persons in Acts who are growing in sanctification, "good men and full of the Holy Spirit" like Barnabas, are often gifted with an infilling of spiritual power and wisdom for specific tasks of witness and ministry. There is no doubt that the whole church in Acts received such a filling for service at the beginning of its existence and that this filling of the entire company of believers was repeated on at least one subsequent occasion (see Acts 2:4; 4:31).

Quite evidently sanctification and empowering for ministry are as inseparable as justification and sanctification. *There is no way that power can be sought and found outside the circle of light which is the truth and holiness of God.* On the other hand, a church which is pursuing personal sanctification is not necessarily one which is powerfully effective in mission, as the Puritans found. There is an additional dimension of corporate waiting upon the Spirit for missionary outreach which is necessary to transcend a self-oriented individualistic piety and begin to carry out the acts of the risen Lord.

2. *Are supernatural gifts of the Spirit available in the present era?* The gifts emphasized in Pentecostalism are the nine listed in 1 Corinthians 12:8-10: the *word of wisdom* (a momentary insight reflecting the mind of Christ toward a particular problem or situation), the *word of knowledge*

(awareness of factual information by direct revelation), *faith* (a special inspiration to believe that God will answer a particular prayer or move in a specific way), *healings* (ability to restore health supernaturally), *working of miracles* (ability to do more extraordinary works such as raising the dead), *prophecy* (contemporary revelation of the mind of God), *discerning of spirits* (detection of demonic influence), *tongues* (fragmentary utterances in other languages, the meaning of which is unknown to the speaker) and *interpretation of tongues* (the ability to reflect the meaning of these utterances, not by translation but by spontaneous revelation).[13]

In several parts of the church there is resistance to the acceptance of these gifts as currently operable in the church. The reasons given are both theological and practical. There is fear that those gifts which involve new revelational content not only may infringe upon the sole authority of Scripture, but often in practice may lead Christians to embrace false doctrine or to put their trust in predictions which fail. The gift of tongues, it is argued, is easily counterfeited and can be divisive in the context of other Pentecostal doctrine. Then, too, all the gifts can easily be abused in the stimulation of credulity and superstition.

It would be theologically and practically convenient for the church not to have to make room for current manifestations like these, but the plain import of the New Testament gives no hint that they are limited to the first century. Several times Paul forbids this easy solution. "Do not forbid speaking in tongues," he urges the Corinthians (1 Cor. 14:39). "Do not quench the Spirit, do not despise prophesying, but test everything; hold fast what is good," he says to the Thessalonians (1 Thess. 5:19-21). There is a vigorous faith in the supernatural operation of God in many Charismatic circles which the rest of the church should emulate.

However, Paul's injunction to test these phenomena must be strictly heeded along with his other cautions on the control of the gifts given in 1 Corinthians 12—14. Demonic counterfeits of many of these manifestations are common in occult circles, and it is not uncommon for Christians to be infected with false charisms if there is an attempt to manufacture a gift in the flesh or a seeking of gifts for wrong reasons. Eager and uncritical seeking after wonders to believe is a work of the flesh, not a grace of the spirit. Superstition was common in pre-Reformation Christianity as any readers of the lives and legends of the saints know. Now that it has been chased out of the church it should not be brought back in under the guise of faith and piety. Parts of the Pentecostal testimony are a jungle of superstition today, although discerning critics in Charismatic circles have carefully sought to correct this situation. It is extremely hazardous to give prophetic utterances and interpretations canonical authority. Any substantial dependence on these can easily lead to a neglect of the whole counsel of God already given to us and a failure in following the Holy Spirit's ordinary leading through the illumination of biblical knowledge. More will be said on this issue in chapter eight.

The graces and fruits of the Spirit are to be sought more earnestly than spectacular gifts. Gifts which edify the minds and hearts of others are to be given priority over those which nourish our own emotional experience. Our aim should be to obey God, and in the process of doing this we should expect God to give us the gifts we need to meet the particular needs in Christ's body that we encounter. As many within the Charismatic or Neo-Pentecostal revival have recognized, there are other less dramatic gifts of the Spirit which are equally significant in the church's life and witness—pre-eminently love, but also those mentioned in Romans 12:6-8: service, teaching, exhortation, giving, leading, showing mercy.

This concept of spiritual gifting underlines the fact that all gifts and graces are manifestations of the love and power of Jesus Christ shining through human experience to encourage and illuminate his people. Neo-Pentecostalism runs the risk of arrogance in calling itself "the Charismatic movement"

when other charisms are distributed throughout the body of
Christ along with many of the nine which are supposed to be
limited to Pentecostal believers. The most common examples of the latter are healings, words of wisdom, and discerning of spirits, but the great evangelical preacher C. H.
Spurgeon experienced the word of knowledge on many occasions.[14]

3. *Is the gift of tongues the initial evidence of a believer's
entry into a full empowering for service* (frequently called
"the baptism of the Holy Spirit")? Now we have come to the
most critical question concerning the gifts of the Spirit. Must
every believer re-experience Pentecost? There are a number
of issues involved here. The most important of these involve
"the baptism" considered as a second distinct work of grace.
Most Pentecostals admit that all regenerate Christians have
some measure of relationship with the Holy Spirit, but insist
that a full immersion in the presence and power of the Spirit
usually occurs subsequent to conversion and is validated by
the sign of tongues.

It is easy to understand how Charles Parham drew this
teaching from the experience of the early church in Acts.
But *subsequence* does not really seem to be the important
feature in the instances used to prove his doctrine. In only
one of the three relevant texts (Acts 8:14-17) do baptized believers in Christ receive the fullness of the Spirit at a second
stage, and the point here does not seem to be that further
seeking of an experience was necessary, but that apostolic
presence was essential (perhaps in order to validate the Samaritan Christians in the eyes of the rest of the church, which
was naturally prejudiced against them). In the other two important texts on this subject (Acts 10:44-48; 19:1-6), the descent of the Spirit occurs simultaneously with full understanding of the gospel, and the use of tongues seems to be a
visible evidence designed to persuade Jewish believers that
Gentiles could be first-class Christians.

The doubt surrounding the importance of subsequence in

these three texts leaves a rather slender base on which to build a doctrine which is almost guaranteed to divide churches. The stock-in-trade of some Charismatic solutions to the problem of church renewal (get the baptism, speak in tongues) does not seem to match up very well with the solution of the New Testament, which is immensely more complex and concerned with the many dimensions of our union with Christ. For this reason and others, young scholars emerging from the Pentecostal tradition have begun to question the doctrines of subsequent and initial evidence and also the phrase "the baptism of the Holy Spirit," since Spirit-baptism, union with Christ, justification and regeneration seem to be indissolubly connected throughout the New Testament.[15]

Those who hold the old Pentecostal theory of the fullness of the Spirit might claim that it is confirmed by experience. This seems true within rigorously Pentecostal churches, but even here many Pentecostals will admit that a second work of grace ("the baptism") is no more a guarantee of spiritual vitality than the first work of grace focused upon by Evangelicals ("being born again"), since there seem to be many "Spirit-filled" individuals in need of a third blessing.

As soon as the field of evidence is opened up, the picture becomes much less convincing. Just as sheltered Evangelicals are surprised to find real and deep graces of Christ among many non-Evangelical Christians, Pentecostals in continuous contact with non-Pentecostal Christians usually become aware of eminent "manifestations of the Spirit for the common good" among those outside their tradition. This experience is probably the main cause of the decline of the doctrine of initial evidence among younger Pentecostal leaders. If the older Pentecostal denominations confine their future leaders to Pentecostal schools, they can stop this process, but it will be at a tragic cost to the church in the isolation of their gifts from those of their other Evangelical brethren.

Nevertheless, the old Pentecostal doctrine accurately fits the experience of many believers, even though many other Christians experience an equivalent infilling of the Spirit at the outset of their Christian lives without the sign of tongues. We need a more general theory which will include and explain the data in the lives of Spirit-filled Evangelicals and Spirit-filled Pentecostals.

Two important factors should be considered here. First, in both Pentecostal and non-Pentecostal Christians who are spiritually vital there is usually a very explicit recognition of the indwelling Holy Spirit as a counselor (parakletos, one called alongside) who is personally real and dynamically active in the life of the believer. In at least one instance in Acts (19:2), a failure to experience the fullness of the Spirit is connected with a lack of awareness of his existence at the root of consciousness.

This failure to recognize the Holy Spirit as personally present in our lives is widespread in the churches today. Sometimes the lack of recognition is intentional and theologically motivated, as in Fundamentalist or confessional churches which are afraid that too much emphasis on conscious communion with the Holy Spirit will lead to a lessened regard for Christ, enthusiasm, mysticism or Pentecostalism. More often it is simply ignorance. Even where Christians know about the Holy Spirit doctrinally, they have not necessarily made a deliberate point of getting to know him personally. They may have occasional experiences of his reality on a hit-and-run basis, but the fact that the pronoun "it" is so frequently used to refer to him is not accidental. If reflects the fact that he is perceived impersonally as an expression of God's power and not experienced continually as a personal Guide and Counselor.

A normal relationship with the Holy Spirit should at least approximate the Old Testament experience described in Psalm 139: a profound awareness that we are always face to face with God; that as we move through life the presence of his Spirit is the most real and powerful factor in our daily environment; that underneath the momentary static of events, conflicts, problems and even excursions into sin, he is always there like the continuously sounding note in a *basso ostinato*.

The typical relationship between believers and the Holy Spirit in today's church is too often like that between the husband and wife in a bad marriage. They live under the same roof, and the husband makes constant use of his wife's services, but he fails to communicate with her, recognize her presence and celebrate their relationship with her.

What should be done to reverse this situation? We should make a deliberate effort at the outset of every day to recognize the person of the Holy Spirit, to move into the light concerning his presence in our consciousness and to open up our minds and to share all our thoughts and plans as we gaze by faith into the face of God. We should continue to walk throughout the day in a relationship of communication and communion with the Spirit mediated through our knowledge of the Word, relying upon every office of the Holy Spirit's role as counselor mentioned in Scripture. We should acknowledge him as the illuminator of truth and of the glory of Christ. We should look to him as teacher, guide, sanctifier, giver of assurance concerning our sonship and standing before God, helper in prayer, and as the one who directs and empowers witness.

We should particularly recognize that growth in holiness is not simply a matter of the lonely individual making claims of faith on the basis of Romans 6:1-14. It involves moving about in all the areas of our life in dependent fellowship with a person: "Walk by the Spirit, and you will not carry out the desire of the flesh" (Gal. 5:16 NASB). When this practice of the presence of God is maintained over a period of time, our experience of the Holy Spirit becomes less subjective and more clearly identifiable, as gradually we learn to distinguish the strivings of the Spirit from the motions of our flesh.

The Holy Spirit should also be recognized as the giver of spiritual gifts, and we should be continually and unreservedly open to receiving these. Part of our reverence toward him, however, should be a marked hesitation toward making any efforts of the flesh to anticipate or force his gifts. Lengthy periods of waiting before God while attempting to "prime the pump" of our speaking faculties, in order to stimulate the gift of tongues and receive assurance of "the baptism," can lead to counterfeit gifts which originate in autohypnosis, the flesh or worse sources. There is no hint of this human forcing of gifts in Scripture; the phenomena in Acts come spontaneously through the sovereign movement of God.

A second factor which should be considered in explaining Pentecostal and ordinary Evangelical experience of the fullness of the Spirit is that many Christians who have spoken in tongues originally were not particularly aiming at that gift but were seeking a deeper level of empowering and effectiveness as Christians. While seeking, they were led to a crisis situation in which they were encouraged to move fully into the light concerning every primary provision of redemption, laying hold of justification, opening their lives unreservedly to sanctification and recognizing the Holy Spirit as sanctifier and empowerer. It is not surprising that in this process they came to a pronounced forward movement in sanctification and a new infilling of the Spirit. Such an experience is guaranteed by Jesus: "Ask, and it will be given you; seek, and you will find; knock, and it will be opened to you. . . . If you then, who are evil, know how to give good gifts to your children, how much more will the heavenly Father give the Holy Spirit to those who ask him!" (Lk. 11:9, 13).

But Pentecostal believers should remember two things about their crisis experience. First, while it represents a high-water mark against which they can gauge their subsequent experience, it is not in itself a guarantee of their remaining filled with the Spirit in subsequent years; that depends upon their continuing in the light and growing in every expression of their union with Christ. Second, non-Pentecostal believers who have entered the light by degrees and without any crisis experience, or in a series of such experiences, may manifest an equal fullness of the Spirit and should not be viewed as second-class Christians because they have developed in a different pattern or because they lack certain gifts.

Fortunately many Christians in the Neo-Pentecostal movement have already moved intuitively toward positions similar to the one outlined here, and the same is true of most Evangelicals. We can hope that in another decade we will not have to deal with two sharply defined areas in the church which are "Charismatic" and "ordinary Evangelical." We should look forward to fully integrated churches in which all the gifts are practiced with restraint and charity, but not by all, in place of churches which are homogeneously Pentecostal or non-Pentecostal, in which counterfeit gifts are being fostered in one area while genuine gifts are repressed in the other. In order to aid this process of normalization, it would probably be helpful if Christians who speak in tongues and practice the other gifts in 1 Corinthians 12 would explicitly abandon the term *Charismatic movement* and substitute the word *Neo-Pentecostal*, indicating that all Christians receive the Holy Spirit at regeneration together with the potential for the development of all his gifts and graces.

Authority in Spiritual Conflict

One of the traditional theories of the meaning of the atonement, the classical or triumphal view, teaches that one effect of Christ's death and resurrection was the defeat and destruction of the powers of darkness. This has been uniformly accepted by most of the church into the period of the Enlightenment and has been restated in this century by Gustav Aulen in his *Christus Victor*.[16] It is clearly a biblical teaching. John says, "The reason the Son of God appeared was to destroy the works of the devil" (1 Jn. 3:8). Paul says that in the cross and resurrection God "disarmed the principalities and powers and made a public example of them, triumphing over them" in Christ (Col. 2:15).

Since the Enlightenment, however, much of the church has been somewhat embarrassed by the literal meaning of this doctrine, and even Evangelicals have been increasingly vague about its practical benefits. The church retains vestigial, folk-religious memories to the effect that the devil's work is to tempt us into sin but tends to regard this idea as a maneuver to shed responsibility. Many Evangelicals are content to affirm that the devil is indeed defeated, shrinking from the notion that Christians might actually run into him in actual combat situations and advising that the wisest course is to keep one's attention on Christ and let God take care of the devil. Recently there has been more talk about the devil because of the occult revival and the rise of Charismatic deliverance ministries specializing in exorcism, but it is hard to tell if these factors will stimulate practical satanology in the church or retard it through the reaction they arouse.[17]

A study of this subject throughout the history of Christian experience reveals that leaders in most other periods of the church's history have found conflict with fallen angels to be a regular feature of their daily existence and have sought to cope with it in biblical terms. We may pass over the experiences of the desert fathers as exaggerated and superstitious, but the "Rules for the Discernment of Spirits" in Ignatius Loyola's *Spiritual Exercises* (still used extensively in Jesuit retreats) indicate that medieval spiritual direction dealt realistically with this dimension of religious experience and left a deposit of accumulated wisdom for later periods in the church.

Two principles from Ignatius's rules were directly assimilated into Puritan pastoral care: (1) conviction of sin wrought by the Holy Spirit always involves a sense of release and joy along with its sorrow, while the satanic counterfeit of this convicting process leads to despair; and (2) genuine illumination by the Holy Spirit leaves residual graces in the life, while the counterfeit peace and illumination of the devil leads gradually to darkness and security in sin.[18] Thus Catholic practical satanology was not discarded by the Reformation as superstitious, since it had a strong biblical foundation. Luther too recognized its validity and conceived of his work as an assault against the entrenched powers of hell within the church. That he was right was verified by his lifelong experience under satanic onslaughts of oppression and accusation.

Subsequent periods of revival in the church have been accompanied by renewed interest in this topic. The proliferation of spiritual battle manuals during the Counter Reformation was matched by the growth of a large Puritan literature on this subject—works like John Downame's The Christian's Warfare; Thomas Brooks's Precious Remedies against Satan's Devices; and William Gurnall's The Christian in Complete Armour, one of the best-selling Puritan works of all time, which was reprinted in many editions through the middle of the nineteenth century and is still in print today.[19] The fearful mental struggles involved in the conversion of leaders like John Bunyan and George Whitefield argue that these men were either psychotic or the victims of satanic attacks like those described by Luther.[20] We have already noted that spiritual conflict was an essential conceptual tool in Edwards's understanding of the dynamics of the Great Awakening.

More recently, the spread of spiritualism and the occult during the 1904-05 revival led to the construction of a rather intricate theology of spiritual conflict by Jessie Penn-Lewis and Evan Roberts, the principal leaders in the Welsh Revival.[21] The sometimes eccentric thrust of this work has been balanced and assimilated by foreign missionaries who, like John Livingstone Nevius, have found that demonic operations on mission frontiers are too obvious to overlook.[22]

Current experience, in which Evangelical Christianity and the occult are again experiencing simultaneous resurgences, has called forth a number of popular works along the same lines.[23] Some of these may be discounted as superficial, but we should remember that as sober and balanced a writer as C. S. Lewis took biblical satanology with dead seriousness.[24]

While the New Testament states unequivocally that Christ totally defeated the powers of darkness in his atoning work, it also makes clear that the results of this victory still remain to be worked out through the increasing liberation of the earth from the occupying army of hostile spirits. Jesus told the disciples, "I have given you authority to tread upon serpents and scorpions, and over all the power of the enemy; and nothing shall hurt you" (Lk. 10:19). It is actually the risen Lord who is striding forth through his body on earth, striking the forces of darkness with the two-edged sword of truth, driving them back and chaining their influence among the nations through the transforming power of the gospel. Paul tells the Roman Christians, "The God of peace will soon crush Satan under your feet" (Rom. 16:20). In folk religion the posture of the Christian toward fallen angels is defensive; in Scripture the church is on the offensive, and the blows it receives from Satan come from a retreating enemy.

This does not mean that these blows are not serious. If the church suffers spiritual decline and the world and the flesh prevail among its members, the enemy can recapture lost ground and imperil the very life of the kingdom. Even when the church is strong and on the offensive the strategies of darkness can be baffling and destructive. But most of the devil's advantage depends on the ability to move among human affairs undetected. If a thorough knowledge of his characteristic devices were widely disseminated among the churches, the Christian warfare for the extension of Christ's kingdom would be immeasurably strengthened. In the present situation we are often operating like an army without intelligence, beating the air and one another at times, fighting flesh and blood instead of the principalities and powers which lie behind them.

As displayed in Scripture and spiritual theology Satan has at least five characteristic strategies:

1. *Temptation.* In Scripture Satan is called *ho peirazon,* the tempter. This is one of the few satanic devices which retains any currency in popular religion. Here it is largely misunderstood as having mainly to do with the efforts of demonic agents to entice believers into isolated acts of serious sin (probably the basis of this conception is the doctrine that salvation can be lost through an unconfessed "mortal sin"). The Bible does contain instances of this sort of temptation. In the case of Ananias and Sapphira the individual sin was quite literally mortal (Acts 5). But usually the enemy strategy here is either to disfigure a Christian's witness through public scandal, to gain some evidence through which his or her conscience can be accused and discouraged, or to weaken faith in the possibility of sanctification in some contested area. Most commonly temptation is directed toward larger ends: involving believers in whole ways of life or patterns of behavior which are subchristian, which will extinguish their spirituality and make them negative witnesses; or luring them into adopting outlooks which excuse or justify sin and which may almost totally obscure their faith.

2. *Deception.* Satan "deceives the whole world" (Rev. 12: 9 NASB) through the activity of lying spirits. Fallen angels are called "powers of darkness" not because they are in any way creatures of night or linked to the common superstitious fear of the dark, but because they are permanent dwellers in a world of lies and ignorance. Living in a mental universe of lies, they persuade men to keep on embracing lies concerning God, themselves and the world, reinforcing the natural affinity of the flesh for darkness.

This deception is both positive and negative. Negatively,

demonic agents induce a strong conscious aversion to biblical truth, an inability to comprehend it and a distaste for
what little can be understood. Negative deception induces
blindness to the truth; thus Satan is called, "the god of this
world [who] has blinded the minds of the unbelievers" (2
Cor. 4:4).

Positively, the forces of darkness inspire and empower
antichristian religious counterfeits (1 Jn. 4:1-3) and can imi-
tate the illuminating work of the Holy Spirit by seducing as
followers those "giving heed to deceitful spirits and doctrines of demons" (1 Tim. 4:1). They can endue these people
with counterfeit graces, "for even Satan disguises himself
as an angel of light. So it is not strange if his servants also
disguise themselves as servants of righteousness" (2 Cor. 11:
14-15). They can even energize counterfeit miracles, "pretended signs and wonders" (2 Thess. 2:9), in order to attest
false religion (Rev. 13:13-14). The deceiving work of Satan
can even be done in and through Christian believers, as
Christ's famous rebuke of Peter shows (Mt. 16:23).

The negative deceiving activity of the devil among Christians is visible in the blindness and unbelief of much theological scholarship since the Enlightenment and in the willingness of the church to accept teaching which clearly con-
tradicts biblical revelation. Positive deception is apparent in
the superstition and idolatry disfiguring much popular Fundamentalism and Catholicism.

3. *Accusation.* The word *devil (diabolos)* means *slander-
er*, and Satan is described as the one who accuses believers
continually in the presence of God (Rev. 12:10). Demonic
agents italicize the defects of Christians and the churches
in the minds of unbelievers and cause true Christianity
to be branded with the image of its own worst exemplars
or to be totally confused with counterfeit religions. They
are also particularly active in dividing Christians from one
another into parties, subtly reinforcing stereotypes in the
minds of believers who are not on guard against this, magni-

fying weaknesses and minimizing virtues to produce divisive caricatures. Unless this stratagem is correctly discerned, Christians can waste a great deal of time buffeting one another in the dark instead of combining forces to face their common enemy. Finally, satanic forces attack Christians directly in their own minds with disturbingly accurate accounts of their faults, seeking to discourage those who are most eager and able to work for the kingdom.

A related affliction which is less frequently encountered is *obsession*, the passage of streams of blasphemous or sinful thought through the mind with strong demonic energy behind it, accompanied by accusations persuading believers that these are their own sins for which they are guilty.[25] Believers in these situations are almost helpless to combat the constant assaults of depression which come upon them with every attempt to engage in mission until they are able to target accurately the source of the streams of accusation entering their minds and erect the shield of faith against these.

4. *Possession.* There is no special word for this phenomenon in Scripture—the New Testament uses *demonization* for any affliction with a satanic origin—but the Gospels plainly describe a condition in which human victims come almost helplessly under control of alien personalities (Lk. 8: 26-33). John Nevius, in his account of this phenomenon on the Chinese mission field, describes a number of situations in which demonic agents had apparently taken over the personalities of individuals, gifting them with paranormal knowledge and healing abilities. This is paralleled in the Eleusinian and Orphic mysteries of ancient Greece, shamanism among primitive tribes, and many sectors in the contemporary occult revival. The servant girl Paul exorcized in Acts 16:16-18 is typical of this phenomenon.

5. *Physical attack.* Jesus says of Satan, "He was a murderer from the beginning" (Jn. 8:44), and the devil is called the destroyer (*ho apolluōn*—Rev. 9:11). From data in the Gospels it appears that demonic agents can occasionally

cause illness, at least psychological and neurological ailments like dumbness and epilepsy (Mt. 9:32-33 and 17: 14-18). It is frequently claimed by demythologizers that the whole biblical treatment of the demonic is just a prescientific way of describing mental and physical illness. But the demonized are usually a separate category from the diseased in the Gospels, and the presence of alternate personalities among them and the personalizing of satanic powers throughout the Bible argue decisively against this.

Normally, however, the destructive malice of Satan against all humanity, and particularly against the church, is channeled through human agents and the systems and institutions they have built. Humanity in general is afflicted by the destroyer through the structures of injustice and oppression of which the flesh and the devil are joint architects, and Christians are murderously attacked by individuals and governments ultimately directed by Satan. The involvement of the forces of darkness in stirring up and shaping these works of destruction against God's creation does not eliminate human responsibility and guilt. It simply explains the fearfully logical strategy often apparent in evil and the blindness and virulent energy present in the human beings involved in such genocidal actions as the murder of six million Jews under Hitler.

It needs to be said immediately that other factors besides demonic agency join in causing almost every aberration mentioned above and that often there may not be any direct satanic activity involved. As Puritan pastoral theory recognized, spiritual pathology can arise from four different sources: physical factors (illness, fatigue, malnutrition or what today might be recognized as glandular or chemical imbalance); psychological factors ("temperament"); fallen human nature; and demonic attack.

The various components of spiritual pathology are often so mixed in any given crisis experience that we would be hard put to separate them, and we might be tempted simply to remain agnostic about the satanic dimension of the problem and deal with the others. But to do so would be against the example and the counsel fo the apostolic church. In attempting to shield the incestuous church member at Corinth from excessive discipline after his repentance Paul assures the Corinthians that he stands with them in forgiving him, "to keep Satan from gaining the advantage over us; for we are not ignorant of his designs" (2 Cor. 2:11). The designs in view here were probably oppression and accusation of this believer, the division of the church over this issue and the alienation of Paul's authority.

The New Testament seems constantly to assume that believers are acquainted with the stratagems of darkness and can recognize them when they run up against them. Thus Peter warns his readers, "Be sober, be watchful. Your adversary the devil prowls around like a roaring lion, seeking some one to devour. Resist him, firm in your faith" (1 Pet. 5: 8, 9). Perhaps it is assumed that the special gift of discerning spirits is widely distributed among the churches. But it also seems evident that any Christian who knows the characteristic methods of demonic agents and who is involved in building the kingdom of Christ under the direction of the Holy Spirit will be alerted to special assaults of Satan simply by the logic, intensity and shape of efforts calculated to undermine the work of God.

In our own time, the sorting out of physical and psychological symptoms which can mimic certain operations of the devil (particularly depression and manic elation, inferiority feelings, and schizophrenia) will have to be carried out by ministers well trained in pastoral psychology. In difficult cases teams of consultants including pastors, psychotherapists and physicians may have to be employed.

Once the activity of Satan has been detected in any situation, unusual caution or elaborate rituals of exorcism are not necessary to handle the enemy forces. Nevius found that the proximity of strong Christians and the reading of

Scripture was enough to drive off many of the possessing spirits he encountered. The Bible says simply, "Submit yourselves therefore to God. Resist the devil and he will flee from you" (Jas. 4:7). The first phrase here might be translated, "Order your lives under God." In effect, it means that a Christian should come fully into the light of Christ's redemptive provisions for him as he opposes the forces of darkness, laying hold by faith of every dimension of strength with which his union with Christ endues him: "I am accepted by God as righteous. I am delivered from the power of sin. I am not alone, for I have the Holy Spirit as counselor. And I have authority against fallen spirits."

This same thrust characterizes Paul's famous discussion of the Christian's armor which heaps up metaphors dealing with the Christian's walking in the light of the knowledge of salvation: the belt of truth, the breastplate of righteousness, the shoes of the gospel, the shield of faith, the helmet of salvation, the sword of the Word and prayer (Eph. 6:14-18). Once this stance is taken, it is simply a matter of resisting the devil steadfastly. He must flee.

The Christian who is substantially walking in light is practically invulnerable to the assaults of darkness as Jesus intimates in the parable of the empty house (Mt. 12:43-45). This is beautifully expressed in John Bunyan's image of the powers of darkness as lions chained on a short tether on either side of the road to the Celestial City. These lions can maul travelers who wander from the middle of the path but cannot touch those who walk precisely in the center. This metaphor emphasizes that Christian warfare is not a conflict in which the sides are in any way equivalent, a Manichaean struggle between equal powers of good and evil. The forces of darkness are so chained by the victory of Christ that they are unable to do anything which does ultimate damage to his glory and kingdom. The battles we fight against them should not be occasions of anxiety. They force us back to reliance on Christ's redemptive work and enhance our dignity and authority as redeemed saints who have the power to judge angels (1 Cor. 6:3).

Charismatic "deliverance ministries" which employ a broad-scale use of exorcism in pastoral care are correct in calling the attention of the church to the reality of spiritual conflict, but they need to be exercised rather carefully within the whole context of the dynamics of spiritual life. It is true that all vital Christians are to some degree "demonized," when *demonization* is defined inclusively to cover every phenomenon from temptation to possession. But the ordinary remedy may not be exorcism but counseling into the fullness of Christ, including an understanding of our authority against demonic agents and a stance of resistance against them in contested areas of the personality.

Some deliverance ministries identify any deep-rooted compulsive pattern of sin as an effect of "demon possession." This is bound to be misleading, although it is an understandable error given the common misunderstanding which identifies sin with voluntary acts and overlooks the compulsive nature of the flesh. But it is important to understand that indiscriminate exorcism for every behavioral problem which does not yield to the immediate exercise of willpower may actually *induce* symptoms of an alternate personality which are hypnotic or psychological in origin. Individual or mass exorcisms which are not accompanied with detailed teaching on the full provisions of redemption may be worse than useless. They may raise false hopes of deliverance from conditions which cannot be cured by exorcism because they originate in the flesh or in psychological or physiological problems. Both Charismatic and ordinary Evangelical ministries need to recognize that deep spiritual problems cannot always be cured by one or two "magic wand" experiences of the infusion of grace. It takes time, and the penetration of truth, to make a mature saint.

At this point, some of those readers with whom I am most concerned to share these insights may be about to give up the dialog. The biblical symbols used have been so debased and trivialized by folk religion that modern imaginations find it hard to reach behind popular stereotypes to apprehend the serious realities described in Scripture. Some may feel that introducing demonic agents into our world encourages irresponsibility with respect to individual sin and corporate structures of evil. But this is readily avoided if our definition of the flesh and the world is accurate. Others may be alarmed that the portraits of God, sin and the powers of darkness presented are too much like the Puritan religion of "hellfire and damnation," and that this kind of spiritual world is frightening and disturbing. But what this outlook seems to lose by its austerity it regains by its close fidelity to Scripture. Multitudes of Christians will undoubtedly be reassured and made secure if the world of their daily religious experience can again be made recognizably similar to the world of the Bible.

Kierkegaard described accurately the sense of disorientation which a tamed modern religion produces in those who read the Bible:

> The New Testament therefore, regarded as a guide for Christians, becomes, under the assumption we have made, a historical curiosity, pretty much like a guidebook to a particular country when everything in that country has been totally changed. Such a guidebook serves no longer the serious purpose of being useful to travelers in that country, but at the most it is worth reading for amusement. While one is making the journey easily by railway, one reads in the guidebook, "Here it is a band of robbers has its stronghold, from which it issues to assault the travelers and maltreat them."[26]

Such a domesticated view of spiritual reality may be superficially comfortable for a while, but eventually it is simply not credible. We will have less anxiety ourselves and more of a hearing from the world if we will believe in and preach the awesome, dangerous, but solid realities taught in Scripture.

SECONDARY ELEMENTS OF RENEWAL

5

THE PROCLAMATION OF THE GOSPEL in depth is the most important condition of the renewal of the church, and for this reason we have dealt with the primary elements contained in the atonement at considerable length. This material is the program source for the church's proclamation, as recorded music is the program source in a stereo system; but it is like a tape recording which has the power to tune the instrument through which it is played until it functions perfectly.

The secondary conditions of renewal are also closely connected with our union with Christ, and they flow out of the primary elements secured in the atonement. *Orientation toward mission* relates Christ's work to the rest of the world, and it is essentially involved in knowing and following the Holy Spirit and correctly using our authority against the powers of darkness. *Dependent prayer* is possible because we are united to Christ, received in his righteousness, sanctified by his life and attuned to his concerns by the presence of the Holy Spirit; and it is necessary because we are engaged in mission against immeasurably superior forces. *Community* grows out of our common life in Christ and joint possession of his Spirit, and is necessary for the full demonstration of his continuing presence on earth. *Theological integration* is necessary because the sanctification of the mind is critically important, leading to a developed understanding of the mind of Christ under the Holy Spirit's guidance and illumination. *Disenculturation* is possible only when we rely fully on Christ for justification and sanctification; it is necessary if we are to be released from the marriage of religion and culture which prevents our reaching all nations and reflecting the diversity of life in Christ.

All of these secondary dimensions of renewal are related and reinforce one another. Mission cannot be effectively pursued without prayer, disenculturation and theological integration. Realistic and effective prayer can only grow out of a community oriented toward mission. Genuine Christian community takes part of its motivation from shared consciousness of mission, grows out of and expresses itself in prayer, and requires disenculturation and theological integration. Further examination of these elements taken separately will indicate how each of them affects the others and how all are rooted in the person and work of Christ.

Orientation toward Mission
At the end of Luke's Gospel, the risen Christ informs the disciples that they are to be witnesses to his resurrection who, beginning from Jerusalem, will proclaim repentance to all nations. At the beginning of Acts, however, they ask him, "Lord, will you at this time restore the kingdom to Israel?" Obviously there is a persistent gravitational pull in their minds away from a task involving unknown spiritual battles and toward the popular messianic concept of instan-

taneous prosperity in which every man can sit under his vine and fig tree, tending his own section of the garden and harvesting its fruits.

This tendency to forget the redemptive emergency in the world and concentrate on enjoying dominion in a part of it has been a continual temptation to the church. The shape of the early church described in Acts, quartered together like an army garrison or a troop of nomadic pilgrims in an alien land, reflects a corrected sense of mission which apparently persisted through the early Christian era until Roman civilization was permeated with witnesses to the gospel.

Moving toward the advent of Constantine, however, the church began to be schizoid in its missionary consciousness. Gradually the great mass of the laity and the regular clergy attending them became a system concerned not so much to advance the kingdom of God as to decorate the occasions of ordinary human existence with religious meaning. Nobles and commoners fixed their attention on tangible goals: survival, security, wealth, power, eminence. At the same time, they employed the church to set moral guidelines for this competition, to illuminate birth and marriage and death with supernatural meaning, providing a kind of insurance policy covering individual sins committed in this pursuit and holding out the probability of a happier existence after death.

This is not necessarily the way the game was perceived by the clergy, of course, and a large group among them, centered around the monastic reformers, made a very deliberate and extreme effort to avoid the goals which had become common in worldly Christianity. It was these ascetic reform movements which continued to spread the church during the medieval era. But the form of Christianity which was planted was still one in which the gap persisted between the few who were concerned for the kingdom of God and the majority who were concerned about the kingdoms of this world. Sometimes this division coincided with that between the clergy and the laity; often, sadly, it did not.

In defense of ordinary parish Christianity, it should be admitted that the form of the kingdom of God in history can better be understood as a transformation of ordinary lifestyles by divine grace than as a set of radical monastic communes abstracted from the ordinary human community. A missionary strategy which calls on its converts to "drop out of the Monopoly game" of normal human activities and become part of a quasi-military commune, like the Children of God, may seem to gain by focusing the attention of its whole membership on proselytizing new members.[1] Ultimately, however, it loses by this approach: it erects too great a cultural gap between the believing community and the surrounding world, and it fails to see that converts are won more by the observable blessedness of a whole way of life than by the arguments of individuals. The trouble with ordinary lifestyles, however, is that it is hard to continue living in them without gradually falling into ordinary motivations. The problem with parish Christianity during its long existence is not that it has failed to be organized strategically, but that it has seldom risen above conformity to the world in its goals, methods and achievements.

It would seem at first that the Reformation should have overcome this problem, since it attacked the separation between lay and clerical vocations, encouraged the priesthood of all believers, and stressed the truths of justification and sanctification through Christ. All these emphases should have helped to release the laity spiritually for missionary concern.

But the kingdom of God continued to be an elusive reality for Protestants. English and American Puritans articulated a missionary concern for the inhabitants of America and acted it out to some extent through John Eliot's ministry to the Indians. But most American Puritans in the late seventeenth century seem to have been caught up in either of two forms of self-absorption: those who were seriously religious were urgently concerned to establish their regeneracy and grow in personal holiness, and those who were only formally pious were mesmerized by their interest in land and business.[2] Edmund Morgan has suggested that the predominant motive of the Puritans in moving to America was not mission but the preservation of godly family dynasties.[3]

It is possible for both individuals and churches to become devoted mainly to personal spiritual culture and forget outreach, especially if the process of reaching out involves touching those who may contaminate us. Thus many Protestant churches have in effect become closed systems for the nurture and servicing of the inheritors of a denominational tradition.

The leaders of the Reformation, of course, engaged in the form of mission appropriate to their calling and possible in their embattled circumstances: the spreading of their approach to church renewal in the waves of influence emanating from Wittenberg and Geneva. With the advent of the evangelical movement, Protestant home and foreign missions began to bloom most remarkably, first in the Pietist missions of Halle and Herrnhut and later in the interdenominational works springing up in England and America in the late eighteenth and early nineteenth centuries. Associated with the verbal presentation of the gospel in this work were tangible demonstrations of physical compassion: food for the hungry, homes for orphans and charity schools for the poor. The home missions work of the Second Awakening also attacked evils within the structure of society, promoting prison reform, temperance, peace, and—with conspicuous success—the abolition of the slave trade and the release of slaves. Both the proclamation and social action components of the evangelical missionary movement were built on a foundation of awareness and concern on the congregational level, nurtured by informed corporate prayer. There was no dichotomy perceived between evangelism and social concern, and no disparity between interest in these forms of mission abroad and willingness to implement them at home.

The disintegration of the American evangelical movement in the early twentieth century due to its own internal weaknesses and the deforming pressure of secular humanism eroded much of this progress in Protestant mission orientation. The antithesis which developed between Christians concerned for social action and those oriented toward personal evangelism impoverished the mission outlook of both groups, particularly in the field of home missions. Among many Evangelicals, willingness to help nonwhites abroad both evangelistically and socially contrasted strangely with ingrown and socially apathetic churches at home. Among many non-Evangelicals, the inability to focus on unregeneracy as the main missionary target and doubts about the proclaimed Word as the main instrument of conversion produced shrinking memberships at home and impermanent gains or bafflement abroad. The main business of the laity of all persuasions was business and not the kingdom of God. The church and religion served as spokes on the wheel of life, the hub of which was personal success.

Despite these weaknesses on the home front in Western Christianity, foreign missions and younger churches in the Third World and parts of Asia have continued to flourish most remarkably in the twentieth century, particularly since the Second World War, as Ralph Winter has shown.[4] The misconception that Christianity is a waning influence in the modern world is partly due to the perspective of Western observers familiar with the disabled home missions of the institutional church and partly to satanically reinforced ignorance of the church's vigor abroad. Much of this growth can be attributed to two factors: continued Evangelical leadership within both denominational missions and the increasing force of nondenominational independent mission works, and new evangelical awakenings in Korea, Indonesia, Africa, Latin America and elsewhere.

While the broad mass of the laity in American churches continue to be exhaustingly absorbed in the rat race of business life, at least a portion of their finances is being diverted to furnish a substantial economic foundation for a remarkable missionary program abroad. One cannot help but wonder what the result would be if this mass of lay people could be spiritually released from their servitude in the American success system and reoriented to channel their major energies toward building the kingdom of God. Foreign missions would be enriched with a new flow of personnel and resources—contrary to some perceptions of the situation there is still room for this—and on the home missionary front there would be not only a surge of evangelism-in-depth comparable to the awakenings on the mission field but also the provision of funds needed for a whole variety of ministries from social compassion to the media. New Christian artists and musicians could be supported in film, television and radio.

A biblical paradigm Western lay people might well consider is the awakened conscience of David: "See now, I dwell in a house of cedar, but the ark of God dwells in a tent" (2 Sam. 7:2). As a result of David's intention to build a better house for God than his own palace, the king in turn was promised that God would build his own household and that he would never lack for a son to sit upon the throne of Israel. The Davidic covenant and the coming of the Messiah were the result of this insight. It would not be extreme to expect an unprecedented rule of Christ in the culture surrounding a church whose members were similarly awakened to build a temple of living stones to proclaim the excellencies of the One who called them out of darkness into his marvelous light (1 Pet. 2:5, 9).

Dependent Prayer

While Jesus left no recorded instruction to the apostles to

prepare themselves for mission by prayer, Luke reports that during the interim until Pentecost "all these with one accord devoted themselves to prayer" (Acts 1:14). When the mission of the new church was threatened by an edict commanding them to cease their witness, the apostles turned to prayer again, and their mission was confirmed by a new spiritual empowering (Acts 4:1-31). The first missionary journey from Antioch emerged from a prayer meeting (Acts 13:1-3). Thus there is an indissoluble reinforcing connection between mission and dependent prayer. Those who realistically face the demanding task of local mission are immediately driven to prayer by the magnitude of the work confronting them. Those who are praying about the needs surrounding them in the world are awakened to the greatness of those needs and the opportunity for the church to meet them.

As we have seen, the Great Awakening was preceded by a period of sterility and stalemate in the life of Western Protestantism in which a few evangelical leaders began to call for and organize prayer for a new Pentecost, an outpouring of the Holy Spirit to carry the church forward at a pace which would accomplish in decades works which had previously taken centuries. The awakening at Herrnhut in 1727 came after the establishment of a round-the-clock prayer meeting for the reviving and spread of the church. The Herrnhut prayer meeting persisted for a hundred years until "the Great Century" of missionary expansion was launched. The regular, synchronized "concert of prayer" for revival among Western Protestants called for by Edwards persisted through the low point preceding the Second Awakening and accelerated from a monthly to a regular midweekly occurrence in nineteenth-century American churches.[5] The "Third Awakening," and to a large extent also the worldwide phenomenon of 1904-05 which Orr documents, consisted mainly of groups of lay people meeting together to pray for the outpouring of the Holy Spirit.[6] Manuals on the technology of revival from Finney's *Lectures* on have stressed the connection between corporate prayer and the outpouring of the Holy Spirit.[7] Ask Evangelicals what the most essential condition of revival is, and they are most likely to point to prayer.

In much of the church's life in the twentieth century, however, both in Evangelical and non-Evangelical circles, the place of prayer has become limited and almost vestigial. The proportion of horizontal communication that goes on in the church (in planning, arguing and expounding) is overwhelmingly greater than that which is vertical (in worship, thanksgiving, confession and intercession). Critically important committee meetings are begun and ended with formulary prayers, which are ritual obligations and not genuine expressions of dependence—when problems and arguments ensue, they are seldom resolved by further prayer but are wrangled out on the battlefield of human discourse. The old midweek prayer meetings for revival have vanished from the programs of most churches or have been transformed into Bible studies ending with minimal prayer.

This was the picture in much of the American church until recently, and it is still almost universally the case in some instruments and organs of the churches which have to do with teaching and administration. Why has this come about? Perhaps it stems partly from the deficient teaching and emphasis on God himself throughout the church, and partly from the man-centeredness of much religious activity. Deficiency in prayer both reflects and reinforces inattention toward God.

Then too, the minimal prayer accompanying many projects in the church may indicate that what is being undertaken is simply what human beings can accomplish pretty well by themselves. In some cases (in religious education, for instance) what is being attempted is genuinely supernatural if compared to biblical models, but those who do the work seem fully confident that they can produce good results simply by their talent, expertise and effort. The weakness here lies partly in oversimplifying the target and partly in failure to comprehend the transforming role the Holy Spirit plays in every redemptive enterprise. Lack of comprehension of primary dynamics of spiritual life leads inevitably to weakness in prayer and other secondary dynamics.

It is hard to avoid the conclusion that much of the absence of prayer in the church is due to a virtual allergy induced by uncomfortable experience with imperfect forms of prayer or to models of the Christian life which require superhuman bouts of prayer in order to qualify at an acceptable level of saintliness. Prayer in a context where all the primary elements of renewal are not functioning can be pathological and deadening.

Puritan piety sometimes re-created the counsels of perfection in monastic spirituality in what it required of the normal Christian prayer life. It was considered good for the young Christian to be challenged with the marathon records of Jesus and the saints. This could be humbling, but it could also cause the young prayer-warrior to buckle under the weight of the armor he felt bound to assume. In such cases prayer was not an expression of faith in God's grace, but a monument erected to attract his attention. Trust was not centered on the God who constantly oversees our paths and knows our needs, but on prayer itself, which must be used as a magical lever to pry answers from an unwilling God.

Since there is a great deal of defective Christianity in existence, it follows that there is plenty of this defective prayer, and one generation full of it can produce a succeeding generation which hardly prays at all. If the parent generation spends its time engaged in bad prayer when it ought to be working, or depends on the Holy Spirit to transform the water of shoddy work into the wine of achievement, a generation of prayerless workers is sure to follow.

Even if the neglect of prayer in some important areas in the church can be explained partly by the formation of allergies to prayer pathology, it cannot thus be excused. The commands and examples of Scripture recommending prayer are too clear. Even bad prayer is better than no prayer. The un-easiness about praying together and the fear of being too pious found among many Evangelicals and non-Evangeli-cals alike must have roots in the flesh. Sometimes this un-easiness springs from an unconscious fear of the entrance into spiritual reality that prayer requires. Persons who are in the dark concerning primary spiritual dynamics have something in their flesh which does not want to face up to the light. The Puritan Thomas Goodwin points out that our fallen nature is actually allergic to God and never wants to get too close to him. Thus our fallen nature constantly pulls us away from prayer.[8]

Part of the reluctance toward corporate prayer may stem from lack of practice in private prayer combined with a fleshly self-consciousness centered on the impression it is making rather than on the truth that God is hearing and an-swering. Or the reluctance to pray with others may reflect estrangement from them and unwillingness to settle disa-greements and close the gap.

Beyond these expressions of the flesh there is a force in our minds resisting prayer like a solid barrier which must be broken. This force seizes on any and all of these good and bad excuses of the flesh and reinforces them in order to dis-courage us from praying. It is sometimes forgotten that if the devil can tempt us to do evil, he can also tempt us not to do good. He can glamorize sin, but he can also paint an ugly picture in our minds of any work which is the will of God, including prayer. Quietly and undetectably, he can embitter the image of prayer in our minds until we will unconsciously go out of our way to avoid it. The reason for this persistence on his part is obvious. It is adroitly summed up in an old couplet: "Satan trembles when he sees/ The weakest saint upon his knees." As Paul says, "The weapons of our warfare are not worldly, but have divine power to destroy strong-holds" (2 Cor. 10:4). The enemy of our souls is painfully aware of the destructive force of even our dullest and weakest prayers and will go to any length to block them.

The reason behind Satan's fear, as well as the key to the critical importance of dependent prayer in spiritual renewal, is twofold. First, the prayer of faith is the instrument which releases the mighty acts of the risen Christ in history. As Jesus promised the disciples on the eve of crucifixion:

> He who believes in me will also do the works that I do; and greater works than these will he do, because I go to the Father. Whatever you ask in my name, I will do it, that the Father may be glorified in the Son; if you ask anything in my name, I will do it. (Jn. 14:12-14)

As he promised them on another occasion: "Whoever says to this mountain, 'Be taken up and cast into the sea,' and does not doubt in his heart, but believes that what he says will come to pass, it will be done for him" (Mk. 11:23). As we grow spiritually and become engaged in the labors of the kingdom, we run into things which block Christ's work in our lives and his work in the world, and however mountainous these are, we have authority to move them out of the way of the victorious Lord. As God alerts us to such blockages and gives us a sense of urgency and intolerance against them, we have the same authority that he promised Jeremiah: "I have set you this day over nations and over kingdoms, to pluck up and to break down, to destroy and to overthrow, to build and to plant" (Jer. 1:10).

Second, prayer is one of the main agencies through which we are brought to understand the mind of Christ toward our particular mission and the work of the kingdom in general. On the night of his betrayal Jesus not only promised his disciples the power to continue his works through prayer, but he also intimated that they would understand the scope and meaning of those works: "No longer do I call you servants, for the servant does not know what his master is doing; but I have called you friends" (Jn. 15:15). The understanding necessary for us to become knowledgeable partners in the redemptive work of Christ comes to us through his Word and through the Holy Spirit's specific application of that Word to situations which are the objects of concerned prayer.

As Christ intercedes for us and for his kingdom at the right hand of God, the Holy Spirit moves our hearts into harmony with God's concerns:

> Likewise the Spirit helps us in our weakness; for we do not know how to pray as we ought, but the Spirit himself intercedes for us with sighs too deep for words. And he who searches the hearts of men knows what is the mind of the Spirit, because the Spirit intercedes for the saints according to the will of God. (Rom. 8:26)

Through the leading of the Spirit in prayer our intercession becomes one with the intercession of Christ, our minds become attuned to his, and his concerns become ours.

Christ's present ministry is described in Psalm 110: "The LORD says to my Lord: 'Sit at my right hand, till I make your enemies your footstool.' The LORD sends forth from Zion your mighty scepter. Rule in the midst of your foes!" (Ps. 110:1-2). In prayer we make use of the privilege which is ours in being seated with Christ in heavenly places and thus join in his counsels and his ruling power. Thus the prayers of believers are a terror to the powers of evil, not simply because of the judgment they bring down on the works of darkness, but because they turn bewildered saints into knowledgeable opponents. "Fear not, you worm Jacob, you men of Israel! I will help you, says the LORD; ... Behold, I will make of you a threshing sledge, new, sharp, and having teeth; you shall thresh the mountains and crush them, and you shall make the hills like chaff" (Is. 41:14-15).

Undoubtedly the small quantity of intelligent intercessory prayer in most twentieth-century congregations is part of the short-circuiting of missionary consciousness among the laity. The establishment of the kingdom of God is an elusive task; we cannot even see what it involves in our vicinity without specific prayer, and we certainly will have little urgency to carry it out unless we are praying.

In recent years the amount and quality of prayer in the American church has been rapidly improving in a number of areas. "Conversational prayer" has abolished the virtuoso art of making long prayers and has made corporate prayer accessible to even the youngest Christian. The small prayer groups emphasized by Samuel Shoemaker's Pittsburgh Experiment and Faith at Work have recently become a widespread phenomenon not only in churches but in businesses and government. Among Pentecostal and Charismatic circles, prayer has continued to hold the primary position it has always been given during spiritual awakenings, and in this respect Pentecostals are perhaps the truest representatives of the Evangelical tradition in the twentieth century. It is not simply intercessory prayer which Pentecostals have emphasized; they have given equal attention to adoration, thanksgiving and confession. This is understandable, since the act of prayer, once we have broken through the prayer-barriers of the flesh and the devil, is one of the closest approaches to the experience of redemption we can have before the eternal state.

Not all of the new profusion of prayer is free from minor pathologies, of course. In Neo-Pentecostal prayer meetings which last hours, sometimes the intelligible content of what is prayed is relatively low, and little care seems to be taken to lay situations out before the Lord in a disciplined and thoughtful way. This does not discount the value of the prayer in terms of God's answering it as Romans 8:26 indicates; but careful, expansive intelligent prayer about the situations which confront us in the world can sharpen our edge to meet them.

In small prayer groups, often the concerns which are shared and prayed about are wholly personal, involved with healing, psychological adjustment and other immediate individual burdens. Larger issues which are closely related to the interests of the kingdom of God are ignored. Groups in which this occurs should make a determined effort to engage in kingdom-centered prayer. The Lord's Prayer is instructive. It is no accident that it begins first with worship of God himself, moves on to involve the doing of his will on earth and the coming of his kingdom, and only then turns to the immediate personal concerns of supply, forgiveness and spiritual deliverance.

Praying too much is probably not a failure in the older generation of Christians today, but fleshly religiosity could make it a problem again in the future. Just how much intercessory prayer is normative for a Christian lifestyle today? Oddly enough, the Scripture does not seem to recommend the long formal bouts of prayer favored by the desert fathers, some of the monastic writers and many Puritans.

> Guard your steps when you go to the house of God; to draw
> near to listen is better than to offer the sacrifice of fools:
> for they do not know that they are doing evil. Be not rash
> with your mouth, nor let your heart be hasty to utter a word
> before God, for God is in heaven, and you upon earth;
> therefore let your words be few. (Eccles. 5:1-2)

Perhaps Jesus had this passage in mind when he cautioned the disciples, "Do not heap up empty phrases as the Gentiles do; for they think that they will be heard for their many words. Do not be like them, for your Father knows what you need before you ask him" (Mt. 6:7-8). These words and the short formula of prayer which follows might seem almost dangerously indulgent to many who have been schooled in a more laborious piety, but their aim is precisely to avoid overloading the conscience of the beginner or the weak believer, to avoid any emphasis on works which will distract us from the recognition of God's grace, and to fix our attention on God who hears and answers rather than on the mechanism of prayer.

But how abbreviated can prayer be before it ceases to have value? Perhaps the biblical examples of short intercessory prayers offered up in the course of a walk with God give us one indication. As one Puritan remarked, "It is best to pray briefly, but often.''[9] A day interwoven with many such prayers may be part of what Paul meant in advising us to "pray constantly" (1 Thess. 5:17).

To the Philippians Paul writes: "have no anxiety about anything, but in everything by prayer and supplication with thanksgiving let your requests be made known to God. And the peace of God, which passes all understanding, will keep your hearts and your minds in Christ Jesus" (Phil. 4:6-7). Evidently one sign of deficient prayer is anxiety. As pain tells us of the need for healing, worry tells us of the need for prayer.

Prayer functions as a safety valve without which informed Christians would constantly be anxious, aware as they are of the spiritual warfare surrounding them. And since faith is the essential grace expressed by and strengthened through prayer, we might say that we have interceded enough when we have held before God the major responsibilities which confront us and any wider burdens which the Holy Spirit may suggest from day to day, and have exercized faith that he is at work in these. This is not at all a difficult labor; there may be times when it can be the work of minutes. Too little prayer is an expression of unbelief in God's love and care; so is too much.

If all regenerate church members in Western Christendom were to intercede daily simply for the most obvious spiritual concerns visible in their homes, their workplaces, their local churches and denominations, their nations, and the world and the total mission of the body of Christ within it, the transformation which would result would be incalculable. Not only would God certainly change those situations in response to prayer—we have Christ's word that if we ask in his name he will do more than we ask or think—but the church's comprehension of its task would attain an unprecedented sharpness of focus. Perhaps much of our prayer now should simply be for God to pour out such a spirit of prayer and supplication in the hearts of his people.

The Community of Believers

Unlike most modern congregations the early Christian church was an integrated community centered around the worship of God and the advancement of his kingdom. Economically it was a commonwealth, which meant that its members were not being pulled apart from one another by the pursuit of individual goals of success; they were devoting everything they were and owned to the strengthening of one another and the cause of Christ. Worshiping and eating together, the members were in constant communication. The religious center of their fellowship was continually reinforced by apostolic teaching, corporate prayer and sacramental worship. Little time or distance separated the members of this body, so there was an unhindered communication of the gifts and graces of each one to the others. Those of us who have experienced something like this life of close community aligned with the purposes of God's kingdom for a few weeks at a good summer conference can witness to the rich vitality and clear spiritual atmosphere which prevail in this kind of situation. Ordinary parish life seems dim and difficult by comparison.

In the early centuries of persecution the church may have maintained this close fellowship. With the development of the church and the influx of large numbers of converts after Constantine's accession a change must have occurred. The adoption of Cyprian's understanding of the New Testament ministry as the antitype of the Old Testament priesthood, now offering an unbloody eucharistic sacrifice in a multitude of churches instead of the original temple, was bound to affect the life of the Christian community. While the ministry of the synagogue had involved considerable lay participation, the temple worship had cast the laity chiefly into the role of hearers of the Law and spectators of the mysterious tableau of the sacrifices. This passive role in worship became once more the normal experience of the people of God as the church developed. Grace was objectified outside the body of believers, specifically in the priesthood and the sacramental system, and its entry into each life became a matter between the individual and "the church," which was no longer regarded as the community of the saints. Paul's description of a congregational meeting at Corinth sounds like a spiritually energized synagogue meeting: "When you come together, each one has a hymn, a lesson, a revelation, a tongue, or an interpretation. Let all things be done for edification" (1 Cor. 14:26). But this does not sound at all like the congregational life of the medieval church.

The change in the conception of normative religious experience between Acts 2 and the end of the third century is indicated by the fact that the ascetic reformers who moved out into the region surrounding Alexandria, the desert fathers, did not seek spiritual perfection in community but in solitude. Gradually some of these hermits discovered that if they banded together in small communities like beehives, they experienced spiritual as well as practical benefits. Over the course of several centuries these cells evolved into increasingly more disciplined communities governed by a rule. At Monte Casino, A.D. 529, this evolutionary process culminated in Benedict of Nursia's establishment of a monastery which became the prototype for a number of other monastic reform movements in the later Middle Ages.

Many of the features of the Christian community in Acts 2 were reincorporated into monastic Christian life. The community's resources were pooled. The Scriptures and other Christian writings were not only privately studied but read aloud during the common meals. The recitation of prayers and singing of psalms occurred seven times a day at regular intervals including the middle of the night. The major difference, of course, was that while the apostolic community was in open contact with the surrounding life of Jerusalem, the monastery was enclosed. Those who ventured outside it for the shortest journey had to return through the air lock of a detailed confession. It would appear that in this instance the cultivation of the microcommunity within the monastery walls had eclipsed the macrocommunity (the rest of the church and the outside world).

But this familiar observation is only one of several Protestant criticisms which do not stand up well under examination. The monasteries were designed to be working models of the kingdom of heaven, earthly copies of the heavenly society, and when they were operating at their best, they became like cities set on a hill. Their walls could not hide the piety and the industry that was generated in these communities when they were healthy, and many of them became civilizing influences on the surrounding towns, exerting a positive influence on their spiritual, economic and social life. The triple vow of poverty, chastity and obedience may be judged to be overkill in the mortification of sin, but at least it was a serious attack on the most common expressions of the flesh: greed, sensuality and pride. The monastery represented a sort of sanctification machine for the postulant longing to become free from his fallen nature, and it could also be a school in which to learn to love God and one's neighbors with the whole heart. Protestants today should ask themselves what comparable mechanisms are operating in their local churches to break down the isolation between Christians and disengage them from conformity to the world, particularly in their unconscious ultimate concern for affluence and success.

To correct this common misconception is not to dismiss the real problems inherent in the monastic community structure, a fact which should be noted by Protestant communes today. Besides the deep theological questions connected with the monastic approach to justification and sanctification, the ascetic abdication of power and wealth by the ordinary monk necessarily concentrated all authority in the hands of the overseer and manager of the community, the abbot. With the normal tendency of absolute power to corrupt absolutely, this could not fail to pose a considerable challenge to the abbot's sanctity. The fate of monasteries with bad abbots was difficult to remedy.

Nevertheless, many monastic communities did serve as nurseries of piety and centers of renewal for the church, and this is true also of the late medieval developments like the Brethren of the Common Life which were derived from the monastic model. One of the most interesting variations of this pattern was an invention of Ignatius Loyola, the temporary monastic retreat, which became an important engine of the Counter Reformation and is the rather unlikely prototype for the Evangelical summer conference experience.[10]

During the Reformation era several alternatives to monastic community appeared. One of the great contributions of the Radical Reformation, along with the doctrine of the separation of church and state, was the expansion of the monastic community pattern to embrace the whole body of believers. The Mennonite communities are in effect geographically separated but open and unenclosed villages of believers, in which there is great opportunity for fellowship and sharing, but ordinarily no abandonment of private property as in the more rigorous Hutterite communities. This kind of community perpetuates some of the best features of monastic life without its more doubtful aspects.

However, there is a danger that the church community will become so self-sufficient that it will be taken out of the world in a way that Jesus explicitly warns against in John 17:15, so that the salt of the earth cannot do its work. The monastic communities were always only a special case within Catholicism where the church retained its contact with the world through the parish network. Connection with more ordinary congregations "dissolved" in the world may always be essential if the microcommunity is not to short-circuit the church's mission and divorce it from the macro-communities of the broader church and human society.

Mennonite self-criticism has recognized this problem: Speaking from an MC [Mennonite Church] background,

John H. Yoder writes that Mennonitism has become "a small Christian body, a Christian corpuscle," into which most members are born and into which few converts are won. "If there has not come into being a 'new humanity,' made up of two kinds of people, some of whom had good strong parents and some who did not, of whom some were born under the law and some were not, and of whom some have the heritage of moral rigidity and some do not, if the marriage of Jews and Gentiles is not happening in every generation, then the work of Christ as described in Ephesians is not happening."[11]

But if the intentional Christian community of the Mennonite variety remains simply one variety among many Christian lifestyles and if it maintains the dynamics of continual renewal with particular attention to orientation toward mission, it is an interesting option for Christians at the end of the twentieth century, not only because it recreates the close community dynamic of Acts 2, but because it is a very efficient way to live in a time of contracting economy.

In the mainline Reformation churches local congregational life became the only form of community normally available to Christians. It soon became apparent that it was not enough. More intensive teaching and fellowship was needed to transform the inert mass of uninstructed laity into parishes which were spiritually alive. In his preface to *The German Mass* Luther suggested that one way in which the church might be transformed was through *ecclesiolae in ecclesia*, little churches within the church, consisting of groups of earnest and seeking lay people meeting for prayer and instruction in homes. He seems never to have followed up on this suggestion, but the Swiss Reformer Martin Bucer was experimenting with small groups in Strassbourg later in the century, and perhaps through his subsequent influence in England, the Puritans adopted this technique.[12] At the end of the sixteenth century Johann Arndt made use of *collegia pietatis*, as the groups were called, and through his influence and that of Dutch Puritanism the collegia were included in Philipp Spener's pastoral work and in his list of suggested reforms in Pia Desideria.[13]

The most deliberate and successful use of the small group principle in history, however, was the band system of Count Zinzendorf. The microcommunity of Herrnhut, which was analogous to the Mennonite open communities in many ways but informed by an urgent sense of mission to send the gospel to the world and to bring renewal to every Christian denomination, was further subdivided into group meetings for sharing, mutual correction and confession, and prayer.[14] The band meetings made much freer use of lay leadership than previous Pietist collegia. They appear to be a literal adoption of the kind of group meetings advised in James 5 (which are, incidentally, the nearest thing to the institution of the confessional mentioned in Scripture): "Is any one among you suffering? Let him pray. Is any cheerful? Let him sing praise. . . . Therefore confess your sins to one another, and pray for one another, that you may be healed" (Jas. 5:13, 16).

In many respects Herrnhut must be considered the most thoroughgoing and fruitful application of the principle of community in church history. Since Zinzendorf started not with an integrated Christian community but with a collection of fragments from widely different ecclesiastical backgrounds who were at one another's throats to begin with, his success in turning Herrnhut into a unified community through the linked use of prayer and small groups serves to demonstrate that Luther's original plan was viable. It also suggests a paradigm for the transformation of the whole church which is the goal of this book.

Zinzendorf's band system was adapted by John Wesley as the basis for his class meetings designed both to nurture converts of the awakening and to transform the Anglican Church according to Luther's strategy. The history of the disappearance of the class meetings in Methodism is one that

I have not traced, but I suspect that it has a lot to do with the weaknesses present in that denomination today. It is startling that a strategy as obvious and effective as small groups could be discovered and widely used in recent history and then apparently lost until its modern rediscovery in popular religious movements. A generation of formal Christians intervening between awakenings appears sufficient to erase them from the church's memory. The loss can only be explained by the resistance of the flesh to the entrance into light which these groups demand when they are correctly handled, and by the hostility and obscuring tactics of the powers of darkness.

Of course there have been ordinary church congregations which have relied neither upon small groups nor on the large intentional community and yet have embodied a flourishing level of Christian fellowship which has born remarkable fruit. One of the best examples of this is the Anglican church at Clapham near London pastored in the early nineteenth century by John Venn. The church developed an intimate community life among its wealthy and politically powerful membership and was one of the main engines of social reform in the English phase of the Second Awakening. Undoubtedly a host of other churches which are historically less visible have achieved a similar depth of community life. What is important is not the *mechanism* of community but the *principle* articulated in the body metaphor used by Paul in 1 Corinthians 12 and Ephesians 4. The latter passage makes it quite clear that full spiritual vitality cannot be present in the church until its macrocommunities and microcommunities consist of fully developed networks of Christians who are exercising their gifts and contributing to one another, so that "the whole body, joined and knit together by every joint with which it is supplied, when each part is working properly, makes bodily growth and upbuilds itself in love" (Eph. 4:16).

The pattern of congregational life established by the beginning of the Middle Ages, in which the laity become passive observers of the redemptive mystery instead of celebrants and participants mutually edifying one another, has resulted in an individualistic spirituality which the church has never quite abandoned. In this model of the Christian life the individual believer is connected to the source of grace like a diver who draws his air supply from the surface through a hose. He is essentially a self-contained system cut off from the other divers working around him. If their air supply is cut off, this does not damage him nor can he share with them the air that he receives. The situation would be no different if he were working alone a hundred miles away.

The organic metaphor for the church used by Paul absolutely negates this conception by asserting that grace is conveyed through the body of Christ along horizontal channels as well as through the vertical relationship of each believer to God. No individual, congregation or denomination of Christians is spiritually independent of the others: "The eye cannot say to the hand, 'I have no need of you,' nor again the head to the feet, 'I have no need of you' " (1 Cor. 12:21). Therefore "the normal Christian life" is not simply a function of an individual believer's relationship to God. If he is isolated from Christians around him who are designed to be part of the system through which he receives grace, or if those Christians are themselves spiritually weak, he cannot be as strong and as filled with the Spirit as he otherwise would be. *Individual spiritual dynamics and corporate spiritual dynamics are interdependent,* just as the health of the body and the health of its cells are correlative. "If one member suffers, all suffer together; if one member is honored, all rejoice together" (1 Cor. 12:26).

The spiritual individualism of congregational life in medieval Christianity was not really overcome by the Reformation. In most instances the passive collection of observers of the redemptive tableau was replaced by a passive collection of listeners to the redemptive message, a sort of weekly class-room of the faith. Participatory liturgies offset this to some extent, and grace certainly was conveyed to each listener, but the interchange of grace between members of the congregation was left for unstructured occasions outside the church.

There was a time when this pattern may have functioned effectively in small communities where there was frequent contact between church members during the week, but the need for the interchange of grace through the spiritual interaction of lay people was seldom articulated clearly. Protestant doctrine defined "the means of grace" as the Word, prayer and the sacraments, and these were usually understood as channels leading directly to the individual Christian, not as streams of grace which necessarily linked him to others. But every one of us can remember times when other believers served as essential channels of grace in delivering us from some agonizing spiritual problem which would never have been handled by our individual use of Scripture and prayer.

At this juncture readers from several denominational backgrounds may be wondering why the sacraments, and particularly the sacrament of the Lord's Supper mentioned in the central text on community in Acts 2, have not been set apart as secondary elements of spiritual renewal. Those who are Roman Catholics or Eastern Orthodox by background, as well as some Lutheran and Anglican Protestants, may feel that the dignity of the sacraments as channels of grace is slighted by incorporating them into the spectrum of other dynamics. If a believer holds the Catholic view that the bread and wine in Communion are transformed literally into the body and blood of Christ so that these become "the medicine of immortality," or the Lutheran belief that the body of Christ is present under these elements and consumed along with them, he may well believe that these have a concrete power to revitalize spiritual life which transcends any of the elements of teaching or structure of which we have been speaking.

The writer, who holds the Reformed position that Christ is spiritually present in the Lord's Supper and imparts genuine spiritual vitality through the reception of the elements, agrees that the Zwinglian understanding of the bread and the cup as purely symbolic (which far too many Protestants have adopted) has robbed Communion of its full significance. I believe that a return to a stronger view of the Supper, and the more frequent Communion advocated by the Reformers, would be immensely helpful to the spiritual life of Protestantism. This is true because the Communion service is the most graphic embodiment of the primary elements of spiritual renewal secured in Christ's death and resurrection, especially his justifying work for us and his sanctifying life in us. It demonstrates the reality of our union with Christ in the most concrete manner possible. It also clearly indicates and celebrates the communion of the saints with one another. At the same time, it is a perfect realization and extension of the Jewish passover and the sacrifices of the Old Covenant.

In the history of movements of spiritual renewal, however, as well as in common observation of parishioners, it is apparent that where the truths embodied in the Lord's Supper are clearly taught and proclaimed, spiritual renewal is present, but where the sacraments are administered without much explanation simply as a kind of spiritual medicine, a palpable deadness may set in. If all parts of the church were to make clear to their communicants the full meaning of the Lord's Supper, we might see spiritual blessing come upon all, but with a special fullness upon the branch of the church with the correct doctrine of the Supper. If that occurs, I would be glad to have this chapter rewritten. In the meantime, history teaches us the danger and futility of fighting and separating over the ceremony that is supposed to unite us instead of living the reality it embodies.

Teilhard de Chardin comments that development in nature is never a matter simply of units piled together, but of "the number and correlative variety of the links formed between these elements. It is not, therefore, a matter of *simple* multiplicity but of organised multiplicity; not simple complication but *centrated* complication."[15] He goes on to say:

> The atom, the molecule, the cell and the living being are real units because they are both formed and centrated, whereas a drop of water, a heap of sand, the Earth, the Sun, the stars in general, whatever the multiplicity or elaborateness of their structure, seem to possess no organization, no "centricity."[16]

It is questionable whether most of the congregations of Christians scattered all over the world at present are much more than imposing human heaps of sand. Of course congregations and denominations have centers and structures of interconnection, politically speaking, and they also have main arteries through which grace is carried. But the fine capillary structure which is necessary for a healthy organism is not yet very well developed in the church.

It is not simply that essential links between individuals and groups are missing, but that persons and parties which ought to complement one another's needs are actively polarized against one another. The political centers and links which are established, which are merely reflections of the sort of personal empire-building attacked by Paul in 1 Corinthians 3:4—4:21, often function as cancers which choke off the life of the body, not as organs which build it. The spiritual gifts of the laity have atrophied, while the responsibilities of ministers and administrators have hypertrophied.

What a flood of spiritual life would be released in the body of Christ if these blockages were removed and the undifferentiated heaps of Christians in churches all over the world were gathered into cells linked together in the great arterial system of grace! The power released could only be compared to the outrush of energy produced in molecular fusion.

Theological Integration
The content of truth needed for the full development and maintenance of spiritual renewal in the church cannot be reduced simply to the four elements of the atonement involved in depth proclamation of the gospel. These constitute the cutting edge of spiritual renewal, and where they are not present the church is weakened spiritually, but they are not sufficient in themselves to complete the Holy Spirit's work in shaping the mind of the church. The mind's natural darkness concerning itself, the world and God is so extensive that it cannot be remedied by a short summary of essential truth. It demands "the whole counsel of God," as Paul says (Acts 20:27): the whole of God's written revelation constantly searched out for its current implications concerning the church and the world in order that "the man of God may be complete, equipped for every good work" (2 Tim. 3:17).

The additional truth that is needed is implicit, first of all, in the whole body of the Scriptures. Even before Pentecost the risen Christ appeared to the disciples, "and beginning with Moses and all the prophets, he interpreted to them in all the scriptures the things concerning himself" (Luke 24:27). This grounding of the redemptive core of truth in the whole context of biblical revelation was probably the content of "the apostles' teaching" in the newborn Christian community described in Acts 2. The content of this infant theology must have been fairly rudimentary, judging from the problems and responses in the early church, so it is obvious that a fully articulated theology is not essential to the flourishing inner life and expanding outward witness of a new Christian community. But the church needed such a theology in order to handle the questions which would confront it during the wider expansion of its missionary witness, and this was provided in God's gift of a theologian through the conversion of Saul of Tarsus (Acts 9:1-31).

Paul's synthesis of Old Testament revelation with the new realm of possibilities opened up by the New Covenant enabled the church to transcend its cultural boundaries and reach the gentile world. His work in relating revealed truth to the situations of the new churches and to their cultural contexts provides us with a paradigm of the function of theological integration in guarding the unfolding embryo of the church from foreign infections and internal disorders, and governing its development toward maturity.

Paul's understanding of gentile culture was sufficiently integrated with his biblical learning that he was able to make use of common-grace preparations for the gospel and unanswered religious questions in his pagan hearers. This is apparent in his conversation with Greek intellectuals described in Acts 17:16-31. On the other hand, his detailed understanding of the contradictions between the non-Christian thought world and the biblical world view gave him intellectual traction in resisting any dilution of the Christian outlook through fusion with antichristian thinking. Hence he plainly states, "the wisdom of this world is folly with God" (1 Cor. 3:19), and warns his readers to take care that no one makes a prey of them "by philosophy and empty deceit, according to human tradition, . . . and not according to Christ" (Col. 2:8).

Clearly Paul does not rule out the possibility of encountering value, truth and beauty in non-Christian culture since he advises Christians to let their minds dwell on "whatever is true, whatever is honorable, whatever is just, whatever is pure, whatever is lovely, whatever is gracious, if there is any excellence [arete, the pagan Greek word for moral excellence which was also used in the Jewish and Christian communities for any manifestation of divine glory]" (Phil. 4:8). "All things are yours," he tells the Corinthian community (1 Cor. 3:21); but he also makes clear that "all things hold together" only in Christ (Col. 1:17). "We do impart wisdom" he argues, "a secret and hidden wisdom of God, . . . 'what no eye has seen, nor ear heard, nor the heart of man conceived, what God has prepared for those who love him' " (1 Cor. 2:6-7, 9).

But the mind of Christ is unfolded to us by the Holy Spirit who searches everything, filtering, unifying and transforming it according to the words which he has inspired (1 Cor. 2:13, 16).

The human mind ordinarily thinks in systems of propositions. If it is not filled with propositional networks which are consistent with biblical truth (even though they do not fully express its meaning), it is likely to be invaded by antibiblical propositions. Therefore it was not a Hellenistic corruption of the gospel for postapostolic Christians to seek to express the essence of their faith in the Rule of Faith which evolved into the Apostles' Creed, or for the theologians of the second century to begin the process of technically defining the deity and humanity of Christ in opposition to the varieties of counterfeit Christianity which were springing up around them.

The early theologians expressed a wide spectrum of attitudes toward the surrounding culture, from Tertullian's contemptuous rejection of the need to have anything to do with it to the openness toward intimations of Christ in the high culture of the pagan world characteristic of Justin Martyr and the Alexandrian school. This tension is effectively resolved by the suggestion of Origen and Augustine that Christians, like the Israelites leaving Egypt, should take the gold and jewels of common-grace truth from idolatrous cultures and reshape these into furniture for the sanctuary of the Christian mind.

Augustine himself forged such a structure of thought, adding usable elements from the Neo-Platonism which dominated contemporary pagan culture to biblical and traditional theological materials. His positive theological contributions built upon the foundation of Paul's thinking. They incorporated a theology of Christian experience based on a much clearer apprehension of the depth of sin and the primacy of grace than is characteristic of the early fathers, and a philosophy of history which accurately defined the church's relationship to the world as a redeemed society bearing an ongoing witness to a fallen one. Augustine largely avoided the error of adopting antibiblical concepts from pagan culture and fusing these into his theology. He was in touch with the secular intellectual environment, but he did not marry it.

On the other hand, he did fuse biblical insights in a conservative synthesis with the structure and tradition of the Western church as they had evolved since the first century. The result was a stabilizing and fixing of the sacerdotal and mediatorial role of the church which has remained until this day in Western Catholicism. In another critically important move, he adopted the principle that heresy should be restrained and punished in a Christian society, thus assuring that a kind of whitewashed Christian culture would prevail in the West until the late Middle Ages, not penetrating the society by spiritual and intellectual power, but sprayed over its surface by political imposition. Nevertheless, the currents of spiritual and theological renewal which continued to run through the church throughout the Middle Ages were almost uniformly Augustinian, probably because of the deep awareness of grace at the heart of Augustine's theology of Christian experience.[17]

As the philosophical basis of Western culture shifted from a Platonic to an Aristotelian outlook, theologians like Albertus Magnus and his great pupil, Thomas Aquinas, in order to maintain a degree of command over the imperfectly Christianized and rapidly mutating medieval mind, began to integrate within their work elements of the new, practical, world-oriented approach which led to the rise of modern science and technology. The great intellectual structures of Aquinas's *Summae* sought to fuse Augustinian theology with elements of truth salvaged from the Aristotelian system. The Thomistic integration was a much more careful, powerful and comprehensive attempt to synthesize Christian theology with secular insights than most Protestants realize, since few take the time to read Thomas. It had, however, several crucial defects. A good many nonbiblical and antibiblical presuppositions from Aristotle slipped through into the system without being filtered out by biblical understanding. The result was that Aquinas often attributed powers and qualities to nature which can only be achieved through grace.

Aquinas's faults at this point derive primarily from his method. The theological material used in the integration was not uniformly the result of biblical rethinking; Aquinas simply used the Augustinian synthesis, which was itself a fusion of biblical insights and churchly tradition, and added to it post-Augustinian traditional elements as well. Thus he created a fusion-theology which was itself based on several fusion-theologies. The result was bound to be several steps removed from firsthand biblical integrity, although it did at least attempt to make comprehensive Christian sense out of the "modern outlook" of the late Middle Ages.[18]

The basic failure of Christian theological integration from the second century through to the Reformation was taking the church's authority too seriously in comparison with the biblical norm. This error was not characteristic of the New Testament church. Jesus condemned the Pharisees for "teaching as doctrines the precepts of men," and he told them, "You leave the commandment of God, and hold fast the tradition of men" (Mk. 7:7-8). Luke commended the Jews at Beroea as "more noble (eugenēs, high-minded) than those in Thessalonica, for they received the word with all eagerness, examining the scriptures daily to see if these things were so" (Acts 17:11). But Paul told those in Thessalonica who did believe, "Our gospel came to you not only in word, but also in power and in the Holy Spirit and with full conviction" (1 Thess. 1:5), perhaps because "when you received the word of God which you heard from us, you accepted it not as the word of men but as what it really is, the word of God" (1 Thess. 2:13). Evidently the process of theological integration is short-circuited and the vitality of the Holy

Spirit's working in the mind of the church diminished either when the words of men are received as if they were the Word of God without biblical testing or when the Word of God is received as if it were only the words of men.

Thus it is not surprising that despite the deep personal piety of Thomas and other theologians in his tradition the scholastic theology somehow lacked the spiritual force of the earlier patristic theology. Much of it was generated by purely intellectual problems, not developed out of new spiritual encounter with the Word of God and centrally anchored to a theology of Christian experience. Perhaps fortunately for the future history of Christian theological integration, it became a weak vehicle for conveying its cargo, which contained some crucial traditional errors, to succeeding generations. For some centuries the real spiritual vitality in the West lay in the popular Augustinianism of mystical and semimonastic movements while the intellectual initiative passed from the scholastics to the gradually secularizing southern Renaissance and the northern Christian Renaissance, both of which were fervently antischolastic.

Probably the best theological integration during the late Middle Ages was done not by the scholastics but by the northern Christian humanists who adopted the Renaissance tools of historical criticism and sought to return to the sources of truth behind previous fusions and adulterations of tradition. The northern Renaissance at its best sought to relate theological insights developed directly from the exegesis of Scripture, with truth gleaned from pagan humanism. There was an existential practicality and personal spiritual relevance to this enterprise which contrasted sharply with most scholasticism. When the fuse of Luther's discovery of justification by faith ignited the northern humanists, there was an explosion of theological integration accompanied by new spiritual life.[19]

The Reformers themselves were principally occupied in reorganizing the church and its central doctrines, retuning

Augustine's fusion of Scripture and tradition. They did not initially address themselves to the integration of theology with the surrounding intellectual culture. Succeeding generations of Protestants had more leisure to attempt this. Peter Ramus sought to replace the Aristotelian philosophical carrier wave for theology with a new common-sense logic.[20] Encyclopedists like J. H. Alsted successfully integrated the first products of Western scientific growth with a Christian outlook. The Moravian J. A. Comenius, the great founder of modern educational theory, conceived the goal of building an immense intellectual synthesis that would successfully integrate all the new knowledge generated by the sciences with biblical theology.[21] In the early years of the Enlightenment, Jonathan Edwards was beginning to construct just such a system when he was interrupted by death.[22]

Meanwhile Lutheran and Calvinist scholastics were building additional wings on Reformation theology through logical extrapolation and intrusions of the older scholasticism, while Puritans and Pietists sought to ground it more firmly in Christian experience with occasional admixtures of legal casuistry.[23] As the eighteenth century moved toward its close, the Protestant humanist synthesis of comprehensive general knowledge and biblically grounded theology was beginning to weaken. Previously the synthesis had successfully focused both general knowledge and biblical theology on the existential requirements of the Christian life. Now it was breaking down into confessional rationalism on the one hand and into a degenerate, anti-intellectual form of pietism on the other.

At this same time the extension of southern Renaissance humanism which we call the Enlightenment completed its own prototype of a comprehensive nonbiblical world view, the *Encyclopedia* of the *philosophes*. The Enlightenment leaders were at their best deistic builders of a world model which could run perfectly well by its own internal mechanisms without any providential assistance from its wholly transcendent and remote Creator. At their worst they were atheistic materialists, sensualists, even occasionally Satanists.[24] All the spiritual illnesses which have gradually taken over Western culture since the eighteenth century were germinally present in a tiny group of intellectual leaders during the Enlightenment. But like diseases which are latent but controlled and suppressed by the body's defense mechanisms, these forms of antichristianity did not gain a strong hold on Western society through the middle of the nineteenth century. They were restrained both by the inertia of custom and by the First and Second Evangelical Awakenings.

In both revivals many of the major leaders were men of both spiritual depth and intellectual force. Men like Timothy Dwight and Charles Simeon in the Second Awakening were able to exert both theological power in the church and apologetic control over the culture.[25] As the divorce between piety and intellect in American Christianity continued to advance, however, evangelical leadership began to fall increasingly into two classes: the evangelistic technicians on the one hand and the orthodox confessional theologians on the other. Imperceptibly the spiritual force of both of these sectors of a divided sensibility began to wane. The intellectual synthesis around a spiritual core foreseen by Comenius and begun by Edwards had no hand to complete it in the midnineteenth century.

Just at this point a new countersynthesis, built from the most virulently antichristian elements in the Enlightenment spectrum, exploded with the impact of a fusion bomb. The new synthesis centered in a cluster of antichristian religions which conferred ultimate significance on the material creation and humanity. It had its own impressive myths, like the concept of development. (Western unbelievers longed for centuries to be able to dispense with even the deist's clockmaker god, but could not do so with intellectual consistency until Darwin proposed a mechanism for evolutionary development.)[26] It had its own eschatologies, the classless state of Marxist communism or the world of prosperous self-interest aimed at by social Darwinism and other forms of capitalist materialism. It even had its own pastoral and priestly leaders, the psychotherapists. Its concept of the historical emergence of the world and humanity seemed to be logically forceful and verified by hard evidence, although it shattered the traditional understanding of biblical cosmology and history. The Bible, which had been the fulcrum from which the Reformers moved the church and the world, was subjected to the most intensive redefinition, attack and ridicule, even in the houses of its friends.

The Christian world was literally stunned. It could be argued that its mind only began to recover full biblical consciousness nearly a century later. Half the church groped about prematurely for ways to fuse its thinking with the strengthening secular currents. The other half climbed into foxholes of pietism or confessionalism and clung doggedly to the heritage of the Middle Ages and the Reformation without looking too closely at the mutating culture around it.

The antichristian systems which intellectually overpowered the church in Western culture were not entirely empty of truth. Some of them had hold of important discoveries which should have formed recognized parts of a Christian intellectual synthesis. (I have in mind Marx's critique of the connection between bad religion and oppressive social systems, and Freud's rediscovery of the unconscious.) The point is, however, that these discoveries were imbedded in anti-biblical religious systems which were dedicated to serving humanity and aligned with an expanding scientific technology which was delivering increasing amounts of tangible goods. Few Christians had comparably integrated systems, incorporating the new knowledge, with which to fight back apologetically. Most of the church, in fact, was extremely divided and disordered by the apologetic impact of secularism within its own ranks.

It is significant that one of the few parts of the church which was still intelligently seeking the biblical-cultural synthesis dreamed of by Comenius and Edwards was one which was still feeling the impact of the Reveil, the European outgrowth of the Second Awakening and the Prayer Revival of 1858. At the end of the nineteenth century, the great Dutch theologian and statesman, Abraham Kuyper, inaugurated a tradition of theological integration which took seriously both the innate enmity of the unregenerate mind toward God and hence toward any truth which points too clearly to him —the antithesis between redeemed and unredeemed thinking—and common grace—God's blessing of all men, converted and unconverted alike, with gifts of truth and beauty and ethical value. Descending from Kuyper and the Free University of Amsterdam, a succession of theologians, philosophers, sociologists and intellectual leaders in other disciplines have sought with varying degrees of success to integrate their fields of knowledge by filtering out presuppositions and theorems that are contrabiblical, and building systems of understanding which incorporate viable common-grace discoveries and insights within a biblical outlook.

While Kuyper himself incorporated a powerful experiential core in his theological outlook, the later Amsterdam School has sometimes been hampered by an incipient aversion to Christian experience, the effect of the reaction in Dutch Christianity against the excesses of Dutch Puritanism. This may explain why the movement has so far failed to have the impact and the growth associated with intellectual leaders in the awakening tradition such as Comenius, Francke, Edwards and Dwight. But where something approaching this emphasis has been reinforced with dynamics of renewal such as prayer and community, as in the L'Abri Fellowship of Dr. Francis Schaeffer, a remarkable moving of the Holy Spirit has been visible. It is not hard to imagine what a powerful intellectual force would be released in Western culture if the Reformed orthodox community and other confessional parties among the churches would recover the dynamics of renewal which characterized the earlier awakenings.

Such a recovery would also renew the church in its internal theological integration and thus unite its divided sectors and parties in the mind of Christ, filtering out the intrusions of antichristian elements in the church's witness. Much of the church rapidly lost the Reformers' consciousness of the noetic effects of sin, the impact of fallen human nature in darkening the unregenerate mind. Later theologians readily forgot that sin generates an unconscious drive to construct systems of understanding the world which suppress the knowledge of the real God, systems which deform and distort the facts and theories they incorporate. Thus the church remained largely paralyzed mentally in the presence of the Enlightenment and post-Enlightenment secular humanist systems, especially after these became entrenched in our systems of education.

In the present century the theological power centers of many larger churches have become so intimidated and mesmerized by this humanism that from time to time they have been reduced to echoing its social moralism. Other leaders who have longed to remain faithful to historic orthodoxy have sought to isolate the realm of faith from the realm of scientifically verifiable history in order to make it invulnerable to the critical erosion of the biblical base and the shifting cosmologies of secular systems.[27] In doing so, however, they have found themselves rulers over a kind of fairy-tale kingdom of meaning beyond history in which the world is not strongly motivated to join them. Non-Evangelical scholarship, especially the work of neo-orthodox scholars, has no doubt produced work of lasting intellectual benefit to the church, and has sometimes broken through to new biblical insights which might not have emerged in some frozen and hardened areas of confessional orthodoxy. But increasingly these modes of fusing with and adapting to non-Christian culture have shown themselves unable to propagate widely among the churches, although they have been very influential in the power centers of the older denominations. They have lacked spiritual power through their loss of many of the primary and secondary dynamics of renewal, and intellectual power through their failure in theological integration.

This is not to say that the record of Evangelical theological integration has been uniformly distinguished in this century. Often it has been content to reiterate earlier systems of orthodoxy without relating to other current theological trends or contemporary thinking, and even without renewed firsthand encounter with the biblical norm. Sometimes it has been intellectually arrogant, as if a high doctrine of Scripture conferred a patent on the ability to discover and believe biblical truth. Sometimes it has been technically careless.

Some Evangelicals have been genuinely obscurantist, addicted to experience and dismissing doctrine and any informed use of the mind as irrelevant to spiritual maturity. In our quest for the fullness of the Spirit, we have sometimes forgotten that a Spirit-filled intelligence is one of the powerful weapons for pulling down satanic strongholds. On the other hand, we have often assumed that the theological task was simply a matter of digging out biblical building blocks and building up logically from them by the exercise of our own inherent brain power, forgetting that only the Holy Spirit can effectively guide us in wielding the sword of the Spirit.

Recapturing the biblical sanity of the professing church is an immense task. So is the projection of a sane theology in a way which will arrest the intellectual decline of our culture. We are not about to achieve these goals without a very close dependence on the Holy Spirit. But if we do attack the task of theological integration with the Spirit's guidance, we are going to succeed. The Spirit will enter into the sanctuary of our minds in fullness and power, and we will lift

from the church and Western culture some of the fog blanket
of intellectual darkness which has been oppressing us since
the late nineteenth century.

Disenculturation
One of the first effects of spiritual decline among the people
of God is *destructive enculturation*, saturation with the godless culture of the surrounding world as we saw in Judges
2:11-13. When men's hearts are not full of God, they become
full of the world around like a sponge full of clear water that
has been squeezed empty and thrown into a mud puddle.
Only the fullness of Christ's life and the transformation of
our minds by the renewing action of the Holy Spirit illuminating the whole counsel of God can effectively prevent this
conformity to the world (Rom. 12:2).

Since the full benefits of union with Christ were not available under the Old Covenant, it was necessary for God to
build around Israel a wall of *protective enculturation* formed
by welding together the Jewish culture with its religious
core. Thus there is a divinely inspired enculturation of religion in the Pentateuch, in which not only the general fabric
of the theocracy but such details as civil law, national holi-
days and dietary taboos are directly imposed by God. If a
sponge is first dipped in oil, it can be thrown in muddy
water without any danger of absorption.

The protective enculturation in the Jewish lifestyle was
an accommodation to the spiritual infancy of Israel. When
we study the near-Eastern peoples who were neighbors and
contemporaries of the covenant people, we discover law
codes, taboo systems and other socioreligious patterns
which duplicate and closely resemble those of Israel. Some
critics have concluded from this that the Judaic cultic system
was merely humanly derived rather than God-inspired, but
it is also explainable as a simple adaptation designed to give
Israel a safe and uncontaminated cultus of its own.

At their level of spiritual development, the Israelites

wanted anything their neighbors had from kings to taboos, and so God gave them a meticulously detailed religious cultus. This cultus served as a tutor to bring them into readiness for the coming Messiah (Gal. 3:24). It was protective, but it was also restrictive of the flesh. This restriction aroused sin and made it visible, producing a guilt which drove the believer to the sacrificial system which pointed toward the coming Lamb of God. Among the devout, it served as a training code which could prepare them for a fully developed spirituality in Christ. The dietary code, for example, was a system of do's and don'ts which accustomed the people to making rudimentary moral distinctions between clean things and unclean. The objects among which they discriminated (pigs, rabbits, lobsters and so on) were morally indifferent from a New Testament perspective (except for occasional marginal symbolic or medical significance), but the constant acts of choice they had to make between clean and unclean items was a kind of game preparation for the serious business of discriminating between the holy and the unholy which is part of a walk in the Holy Spirit.

Connected with this protective enculturation under the Old Covenant was an attitude toward race or blood lineage which seems at times to border on prejudice and yet has a divine rationale. On the one hand, the seed of Abraham was promised as a blessing to all nations, and members of other nations (even those under a divine curse, as in the case of Rahab the Canaanite) were welcomed into the covenant if they espoused Israel's God. On the other hand, marriage within the "line of promise" was deeply desired from Abraham onward, and in Ezra's time mixed marriages among idolatrous peoples were actually broken up by divine command (Ezra 10:9-15).

It seems that mankind always retains a kind of rudimentary awareness that there are two kinds of people in the world —the seed of the serpent and the seed of the woman, the City of Man and the City of God—but it is of course a matter of

extreme spiritual subtlety to discern the two types accurately. Once again, God adapted his commands to the spiritual
minority of the Israelites and gave them a simple rubric
under which to operate: Jews are safe, Gentiles are acceptable only under certain conditions. By the time of Jesus,
Pharisaic Judaism had intensified this racial barrier so that
even believing Gentiles were required to be segregated at
meals. It had also elaborated the rest of the protective cultus
into a scrupulous legalism which tithed herbs and scrubbed
exteriors to erase its guilt over violation of weightier matters
of the law.

In the ministry of Jesus there is an ambivalent response
to the wedding of culture and religion in Judaism. He is
"born under the law" (Gal. 4:4), and therefore observes the
inspired ceremonial and ritual regulations although he decisively rejects the legalistic elaborations of the Pharisees.
In the parable of the good Samaritan (Lk. 10:29-37) he indicts
Jewish racism, but in the case of the Syrophoenician woman
(Mk. 7:24-30) he shows a consciousness of the difference
between the elect people and others under the Old Covenant.
Perhaps Jesus' most decisive break with the Old Covenant
perspective is his rejection of the Zealot patriotism which
would have made him a revolutionary leader against the
Romans and, if it could, the ruler of an earthly kingdom.
Obviously there is a transition here to a posttheocratic situa-
tion.

After the cross and the resurrection, a wholly new state of
affairs comes into being. The kingdom of God which has
been established is not an earthly cultural and political organization but a process of spiritual transformation energized by the Holy Spirit using the catalyst of the gospel message which will spread like leaven among all cultures. The
message must therefore be *disenculturated*, freed from its
protective shell, so that it may take root in a thousand different cultural and political soils and bring them to full self-
expression. The oil must be wrung out of the sponge, in order

that it may be filled with wine.

Of course the disciples do not comprehend this at first. They must be led by the hand into a fuller understanding by means of epiphanies, miracles, visions, persecutions and finally a severe internal struggle. The ascending Lord repeals the theocracy (Acts 1). The universal offer of the gospel is intimated in the tongues of Pentecost. When the offended cultural pride of Judaism strikes back in persecution, the disciples are driven into Samaria and converts are made there, across one of the strongest cultural barriers dividing Judaism from the rest of the world. And then an elaborate drama is played out (Acts 10 and 11) in which Peter is convinced by dreams and by actual conversions that the whole Old Testament marriage of culture and religion is now dissolved and the ceremonial law abrogated. When this is contested by Judaizing teachers (Acts 15), Peter refuses to permit them to weld the protective enculturation and legal requirements of the Old Covenant to the New Covenant lifestyle, to put "a yoke upon the neck of the disciples which neither our fathers nor we have been able to bear "(Acts 15:10).

The council decision reaffirms the separation of cultural Judaism and the gospel core, although for strategic purposes in the mission to the Jews it cautions Gentiles not to flaunt the law by eating things strangled or sacrificed to idols. Now the gospel is free and unencumbered in its outward spread. The rest of Acts serves as a paradigm of the success in mission which occurs when the catalyst is kept clean of cultural rust, for the message penetrates and reaches a variety of different cultures until it strikes home at the heart of Roman civilization.

Paul's attitude to the problem of culture and gospel in mission is subtle and ambivalent. On the one hand, he refuses to have any part of either soteriological legalism (circumcision and the law as essential to salvation) or the cultural muzzling of the gospel core. We all know the story of his stand against the compromising legalism of a somewhat eroded Peter told in Galatians 2. He was willing, however, to have Timothy circumcised for appearance's sake, and we find him going along with ritual Judaism right up to the time of his arrest. To the Corinthians Paul explains his major principle of conduct:

> For though I am free from all men, I have made myself a slave to all, that I might win the more. To the Jews I became as a Jew, in order to win Jews; to those under the law I became as one under the law—though not being myself under the law—that I might win those under the law. To those outside the law I became as one outside the law—not being without law toward God but under the law of Christ —that I might win those outside the law. To the weak I became weak, that I might win the weak. I have become all things to all men, that I might by all means save some. I do it all for the sake of the gospel, that I might share in its blessings. (1 Cor. 9:19-23)

Many of us have been so nervous about the dangers of wrong applications of this passage that we have failed to note the marvelous principles of cultural freedom in mission that it contains. From this statement and from Paul's other conduct we know that he considered the gospel to be a transcultural message of repentant faith in Christ designed neither to bind people to a form of culture alien to their own, nor to eradicate the distinctive features of their own culture. Paul could even live comfortably with Jewish Christians still being circumcised and observing their traditions so long as their soteriology was straight. Just as the gospel was to set free an infinite variety of individuals, developing their distinctive gifts and kinds of beauty rather than stamping them into a mold of conformity, so it was to come to whole cultures, with their dance patterns of folkways and institutions, and to lift these to the highest level of individual expression, erasing or cleansing only those with idolatrous implications. Thus the gospel is free to become encultured—to wear many forms of cultural expression, with perfect freedom to change these expressions like clothing when the need arises—only when it has been *disencultured.*

Elsewhere Paul suggests that spiritual freedom in the fullness of Christ and protective enculturation are mutually exclusive alternatives. Once we have learned to walk in the Spirit, we cannot lean on the legal training code as if it were a child's walker. But if we fail to put on the full provision of Christ, we are bound to fall back into an enculturated lifestyle.

> As you therefore have received Christ Jesus the Lord, *so* walk in Him, having been firmly rooted *and now* being built up in Him and established in your faith. . . . See to it that no one takes you captive through philosophy and empty deception, according to the tradition of men, according to the elementary principles [training codes] of the world, rather than according to Christ. (Col. 2:6-8, NASB)

Paul goes on to give a concise and complete statement of the benefits of the atonement for us through our union with Christ, including justification, sanctification and authority over the powers of darkness. He continues by warning against any return to protective enculturation:

> Therefore let no one act as your judge in regard to food or drink or in respect to a festival or a new moon or a Sabbath day—things which are a mere shadow of what is to come; but the substance belongs to Christ. . . . If you have died with Christ to the elementary principles [training codes] of the world, why, as if you were living in the world, do you submit yourself to decrees, such as, "Do not handle, do not taste, do not touch!" (which all *refer to* things destined to perish with the using)—in accordance with the commandments and teachings of men? These are matters which have, to be sure, the appearance of wisdom in self-made religion and self-abasement and severe treatment of the body, *but are* of no value against fleshly indulgence. (Col. 2:16, 20-23 NASB)

In the next chapter Paul urges that life in Christ can and must
deal effectively with the flesh. Paradoxically enough, it appears that when the church begins to draw up codes and
taboos which separate it from the world, it is most worldly,
most in conformity with the world's understanding of holiness and spirituality.

At first glance, the early Christian church may seem to
have avoided this trap and achieved a kind of transcultural
planting of the gospel in different soils. The second-century
Epistle to Diognetus gives witness to a measure of cultural
adaptability when it speaks of Christians as a "third race"
identified neither with Jews nor Greeks, neither with Romans nor barbarians: "For Christians cannot be distinguished from the rest of the human race by country or language or customs. They do not live in cities of their own,
they do not use a peculiar form of speech, they do not follow
an eccentric manner of life."[28]

A distinctively intellectual brand of Christian culture developed in Alexandria, the great Egyptian center of learning;
other idiomatic cultures flowered at Jerusalem, Antioch,
Byzantium and Carthage. Karl Adam, the eminent Catholic
apologist, says that the genius of the Roman Church has been
its ability to coexist in symbiosis with differing cultures, so
that like a great tree she sucks up into her structure enriching
elements from all the various soils into which her roots
probe.[29]

But symbiosis is a different metaphor from that of the
leaven working in various cultures. It suggests that the early
church was once again protectively fusing itself with a culture, this time with the rather diverse and eclectic culture
of the Roman empire. We would expect this to be the case,
since by the second century the church had lost track of an
important element in the saving work of Christ and was
teaching that believers are justified not by faith but by being
sanctified. As a result it became very easy for the church to
revert to an Old Covenant lifestyle and adopt a form of dis-

guised Judaism, with circumcision reinterpreted as baptism, the temple liturgy resurfacing in the mass and the cycles of festival days reappearing as fast and saint's days.

Uneasiness about justification produced a flowering of asceticism reflecting an unconscious need for lists of clean and unclean activities and a rebirth of Pharisaism. Hard-line fundamentalists like Tertullian ruled out many intellectual activities: the theater (because of its origins in pagan worship), the dance (because it might inflame ill-controlled sexual passions) and cosmetics (if God meant you to smell like a flower he would have given you a crop of them on your head!).[30] As Eastern asceticism infiltrated the church, the reform element within it embraced cultural masochism. If a practice or a department of human culture happened to be infected by sin or idolatry, they gave a "counsel of perfection": amputate that part of your experience.[31]

When the Constantinian revolution placed Western Christians politically on top, they were able to revert entirely to the Old Testament style of religiocultural amalgamation, and they attempted to construct a theocracy. Yet at the same time this effort at cultural purgation and protective enculturation was being made, popular Christianity was assimilating some of the worst elements of the polytheistic surrounding culture, aping its superstitions and translating into the cultus of the saints its multitude of patron spirits, which as Augustine tells us, brooded over every aspect of pagan life.[32] The missionary expansion of this modified theocracy was a genuine work of God's grace, and yet it left the worst features of converted cultures intact or assimilated them into Catholicism while covering them over with a surface conformity to Roman ritual, theology and governmental hierarchy.

Apparently if the church has not fully appropriated the life and redemptive benefits of Jesus Christ, it will inevitably be subject to two forms of re-enculturation. Either it will suffer destructive enculturation, absorbing elements of its host cultures which it should discern and suppress as unholy, or it will try to re-create once again the Old Testament protective enculturation, fusing itself with certain aspects of Christianized culture until the gospel is thought to be indissolubly wedded to those cultural expressions.

Until recently, Western Catholicism, sprayed with theological fixative by the Council of Trent, was a kind of living fossil demonstrating a phase of re-enculturation which took place in the first five or six centuries of the Western church. Once this re-enculturation had taken root, becoming a Catholic meant not simply accepting the radical core of the gospel but changing one's culture to conform to the Catholic way of life. In an ironic inversion, the gentile Christians, who had been persecuted by Jewish racists and threatened with cultural imperialism by Judaizers in the church, became racist persecutors of the Jews, insisting that conversion must mean abandonment of the Jewish culture and adoption of the culture of Christian Gentiles. This kept many potential converts from coming in. Of course, it also kept many rather nominal Christians in "Christendom" from dropping out, a rather questionable advantage.

But is Protestant Christianity free from the gravitational force toward re-enculturation? Karl Holl has written of the great transformation in Western culture which ensued when Luther's attack on sacerdotal monopoly, seen particularly in his teaching on vocation and the priesthood of all believers, released the catalyst of the Word from its cultural container into the bloodstream of European society.[33] On the other hand, the theocratic ideal died hard, as we can see in Calvin's Geneva and Puritan New England. Protestants influenced by Zwinglian biblicism were inclined to ask Old Testament questions of the New Testament, like those answered in Leviticus: What is the perfect way to run a worship service? Should we use organs? How do you baptize people? What is the inspired form of church government? And since the biblical answers were deliberately meager or equivocal, a host of differing leaders and denominations arose, each making absolute claims, leaving us today with a variety of seventeenth-century Protestant fossils still littering the scene.

Since destructive enculturation remained widespread among the Protestant laity, reform movements from the late sixteenth century on, such as Puritanism and Pietism, sought to develop a Protestant style of piety by tinkering with monastic spirituality and adapting it to a Reformational theological base. This inevitably sent them back to the ascetic ideals of the early church fathers, which they did not entirely rethink. And so the Puritans, shuddering a little at Luther's "freedom of the Christian man" which they feared would lead to licentiousness and dead orthodoxy, reintroduced the training-code morality which forbade the theater, the dance, cosmetics and novel clothing style, and added to the older list taboos on the use of playing cards, religious graphic art, the employment of musical instruments in worship, the celebration of Christmas and other indifferent things. Abandoning the Reformers' use of Sunday as a day of rest, recreation and reflection on the works of God, they turned the Sabbath into a day of strenuous holy work with recreation tabooed. They rigorously abandoned holy days like Christmas and Easter but introduced in their place fifty-two new fast days per year.

Out of Puritanism, however, evolved a kind of Protestantism which was less enculturated: the evangelical movement. In the seventeenth century, English and American Puritans gradually began to abandon the theocratic pattern of enforcing religion, adopted the leavening strategy of the New Testament and began to pray for spiritual awakening to reshape the church and the culture by internal transformation instead of external imposition. Many Puritans and Pietists began to seek to transcend theological and denominational differences to form a union of Protestants on the basis of a common recognition of godliness in one another. The most radical of these leaders, Count Zinzendorf, consciously limited his concern in missions and ecumenism to the core of biblical teaching in the New Testament which deals with spiritual renewal and insisted that political unification or cultural homogenization of the church was useless and unnecessary. Zinzendorf discouraged legalism and fostered Christian freedom to such an extent that observers like Wesley found him almost antinomian.

The evangelical stream, however, was only partially disenculturated, and it became increasingly less so, for reasons which will be clarified in a subsequent chapter. At its highest point it aimed to transcend the diversity of cultic practices to establish an ideal spiritual unity of Christians across denominations and cultures. But it was still largely wedded to the Puritan version of the training-code morality, which caught on in Pietist circles also. As the understanding of grace declined in revivalism, evangelicalism erected a stronger shell of protective enculturation to guard it from the world. Not only did it cling to the Puritan taboos, but in the nineteenth century it added more: wine and tobacco, both of which had been consumed by both Reformers and Puritans. The early Temperance movement was motivated by social compassion for the victims of distilled liquor during the stresses of the Industrial Revolution, and it really called for temperance. When moderation seemed too difficult a spiritual discipline and too slow a remedy, the revivalists of the 1820s and 30s moved on to redefine temperance as abstinence, to the horror of Charles Hodge, who protested that the replacement of Communion wine with grape juice was an insult to Jesus and to biblical ethics.

A few decades later, coffee and tea were added to the taboo list by revivalist Charles Finney. It is significant that Finney's understanding of justification and sanctification were essentially severed from any doctrine of union with Christ; in effect, he taught justification by sanctification and not by faith, and sanctification by will power more than by grace. As succeeding generations of revivalist leaders had less and less grasp of the dynamics of spiritual life, the drift toward training codes and protective enculturation became stronger and stronger.

Worldliness, for the Puritan, had meant "excessive love for the wealth, affluence and pride of the world." For the late nineteenth-century evangelical, however, it increasingly came to mean the presence of certain visible habits of behavior which marked the nonevangelical off as nonkosher. At the same time, an insidious process of cultural fusion was going on in which Christianity was gradually identified with Americanism, patriotism and the preservation of the status quo.

By the 1930s the average American Fundamentalist was not, at least, a proponent of theocracy, but he did have a way of confusing America, the Republican Party and the capitalist system with the kingdom of God. He did not practice circumcision, but he did assume that only those who had gone through a certain form of conversion experience were "born again" and that the salvation of these persons was either unquestionably sure or else maintained by works of personal morality. Sanctification was not a subject he was used to hearing about—at least, not in terms of Pauline doctrine—but he had an extensive behavioral code by which to distinguish dedicated Christians from liberals, the unsaved and the backslidden. He felt that black people, including black Christians, were all right in their place (and that included a separate place of worship), but he was ready to focus all the hidden fears and pooled hatreds of his heart on those who did not stay in their place, and also on Communists, Jews and sometimes even Democrats. If sufficiently well-trained, he could recognize the fact that theological liberals were Sadducees, but very rarely could he see the point of the liberal contention that he himself was a Pharisee.

By this point, it becomes somewhat hard to discern whether the enculturation of Evangelicalism was protective or destructive, as in the parallel case of the Pharisaic distortion of the Israelite training code. It is certain, however, that what happened to the liberal wing of the church was no less destructive. Non-Evangelical Protestantism became fused in varying degrees with the secular humanist culture which burgeoned in the century after Marx and Darwin. Its confidence in the radical authority of the Bible was jammed by the strong signal broadcast by secular skepticism. Since biblical authority had served as a kind of discriminator circuit filtering out the counterbroadcasts of non-Christian culture, the program of the church was increasingly dominated by the concerns of social humanism.

The Old Liberalism totally lost the biblical gospel, redefining Jesus as a social reformer aiming at the introduction of an earthly kingdom of justice and the equal enjoyment of material benefits. Neo-orthodox theology restrained some of the worst of these distortions in the 1930s, but again and again in later decades a sort of zealot theology recaptured the mind of the church, ignoring the basic human problem of sin and the supernatural provisions in Christ for its solution, and focusing on liberation from human tyrannies and worldly needs.

Some of the emphases of liberation theologies are not in themselves illegitimate, and their absence in Evangelical circles is itself a grave defect of enculturation. It is also true that when the church loses its own Spirit-directed social initiative, that initiative passes to common-grace movements within the fallen world, for God's compassion for humanity will not be frustrated by the church's failure. In such a situation, the church may do better to climb on secular bandwagons than it would do by remaining socially passive.

But neither the socially conservative enculturation of the Fundamentalist nor the compulsive harmony with the latest cause of humanistic liberalism of the social gospeler is a healthy expression of the mind of Christ. Non-Evangelical Protestantism has too often been "The Church of What's Happenin' Now," to use a black comedian's accurate label.

Most sectors of the church have been helped by the black liberation movement. They have been both helped and hindered through an uncritical adoption of all the stresses of the women's liberation movement. But now some sectors of the church are in danger of being destroyed by conformity to the movement of gay liberation, as they consider accepting the ordination of homosexuals and the introduction of an antinomian sexual lifestyle based on man-centered situation ethics.

Enculturation is the net result of the church's failure to understand and appropriate the primary and secondary elements of renewal which define the meaning of fullness of life in Christ. It almost inevitably appears over a period of time in which any of these dynamics is substantially missing in the church. It is a kind of rust which forms on the surface of the church's witness and clouds the glory which ought to shine out from it to illuminate the nations. At its worst, it destroys the church's life. At best, it freezes the form of the church and produces a sanctified out-of-dateness which the world can easily learn to ignore. In periods of awakening, the church is all growth and movement as new and creative expressions of the gospel are shaped to communicate to the surrounding culture. With the onset of spiritual decline, the church's expression ceases to be creative and becomes mere rehearsal of the forms that once expressed life and spoke to the world with arresting power.

Despite their weaknesses, the religious language and hymnody of the Moody era came out of such a vital movement of the Holy Spirit. But their continued dominance in many sectors of Evangelical church life a hundred years later is not a testimony to their spiritual power but to the deadness of twentieth-century Evangelicalism. The church ought to be like a mobile sculpture in which fixed forms of truth and fellowship are constantly shifting their relationship to harmonize with the decor of the social and cultural environment. Enculturation freezes the form of the mobile until it becomes a static monument, a reminder of the past which appears to have no relevance for the present.

Paul's self-analysis in Philippians shows the psychological mechanism through which enculturation occurs in the church and suggests the way it can be overcome. He speaks of the Judaizers, those who were trying to bind the expression of the gospel to a single cultural form, as those who "mutilate the flesh" by holding an excessive confidence in it. By "confidence in the flesh," Paul means the reliance on our gifts, descent, achievement, righteousness and cultural surroundings for identity and standing before God. Paul had to learn to empty himself of this confidence before he could enter the fullness of spiritual life:

> If any other man thinks he has reason for confidence in the flesh, I have more: circumcized on the eighth day, of the people of Israel, of the tribe of Benjamin, a Hebrew born of Hebrews; as to the law a Pharisee, as to zeal a persecutor of the church, as to righteousness under the law blameless. But whatever gain I had, I counted as loss for the sake of Christ. . . . For his sake I have suffered the loss of all things, and count them as refuse, in order that I may gain Christ and be found in him, not having a righteousness of my own, based on law, but that which is through faith in Christ, the righteousness from God that depends on faith. (Phil. 3:4-9)

Thus men who are not secure in Christ cast about for spiritual life preservers with which to support their confidence, and in their frantic search they not only cling to the shreds of ability and righteousness they find in themselves, but they fix upon their race, their membership in a party, their familiar social and ecclesiastical patterns, and their culture as means of self-recommendation. The culture is put on as though it were armor against self-doubt, but it becomes a mental straitjacket which cleaves to the flesh and can never be removed except through comprehensive faith in the saving work of Christ. Once faith is exercised, a Christian is free to be encultured, to wear his culture like a comfortable suit of clothes. He can shift to other cultural clothing temporarily if he wishes to do so, as Paul suggests in 1 Corinthians 9:19-23, and he is released to admire and appreciate the differing expressions of Christ shining out through other cultures.

Disenculturation through the full appropriation of life in Christ is vital to the church's missionary expansion. If the apostolic church had failed to take the steps described in Acts 10—15, its spread among the nations would have stopped dead, and the power of God would have been withdrawn from its inner life. In just the same way, the church's foreign missionary witness would have been short-circuited in this century if it had not learned something about distinguishing the heart of the gospel from its cultural and traditional packaging. Disenculturation of home missions has lagged behind the foreign field, perhaps because Christians have assumed that their antique style was adequately communicating the gospel to a surrounding society which at least speaks the same language.

Since renewal and reform in the Evangelical community began to escalate around the middle of the century, however, this picture has been changing. Our young people are breaking out of much of the enculturation which bound us. The seminary students I train are zealous to test everything by Scripture and to sit loose to that which is merely tradition. They earnestly want to break down the false walls which legalism has erected between them and the cultures they long to reach with the gospel. They want to scrub the rust off the gospel catalyst. If this process continues, separated parties in the church may be reconciled by the dissolution of the cultural barriers between them, and many parts of Western society which have been closed to the gospel may become open. There is particular hope that the Jewish community may be drawn to receive its Messiah once it clearly sees that this will not mean cultural suicide but rather the completed blooming of the vine God planted.

But if the basic principles of the dynamics of spiritual life are ignored or mislaid in all the creative innovations which are sweeping through a renewed Evangelicalism, enculturation will surely set in again. It is already visible in many areas of the Jesus movement, and it is bound to recur in places where pop psychology and experiential froth are being substituted for biblical spiritual theology. And the large continent of still-enculturated Fundamentalists in America and the great mass of the Middle-American laity are not going to be wakened from their deathly sleep in the cradle of a training code except by the preaching of the cross in its fullest dimensions. For it is not merely new methods, new insights and clearer theologies which will advance the gospel at the close of the twentieth century. It must be a cleansing of man's spirit, and therefore a pouring out of the Holy Spirit of God.

RENEWAL
IN THE
CHURCH

PART
II

THE RENEWAL
OF THE
LOCAL
CONGREGATION

6

AMERICAN HOME MISSION TO YOUNG people in the early 1970s
achieved a measure of disenculturation, and the result was a
remarkable openness to the gospel among counterculture
dropouts and straight college students on the secular campuses. Whether or not the wave of response to the Christian
message in these circles marked the beginning of another
Great Awakening, it is certain that a flood of new leadership
has entered the body of Christ. Communes, house churches
and campus gatherings have been filled with converts dedicated and hungry for instruction.

But whether or not this awakening will have a lasting positive effect on the *church* remains a question, as we have already observed. Ministers may be aware of the new things
that have happened, but their congregations tend to slumber
peacefully on, and even when they are partially awake, they

are nervous. The generation gap and the culture gap are often sufficiently great between these young people and their elders that they form a firebreak to prevent the spread of the revival. In a recent mission at a large Eastern university, I found the college Christians linking forces with a converted Hell's Angel to minister to the drug culture on campus and among the street people in a nearby city. But the local pastor who was trying to bring both of these forces to bear on his congregation (which consisted of about twenty-five persons, with at least five desperate pastoral problems among them) was totally frustrated. His people actually seemed to resent the vitality of the college young people, as well as their mildly different cultural style.

And yet the continuing health of the young people, as well as the revitalization of the Middle-American church, is dependent on the establishment of a liaison between older and younger Christians. The young converts are new blood intended to quicken the body of older Christians, and the latter, despite their partial enculturation, have much to offer in stability and tradition which can prevent the youth culture from going cultic and insular. If new waves of converts do not receive sound instruction in the theology of the Christian life, in ten years they will be just as dormant and derailed as their elders. It is therefore vital that the revival spread across the cultural firebreak into the heartland of the American church, the local congregation.

In order to see how this goal can be reached, we should first review the condition of enculturation prevailing in many congregations. Assuming pastors themselves have become aware of the degree of their own unconscious enculturation, what do they face in their own parishes?

In most cases what they confront is a style of living very unlike the spiritually vibrant mission station described at the end of Acts 2. The "ultimate concern" of most church members is not the worship and service of Christ in evangelistic mission and social compassion, but rather survival and success in their secular vocation. The church is a spoke on the wheel of life connected to the secular hub. It is a departmental subconcern, not the organizing center of all other concerns. Churchmembers who have been conditioned all their lives to devote themselves to building their own kingdom and whose flesh naturally gravitates in that direction anyway find it hard to invest much energy in the kingdom of God. They go to church once or twice a week and punch the clock, so to speak, fulfilling their "church obligation" by sitting passively and listening critically or approvingly to the pastor's teaching.

Sometimes with great effort they can be maneuvered into some active role in the church's program, like a trained seal in a circus act, but their hearts are not fully in it. They may repeat the catchwords of the theology of grace, but many have little deep awareness that they and other Christians are "accepted in the beloved." Since their understanding of justification is marginal or unreal—anchored not to Christ, but to some conversion experience in the past or to an imagined present state of goodness in their lives—they know little of the dynamic of justification. Their understanding of sin focuses upon behavioral externals which they can eliminate from their lives by a little will power and ignores the great submerged continents of pride, covetousness and hostility beneath the surface. Thus their pharisaism defends them both against full involvement in the church's mission and against full subjection of their inner lives to the authority of Christ.

Their religious lives, however, do not satisfy their consciences at the deepest level, and so there is a powerful underlying insecurity in their lives. Consciously they defend themselves as dedicated Christians who are as good as anybody else, but underneath the conscious level there is deep despair and self-rejection. Above the surface this often manifests itself in a compulsive floating hostility which focuses upon others in critical judgment. Thus a congregation of

Christians who are insecure in their relationship to Christ can be a thorn bush of criticism, rejection, estrangement and party spirit. Unsure in the depth of their hearts what God thinks of them, churchmembers will fanatically affirm their own gifts and take fierce offense when anyone slights them, or else they will fuss endlessly with a self-centered inventory of their own inferiority in an inverted pride.

They will also become entrenched in their own enculturation and set up mortars with which to shell those in other cultural molds. Alienation from other races, political persuasions and the kids with their long hair will be badges of honor for them. They will take good principles and sound doctrine and affirm them in a way which attacks and hurts others unnecessarily. Confronted with a change in the church's program, their response will be a frantic clinging to past precedents: "But we always did it this way." Their church life is a desperate effort to maintain allegiance to a Leviticus written forty years ago. Their ability to follow Christ into constructive change is severely limited by their bondage to cultural supports for their insecurity. I suspect that this portrait applies equally to Evangelical and non-Evangelical churchmembers. In the case of the former, it is no wonder that their word for the Evangelical faith is "conservatism."

Pastors will often find that those who have risen into leadership (or thrust themselves into it) within the congregation are persons in this state of insecurity and bondage. Lay leadership is frequently so bound by cultural defense mechanisms and prerational conditioning that it is unable to "contend earnestly for the faith" in the liberty of the Holy Spirit. Hence even those who aim at good goals and try to follow the Spirit in their behavior end up handling situations in the flesh because of their domination by unconscious compulsions. A typical example of this in current church life is the lay leader in a church judiciary who, confronted by ministers promoting the ordination of homosexuals, pub-

licly explodes like a tin drill bit hitting steel, throwing fragments in all directions.

Confronted with this kind of violent reaction when they
seek to mold their congregations into instruments of evangelism and social healing, pastors gradually settle down and
lose interest in being change agents in the church. An unconscious conspiracy arises between their flesh and that of their
congregations. It becomes tacitly understood that the laity
will give pastors places of special honor in the exercise of
their gifts, if the pastors will agree to leave their congregations' pre-Christian lifestyles undisturbed and do not call for
the mobilization of lay gifts for the work of the kingdom. Pastors are permitted to become ministerial superstars. Their
pride is fed and their insecurity is pacified even if they are
run ragged, and their congregations are permitted to remain
herds of sheep in which each has cheerfully turned to his
own way.

The dissatisfaction of the rising leadership among youth
with the traditional form of the institutional church may well
be simply a refusal to enter situations which will inevitably
stamp them into this kind of mold. Many of them would
much rather enter communes of younger Christians who are
uniformly oriented toward mission instead of pursuing it
haphazardly as a sideline while devoting most of their energies to the rat race for success. Since the finest leaders among
our children are determined not to play in this kind of game,
the churches are going to have to change if they want to retain this leadership.

But there are many other pressures toward change. Chief
among them is the radical cultural pluralism which, as the
futurologists have told us, is emerging as the twentieth century moves onward. So many subcultures are proliferating
that Christian lay people almost need disenculturation to
preserve their sanity. As Alvin Toffler says, the future is
arriving early in countless new and disconcerting forms.[1] In
order to cope with this catastrophically shifting environ-

ment, the Christian needs to be very deeply rooted in the cross of Christ.

Some critics of the institutional church question whether it is possible for it to achieve disenculturation and would insist on new bottles to hold the new wine. Others who are pastors may theoretically be convinced that the transformation is possible but may feel that the inertia and hostility to change present in the average congregation make the job so difficult as to be hardly worth the cost.

But would starting over with new congregations in new shapes of mission avoid the problem of enculturation? It is a practical certainty that every new gathering of Christians will recapitulate the crisis of disenculturation experienced by the early church as recorded in Acts. Unless new converts are persuaded to stop leaning on their culture and the law and to lean fully on Jesus Christ in every phase of their lifestyle, their spiritual lives and the mission of the church will inevitably be short-circuited by the process of enculturation. As for the old converts who are unconsciously trapped in hardened shells of protective enculturation, it would be disloyalty to them (and to Christ's mission through them) to allow them to continue to exist without the full deliverance available in Christ.

The shape of the Christian movement as a constellation of local congregations needs to be renewed and continued, not scrapped and superseded, for both theological and practical reasons. While the New Testament nowhere presents a Levitical set of commands for congregational worship and church government, it obviously takes over and adapts the synagogue structure as a framework for local fellowship and nurture. This is fitting, since the synagogue was the local meeting place for Jews who were too distant to attend the Temple where the sacrifices were held, just as we are currently at a distance from the heavenly sanctuary where the Lamb of God is physically present. The apostles were aware of the need for new wineskins, but they sought for these in the process of disenculturation, not in any radical reshuffling of polity.

There is a principle of the *conservation of structures* in the precedent they set, and there are many practical reasons why this principle needs to be followed today. Lines of communication along which renewal can travel can easily be dismantled in any wholesale creation of new structures. A dissolving of local congregations into house churches, independent communes or elite task forces would not only disrupt communication, it might create structures which do not by themselves have the power to carry the whole people of God forward through history with the same effectiveness as parish churches. The local congregation is like a whaling vessel. It is too large and unwieldy in itself to catch whales, so it must carry smaller vessels aboard for this purpose. But the smaller whaleboats are ill-advised to strike out on their own apart from the mother ship. They can catch a few whales but they cannot process them, and the smaller boats can easily be destroyed by storms.

Nevertheless, if the local congregation is not to be abandoned and by-passed in the renewal of the church, it must be itself renewed and disenculturated. How can this be done? I am reluctant to speak on this issue. For one thing, it is presumptuous to do so. No single individual has the pastoral expertise necessary to qualify for this task. And the strategy of renewing congregations must differ from case to case so that generalizations may be misleading. The wide differences in "parish ethos" among Catholics and the different sorts of Protestants complicate the matter. It might be better simply to call for an application of the biblical truths behind the primary and secondary elements of renewal tailored carefully to each local situation. But perhaps some general guidelines which will apply to all congregations may be distilled out of what has been said already. Although most Evangelical approaches to revival have dealt primarily with individual regeneration or awakening, this account will try to

deal with two tasks which are interrelated and mutually reinforcing but nevertheless distinguishable: the renewal of individuals and the renewal of the church's corporate structure.

Individual Renewal

The beginning place for personal renewal in most congregations is a preaching and teaching ministry which emphasizes
primary elements of spiritual dynamics: depth proclamation
of the gospel. The aim of the minister should be to encourage
in every parishioner an intelligent response of faith laying
claim to the provisions of Christ's redemptive work, a daily
standing on the four platforms discussed in chapter four:
*You are accepted, you are delivered, you are not alone, you
have authority.* At the same time that this good news is given,
the "bad news" to which it is the answer must be presented:
the depth and gravity of sin in the light of God's holiness and
righteousness, and the problems likely to be encountered in
spiritual conflict with the powers of darkness. The balance
and proportion of these positive and negative materials of
preaching, and the order in which they are approached, is a
subtle matter which depends on the spiritual profile of each
congregation.

Preaching and Teaching for Individual Renewal. Churches
which have been fed on a heavy diet of "legal terrors" or
moralism will need to be addressed with a strong positive
emphasis on the grace of God, in line with the Lutheran tradition, before they are led into any deeper examination of the
darker or more awesome background of the gospel which
gives it meaning. Churches which have been raised on cheap
grace (and this may include most congregations today, Evangelical and non-Evangelical) might be handled with the
typical Puritan approach, the presentation of the majesty of
God and a searching "law-work" leading to conviction of sin
which will awaken a hunger for the gospel and a full appreciation of the saving work of Christ. But this could create a
serious credibility gap between the preacher and his or her

audience, since such preaching is widely thought to be extinct except in backwoods revivalism. Probably the Lutheran Formula of Concord is correct when it recommends that a full explanation of grace precede the preaching of the law in order to establish enough confidence in the congregation so that it can be led fully into the light.

While Evangelical churches have been preaching incessantly on the love of God since the Moody era, in far too many instances the justifying work of Christ has not been spelled out clearly and balanced by an equal stress on sanctification, so that the grace of God can be both intelligible and credible for the individual believer. Many of our people are severely enculturated because their relationship to Christ is so insecure that they are not free to cut loose from cultural support. So we must first make real to them the grace of God in accepting them daily, not because of their spirituality or their achievements in Christian service, but because God has accounted to them the perfect righteousness of Christ.

This may seem to be the most elemental concept in the Protestant tradition but is just as rare an act of faith among Protestants as among Catholics. We all automatically gravitate toward the assumption that we are justified by our level of sanctification, and when this posture is adopted it inevitably focuses our attention not on Christ but on the adequacy of our own obedience. We start each day with our personal security resting not on the accepting love of God and the sacrifice of Christ but on our present feelings or recent achievements in the Christian life. Since these arguments will not quiet the human conscience, we are inevitably moved either to discouragement and apathy or to a self-righteousness which falsifies the record to achieve a sense of peace.

Much that we have interpreted as a defect of sanctification in churchpeople is really an outgrowth of their loss of bearing with respect to justification. Christians who are no longer sure that God loves and accepts them in Jesus, apart from their present spiritual achievements, are subconsciously radically insecure persons—much less secure than non-Christians, because they have too much light to rest easily under the constant bulletins they receive from their Christian environment about the holiness of God and the righteousness they are supposed to have. Their insecurity shows itself in pride, a fierce defensive assertion of their own righteousness and defensive criticism of others. They come naturally to hate other cultural styles and other races in order to bolster their own security and discharge their suppressed anger. They cling desperately to legal, pharisaical righteousness, but envy, jealousy and other branches on the tree of sin grow out of their fundamental insecurity.

The natural tendency of ministers is to lash out at all this baptized depravity with the stinging rebuke of the law. Sometimes this is the right course. But it is often necessary to convince sinners (and even sinful Christians) of the grace and love of God toward them, before we can get them to look at their problems. Then the vision of grace and the sense of God's forgiving acceptance may actually cure most of the problems. This may account for Paul's frequent fusing of justification and sanctification.

It is often said today, in circles which blend popular psychology with Christianity, that we must love ourselves before we can be set free to love others. This is certainly the release which we must seek to give our people. But no realistic human beings find it easy to love or to forgive themselves, and hence their self-acceptance must be grounded in their awareness that God accepts them in Christ. There is a sense in which the strongest self-love that we can have, in the sense of *agapē*, is merely the mirror image of the lively conviction we have that God loves us. There is endless talk about this in the church, but little apparent belief in it among Christians, although they may have a conscious complacency which conceals the subconscious despair which Kierkegaard calls "the sickness unto death."[2]

As P. T. Forsyth says, "It is an item of faith that we are children of God; there is plenty of experience in us against it."[3] The faith that surmounts this evidence and is able to warm itself at the fire of God's love, instead of having to steal love and self-acceptance from other sources, is actually the root of holiness:

It is a fatal mistake to think of holiness as a possession which we have distinct from our faith. . . . Faith is the very highest form of our dependence on God. We never outgrow it. . . . Whatever other fruits of the Spirit we show, they grow upon faith, and faith which is in its nature repentance. . . . Every Christian experience is an experience of faith; that is, it is an experience of what we have not. . . . We are not saved by the love we exercise, but by the love we trust.[4]

But as Forsyth points out, justifying faith must necessarily be repentant faith. It must be the kind of faith which proceeds to sanctify the whole life. Where justification is preached without an equal stress on sanctification, the good news is always perceived as "too good to be true." People may say they believe it and try to pacify their consciences with the message of cheap grace, but they will not succeed in believing the truth about God's grace until they believe the truth about themselves and begin to strive to change what they see.

We cannot claim Christ's justifying work without claiming at the same time his delivering power for sanctification. Thus Paul says, "We are convinced that one has died for all; therefore all have died. And he died for all, that those who live might live no longer for themselves but for him who for their sake died and was raised" (2 Cor. 5:14-15). Real justifying and sanctifying faith involves death and resurrection for the believer; it involves being born again. Every minister who is aiming toward a renewed congregation must seek to bring every individual member into the light concerning the depth of his or her need to appropriate the justifying and sanctifying work of Christ through a response of faith.

This does not mean that everyone must go through the same conversion pattern or must be able to remember the time and circumstances of conversion. As the great Pietist Francke said, "We do not have to ask, 'Are you converted? When were you converted?' But rather: 'What does Christ mean to you? What have you personally experienced with God? Is Christ important to you in your daily life?' "[5] If these questions elicit a reply which indicates repentant faith in Christ and a reliance on him for justification and increasing victory over sin, we can presume that we are dealing with a regenerate Christian.

Beyond the goal of a regenerate congregation, the minister aiming at renewal must work toward one in which the members are growing in sanctification and making progress at conquering sin in their lives. Probably every ministry strives in this direction; straightening out the lives of parishioners is the stock and trade of the pastorate. But much of this straightening is often unrelated to Christ and the real depth of congregational problems. Moralism, whether it takes the form of denunciation or pep talks, can ultimately only create awareness of sin and guilt or manufactured virtues built on will power. A ministry which leads to genuine sanctification and growth, on the other hand, avoids moralism, first by making clear the deep rootage of sin-problems in the flesh so that the congregation is not battling these in the dark, and then by showing that every victory over the flesh is won by faith in Christ, laying hold of union with him in death and resurrection and relying on his Spirit for power over sin.

Presented in this context, even the demand for sanctification becomes part of the good news. It offers understanding of the bondage which has distorted our lives and of the promise of release into a life of Spirit-empowered freedom and beauty. Ministries which attack only the surface of sin and fail to ground spiritual growth in the believer's union with Christ produce either self-righteousness or despair, and both of these conditions are inimical to spiritual life.

Every Christian congregation should be at least as well instructed in the biblical treatment of the person, gifts and graces of the Holy Spirit as the average Pentecostal church. This means that the person and work of the Holy Spirit should be adequately covered every time the application of redemption in Christian growth is dealt with, since this is his particular office. His work in the believer's life should be given full sermonic treatment more often than once a year at Pentecost. Churches which have a serious practical ignorance about what it means to walk by the Spirit should be given a series of studies handling the major texts which have to do with his person and work, fully explaining the gifts of the Spirit and his ministries of sanctifying, teaching, guiding, empowering for witness, enabling in prayer, comforting and assuring. These are not themes which can be sounded once a year with any lasting benefit to the congregation.

The relationship of believers to the Holy Spirit is the most important experience of fellowship they have, but it is also the most elusive. It requires careful cultivation until a habitual recognition of the Spirit is established as a constant attitude of the heart. Ministers should do everything they can to lead their congregations into this recognition. Ministers who are shaky about their own relationship to the Holy Spirit—and who among us are not?—should enter the project as a joint venture of discovery with their congregations, confident that "every one who asks receives, and he who seeks finds" (Lk. 11:10), and that therefore the heavenly Father is sure to give the Holy Spirit in increasing measure to those who ask Him.

Since the activity of Satan is one of the most important roadblocks a Christian encounters in his efforts to serve God, the existence and devices of fallen angels should be adequately understood by every serious churchmember. A small amount of instruction in the strategies of darkness would save most ministers a good deal of wear and tear in church conflicts where the works of the flesh are triggered and reinforced by satanic accusation and deception. Unfortunately many ministers will hesitate to deal with this subject at any length and in any connection other than a treatment of the occult because of fear of being thought superstitious or morbid. Some will have an uneasy feeling about devoting time to something which seems to divert attention from God. Others will just have an uneasy feeling, one which is echoed by a few uncomfortable churchmembers. Puritans, Pietists, Catholic spiritual directors and others who have had to be realistically biblical about the negative factors in Christian experience would interpret this pressure as a stratagem of the enemy to avoid disclosure. It may be that the most fruitful handling of this subject occurs in pastoral counseling, where it can be directly and accurately related to concrete problems in the believer's life.

Counseling for Renewal. A fully developed counseling ministry is normally essential to the renewal of the local congregation. Ministers in the Puritan and Pietist traditions soon discovered that they needed Protestant equivalents for the Catholic instruments of spiritual direction and the confessional. The revival at Kidderminster parish under Richard Baxter's ministry was largely the result of systematic pastoral oversight in which catechetical instruction was the means of opening up spiritual needs which could be met by a direct application of biblical truth impossible in the preaching situation. Baxter's *Reformed Pastor* describes a pastoral program which generations of evangelical ministers have tried to emulate.[6]

Philipp Spener, Baxter's contemporary in Lutheran Pietism, discovered in his pastorate at Frankfurt that it was impossible to produce a transforming understanding of the gospel in the mass of parishioners using the pulpit ministry alone. In *Pia Desideria* (1675), he recommended augmenting this with group discussions, catechetical visitation and a strategic use of confirmation and confession. The Great

Awakening in the Middle Colonies in America was carried forward by house-to-house pastoral visitation combined with counseling.

Individual counseling has continued to be a major instrument through which evangelical ministers have sought to counteract the tendency of lay people to "play church," hiding their real needs in the crowd of passive spectators at the weekly liturgy or lecture. The clear biblical precedent for this dimension of ministry is the example of Paul, who taught both "in public and from house to house" (Acts 20: 20), "warning every man and teaching every man in all wisdom," in order to "present every man mature in Jesus Christ" (Col. 1:28).

In the present century ministers have had to deal with the development of secular psychotherapy which has had an ambivalent impact on pastoral counseling. On the one hand, the various schools of psychology have cast considerably more light on the physical and temperamental factors in pastoral problems of which the Puritans and other earlier counselors were dimly aware. On the other hand, psychotherapy has sometimes seemed to be little more than a costly and problematic rival to Christian counseling. Some therapists have intimated that ministerial counseling is a sort of pre-scientific substitute for adequate psychotherapy.

Pastoral psychologists have tried to bridge the gap between the disciplines and create an acceptable Christian integration of psychological theory with pastoral technique. But this task has often been complicated by a weakening of the current Christian understanding of spiritual dynamics and the consequent difficulty of filtering out nonbiblical presuppositions and practices in the process of synthesis. Some Evangelicals have jumped to the conclusion that any unusual spiritual difficulty must be psychological in origin and have sent for the psychotherapists in cases which would have been routine for Puritan pastoral counselors. (I cannot escape the feeling that Luther, Bunyan and the apostle Paul would be referred to psychotherapists if they appeared in the Evangelical community today. Any leader strong enough to attract severe demonic harassment would appear unbalanced by our standards.)

Recently counseling theorists attempting to follow the Amsterdam tradition have protested against illegitimate fusions of pastoral and psychological approaches. They have asserted that most "psychological" problems are really rooted in sin and have defended the competence of pastors to deal with these problems by fairly direct exhortations to stop sinning and to follow scriptural examples and precepts. This "nouthetic" approach to counseling (from the Greek *noutheteō*, to admonish, warn, rebuke, see Col. 1:28) has confirmed the intuitive sense of rightness that most Evangelical pastors have felt in their attempts to apply biblical teaching directly to spiritual needs under the guidance of the Holy Spirit. It has served as a pointed reminder of Kuyper's warning that there is a necessary antithesis between non-Christian thinking and Christian thought unless the former is restrained and corrected by common grace, and it has warned Christian counselors not to import antibiblical defective theories and techniques from secular psychotherapy. It has also helped a great many people—especially Christians with a tendency toward passivity or quietism. The counseling approach which is most likely to help in congregational renewal is a tuned and adapted form of nouthetic counseling.

But the nouthetic approach has been criticized on several counts, and it needs to be extensively reworked in two areas. First, its attitude toward psychotherapy must be moderated. It tends to write off all non-Christian psychological theory and practice as erroneous because of their lack of ultimate biblical presuppositions, and overlooks the possibility that techniques and conclusions may be valid even when their theoretical foundations are unsound. The right thing can often be done for wrong reasons. Elements of truth can be found in almost any system, if not because of common grace, then because the devil needs an admixture of truth in order to market a lie successfully. The most effective heresies have capitalized on important elements of truth which were lacking in current Christian understanding.

We must guard against the assumption that all the truth that is needed for the most effective counseling is contained in Scripture. Biblical truth is not a compendium of all necessary knowledge, but a touchstone for testing and verifying other kinds of truth and a structure for integrating them. It is not an encyclopedia, but a tool for making encyclopedias. If Paul was unaware that chemical and physiological factors could enter into spiritual problems, this is not reason for us to overlook the evidence that they do. If the biblical writers did not explicitly state that our interaction with our parents colors our attitude toward God or that our experience of early rejection can dispose us toward spiritual depression, this does not mean that these facts cannot be immensely illuminating and releasing.

To assume that there is almost no such thing as psychopathology, only malingering disobedience, so that every problem should be met head-on with a strong moral imperative, is to run a severe risk of misdiagnosis and malpractice. Pastors need to be alert to the fact that they may be feeding their religious "talk therapy" into people who are chemically imbalanced or undergoing a postpartum or menopausal depression, whose only possible response may be to make their religion part of their illness.

Pastors likewise must recognize that the fallen world system (especially in its expression within the family) may impinge on the development of growing children to cause distinctive psychospiritual problems through the repression of traumatic events, through "operant conditioning" of pathological behavior or through other mechanisms as yet undiscovered. The fact that such mechanisms are operating does not remove the guilt of sin, but it does help explain the *shape* of an individual's characteristic flesh. For example, the

sexual drive under the bondage of sin may be channeled
(either by parental interaction or conditioning experience)
into a heterosexual adulterous expression in one person, into
homosexual expression in another and into total repression
in a third. Understanding the psychological mechanism by
which the flesh has been shaped may prove to be an important factor in gaining practical freedom from the power of sin.

While Freud, Skinner and others may not be our best
guides to redeemed behavior, they may be able to tell us quite
a bit about the way fallen human nature works and is shaped
in the experience of development. Christian counselors
should therefore look into all the psychological schools and
make an eclectic use of discoveries which are not contrabiblical and which appear to work in practice. And they should
also be alert to refer counselees to physicians and psychotherapists (preferably Christians who have made progress in
integrating their discipline) when this is necessary. On the
other hand, we cannot isolate "spiritual" problems from psychological" problems and treat the latter nonspiritually because the human soul is a psychospiritual continuum in
which psychological stress, physiological conditions and
spiritual states are deeply interrelated.

An even more serious fault of some nouthetic counseling than its disdain of all non-Christian psychological
theory is its failure to incorporate a full understanding of
spiritual dynamics. Such counseling simply operates with
the Pelagian model of the Christian life common in modern
Evangelicalism, assuming that sin problems are only habit
patterns of disobedience which can be broken down by the
application of will power in a process of dehabituation. This
is a view of sanctification which will work in some instances,
especially on persons who have been looking for easy vic-
tories through faith and neglecting the vigorous engagement
of the will. But it does not penetrate the depth of the problem
of indwelling sin and provide a dynamic to overcome it.
Thus at times it will amputate the surface manifestations of

sin without disturbing the roots of the flesh and produce a pharisaical self-righteousness. In other cases it can lead almost to despair as the counselee attacks an iceberg of concealed sin with efforts at discipline and will power. This approach to counseling is fully consistent with the legal approach to sin in Scripture which points out sin and calls for a change in behavior, but it is not sufficiently evangelical because it fails to see that progress must be grounded in the appropriation by faith of the benefits of union with Christ.

This model of pastoral counseling may fail not only because it follows a Pelagian approach to sanctification, but also because it limits itself to sanctification and overlooks the other dynamics of spiritual life. None of the primary elements of spiritual renewal can operate entirely independent of the others. Christians cannot remain assured of justification without being committed to sanctification, without being in touch with the Spirit of adoption who confirms our sonship and without being released from deception under the counterfeit conviction of satanic accusation. They cannot proceed to grow in sanctification unless they are sure that they are accepted by God through the righteousness of Christ, unless they are in a vital dependent relationship with the Holy Spirit and unless they are confident that they can resist the devil and retake the ground in their lives that has belonged to the enemy through its subjection to the flesh. Believers cannot know the Holy Spirit fully unless they are secure in their adoptive sonship, contending with the Spirit against their flesh, and able to discern and withstand opposing spiritual forces. Any assault against the powers of darkness is of course hopeless without the full armor of justifying and sanctifying righteousness and without vital dependence on the Spirit.

Therefore counseling which brings spiritual release and renewal must explore each of these areas with great sensitivity to determine whether or not a vigorous response of faith is appropriating each of these benefits of union with

Christ. It is not enough merely to locate the most obvious outcroppings of the flesh and to encourage the counselee to strive against these. What is needed is a total evaluation of the counselee's present ability to abide in Christ by faith. Each of the primary elements of renewal must be explored and carefully tuned, and the same is true for the secondary factors. Spiritual difficulties rarely have only one root; they are more often the composite result of deficient faith in several areas. Often in the process of exploring these the counselor will become aware of problems and dimensions of the flesh which should be noted but not explicitly handled at this point in the counselee's developing spiritual life, because they do not seem to be at issue in his or her current need.

Obviously an immense amount of tact and discernment is required for this kind of counseling, more in fact than any human counselor possesses. Therefore it cannot be too strongly emphasized that the counselor cannot arrive at the heart of the counselee's current need without extraordinary dependence on the Holy Spirit and a close following of his leading during the counseling process. Conversely, the counselee will not obtain full insight and healing in this process unless his or her primary dependence and awareness are focused not on the human counselor but on the Holy Spirit.

Counseling sessions should begin with a mutual or group recognition of the presence and leading of the Spirit. If this pattern is followed, it will not be unusual for the counselor/ counselee roles to shift somewhat during the session as both participants find themselves being counseled by the mind of Christ expressed in the application of biblical truth. For this reason, fairly nondirective small groups can often function as very effective counseling media where full honesty before a number of persons is possible. The model of the counselor as an omnipotent spiritual director whose insights and commands virtually become the voice of God for the counselee must be avoided at all costs. If counseling is not theonomous, grounded in the counselee's perception of the Word and Spirit of God, it does not bring spiritual renewal but a condition of bondage and dependence on other human beings.

What is true of the Holy Spirit's role in the counseling procedure is equally important in the pulpit and teaching ministry of the pastor directed toward the whole congregation. If it is difficult to do spiritual surgery in the life of one parishioner in the counseling situation, it is even more difficult to take aim at the spiritual needs of a group without explicit direction from the Holy Spirit. Many texts and many sermons may be appropriate in a general way to congregational needs. But the pastor who is working for congregational renewal will learn not to fix on any of these possibilities prematurely, until the quiet imprimatur of the Holy Spirit's direction illuminates the thrust and strategy which is most strategic for spiritual release. While many pastors try to use their own gifts and personalities as instruments of renewal, fixing the attention of their people on them, the clearest road to spiritual awakening in a congregation is to develop the independent relationship of each churchmember with the Holy Spirit, so that every parishioner is constantly looking beyond personalities and listening for the voice of God.

Corporate or Structural Renewal
Not much has been said above about teaching and counseling focused on the secondary elements of spiritual renewal. But the same effort that is devoted to depth proclamation of the gospel and depth counseling with respect to the primary elements of renewal must be devoted to establishing each churchmember in a witnessing stance, in a personal discipline of prayer, in a productive relationship with the larger church community and supportive smaller groups, in a developed theological integration, and in freedom from dependence on cultural supports.

Beyond this individual attunement, however, there are

structural implications of the secondary dynamics of renewal which may have to be implemented if a congregation's
full potential for renewal is to be released. It is not enough
to renew individual hearts for churches to be renewed, although it is probably true that structural renewal cannot
progress very far unless it is preceded by a great deal of individual awakening. Because individual Christians—and
even local congregations—are not ultimate ends in themselves, but cells in the body of Christ, reconstitution of these
cells is often necessary for spiritual health and the fullness of
Christ to be present in the church.

Most of the corporate dimensions of renewal follow directly from the dynamic of community, although they also involve by implication the elements of mission, prayer and
disenculturation. First in importance is probably the effective realization of Luther's concept of the priesthood of all
believers. One of the clearest themes in the history of awakenings is the increasing importance of lay leadership in the
church's life. But it is still true that the model of congregational life in the minds of most clergy and laity is one in
which the minister is a dominant pastoral superstar who
specializes in the spiritual concerns of the Christian community, while the laity are spectators, critics and recipients
of pastoral care, free to go about their own business because
the pastor is taking care of the business of the kingdom.

The pattern followed is still that of the temple, not the
synagogue. Some experiments at breaking up this model
have shown that there is an important continuing role for the
educated clergy in preventing the loss of Christian culture
and the collapse of the church into folk religion or moralism.
Perhaps the most successful attempt to restructure this feature of church life is that of modern Pentecostalism, which
has retained the professional clergy as leaders and coaches
but has emphasized "body life" through the gifting and leading of the Holy Spirit granted to each churchmember. Just as
the ideal Pentecostal worship service is decentralized, with

every member stirred up to active participation in the experience, so the Pentecostal congregation depends on its whole constituency to carry forward the work of the kingdom without delegating this impossibly heavy task to the pastor alone. The elimination of pastoral elitism is probably one of the principal reasons why the Pentecostal "third force" has grown so rapidly, especially in Latin America.

How can the pattern of lay passivity and pastoral dominance be broken up in non-Pentecostal congregations? First of all, it is necessary for ministers to be aware of the problem and determined to see it corrected. This will require a certain relinquishment of power in democratizing the congregational pattern; pastors must decrease in order that the laity may increase. Since some ministers are using their congregations as private kingdoms which contribute to their own emotional support, this will require a thorough work of the cross in renewing the pastors' own lives. They will have to refuse the bargain which the lay people unconsciously offer them: an empire of unrestricted authority in return for an assumption of most of the church's spiritual responsibility.

Ministers who are spiritually liberated in this manner will have to make the decentralization of ministry within the church part of their initial negotiations with local congregations. Just as the partners in a marriage reach an understanding of their parity and mutual responsibilities before the match is sealed, ministers will have to raise the consciousness of churches before which they are candidating to an awareness of the structural error in the tradition of clerical domination, and they will have to avoid accepting churches which will not see the problem. If enough local churches can break up this pattern, popular expectations will change and the decentralized congregation which fully utilizes the gifts of its members and relies on the trained pastor only as a resource person will become the norm.

A second major area of structural renewal needed within the local congregation is the formation and strengthening of nuclear subcommunities within the larger church community. To restate Teilhard's metaphor, many large congregations are like piles of iron filings which have been accumulated by the magnetism of a preaching ministry. There is no real life and virtue in such heaps of disconnected Christians. Vitality in the church of Christ gathers around centered groups of Christians who are interacting with one another and with other groups like cells or organs in a body. The most natural microcommunity in the church is the Christian home, and pastors should work to build up this unit into the functional strength it enjoyed in Puritanism (or in the patriarchal household in the Bible, which was the Puritan model).

But there are many younger and older people in our society who are outside any natural family cell unit. For this reason it seems wise to work toward the formation of an additional class of "family units" or pastoral cell groups cutting across family lines, usually in the form of support groups meeting in homes for study, sharing, prayer and mutual pastoral oversight. These house meetings are already proliferating widely among the American churches, as if they were a natural further development in the maturing of the body of Christ. They can function as diversified prayer centers replacing the old midweek prayer meetings for revival, and as originating centers for pastoral care and community concern growing out of this prayer. Without such mechanisms for the interchange of grace and the movement of known truth into action, the weekly pattern of Sunday church attendance can become a stagnant routine consisting of passive intake of truth which is never turned into prayer and work for the kingdom.

If the main locus of prayer in the church is transferred to these cell groups and to the committee structures within the congregation, great care must be taken to keep the groups informed of broader prayer needs for the reviving of the local church, the work of God in the community considered cross-denominationally, the denomination, home and foreign missions, and the human community in general, ranging from the immediate area through national and international concerns. Otherwise the cell groups can become excessively ingrown and shortsighted in their intercession.

The main instrument through which the kingdom of God can be understood and advanced by churchmembers is prayer, and it is important that every member be involved in some prayer center whose vision is comprehensive. Unless the midweek prayer meeting is revived or reinstituted, perhaps the best source of this comprehensive vision is the "pastoral prayer" section of the Sunday general service, which ought to be broken out of its rusty traditional mold and turned into a vital medium for stirring up prayer concern in the church, perhaps with more congregational involvement helping to offset the lengthy ministerial cadenza which might otherwise result.

The restructuring of the local congregation inwardly, forming it into a cellular network of microcommunities, must be accompanied by an outward restructuring of its awareness and contact with macrocommunities: other local churches of various denominations, its own denominational network and the relations of denominations with one another, and the local and national human communities and their needs. This restructuring may end in new systems of communication linking these elements together in productive labor for the advancement of the kingdom, but it must begin with concerned corporate prayer. Dissension and division within a congregation can short-circuit the work of God there, grieving the Holy Spirit and extinguishing his power. But it is also true that any absence of concern and charity for other parts of the body of Christ on a larger scale can diminish the fullness of Christ within a church or a denomination. This is one reason why many orthodox groups with a strong concern for doctrinal purity operate in an atmosphere of sterility and spiritual deadness.

The current awakening has provided us with a variety of

examples of structural renewal in the local church. One of the most interesting of these is the Episcopal Church of the Redeemer in Houston, Texas. Following an experience of new infilling with the Holy Spirit, the pastor, Graham Pulkingham, began to observe and promote a community-gathering process within his congregation in which individuals and families began to band together in close groups for nurture and prayer. Many moved into one section of urban Houston so they could be together and in some instances set up communal households. Part of this process of gathering was an inevitable shift of the center of gravity of personal concern in each family, so that the kingdom of God and not personal success became the dominant factor in decisions and outlook. Gradually a strategy of congregational mission and ministry was unveiled: the church was to pour itself out in meeting the needs of its local community, both in evangelism and in works of social compassion.

The congregation appears to be thriving on this kingdom-centered approach. Some members have turned down promotions in their ordinary vocations in order to remain with the community and carry on its work. The ideal of the church as a servant people to heal and help the world, often articulated in non-Evangelical circles but usually lacking the dynamic necessary to bring it to realization, began to operate almost automatically in this congregation as it was knit together in community and filled with the Holy Spirit. The result is a working model of a balanced ministry of love expressed both in evangelism and social action which re-creates the normal pattern of past evangelical awakenings.[7] If a great number of congregations could experience this kind of individual and structural renewal, the rest of the church could overcome the sterile division between evangelism and the social expression of Christianity which has sapped the energy of the American church since the beginning of this century, and the church could unite in promoting a program of spiritual and social renewal at the grassroots level.

THE
SANCTIFICATION
GAP

7

IN 1952, WHEN I WAS TWENTY-ONE AND still an atheist studying philosophy at Yale, I picked up a copy of Thomas Merton's *Seven Storey Mountain* and began to read about the author's pilgrimage from secular intellectualism to the Trappist Order.[1] As I read, my mind became enlightened by the reality of the presence of God. It suddenly became clear that behind all the beauty and order in nature and human art there lies a divine creative wisdom, an infinite personality whose beauty is past change. In Merton's metaphor, it seemed as though a window in the depths of my consciousness, a window I had never seen before, had suddenly been opened, allowing a blazing glimpse of new orders of existence. My mind was suddenly filled with streams of thinking which reordered my understanding around the central fact of God, streams which I knew were not rising from any source within

my natural awareness, which now seemed a desert by comparison. Immediately, irrevocably I was no longer an atheist.
If someone had spoken to me about a "leap of faith," I would
not have known what they were talking about; for there was
no gap to leap. I felt that I was in contact with God.

It was natural that I should plan to become a Trappist and
immerse myself during the next year in John of the Cross and
other mystical authorities. Liberal Protestant friends delighted in my new found theism and sought to persuade me
away from the dangers of the Catholic system, but I did not
take them seriously. As Merton pointed out, their faith
seemed eroded and desupernaturalized; it was altruistic
moralism, not piety. The Church was the sole possessor of a
great tradition of doctors of the spiritual life, physicians of
the soul who walked in the light of God's presence. As for
Protestant theology, it was as supernatural as a Sears Roe-
buck catalog.

However, I did take seriously one friend's injunction to
read the Bible, since that was part of the regular Catholic apparatus. That step led to massive change. Suddenly I became
aware of an unbridgeable gulf of sin and guilt which lay between me and the God who was formerly close at hand. The
words of Christ echoed in my mind and brought terror: "Unless your righteousness exceeds that of the scribes and Pharisees, you will never enter the kingdom of heaven.... The
gate is narrow and the way is hard, that leads to life, and
those who find it are few" (Mt. 5:20; 7:13). Few of my friends
seemed to understand my problems. If they had heard of
Luther's struggles, they did not connect them with mine. I began to beat the bushes for spiritual counselors who might
know the way out of this condition, but all my confidants
seemed to assume that I was caught in a pathological delu-
sion. Twice I made a full life's confession to priests who did
not seem to know much about John of the Cross, and was
warned against scrupulosity and advised to follow a rule of
prayer. I investigated one Fundamentalist church, but the

apparent shallowness of the activity, the singing and the preaching, and the absence of any sense of luminosity in the people discouraged me from seeking counsel.

Shortly after this, however, I did find Protestants who understood the dynamics of spiritual life, whose spirituality commanded my respect as much or more than the Catholic mystics formerly had, and who had biblical answers for the troubles in my soul. Later I came to realize that they were the historical result of a transformation of "deeper life" teaching by Reformed theology, drawing upon a tradition of Protestant spirituality which went all the way back to the English Puritans.[2]

In seminary and graduate school I studied the history of Christian experience beginning with the Puritans and moving on through the great streams of evangelical revival springing from Puritanism and German Pietism, especially that greatest of all Protestant theologians of the spiritual life, Jonathan Edwards. I was amazed to find that most Protestants were ignorant of the body of tradition which seemed to me to be the living heart of the Reformation heritage. There was not even a name among Protestants for the sort of thing I wanted to study. Catholics had one—spiritual theology— but Protestant scholars, except in the heart of the firestorms of revival, did not seem aware that there was something else to the faith besides catalogs of doctrines and institutions. Yet there seemed to be an increasing hunger for my subject among the scholars of this century, and more and more work seemed to be building up, often among authors who were not card-carrying Evangelicals. It occurred to me that the success of neo-orthodox theology in capturing the center of the church and the inexplicable failure of confessional ortho- doxies in holding their own might be due in part to the grop- ing interest of the former in Christian experience and the relative neglect of this by the latter. A living dog, after all, is better than a dead lion.

What was true among scholars seemed doubly true in the

life of the church. There seemed to be a sanctification gap among Evangelicals, a peculiar conspiracy somehow to mislay the Protestant tradition of spiritual growth and to concentrate instead on frantic witnessing activity, sermons on John 3:16 and theological arguments over eschatological subtleties. Other sectors in the church argued over issues of real substance, but with such rancor and exaggeration that one wished that some attention had first been given to sanctification.

Not that the gap was not being filled in some quarters. Enclaves of "deeper life" teaching in various conferences sought to hang on to the revival tradition. Pentecostalism and later the Charismatic movement offered models of the vital Christian life through which many satisfied their hunger for communion with God. Free-style movements stressing prayer or Christian experience sought to transcend the theological battle lines in the church. Psychedelic experimentation in the youth culture during the 1960s seemed to be another inarticulate expression of the parching thirst for spiritual reality which young people were not finding in standard-brand churches. On the brink of the 1970s, as denominational leaders moved more and more toward secular theologies and ministries of social relevance, the secular city itself seemed about to pass the church going in the opposite direction, searching for oases of living water amid the deserts of technology.

The Origin of the Gap
If the sanctification gap does exist within Protestantism—and the reader may at least grant that it does in sectors of the church other than his or her own—why has such a thing developed? This can be answered simply by saying that there is always a conspiracy against spiritual power in the church on the part of the world, the flesh and the devil. Cotton Mather saw this conspiracy as the underlying cause of the process which prompted Francis Bacon's observation that all

that is weighty in history sinks to the bottom of the river where it cannot be seen, while straw and stubble rise to the top.[3] But it is also true that the historical development of Protestant Evangelicalism has predisposed it to lose sight of the central importance of sanctification.

The English Puritans, concerned that the Reformation had been only a "half-Reformation," introduced into Protestantism a tremendous stress on initial conversion. Their object was to counter dead orthodoxy, mere "notional" or historical faith, by the doctrine of regeneration. Unfortunately, as the result of a rational manipulation of Reformed doctrine which went far beyond Calvin into hypercalvinism, they loaded into the conversion experience so much of the developed content of Christian growth that in effect they required believers to become practicing mystics before they could be counted Christians. Many Puritans insisted on telling the subjects of their evangelism that they were unable to turn to God without the sensible assistance of grace and that the sovereign God might well refuse the nonelect entrance no matter how hard they sought. Not simply faith on the promises of God's general offer of salvation but mystical assurance of one's individual acceptance with God was therefore necessary for valid church membership.[4]

This approach to evangelism, which might keep the potential convert striving for months in a maze of subjective difficulties before reaching assurance, produced some great saints, men and women who were in a sense "presanctified," searched out in the deepest aspects of their lives and transformed. But while this net caught a few whales, it must have discouraged thousands of smaller fish. Some Christians, D. L. Moody for instance, start poorly in the first act of the Christian life but come to real magnificence in the third or fourth. Therefore it is not surprising that although Jonathan Edwards continued the Puritan teaching on conversion during the revivals of the 1730s and 40s, most of Christendom was skeptical by the end of the eighteenth century. The

popular jingle summed up the perplexities of hypercalvinism fairly well: "You can, but you can't; you will, but you
won't; you're damned if you do, and damned if you don't."

The nineteenth-century heirs of the revival tradition
modified the Puritan system by allowing easier standards of
initial conversion. "I wish I could tell you about my therapeutic theology," said Lyman Beecher, "I have retrieved
hundreds from the sloughs of High Calvinism."[5] The ultimate simplification, of course, was Charles Finney's call for
instantaneous commitment and instantaneous conversion
with no waiting period to allow election to set in. The nineteenth-century revival leaders were like mechanics examining an engine in which the power train has somehow been
attached to the carburetor; the whole of sanctification had
been inserted into conversion. Seeing that there was no
biblical warrant for this, and overreacting from hypercalvinism into Arminianism, they proceeded to do the right thing
for the wrong reasons: they disconnected sanctification from
conversion and made it easy for men to enter the kingdom on
the basis of simple faith and initial repentance. Having un-
loaded conversion, however, they failed to reinsert sanctification in its proper place in the development of the Christian life and left the engine with no power train at all. The
divorce from Puritanism was effected, and the sanctification
gap was born.

Something, of course, had to be done to make the converts
grow; some explanation had to be given as to why the new
believers, no longer presanctified, often proved so fruitless.
Finney, who had experienced a postconversion "baptism of
the Holy Spirit" empowering him for service, adapted the
two-stage model of the Christian life proposed by John
Wesley in his theory of Christian perfection.[6] If being born
again would not entirely equip the convert, a second experience would surely solve the problem. D. L. Moody, fortunately uninfluenced by most of Finney's theology, fell in
with the same two-stage theory, and he and R. A. Torrey

wrote pamphlets urging "the baptism" on ordinary Christians.[7] Meanwhile, in England, the Keswick Conference was developing principles of continuous ("n-stage") sanctification, and this "deeper life" tradition ultimately captured a place in Moodyan evangelicalism in America.

Beginning in 1901, however, a more spectacular development of the Finney-Moody concept of the baptism of the Spirit began to flower into modern Pentecostalism. This left some of the American church filling the sanctification gap with a Pentecostal experience and some of it adhering to the strain of progressive sanctification developed in the deeper life movements. But in far too many of the Evangelical churches, little emphasis on sanctification remained at all, except in terms of adherence to a cultic legal code of "separation" inherited from the Puritans. What was best in Puritan mysticism was forgotten, and what was most questionable was kept.

It is hard to overestimate the damage done through this traumatic loss of bearings in the Evangelical tradition. One effect was the division of sensibility in the churches since the time of Moody, in which socially concerned churchmembers have found themselves pitted against Fundamentalists concerned mainly for conversion and code moralism. It is too much to say that this rift would not have occurred had there been no sanctification gap. But at least there would have been less excuse for it if the Evangelical church had been pursuing sanctification, rooting out pride, race prejudice, covetous immersion in affluence and all the deeper forms of sin which easily hide beneath a cover of pharisaic respectability. After all, the major argument many Protestant liberals have against "supernatural conversion experiences" is the distinctly natural lives led by many "born again" congregations.

Closing the Gap
What can be done about the sanctification gap? The first

thing is simply to see that it is there. Evangelicals can retool, tune up and debug their tradition endlessly in pursuit of the American version of *aggiornamento;* but unless there is a deepening in the heart of their faith, new methods and new masks are not going to help much. Evangelism-in-Depth and two-by-two house evangelism can expand the trade routes of the gospel outside our church walls, but unless what we export is more than a two-dimensional caricature of Christian spirituality, we will not overcome the credibility gap among consumers.

A second step must be the forging of a valid biblical model of spiritual life for Christians in the late twentieth century. To forge such a model we must, of course, restudy the Scriptures. But we will also do well not to overlook the insights of elements in the Catholic tradition and in subsequent renewal movements. I am convinced that our efforts must be directed along the lines of the Reformed doctrine of progressive sanctification—n-stage rather than 2- or 3-stage growth. This is to be preferred to the simpler model employed by many Pentecostals. "The vigor and power of the spiritual life," says John Owen, "depend upon the mortification of sin."[8] The vitality of true revival preaching has always come from its keenness in penetrating defense mechanisms, uncovering hidden sin and leading people—Christians and unbelievers alike—to repentance. It is this kind of prophetic preaching and counseling which can bring revival again today. But these tools must not be employed to move people once more into obedience to cultic legal codes. To maintain their spiritual vigor and to carry out their mission properly, Christians must be removed from the training devices of legalism and allowed to walk as those liberated by the work of the cross, freed from human regulations and entrusted to the communion of the Holy Spirit who guides believers through the application of biblical principles and precepts.

A third step involves a reclaiming by contemporary Evangelicals of the explosive heritage of spiritual renewal which lies behind them in the eras of revival. The pan-denominational consensus which is Evangelicalism was forged in the aggressive revivalist ecumenism of Zinzendorf, in the hundred-year prayer meeting at Herrnhut for the renewal of world Christendom and in the miraculous outpourings of the Holy Spirit which took place through the late nineteenth century in the Western churches and in foreign missions. Compared to the Log College, to Edwards, Whitefield, Wesley and the others, modern Evangelicalism is in danger of becoming a tame lecture circuit, a kind of sanctified show business. Here is where Pentecostals and Charismatics reflect the authentic revival tradition of Protestantism. When they commence a venture, it is with hours of prayer, while with ordinary Evangelicals it is with hours of talk and organization. The result is often that the Charismatics achieve supernatural results, while the rest of us obtain what is organizable. Since the work of the Holy Spirit in lives is intimately related to mission, it is unlikely that we can close the sanctification gap until we approach our mission in this dangerous age with the same fear and trembling, the same prayer to be endued with power from on high, that characterized the first apostles. My prayer is that this urgency will return to all the Evangelical church today, and my confidence is that this is already occurring.

HOW
REVIVALS
GO WRONG

8

IN WHAT HAS ALREADY BEEN SAID ABOUT the Jesus movement and the Charismatic renewal, it is clear that not everything which accompanies a renewed surge of vitality in the church is necessarily healthy, productive and purely of the Holy Spirit. Almost every major revival recorded, in fact, has been surrounded by an aura of irregular religious activity and has also been centrally affected by elements of weakness and sin. As a result, successive eras of churchleaders have found it easy to immunize themselves and their followers against awakening movements by applying caricatures stressing the worst features of past revivals.

Some of these stereotypes are surprisingly different from age to age. During the Great Awakening the revival preachers were accused of radical innovation in doctrine and practice. The "Old Light" antirevivalists did not perceive that the

"New Light" evangelists were simply restoring and reiterating the original Puritan emphasis on live orthodoxy in place of its rationalist erosion in the early eighteenth century. As often happens, yesterday's modernism had become today's dead hand of tradition. In the late twentieth century, on the other hand, proponents of live orthodoxy are most likely to be charged with being out of date and tarred with the brush of fundamentalist obscurantism. Two charges recur in the same form in almost every context, however: revivalism is said to be divisive, and it is accused of fanaticism or "enthusiasm." The first of these accusations is important enough to merit an entire chapter later in this study, weighing its pros and cons. The charge of fanaticism, along with the evidence behind it, is the main subject of this chapter.

"Enthusiasm" has been a code word for the excesses of spurious revival since the days of the Reformation when Luther found his work of rebuilding blocked and discredited by the extremism of some left-wing leaders.[1] Neglect of the written Word and an overdependence on the inspiration and leading of the Holy Spirit seem to be the central weaknesses of the Zwickau prophets and the Anabaptists of Münster. The same pattern was observed and attacked by English Puritan leaders of the revolutionary period in the Seekers, Quakers and other left-wing sects.[2] The etymology of the word *enthusiasm* points to a delusive confidence in certain believers that they "have" or contain God's Spirit to such an extent that their thoughts and actions are inspired and free from the sin and error of ordinary believers. Thus the label *enthusiast* is frequently applied to those who are perfectionist as well as spiritualist in their leaning.

Ronald Knox, in a study of this subject which is both fascinating and at times irritating because of its critical chauvinism, includes a wide range of historical movements under the rubric of enthusiasm: the Corinthian charismatics, the Montanists, Donatists, medieval perfectionists, both the Anabaptists and the magisterial Reformers, the Quakers, the Jansenists, the Quietists, the Moravians and the Wesleyan

Methodists. This rather mixed list effectively shows how false and defective revival can be generalized to discredit genuine movements of awakening. It ranges from groups which are not even Christian, such as the Albigenses, through a number of aberrant forms in order to reduce the standing of the Reformers and the awakeners of the eighteenth century.[3]

The characteristics which Knox ascribes to most enthusiasts include "ultrasupernaturalism" (the expectation that transforming and sanctifying grace should raise all believers above the dullness of ordinary Christianity and create a church of saints); Donatism (separation from the church when it rejects the ultrasupernaturalist ideal to form a sect of pure believers); a bias against sacraments, liturgy, icons and other condescensions to the dim spiritual vision of most churchmembers; a man-centered emphasis on piety which loses sight of the central glory of God; a tendency to ignore or despise the faculty of reason and the normal fabric of human society and culture; an unbalanced emphasis on miracles and ecstatic or charismatic behavior; and a chiliastic expectation that the end of history is at hand. Knox traces all of these deviations to one central error, the notion that grace destroys and replaces nature rather than perfecting and ennobling it.[4]

This error may express itself either in a mystical or Platonic enthusiasm which takes grace and salvation for granted, or in an "evangelical" enthusiasm which places the question of salvation in the center of its concern. Knox admits that evangelical enthusiasm is usually found to have an Augustinian theological base, since he feels that Augustine's anti-Pelagianism overstressed the distance between nature and grace and "darkened ... the outline of St. Paul's world picture."[5] This insight into the Augustinian influence on the tradition of live orthodoxy, which I believe to be correct, should have alerted Knox to the presence of a great deal of evangelical enthusiasm in some segments of Catholic mys-

tical spirituality that he chose to overlook in his effort to discredit gently a number of the kindred spirits among evangelical Protestants. And yet Knox's analysis does contain a
good deal of useful medicine for the defects in the Protestant awakening tradition, as we shall see, although it is rather
disquieting to see him profess that an attack on reformers
and awakeners of the church is his most important work.

Another significant attack on revival as enthusiasm, much
earlier and far less moderate, is Charles Chauncy's *Seasonable Thoughts on the State of Religion in New England*,
issued in 1743 as a broadside against the Great Awakening.
Chauncy manages to find instances in the awakening of
nearly every form of spiritual pathology in the church's history. Chauncy felt that the entire thrust of the awakening fell
into the classic pattern of enthusiasm feared by New Englanders since the trial of Anne Hutchinson in Boston in the
1630s: an unguarded stress on the immediate witness of the
Spirit and an antinomian stress on justification to the neglect
of sanctification and good works. In his view the awakened
masses were being induced to rest content with an emotional
experience which did not result in life transformation and
the production of the fruits of the Spirit.

Chauncy felt that an unusually large number of those professing conversion were falling away from the faith soon
afterward and that those who did not apostatize were puffed
up with pride, contemptuous of the rest of the church including "unconverted" ministers, and full of spiritual intoxi-
cation leading to uncontrolled celebration and dependence
on visions and trances. The order of the church was being
broken up at every level. Worship services were chaotic, lay
people were preaching and exhorting, and itinerant evangelists were invading other men's parishes and undermining
their pastoral authority.

Chauncy accused the revival preachers of manipulating
the populace emotionally through hellfire preaching and
propagating a number of theological errors in their evangel-

istic work: Donatism; separatism; presumptuous dependence on the Holy Spirit and despising the use of means including the Bible, scholarship and reason; and insisting that
a knowledge of the time of one's conversion was essential
to assurance, and assurance necessary to salvation. Chauncy
felt that these items were not incidental blemishes on the
awakening but essential elements in its nature, and that the
spread of these aberrations was so rapid and powerful that
it must almost be attributed to demonic agency.[6]

It is obvious that Chauncy's attack voices a number of objections to the evangelical tradition that have become so
deeply rooted in the American subconscious that they are
like conditioned reflexes. This is remarkable since Chauncy's work did not obtain a fraction of the popular attention
gained by Jonathan Edwards's answers to his critique. We
may conclude that Chauncy is relevant to the continuing
attitudes among American churchpeople, not because of the
influence of his work, but because he is describing a constantly recurring pattern of aberrations in the history of
American awakenings.

With the hindsight afforded by history we know that some
of Chauncy's complaint issued out of his own incipient
rationalism, which moved increasingly from Puritan Calvinism toward Unitarianism in subsequent decades. But Edwards took Chauncy's complaint seriously. Where he could
not contest Chauncy's findings, he incorporated them and
restated them more strongly. Perhaps one reason Chauncy's
book failed to sell was that Edwards's *Thoughts on the Revival in New England* and *Religious Affections* reiterated
everything that was valid in Chauncy's critique and focused
it to heal the defects of the awakening. These works are a
model of evangelical self-criticism.

It is not too strong a statement to contend that the whole
career of evangelicalism in America would have been
cleansed of its distinctive scandals if Edwards had remained
alive in the memory of the revivalists. In the analysis which

follows, therefore, I have made a generous use of Edwards's critique of the pathology of awakenings. I have attempted to distill out of his work a summary textbook on the dangers of diluted and counterfeit revival. I hope this summary will remain in the foreground of the church's mind as it confronts future movements of renewal and that Evangelicals will especially remember when they try to understand the church's resistance to their own movement and seek for keys to unlock that resistance. I have reordered Edwards's material within the triple framework of negative elements in Christian experience already unfolded in chapter three and have amplified it where necessary with other biblical and theological insights.

The Flesh and the World as Factors in Aberrant Revival

In answering Chauncy's charge that the awakening had so many defects that it must be essentially destructive, Edwards had to explain how an outpouring of God's grace could result in so many works of darkness. How could a season of spiritual growth produce so many weeds? Edwards found one explanation for the aberrations of revival periods in the concept of *mixtures of grace and carnality* in the subjects of revival. Indwelling sin is a constant factor in earthly human experience, he argues, and it may erupt in spectacular ways at the time of conversion. It might appear that the outpouring of the Spirit should quench the fire of sin, and this is certainly true in some measure. But there are times when that outpouring causes sin to flare up like a fire which has just been drenched in kerosene. Sin, rather than being quenched, is merely diverted into new channels.

The convert who has turned his back on the patterns of the flesh which are common in the world may develop new and sublimated patterns of sin which are largely unconscious but extremely destructive, ugly forms of *spiritual flesh*, or *fleshly spirituality*.[7] As John of the Cross points out, the seven deadly sins of the non-Christian have their spiritual counterparts within the growing Christian, as the gravitational field of self-centeredness seizes and bends the elements of the new life into old carnal patterns.[8] New Christians may envy the spiritual gifts of others and covet them. They may become preoccupied with the emotional side effects of Christian experience and lapse into spiritual gluttony, lusting after joy and ignoring its giver and the responsibility of an obedient walk of faith. Wrath may find its counterpart in censorious judgment. But the most dangerous form of religious flesh is spiritual pride.

Edwards takes up the effects of pride on the aftermath of revival in a classic section of *Thoughts on the Revival in New England*. He judges it to be the greatest single cause of the miscarriage of revivals because it affects those who are most zealous to promote them:

> This is the main door by which the devil comes into the hearts of those who are zealous for the advancement of religion ... the chief inlet of smoke from the bottomless pit, to darken the mind and mislead the judgment ... the main handle by which the devil has hold of religious persons, and the chief source of all the mischief that he introduces, to clog and hinder a work of God.[9]

Pride drastically hinders revival because it padlocks the spirit, shutting the soul off in its own darkness and blocking it from dealing not only with pride itself (for "those that are spiritually proud, have a high conceit of these two things, viz. their *light*, and their *humility*")[10] but with every other area of the flesh. Because spiritual pride is so secretive, it is hard to detect except through its effects. Edwards proceeds therefore to analyze these effects, noting that they are generally opposite counterparts to the fruits of the Spirit:

> Spiritual pride is very apt to suspect others; whereas an humble saint is most jealous of himself, he is so suspicious of nothing in the world as he is of his own heart. The spiritually proud person is apt to find fault with other saints, that they are low in grace; and to be much in observ-

ing how cold and dead they are; and being quick to discern
and take notice of their deficiencies. But the eminently
humble Christian has so much to do at home . . . that he is
not apt to be very busy with other hearts. . . . He is apt to
esteem others better than himself, and is ready to hope
that there is nobody but what has more love and thankful-
ness to God than he, and cannot bear to think that others
should bring forth no more fruit to God's honour than he.[11]
Pride magnifies the faults of other Christians and diminishes
their graces, while it diminishes the faults and magnifies the
graces of its subject. It is apt to treat the needs of others as
occasions of contempt and laughter rather than as sources
of concern or shock. All of this may seem conventional
enough today until we begin to measure it against the history of American revivalism or the current behavior of both
liberal and conservative leaders.

Under the guise of prophetic righteousness, pride can
move awakened believers to censorious attacks on other
Christians, a lack of meekness in rebuking those who really
need it and a hair-trigger readiness to separate from those
less holy or less orthodox. It can do things to Christians
which make their religion grate painfully on the sensibilities
of fellow believers. It can engender an unholy boldness before God which expresses itself in undue familiarity and
effusive religious talk. It can make people proud to be weird
for Jesus and grateful for the persecution this provokes. As
Edwards says, "Spiritual pride often disposes persons to
singularity in external appearance, to affect a singular way
of speaking, to use a different sort of dialect from others, or
to be singular in voice, countenance, or behaviour."[12] Both
the institutionalized strangeness of Fundamentalism and the
invented strangeness of the Jesus movement come into view
here, along with many things which pass for religious communication on radio. Edwards notes further:

Spiritual pride commonly occasions a certain stiffness and
inflexibility in persons, in their own judgment and their

own way; whereas the eminently humble person, though
he be inflexible in his duty, and in those things wherein
God's honour is concerned ... yet in other things he is of
a pliable disposition ... ready to pay deference to others'
opinions, loves to comply with their inclinations, and has
a heart that is tender and flexible, like a little child.[13]
Dogmatic orthodoxy and heterodoxy, on the other hand, are
generally proud of their inflexibility, mistaking it for conviction.

Edwards goes on to say of the humble person:
And though he will not be a companion with one that is
visibly Christ's enemy ... yet he does not love the appearance of an open separation from visible Christians ... and
will as much as possible shun all appearances of a super-
iority, or distinguishing himself as better than others.[14]
We may note that theological and social singularity, on the
other hand, often function as masks and supports for a weak
ego.

Edwards further points out that "spiritual pride takes great
notice of opposition and injuries that are received, and is apt
to be often speaking of them, and to be much in taking notice
of their aggravations, either with an air of bitterness or contempt."[15] The absence of genuine dialog between conservatives and liberals during this century is usually traceable to
just such mutual contempt. Pride forces believers to either of
two extremes in handling opponents: spiteful polemics or
refusal to dialog. Edwards sees the problem and offers a
motive for a change in behavior:
As spiritual pride disposes persons to assume much to
themselves, so it also disposes them to treat others with
neglect. ... Indeed to spend a great deal of time in jan-
gling and warm debates about religion, is not the way to
propagate, but to hinder it. ... But yet we ought to be very
careful that we do not refuse to discourse with men, with
any appearance of a supercilious neglect, as though we
counted them not worthy to be regarded; on the contrary,

we should condescend to carnal men, as Christ has con-
descended to us, to bear with our unteachableness and
stupidity.[16]

It has been said of some religious leaders that they have the
unusual ability to be able to strut sitting down. Against this
pattern of behavior Edwards sets out an ideal portrait of
Christian humility:

The eminently humble Christian is as it were clothed with
lowliness, mildness, meekness, gentleness of spirit and
behaviour, and with a soft, sweet, condescending, winning air and deportment; these things are just like garments to him, he is clothed all over with them. . . . Pure
Christian humility has no such thing as roughness, or contempt, or fierceness, or bitterness in its nature; it makes a
person like a little child, harmless and innocent, that none
need to be afraid of; or like a lamb, destitute of all bitterness, wrath, anger, and clamour; agreeable to Eph. iv. 31.
. . . [Ministers] ought indeed . . . not to be gentle and moderate in searching and awakening the conscience, but
should be sons of thunder. . . . Yet they should do it without judging particular persons, leaving it to conscience
and the Spirit of God to make the particular application.
But all their conversation should savour of nothing but
lowliness and good-will, love and pity to all mankind; so
that such a spirit should be like a sweet odour diffused
around them wherever they go. They should be like lions
to guilty consciences, but like lambs to men's persons.[17]

Unfortunately this description is that of a finished saint with
some years of mellowing and maturing, and not a picture
of a new convert in a religious awakening. But all too often
a pattern of behavior which falls far short of this ideal becomes an institutional norm for religious leadership, so that
we stop striving to grow in this direction as we govern the
church or seek to control and orchestrate a burst of renewal.

Responding to Edwards's analysis from a twentieth-century perspective, we can see that spiritual pathology and

psychopathology are closely intertwined in producing aberrant revival. What we call pride is usually not an expression of serious self-appreciation but a defense mechanism compensating for unconscious feelings of inferiority. A new influx of spiritual life and gifts should ordinarily eliminate the psychological need behind compensatory egoism and thus attenuate the sin of pride in the believer. But where there is any tinge of guilt or insecurity present in the believer (and Evangelical Christianity can create them easily unless the depth of its challenge is held in exquisite balance with the doctrine of atonement), any unhealed traumas stemming from past rejections or any shade of hidden alienation from God, the graces which should become a support for the believer's legitimate self-regard are transformed into a shield for sin or a defense against inferiority feelings. Orthodoxies of one sort of another, Christian experience and spiritual gifts can all be abused in this manner, and much of the pathology of revival springs from this mismanagement of grace.

Much of the contention and lack of charity in the wake of revival is simply the necessary reflex of the soul which secretly doubts itself and seeks relief in casting doubt on others, as Cotton Mather long ago suggested:

> The zeal of many is but a meer composition with conscience, for some favour unto some detestable ungodliness.... A man does not keep his heart with all diligence; does not walk in the fear of God continually ... does not lead a life of communion with heaven; does not love his neighbour, and seek his wellbeing, and rejoice in it. And now he compounds with his conscience, to make a mighty noise about something or other, that is not essential to Christianity. Oh! the deceits, the deceits, of wretched hypocrisy![18]

Along with the *mixture* of flesh and Spirit in the experience of revival, Edwards focuses on the *degeneration* of experience as a source of aberrant revival. Some religious experience is not gracious at all. It does not emanate from the Holy

Spirit and it does not touch the heart; it issues merely from some source within human consciousness and acts upon the surface of the imagination. But even when Christian experience involves genuine contact with God which penetrates and transforms the heart in some measure, the vitality of grace may gradually and insensibly decay even though a person remains constantly assured that he or she is walking with God in full spiritual vigor. The convert who began new life filled with love toward God and others may soon lapse into a state of deception, filled with projected self-congratulation and "spiritual" self-interest. This is particularly likely to occur when a convert receives little instruction after initial commitment, or when the instruction received neglects the dimension of sanctification or focuses too narrowly on interior emotional states and fails to stress the responsibility for active practical love directed toward others, including social concern and action.[19]

Charles Chauncy was therefore correct in calling for spiritual reality rather than emotional fireworks and for a perseverence beyond conversion in the direction of sanctification and good works. Edwards incorporated Chauncy's critique and passed it on to the American church in a form which would have prevented the abuse of cheap grace in American revivalist culture if it had continued normative for later evangelicalism. But later revivalists ignored his insight into the essential unity of the faculties of understanding, will and emotion, which he saw as three branches diverging from a common trunk, the center of personality controlling every aspect of the soul.[20] Edwards based his theology of revival on the truth that "out of the heart are the issues of life." Later evangelicalism lost his vision of the heart and disintegrated the unity of the faculties to form three different false pieties: one based on emotional tastes divorced from works and theological depth, another based on will power and works, and a third consisting of notional orthodoxy. It is not hard to sort out these strains in nineteenth-century Christianity or to identify descendants in the current religious scene.

Christian experience can only be kept from degeneration by an insistence that it penetrate the heart and thus transform all of the personality by touching it at the root. It is significant that Scripture guards its presentation of normative Christian experience by balancing affective, intellectual and volitional parameters against one another. A hollow and heartless works religion is rejected: "If I give away all I have, and if I deliver my body to be burned, but have not love, I gain nothing" (1 Cor. 13:3). The eyes of the heart must be enlightened in faith and love; and yet on the other hand, as James makes clear, the heart has not really been touched unless there is an outflow of loving action (Jas. 1:22-27; 2:14-26). Neither action nor emotions can validate a piety which is not anchored and nurtured in sound and comprehensive doctrinal understanding.[21] Thus any movement of awakening which does not aim steadily at a comprehensive renewal of the heart registering at all these levels of the personality is bound to miscarry.

There is one further intrusion of the flesh into the course of awakenings which should be noted: counterfeit revival in which the flesh simulates the effects and results of the Holy Spirit without consciously intending to do so. This may occur simply as imitative herd behavior, in which numbers of false conversions follow in the wake of those which are genuine because Christianity is suddenly in vogue. As Edwards notes:

> In the spring innumerable flowers and young fruits appear flourishing and bid fair, that afterwards drop off and come to nothing.... So a shower causes mushrooms [toadstools] suddenly to spring up, as well as good plants to grow, and blasts many fruits as well as bring[s] others to perfection. In the spring of the year when the birds sing, the frogs and toads also croak.[22]

This pattern is familiar from the ministry of Jesus, and it is clear that the apostasy of his temporary followers does not discredit the genuineness of those who persevered.

It is possible, however, for a revivalist in deliberate fashion to generate counterfeit revival by emotional manipulation of an audience. Intentional deceit is not the problem, but defective theology. If evangelists conceive of the rebirth of their hearers as a responsibility resting solely on them, so that instead of being midwives to works of sovereign grace they must somehow convince human wills to turn to God by every means at their disposal, then they will quite naturally make use of any means which works. A theology of conversion like Charles Finney's, which conceives of revival as galvanizing the emotions of an audience in order to move their wills toward obedience, will necessarily lead to manipulation: multiple repetitions of hymns during lengthy invitations, hard-sell salesmanship aimed at immediate decisions and the rest of the trappings of much post-Finneyan evangelism.[23] If these means are not used, after all, there may be some who will fail to decide and be lost.

We cannot discredit mass evangelism which uses this style simply because it has become a traditional model. But we can predict that broad areas within the church are likely to resist paying very much attention to our evangelism unless it clears up these surface blemishes, evolves a style which is more credible and more dignified, and restores evangelism to its proper place within the constellation of factors involved in total church renewal.

When the influence of the world on revival in America is mentioned, it is usually these manipulative aspects of mass evangelism which are in view. More technically speaking, the effect of corporate flesh upon revival is, first, to spread the carnal admixtures in its development very rapidly from one locale to another and, second, to limit and condition the thrust of the awakening by concealing and preserving large areas of sin which are culturally normative in a given region. Not just individuals, but nations and smaller social groupings have their own patterns of characteristic flesh which are extremely resistant to detection and change. These patterns are so universal within a local culture that they are as un-detectable as the air we breathe and just as powerful in their effects. They are also socially reinforced, and often defended and legitimated by local mores, mythology, politics and even religious rationales. Consequently, they are very hard to penetrate and transform, especially if the tool used is an individualistic and moralistic style of revivalism.

It is hard to generalize about a whole nation as large and complex as our own, but it might not be far wrong to say that the characteristic flesh of America is compounded of cov-etousness, gluttony, egocentric libertarianism and pride, all of which have been selectively bred into our culture because of the types of sinful people we have attracted and the be-havior which our political and economic system has stressed and rewarded. It is true that all of these vices are simply distortions of virtues which are part of the American ideal (ambition, enterprise, freedom, self-respect). But our im-mediate tendency to defend ourselves when accused of these defects is usually a sign of that unconscious subjection to universal sin which corporate flesh involves. The Chris-tian cultures of other nations, especially those of third-world Evangelical churches, can easily detect the fact that most American Christians have their lives organized around the kingdom of business success and not the kingdom of God.

Why has American revivalism failed to breed these pat-terns out of American churchmembers? Largely because the ideals of the two kingdoms have been subtly fused together in a gradual process of compromise, mutual support and en-culturation which results in an uneasy symbiosis. The ques-tion is often asked why the Evangelical religion of the Bible Belt in southern America failed to eradicate racism despite its relatively pervasive influence on southern life. The impli-cation is drawn that "being born again" in an evangelistic meeting really changes very little in the lives of converts, and sometimes it is even said that racist Christians cannot be regenerate. Of course this is nonsense, unless we are prepared to pronounce as unregenerate every Christian who is imperfectly sanctified. But many areas of sin are virtually invisible within particular cultures. As Reinhold Niebuhr has shown, we are all guilty of corporate sin in ways which are almost too numerous to chart.

Once this is recognized, however, it is the responsibility of Christians (and especially Evangelicals) to turn the spotlight of the Word of God on the corporate flesh of their region and call for repentance among Christians who should become the vanguard of cultural transformation. The same spotlight should be directed at non-Christians in the work of evangelism; the "invisible sins" of a society should be presented as material for repentance along with those which are more obvious to the natural conscience. If this kind of assault could be made by Christian leaders on the patterns of flesh which up to now have been accepted simply as normal modes of behavior, how much blocked energy could be released within Western Christianity!

Satan as a Causative Agent in Aberrant Revival

A great deal of the pathology, confusion and opposition which have arisen in connection with revival movements can be understood purely in terms of visible, immanent causes. Individual and corporate flesh are certainly the main agents here, adulterating the work among its Christian adherents and reacting against both its virtues and defects among Christian opponents and unbelievers. And since religious renewal is a profound agent for social and psychological change, it is also often an occasion of disorder and resistance. Those who promote revival are not always animated by the Spirit, and those who oppose it are not necessarily motivated by flesh. Granting all of these qualifications, however, we must go beyond this to recognize that there are

satanic factors at work in the pattern of every revival movement, and that their effects are apparent among both its opponents and proponents. Chauncy was not wrong in suggesting that the aberrations of the Great Awakening spread too
fast to be attributed simply to human weakness, although he
failed to suspect that his own blindness to the awakening's
values may also in part have been supernaturally induced.

As we have already indicated, Scripture portrays Satan
as the adversary of God and his kingdom, as a liar, a murderer
and "the accuser of the brethren." The Revelation of John
strips away the surface of history to display the demonic
force opposing the church as a dragon pursuing the bride
of Christ into the wilderness, attempting to drown her in a
river of lies poured out of his mouth (Rev. 12:1-17). The dragon is presented as a motivating power behind persecuting
governments and false religions, both of which are satanic
instruments of war against the kingdom of God. The apostles
sensed that in working for the expansion of the kingdom they
were hand-wrestling with personal agents of spiritual darkness. Both the Gospels and the history in Acts record many
occasions when this hidden struggle breaks out into the
open. Paul teaches that the strength of the sin's grip on
people's lives is reinforced by an underlying demonic power
and that their blindness in resisting the gospel is due in part
to a satanic veil cast over their minds (2 Cor. 4:4). Other passages in the Gospels and the Epistles indicate that demonic
control and direction is possible even in the thoughts and
acts of believers through unmortified areas of the flesh (Mt.
16:23; Eph. 4:27). John and Paul both teach that the energy
and direction behind false religion is demonic (1 Jn. 4:1-3;
2 Cor. 11:13-15).

With these New Testament insights into the underlying
struggle involved in the growth-spread of the rule of Christ,
we can discern demonic strategy reinforcing and directing
the fleshly motivation of many opponents of the kingdom in
the Old Testament. Another hand besides Cain's is active in

the murder of Abel. Another mind besides Pharaoh's directs
the slaughter of the innocents intended to murder Moses, as
later in the case of Herod. Saul's murderous rage against
David is caused by "an evil spirit from the Lord," and so is
the religiosity of the false prophets in Ahab's time (1 Kings
22:19-23). While it is true that in many of these instances
Scripture expressly states that the evil spirits themselves
were sent by and ultimately under the control of God, so that
their activity could only accomplish God's purposes by ex-
hibiting his glory and serving as grist for the mills of sanctification, it is also true that the powers of darkness are engaged in real warfare against the expansion of the kingdom
of God and that their strategy is designed to limit and to defeat any movement of renewal within the kingdom.

A good deal of the church's history becomes somewhat
more intelligible if biblical principles for the discernment
of spirits are employed. They must be applied with exquisite
caution. But some rather tumultuous periods of renewal,
counterinfiltration and counterattack can only be sensibly
interpreted with their use. Otherwise the scene is as confusing as a football game in which half the players are invisible.

Jonathan Edwards sets down a foundational principle for
understanding the interior and exterior problems of revival
movements: revivals of religion are advances in the progress
of the kingdom of God which inevitably occasion countermovements on the part of the powers of darkness. Periods
of renewal are therefore times of vigorous activity both
among agents of God and agents of darkness. Behind the
scenes of earthly history in awakening eras we can dimly
discern the massing and movement of the invisible troops of
darkness and of light.[24] While this may seem fanciful to anyone in the twentieth century, it is simply realistic according
to the biblical world picture, in which the angels of God are
portrayed as locked in combat with the occupying powers of
darkness at critical junctures in the unfolding of world history.[25]

The strategy of darkness against revival is threefold: (1) to destroy the work either by persecution or by accusation which will discredit it and limit its growth, (2) to infiltrate the work and reinforce its defects in order to provide more evidence for accusation, and (3) to inspire counterfeit revival which may deceive the elect and further confuse and alienate the onlooking world.

The first of these tactics, direct attack upon a renewal movement, is exemplified by countless situations in history. There has never been a revival which has not been severely attacked. Every advance of the kingdom of God has occasioned an explosion of conflict and contention. In occupied territory in which the gospel has not yet penetrated or has never taken hold vigorously, this counterattack usually takes the form of outright persecution, ending either in death or in serious personal losses and restrictions. The initial surge of Christianity within the Roman Empire, the battle for the reformation of Western Catholicism in the sixteenth and seventeenth centuries, and the present situation of Christians in the Iron-Curtain countries and in some Islamic areas are a few major examples. Along with this overt persecution, Christianity in these situations has also had to deal with persistent misunderstandings and misrepresentations. Often there are plausible, immanent causes for the cloud of accusations. The early Christians who were accused of atheism, incest and cannibalism, for instance, were holding secret and closed meetings. In baptism and communion there were ample reasons for their unbelieving neighbors to misunderstand their practices. But the intensity, the bitterness and the strategic usefulness of the charges all have a diabolical smell about them.

Where the gospel has taken substantial hold in a culture, there is less chance that the opposition to a work of renewal will take the form of overt persecution. Just as the spread of civilization gradually eliminates or restricts to a manageable level the predators, pests and diseases in a region, the progress of the church's mission restrains and drives back the occupying darkness and makes a clearing in the world's jungle. The Constantinian establishment achieved such a clearing for Western Catholicism, but Augustine's endorsement of the corporal discipline of heretics left room for a new growth of demonic resistance at the time of the Reformation. When the Protestant and Catholic forces agreed to renounce their pretensions to theocratic discipline and joined forces with the Enlightenment in promoting an open market of ideas in the Western world, the largest clearing of relative safety for the kingdom of God in the world's history was established. Now at least in part of the world the gospel can move across the boundaries of nations and minds with relative impunity.

Even here, however, the church and every movement which renews it are subject to the milder forms of demonic attack. When they are not directly misrepresented and misunderstood, they are mysteriously ignored, encased in an insulating wall of neglect which restricts their impact upon the rest of society. This sort of quiet opposition to renewal is not confined to the world, of course. It appears in its most mischievous forms within the church, where Christians of differing parties have their natural tendency to ignore and stereotype one another quietly reinforced by the real enemy. Those who have unintentionally become the bitterest opponents of renewal in the church have often been professing Christians usually either to the right or the left of live orthodoxy. Sometimes the opposition has come from both sides at once. Established confessional orthodoxy lends itself to the interests of darkness in these encounters whenever it accepts Satan's estimate and mistakes a sound movement for a Trojan horse with attractive camouflage.

Counterattack against revival can also take the form of psychological assault upon the leaders and subjects of revival. It is characteristically hard to sort out the various physical, psychological and spiritual factors involved in this kind of attack. But where interior accusation and oppression are apparently part of a concerted strategy against revival, and when these come with a particular intensity, we should at least suspect satanic involvement.

The dampening impact of the depression and suicide of one participant in the 1734 Northampton awakening is a case in point.[26] Edwards analyzes the interweaving of causes in this sort of attack with a degree of psychological insight which is remarkable for the eighteenth century:

[Some] have often suffered many needless distresses of thought, in which Satan probably has a great hand, to entangle them, and block up their way. Sometimes the distemper of melancholy has been evidently mixed. . . . One knows not how to deal with such persons; they turn every thing that is said to them the wrong way, and most to their own disadvantage. There is nothing that the devil seems to make so great a handle of, as a melancholy humour; unless it be the real corruption of the heart.[27]

The second demonic strategy for the defeat of revival, discrediting a movement by stirring up and reinforcing its defects, is one which Edwards analyzed in great detail. Edwards describes the devil as using the momentum of carnal zeal in the agents of revival somewhat as a Japanese wrestler uses the motion of his opponent to secure his defeat:

If we look back into the history of the church of God in past ages, we may observe that it has been a common device of the Devil to overset a revival of religion, when he finds he can keep men quiet and secure no longer, then to drive 'em to excesses and extravagances. He holds them back as long as he can, but when he can do it no longer, then he'll push 'em on, and if possible, run 'em upon their heads.[28]

Much of this opposition simply involves blinding Christians to the operation of their own flesh, particularly in the area of pride, and reinforcing the strength of carnal drives and responses. When opposition to the awakening rises, a great advantage can be gained if proponents of revival can be de-

ceived into responding with anger and denunciation, publicly ruling their opponents out of the kingdom in the manner
of James Davenport, Gilbert Tennent and George Whitefield
in the Great Awakening. This will set up a feedback cycle
in which each side's resistance to the other is increased, and
the effects of the revival will be contained and discredited.

Ironically, if the revival leaders in this kind of situation
even intimate that there is fleshly and demonic motivation
behind their opposition, they are likely to fan the flames
of resistance and decrease the possibility of communication
and healing. If the Accuser can persuade the agents of renewal to accept his picture of their opponents and to broadcast this caricature to the world at large, this is quite as helpful to his purposes as a frontal attack on their own weaknesses.

Edwards observes that the devil's tares sown in the field
of renewal can mislead both opponents and adherents.

> I don't know but we shall be in danger by and by, after our
> eyes are fully opened to see our errors, to go to contrary ex-
> tremes. The Devil has driven the pendulum far beyond its
> proper point of rest; and when he has carried it to the ut-
> most length that he can, and it begins by its own weight to
> swing back, he probably will set in, and drive it with the
> utmost fury the other way; and so give us no rest; and if
> possible prevent our settling in a proper medium.[29]

> The Devil in driving things to these extremes ... has, I
> believe, had in view a twofold mischief hereafter, in the
> issue of things; one with respect to those that are more cold
> in religion ... to tempt them entirely to reject the whole
> work as being all nothing but delusion and distraction.
> And another is with respect to those that have been very
> warm and zealous ... to sink them down in unbelief and
> darkness. The time is coming, I doubt not, when the bigger
> part of them will be convinced of their errors; and then
> probably the Devil take advantage to lead them into a
> dreadful wilderness, and to puzzle and confound them

about their own experiences and the experiences of others; and to make them to doubt of many things that they ought not to doubt of, and even to tempt them with atheistical thoughts.[30]

Anyone who has dealt with the burned-over aftermath of the extremes within the Jesus movement and Charismatic renewal can confirm this estimate.

The third strategy of darkness in opposing revival, the intrusion of counterfeit movements to capture those seeking salvation and further discredit genuine renewal, is also especially apparent today. The Jesus movement, which was at times a patchwork of carnal religiosity, has been followed by a circus of occult and Eastern sects promising spiritual fullness and reality. Campuses which were recently penetrated by a new Evangelical witness are now drowning in mystical propaganda. In some cases this has had the expected effect, and current Evangelical renewal is dismissed as part of the wave of Aquarian religiosity and superstitious nostalgia. This is a familiar pattern from past history. The early fathers who discerned Satan behind the waves of persecution they suffered saw his hand also in the gnostic counterfeits multiplying around the church, and even in the mystery religions which caricatured its theme of regeneration through the dying and rising God. This explanation may itself seem facile and superstitious. But the fact remains that the apostolic writers regarded false religion as an antichristian weapon forged by the powers of darkness and expected its growth to parallel that of the expanding church.[31] It may be unsophisticated to reject their guidance.

Theological Factors in Aberrant Revival
Even where the flesh, the world and the devil are relatively inactive in distorting or resisting an awakening, the adoption of false principles is likely to upset its course. And bad theology can make a work extremely vulnerable to the flesh and the devil. Thus a shallow understanding of sin and the

leaven of asceticism have deeply deformed American evangelicalism since the early nineteenth century. The revivals of Billy Sunday were real and powerful manifestations of the Holy Spirit according to living witnesses who worked in them, but they produced Christians who were shallow, moralistic and culture-bound. For the purity of a revival is intimately related to its theological substance. A deep work cannot be done without the sharp instruments of truth. Unless revival involves and issues in theological reformation, its energy will be contained and its fruits will not last.

The Charismatic renewal, as we have seen, is programmed to divide the church unless the old Pentecostal theology is broadened and modified. There are other disquieting aspects woven through the movement which disturb even its leaders and adherents. Thus while the Catholic Charismatic sector is in many aspects among the most balanced and beautiful in this renewal, no one doubts that eventually hard theological issues will have to be faced: justification, assurance, the veneration of saints and all the other machinery of popular piety, and the question of ultimate authority.

Among the distinctive emphases of glossolalic Christianity is one which has caused a great deal of difficulty in past awakenings and which continues to be problematic today: the doctrine that the gift of prophecy is still to be expected and enjoyed by the church. It seems difficult to frame a very strong biblical argument for limiting prophetic utterance to the apostolic period. And yet the church in later eras has repeatedly found that when it goes beyond the canon of Scripture to recognize new revelations, it soon finds itself dealing with severe problems. Outbreaks of fanatical enthusiasm in church history have always been accompanied by a belief in contemporary revelations of the Spirit. An early instance of such enthusiasm was Montanism, the second-century sect which practiced glossolalia and predicted the imminent return of Christ to the town of Pepusa in Asia Minor. This became the first major instance of a prophecy which failed, a recurring phenomenon which often has traumatic effects on the Christians involved.[32]

During the sixteenth century, the Zwickau prophets attacked Luther's reform with a fanatical zeal they attributed to the Spirit's leading, and another group of enthusiasts attempted to establish a theocratic commune complete with polygamy and a strategy for conquest by the sword. Some Reformation groups which began by stressing the contemporary revelation of the Spirit soon ended by treating the Scripture as an addendum which was more or less unnecessary once a Christian obtained direct access to the mind of God through the Spirit.[33] This pattern recurred during the Revolutionary period in seventeenth-century England. Left-wing prophets claiming to be led by the Spirit scandalized conservative Puritans by marching naked into towns proclaiming their downfall, and some of these so-called prophets wandered into delusions like that of James Naylor, who claimed that the Spirit had assured him that he was Jesus Christ.[34]

In order to guard against the prophetic pretensions of the enthusiasts and the Roman Catholic appeal to the guidance of the Spirit in her magisterium, the Reformers and the Puritans strongly guarded their doctrine of the Holy Spirit by a stress on the objectivity of the written Word. In the Reformed tradition, *revelation* was confined to Scripture, although it was acknowledged that *illumination* by the Holy Spirit was necessary for the understanding and application of the Word. Alarmed by the enthusiasm of Anne Hutchinson's group in New England and the left-wing sectaries in the mother country, most Puritans sought to rule out new revelations of the Spirit, although there were streams within Scottish and American Puritanism which had a livelier view of the contemporary operations of the Spirit.

During the Great Awakening, confronting an outbreak of popular enthusiasm and the embarrassment of Whitefield's claim to be directed by the Holy Spirit, Edwards readily adopted the standard Reformed position against new revelation. In his first sermon on 1 Corinthians 13, he asserts that the gift of love is worth more than all the miraculous and extraordinary operations of the Spirit during the apostolic period and states his opinion that such extraordinary operations have ceased. His analysis of the problems involved in the awakening casts light on our own situation today. In the section devoted to this matter in the *Thoughts on the Revival in New England,* he rejects new revelations, guidance by motions or impulses which are thought to be from the Spirit, and even direction by scriptural texts which seem to come to the mind with the impress of the Spirit but are interpreted out of context and import a new meaning not rationally derived from their basic sense.

Edwards warns that unless the church is rigorously critical of such procedures it will suffer serious damage in several ways. People who begin by being open to extrabiblical revelation will give Satan an opportunity to wean them gradually away from Scripture and establish himself as ultimate authority. Persons who suppose they are immediately guided by the Spirit will be incorrigible when they fall into error, since they suppose that they are inspired. Prophecy will fail and darkness will result. Individuals who suppose that they have assurance that a particular prayer will be answered because they experience the Spirit's assistance as they make it will be thrown into despair. Christians will do jarring and unseemly things without considering the impression they are making on others, including unbelievers, because they believe they are moved by the Spirit. Those who are seized with a strong spiritual concern will give themselves over to relentless and imprudent activity without rational control. Those experiencing strong emotions of joy or concern will express these to others without discretion. Leaders will abandon careful planning and trust themselves to the immediate direction of the Spirit without regard for future consequences. All will be filled with a powerful but indiscreet zeal which has its roots in the flesh and is even tinged with the interference of the devil, who can use this to discredit both revival and Christianity.[35]

The common denominator of all of these aberrations is a reliance on subjective experience divorced from the objective control of reason and the written Word of God. The neglect of rationality is a prime example of the central error of all enthusiasm according to Ronald Knox, the idea that grace destroys nature rather than perfecting it. Christians who block out their minds in the process of attuning themselves to the Spirit are trying to replace an essential human attribute by the gift of the Spirit which is meant to transform that faculty, not to replace it. To relinquish the guiding and superintending function of the intellect in our experience seems pious at first, but in the end this course dehumanizes us by turning us into either dependent robots waiting to be programmed by the Spirit's guidance or whimsical enthusiasts blown about by our hunches and emotions. God has provided us with the ability to gather information and to make rational decisions in the light of this information in conformity with his revealed will in Scripture. Any method of guidance which habitually detours around reason is crippling and dehumanizing. It will lead to indecision, hesitation to act where the imperatives of action are plain to reason informed by Scripture, and inability to plan properly and to maintain or adapt plans when made.

If the direction of our lives is reduced to a function of reason alone, however, there is something wanting, something which does not harmonize well with Paul's description of Christians as those "who are led by the Spirit of God" (Rom. 8:14). The Christian is then reduced to a closed and isolated rational computer, making decisions without any conscious sense of the Spirit's leading and approval, which does not agree either with Scripture or with common Christian experience. Edwards is aware of this and moves as far as he can to balance his stress on reason with an emphasis on the illumination of the Spirit.

> There is a more excellent way in which the Spirit leads the
> sons of God, that natural men cannot have; and that is, by
> inclining them to do the will of God, and go in the shining
> path of truth and Christian holiness, from a holy, heaven-
> ly disposition, which the Spirit of God gives them, and
> which inclines and leads them to those things that are ex-
> cellent and agreeable to God's mind, whereby they "are
> transformed by the renewing of their minds, and prove
> what is that good, and acceptable, and perfect will of God,"
> Rom. xii. 2 .... The Spirit of God enlightens them with
> respect to their duty, by making their eye single and pure,
> whereby the whole body is full of light. The sanctifying
> influence of the Spirit of God rectifies the taste of the soul,
> whereby it savours those things that are holy and agreeable
> to God's mind; and, like one of a distinguishing taste, it
> chooses those things that are good and wholesome, and re-
> jects those that are evil. The sanctified ear tries words, and
> the sanctified heart tries actions, as the mouth tastes meat.
> And thus the Spirit of God leads and guides the meek in his
> way, agreeable to his promises; he enables them to under-
> stand the commands and counsels of his word, and right-
> ly to apply them.[36]

Edwards argues that the reception of new revelations is not a
very high spiritual function. It is more suited to a secretary
than to a saint. Thus his formula for the leading of the Spirit
might be summed up as *communion without communication,* or at least without the addition of communicated data
in addition to the content and implications of the written
Word:

> Why cannot we be contented with the divine oracles, that
> holy, pure word of God, which we have in such abundance
> and clearness, now since the canon of Scripture is com-
> pleted? ... Why should any desire a higher kind of inter-
> course with heaven, than by having the Holy Spirit given
> in his sanctifying influences, infusing and exciting grace

and holiness, love and joy, which is the highest kind of intercourse that the saints and angels in heaven have with God, and the chief excellency of the glorified man Christ Jesus?[37]

Edwards does not deal directly with the gift of prophecy, but what he might say about it can be deduced pretty clearly from what he says about the Spirit's direction in preaching:

The gracious and most excellent assistance of the Spirit of God in praying and preaching, is not by immediately suggesting words to the apprehension, which may be with a cold, dead heart; but by warming the heart, and filling it with a great sense of things to be spoken, and with holy affections, that these may suggest words. Thus indeed the Spirit of God may be said, indirectly and mediately, to suggest words to us, and indite our petitions for us, and to teach the preacher what to say; he fills the heart, and that fills the mouth. . . . But since there is no immediate suggesting of words from the Spirit of God to be expected or desired, they who neglect and despise study and premeditation, in order to a preparation for the pulpit . . . are guilty of presumption.[38]

Much of what in glossolalic circles is assumed to be prophecy (words addressed to the body as first-person utterances from God himself) might better be explained in terms of the process Edwards described. Such an understanding would preserve the integrity and supreme authority of Scripture and guard it from being undercut by an ever-increasing volume of new revelations. Most of these prophecies have a timbre which differs from the ring of unalloyed truth in Scripture and which argues for something less than biblical inspiration in their creation. A steady diet of semi-inspired prophetic counsels weakens the palate (and perhaps the appetite) for the Word of God, unless such counsels are distinctly subordinated to Scripture.

There is one way of handling prophetic gifts which can be very dangerous and in fact destructive of the ordinary Chris-

tian's relationship with the Holy Spirit. This is the power
structure sometimes found in glossolalic groups, where an
almost infallible authority comes to rest on certain individuals who are assumed to have the gift of prophecy. There
are small groups today which are tight little papacies in
which the will of God must always descend from human
authorities, and this pattern may be at work in some of the
more extended glossolalic ministries as well. Some glossolalic teaching now is emphasizing that believers should subject themselves to the discipline of total obedience to Spirit-
directed elders.

No doubt this has an appearance of wisdom; it is not unlike the monastic pattern of absolute submission to the abbot
which is echoed in the Roman Catholic tradition of spiritual
direction. The monks who did not fully grasp the complete-
ness of the atonement wrought by Christ sought to strap
themselves into the sanctification machine of the monastic
system because they found difficulty in mortifying their
pride by other means. And of course the system worked, but
only when it involved a very saintly and sensitive abbot.
Even then, it brought the person sanctified into closer dependence on human authorities than on the Holy Spirit, who
alone can truly mortify pride and who alone should be our
guide.

In the wrong hands, this practice can be absolutely destructive of a Christian's conscience and personal relationship with God. And it is almost always in the wrong hands.
Many young converts today are extremely open to this sort
of counsel because they are both eager for sanctification and
ignorant of the resources of grace through which it can be
effected. Glossolalic leaders may consider it a valid strategy
to take advantage of this willingness and thus create a host
of shock troops for the advancement of the kingdom. But the
end of this procedure will be exhaustion, disillusionment
and desertion of the troops.

In order to guard against this error, believers should maintain a lively awareness both of their own fallibility and that of all other Christians, especially those in authority. If prophetic gifts and the guidance of the Spirit are acknowledged, they should never be institutionalized. Christians should remain open to the Spirit's direction coming from any part of the body of Christ and should always seek to confirm any course they adopt by reason, Scripture and the underlying witness of the Spirit in their hearts.

Despite all these warnings, however, and beyond all that Edwards says to guard against subjectivism, it is my judgment that it is neither prudent nor biblical to rule out contemporary manifestations of the communication of the Holy Spirit in guidance and in prophetic gifts. Limiting these phenomena to the apostolic age solves some practical problems in the church, but it creates many others. It has an extremely speculative theoretical base which seems to have been derived not from the plain sense of Scripture but from the Reformers' necessity to fight a two-front war against papists and enthusiasts. The Reformers' stress on objectivity has often degenerated into a positive neglect of the doctrine of the Holy Spirit and of dependence on him. This in turn has only led to enthusiastic overreactions. We are not likely to arrive at a mean between deadness and fanaticism unless we give to the Holy Spirit exactly that place which the Scripture gives him as the architect of the kingdom of God.

There is a dimension of openness to the Holy Spirit which allows him the sovereign right to intervene and override the rational guidance system, to go beyond the written revelation if he chooses, which must be preserved, or else we will fail to do justice both to Scripture and to our common experience. The normal conduct of our ministries must be under the careful control of the sanctified reason reflecting on the Word. But often in the background of our minds there is an awareness of the One called alongside us, of his approval or displeasure with the course we are taking, and of our need to depend on him for the checking and quickening of our decisions.

Even when we are intelligently pursuing the will of God with the aid of Scripture and illumined reason, we should be open to a witness of the Spirit halting and redirecting us, just as the apostolic missionaries were when they were trying to go into Bithynia but "the Spirit of Jesus did not allow them" (Acts 16:7).

There is a good deal of spiritual pathology that can be generated from a belief in contemporary prophetic gifts, unless this is carefully guarded by an awareness of some of the dangers we have discussed and the emulation of Edwards's deliberately antisensational approach to the ministry of the Spirit. Much that passes for prophecy needs to be recognized as part of the normal and unspectacular working of the Spirit, and not inflated into something miraculous and infallible. Many prophecies should be recognized as manufactured by the flesh and the imagination, and discarded with some effort to correct their source by counseling. Others should probably be rejected as demonic counterfeits. Prophecies that seek to spell out the future should be noted and filed in a special compartment of the mind that combines memory with suspended judgment; then from time to time they can be brought out and examined to check their plausibility. But perhaps a very few prophecies, those bearing the ring of truth, should not be ruled out of court before they have been carefully tested. Scripture is more generous here than our efforts at safeness and systematic consistency: "Do not quench the Spirit, do not despise prophesying, but test everything; hold fast what is good, abstain from every form of evil" (1 Thess. 5:19-22).

LIVE
ORTHODOXY

9

ONE OF THE CENTRAL THEOLOGICAL issues confronting the Christian church in our generation and seriously dividing it is the problem of the function of sound teaching in the body of Christ. Is intellectual assent to creedal propositions essential to the health and even the life of churches and individuals? Or is a free-ranging mind unanchored to biblical thought-structures, but personally committed to Christ, a safer option for the educated Christian who wants to preserve integrity and commend a plausible faith to outsiders who stumble at traditional doctrines? There are large numbers of professing Christians attached to each of these options, and the two groups tend to make one another extremely uneasy.

The difficulty here has been with us for several centuries. In early and medieval Christianity neither the orthodox nor heretics doubted the importance of their respective creeds.

But in the aftermath of the Reformation, which was a golden age of creed making, an anticreedal mood appeared in Western Christendom. Nonclerical observers noted the uncomfortable and sometimes lethal effects which creedal differences produced among Catholics, Calvinists, and Lutherans, and later among baptists and pedobaptists. Many decided that lists of opinions which fractured the church into parties literally at war with one another might not be indispensable to Christian life. They also noted that orthodoxy and Christian behavior did not always exactly correlate and were sometimes found in inverse proportion.

Eighteenth-century rationalism distrusted creeds because they were full of irrational mysteries like the Trinity, and not clear and reasonable like the Bible. Nineteenth-century Romantics, on the other hand, found an excessive clarity in systems of doctrine which contrasted harshly with the mystery and wonder of biblical religion. At the end of the century Adolf von Harnack, the great historian of dogma, articulated the Romantic approach in a formula which has remained axiomatic for many subsequent theologians: early orthodoxy took the noncerebral activism of Hebrew thought and Hellenized it into technical scientific categories alien to the spirit of primal Christianity.

Early twentieth-century Liberalism, as expressed in Harnack's own Ritschlianism, was itself a rather clear and simple creed. The dialectical theology which opposed and superseded it, however, improved on the Romantic approach with considerable subtlety. One of the most effective statements in this line of development is found in the theology of Emil Brunner, which insists that encounter with the divine presence is far more important in producing healthy Christianity than assent to propositions. The system building of Protestant orthodoxy, Brunner says, produces great structures of thought which appear to us "like a frozen waterfall— mighty shapes of movement, but no movement." Christian faith is not intellectual commitment to such systems but repentance and personal trust in Jesus Christ, the incarnate Word who alone expresses the mind and character of God which no verbal structures can convey.

Although Brunner admits that some objective propositional content must be present at the core of the divine-human encounter, he holds that wherever doctrines or even biblical assertions are regarded as "revealed truths" to be believed objectively by the faithful, irreparable damage is done: "From being a fellowship of disciples the Church has become a school."[1] It would appear to follow that for Brunner any orthodoxy carries within it the seeds of its own death. The frequency with which we can apply the phrase "dead orthodoxy" to whole eras of illness in the church's history almost seems to bear this out.

It is obvious, however, considering the length of their own doctrinal writings, that what Brunner and Barth are aiming at is a "live orthodoxy," and not an abolition of all teaching in the church. Evangelical Christians who have squared off against neo-orthodoxy in stressing objective propositional revelation should recognize that this quest for live orthodoxy is at the heart of their own historical tradition, embodied in those twin expressions of experiential Christianity, Calvinist Puritanism and Lutheran Pietism. Brunner himself comments that the best insights the dialectical theology had when it began were derived from Pietism, although he repeats Ritschl's incorrect judgment that all Pietists were radical subjectivists.[2] There are other roads to live orthodoxy than the one dialectical theologians have taken. Since valuable and viable insights which offer keys to modern problems often get lost in the church's history, it might be profitable for us to examine for a moment the Pietist and Puritan prescriptions for live orthodoxy.

Pietist and Puritan Prescriptions

In the late sixteenth century the first Puritan pastors in England and Johann Arndt, the early German Pietist, began independently to assert that the first essential for live orthodoxy was the appearance of a body of Christians who were not merely nominal or professing believers but who had been made spiritually alive by supernatural rebirth. The accompanying signs of this regeneration were the products of an encounter with the living and holy God: repentance—a heart broken because of sin and committed to obey the divine lordship—and evangelical faith in Jesus Christ focused upon his atoning sacrifice. The Puritans carefully distinguished between a mere "notional" orthodoxy (belief in miracles, faith in the historical record of Scripture and mental assent to the gospel without a change of heart) and "saving faith" (defined by William Ames as "a resting of the heart in God," combining acceptance of all the notional elements with personal trust in the Author of doctrine). It was assumed that grace normally entered the life through the understanding, but that understanding alone was incomplete and ineffectual without grace.

In the Lutheran situation, Johann Arndt found himself contending against an unbalanced stress on the doctrine of justification by faith alone, which deprecated or ignored sanctification and good works, and encouraged the growth of what Dietrich Bonhoeffer has called "cheap grace."[3] Arndt observed that orthodox doctrine was brandished like an axe in the hands of unsanctified theological leaders and driven by the flesh as a weapon of destruction instead of serving as a tool of healing surgery. Arndt himself was attacked by the orthodox as unsound on the doctrine of justification, but he continued to insist that Luther's original balance of "two kinds of righteousness" must be maintained and that the justifying faith of the truly regenerate would prove itself by growth in sanctification and an outpouring of works of love.

The Puritan approach to the function of orthodox teaching was also heavily focused on sanctification and practical Christian living, for doctrine was "in order to godliness."

William Perkins defined theology as "the science of living blessedly forever"; his pupil William Ames defined it as "the doctrine of living unto God."[4] Both men tended to avoid speculative subtleties which were unrelated to the Christian life. This approach could easily lose its balance and topple into a pragmatic anti-intellectualism. But it also reflects elements of the New Testament pattern in which doctrine is always existentially focused on practice.

A Puritan sermon was never a tape-recording session in which abstract doctrinal information was transferred from the pastor's memory to that of the congregation. It was always an operation on the spiritual lives of the hearers in which no doctrinal tool was used which did not vitally relate to the needs of some class among them. The preacher who was content to rehearse and admire doctrines without applying them to the life and world of the congregation in such a way that believers sensed the guiding control of the Holy Spirit and heard the voice of God addressing them in concrete situations, was not for the Puritans a physician of souls, but an aesthetician or tool-salesman, displaying the instruments of healing but refusing to employ them.

The vital difference here is well expressed by Lyman Beecher, representing the nineteenth-century evangelicalism which developed from the Puritan base. Beecher's preaching, according to Harriet Beecher Stowe,

> consisted invariably of two parts: first, careful statement and argument addressed purely to the understanding, and second, a passionate and direct appeal, designed to urge his audience to some immediate practical result. . . . A sermon that did not induce anybody to *do any thing* he considered a sermon thrown away. The object of preaching, in his view, was not merely to enlighten the understanding, or even to induce pleasing and devout contemplation, but to make people set about a thorough change of heart and life.[5]

Beecher's version of orthodoxy compelled him to fight

against false doctrine, but it was a different sort of battle from the polemics of dead orthodoxy:

> I did not attack infidelity directly. Not at all. That would have been cracking a whip behind a runaway team—made them run the faster. I always preached right to the conscience. Every sermon with my eye on the gun to hit somebody. Went through the doctrines; showed what they didn't mean; what they did; then the argument; knocked away objections, and drove home on the conscience.[6]

Beecher's imagery is belligerent, but his motivation was loving concern for the health of souls which showed itself in searching attention to spiritual needs. Mrs. Stowe comments:

> As he preached he watched the faces of his hearers, and when he saw that one moved he followed him. "A_____ B_____ has seemed to feel a good deal," he would say, "these several Sundays. I must go after him. Something seems to block his wheels." Often he used to say to me, speaking of one and another with whom he had been talking, "I've been feeling round to find where the block is. I put my finger on this and that, and it don't move; but sometimes the Lord helps me, and I touch the right thing, and all goes right."[7]

Perhaps the keenest expression of the Puritan theology of live orthodoxy is the work of Jonathan Edwards. Edwards inherited a congregation in Northampton which was outwardly respectable and had correct, if dim and fading, views of doctrine but which was spiritually lifeless. The awesome realities which the people professed to believe had little hold on their attention or their energies. Like most New Englanders before the Great Awakening they were not absorbed in God and his kingdom as ultimate concerns but were principally occupied with the natural concerns of fallen men: land, business, affluence. During the course of the awakening, Edwards observed the appearance of a new "sense of the heart" among numbers of his parishioners as the doctrines in which they had professed belief suddenly became transparent media through which they could see the glory and holiness of God, the depth and wretchedness of their sin, and the beauty and compassion of the redeeming Christ. The orthodoxy they still held was no longer a cryptic map of distant territories they had never visited, but a vital guide to regions of experience through which they were moving daily. Edwards's private notebooks comment that men can manipulate symbolic counters which denote supernatural realities even if they have no direct experience of the referents to which those symbols point, and are in fact alienated from the life of God. Live orthodoxy, however, is only found where the Holy Spirit opens the eyes of the heart and imparts a vision of the true God and the actual human condition. This vision changes the whole direction of life.

The form of orthodoxy against which Edwards contended divided the human personality into three independent compartments—mind, will and emotions—and assumed that these could be rectified separately in redemption. The mind could be filled with correct information; the will could be directed toward good works; and—somewhat as an afterthought—"devotion" could be cultivated as an emotional frosting on the cake, if one cared for that sort of thing. Against this Edwards contended that all the faculties were rooted in the heart, the subconscious wellspring from which flow all the issues of life. He held that redemptive truth could not produce a genuine change in mind, will or emotions unless it had entered the life through a work of the Holy Spirit which renewed and purified this wellspring, producing a new "sense of the heart" which could energize the whole personality through the vision of God. Paul Tillich comments that spiritual experience is not a source of theological truth, but that it is an essential medium through which live theological reflection must pass. Edwards would agree.

All the prescriptions for live orthodoxy mentioned thus far involve the application of the work of redemption to the lives of believers by the Holy Spirit. Regeneration, subsequent sanctification, the focusing and empowering of preaching, and the illumination of the symbols preached are all part of the process by which the Holy Spirit works to reproduce in Christians a continuing presence on earth of the mind of Christ, which alone holds an orthodoxy which is living and active. The longest texts on the work of the Spirit in the New Testament, John 14—16 and 1 Cor. 2, both center on the teaching ministry which transforms the believer by the renewal of his mind. It would therefore be easy to rest in the assumption that the key to live orthodoxy is the role of the Holy Spirit.

Both Puritans and Pietists, however, were concerned to guard against the subjectivism which might result from a unilateral emphasis on the Spirit, and they balanced that emphasis with a stress on the objective Word. The opening section of the Westminster Confession states this balance with exquisite care. It grounds our acceptance of Scripture itself on the internal testimony of the Holy Spirit while it pits biblical authority both against the heteronomy of church supremacy and against the autonomy of the Puritan left wing, which deprecated doctrinal structures and the historical Jesus, replacing them with the experience of encountering the living Christ, the "inner light." Puritans and Pietists correctly sensed that the radical wing of their experiential movement would rapidly degenerate into rationalism or moralism if it was not anchored in objective revelation. Consequently, the function of the Spirit in the normative center of both traditions was not that of revealing new truth, but of illuminating truth already given, making it real in the minds and lives of believers.

The Pietism of Spener and Francke stressed also the primacy of biblical revelation over confessional doctrinal structures, holding that another cause of dead orthodoxy was reliance on purely manmade objective formulations rather than on the God-inspired objectivity of Scripture. The complicated system building of some forms of Protestant scholasticism, which asked the Bible questions it is not designed to answer and extrapolated great leaning towers of theory from a few scriptural loci, was alien to the practical spirituality of the Pietists. Like Luther, they were interested in a theology of the cross, not a "theology of glory" which sought to read the mind of God between the lines of what was clearly revealed.

We may conclude therefore that the key to live orthodoxy offered by the Puritan and Pietist traditions is the proper balance between the Spirit and the Word with appropriate attention given to the role of each. What this really means is that to proclaim Christ in living power it is necessary for us to depend on him in a double way. On the one hand, for accurate knowledge of the incarnate Word, we must look back in dependence on the written Word which he inspired through the Spirit and which is the continuing instrument through which his mind is made present among believers. On the other hand, for illuminated understanding of the written Word and power to transmit it to others, we must look up in dependence on the risen Word, who alone is able to enliven the dead conceptual knowledge of the fallen human mind through the sanctifying operation of the Holy Spirit, and to focus it existentially so that it will be wisdom in the biblical sense and not mere knowledge.

Proposals for Today

What implications do these conclusions have for the modern church as it confronts the problem of the function of orthodoxy? At first glance it would seem that at least some segments of the church understand the balance of the Spirit and the Word, since both neo-orthodox and Evangelical Christians profess allegiance to it. On closer examination, however, we may question whether any large sector of the church possesses this balance in its practice.

Although Brunner[8] builds his whole theory of live ortho-

doxy on the balancing of Word and Spirit and claims to find
a middle way between false subjectivism and false objectivity, in practice his approach can lead to an encounter-mysti-
cism as unanchored to the biblical thought world as the
original Quakerism. This has apologetic advantages, of
course. It enables the theologian to use the trump card of the
Word while ignoring niggling attacks on historical and cosmological details in it. But for a second and third generation
who have been trained to subject their minds only to portions
of Scripture which seem especially endorsed by the Spirit,
the objective Word may well become a rubber knife instead
of the sword of the Spirit, powerless to discern the heart and
do surgery on the spirit. And the apologetic value of being
able to retreat like a cuttlefish into a cloud of philosophical
subtlety when one's facts are menaced may appear less de-
sirable than the relative clarity of a demythologized faith or
a secular religion which has placed a moratorium on God-
talk.

On the other hand, the Evangelicalism which claims to be
a reformed continuation of the Puritan and Pietist traditions
has also imperfectly realized the balance between the Word
and Spirit. Some areas within it are heir to the apparently
congenital illnesses of former orthodoxies: confessionalism,
polemic self-righteousness, the twin opposing plagues of
irrational enthusiasm and allergy to Christian experience,
preaching which is spiritually and socially irrelevant, neglect of sanctification, and consecration of the status quo.
In some instances doctrinal fidelity has been given such
primacy over spiritual reality that those with the wrong system or the wrong theory of inspiration have been read out of
the kingdom as worshipers of a false and unbiblical Christ.
This is an error which earlier Reformed theologians such
as Hodge or Machen would never have made. In reaction to
all of this, other Evangelical movements stressing spiritual
renewal are leaning toward subjectivist extremes, teaching
that doctrine divides while Christ and the Spirit unite, and

aiming for a warm emotional glow rather than for the sharp edge of reality present where revival is defined in terms which include Spirit-empowered biblical thinking.

At the end of the nineteenth century the ancestors of most of today's Evangelicals and conservative neo-orthodox Protestants were united under the banner of D. L. Moody's revivalism. In the early twentieth century the immense thought storm of secular humanism, made up of apparently consistent and convincing alternates to the biblical world view, burst upon the church and shattered the clarity of its thinking and hence the unity of its forces. Live orthodoxy might have weathered the storm and risen to the educational challenge humanism presented, setting out to construct a consistently biblical counterposition which would seek to integrate all the new data pouring into human consciousness. But what we had under Moody's leadership was not equal to the strain, and it broke in two. Half of it emulated the ostrich, turned its back on the culture, immersed its head in the biblical world and almost became an enculturated folk religion. The other half grappled with the task of integrating modern and biblical thought but often lost its biblical moorings and slipped away into another kind of enculturation: conformity to the secular mind. Theologians who built some of their thought on contrabiblical building blocks often found that the strain of doublethink can collapse a mind into consistent secularism.

Neither wing of the church can be uniformly proud of its performance thus far in the twentieth century. Fundamentalism broadcast packaged answers from its cultural ghetto without engaging the modern world in intelligent dialog. Opposing parties too often echoed the world's confusion. On the other hand, neither wing of the church was a total failure. Evangelicalism kept the faith and led multitudes into an attenuated form of authentic Christian spirituality. Non-Evangelicals built a social witness which was sometimes impressive and in their scholarship uncovered new biblical and historical insights. The scene was often drenched in the light of irony, as some workers who affirmed the inerrancy of the written Word of God remained on the periphery of its vineyard, while some who were less clear in their allegiance were led past them by the Spirit.

The time may now be ripe for the reunification of these tribes within the Christian movement. If dead orthodoxy is the brittle fault which leads to the splintering of Christendom, perhaps live orthodoxy is the element which can bridge and heal its divisions. Let me suggest some principles bearing on the function and the limits of orthodoxy which could conserve the essential insights of both sides and which may serve as a basis for unifying dialog.

(1) *Biblical doctrine (spiritually energized and illuminated propositional truth) is normally the instrument through which regenerative transformation of the human personality takes place in the Holy Spirit's application of redemption* (1 Pet. 1:22-23; Rom. 10:9, 17). Since spiritual death enters the world through humanity's flight from divine reality into a mental universe of lies in which God's character and purposes are falsified, it is natural that spiritual life should be associated with a mental universe of *truth*, reached through repentance (*metanoia*, change of mind and heart) and *faith* (acceptance of the biblical portrayal of God, humankind and the world). "You will know the truth," Jesus said, "and the truth will make you free" (Jn. 8:32).

Propositions fall far short of the splendor of the One who is the Word and the Truth, it must be admitted. But by the power of the Spirit of truth they can be the medium of conveying to us the mind of Christ. The Christian who wants to encounter God without listening to what he has to say may remain in the condition of a smilingly subliterate and disobedient two-year-old. Sanctification of the mind is of pivotal importance in sanctification of the whole life, and sanctification of the mind involves an increasing ability to think biblically under the empowering of the Spirit.

Our knowledge must extend far beyond the biblical revelation, but principles of biblical truth, under the Spirit's
illumination, must function as a kind of clarifying lens
through which we view all things. Of course, a delicate her-
meneutical task is posed here. Thinking biblically does not
involve confinement to cultural and cosmological details
which are only incidental to the main thrust of biblical teaching. The biblical cosmology, however, is far more sensible
than some of its caricatures indicate. To "demythologize" it
is often to confine our thinking in modern mythologies
which are far less durable and significant.

(2) *Biblical doctrine is therefore essential both in evangelism and in the church's prophetic social witness.* A strategy in which the church becomes a silent presence in the
world is therefore an ineffectual form of mission, which reveals to non-Christians our doctrinal confusion and spiritual
impotence rather than commending our humility. Good
works done in silence are often a necessary part of pre-evan-
gelism, but in themselves they can only win others to moralism or repel them in bafflement. The sheep can be led into
social righteousness, but they will not follow unless they
hear the voice and the words of the Shepherd. The church as
an instrument of mission may be compared to a cutting tool
whose steel shaft is works of justice and mercy, but whose
diamond edge is the proclamation of truth. This is confirmed
not only by biblical data (in the *euangelion* and *kerygma*,
and in the symbolism of the miracle of tongues in Acts), but
also by the history of spiritual renewal in the church, in
which awakenings travel by means of news along routes of
verbal communication and are often contained by linguistic
barriers.

(3) *Doctrine is a reliable indicator of the kind of spiritual
life or motivating force within a person or movement; for
life expresses itself by affecting thought and teaching.*[9] There
are occasional biblical statements which imply that we are

not to limit ourselves to doctrinal criteria in testing the spirits. The portrayal of the final judgment in Matthew 25 divides the agents in history according to whether these have ministered through works of love to the edification of the body of Christ or have neglected to do this. Nevertheless, the main thrust of the New Testament is that persons or movements emit ideological signals through which their force is propagated and by which they can be identified. The discernment of spirits is difficult to pursue through the inspection of works alone, since the agents of darkness can disguise themselves as servants of righteousness (2 Cor. 11: 14-15).

(4) *However, sound doctrine does not necessarily guarantee spiritual life or force within a person or a movement* (2 Tim. 3:5; 1 Cor. 13:1, 2; Rev. 2:2-4). The written Word and its doctrinal derivatives are not the sword of the Spirit unless his hand is upon them, and they are being wielded at his direction. Some of the factors which determine the difference between dead orthodoxy and "the power of godliness" have been spelled out in preceding pages. The general precondition of live orthodoxy is the presence of the Holy Spirit, endorsing and applying sound doctrine, using at least minimal relevant quanta of biblical truth to realize the life of Christ in believers. The main condition of spiritual life, according to 1 John 1, is fellowship with God; and the prerequisite for communion with God is "walking in the light" (1 Jn. 1:5-10), which may be defined as an honest heart awareness of the truth about the condition of one's life and the truth of God's grace, which both covers sin and provides a dynamic of sanctifying transformation. Live orthodoxy is found, not among those who wave the flag of commitment to biblicism, but among those who live in this focused spotlight of applied biblical truth. "I have no greater joy than this," says John, "to hear of my children walking in the truth" (3 Jn. 4 NASB).

(5) *Some measure of the life and power of the Holy Spirit*

can on occasion be found in persons and movements which
have had little or no contact with doctrinal truth (Mt. 2:1-12;
Ezra 1:1-4). These may be instances of God's common grace,
or they may be recipients of the beginning stages of redemptive grace who will respond in repentant faith when exposed
to truth.

(6) *Doctrinal error can destroy spiritual life.* Jesus warned
the disciples to beware of the leaven of the Pharisees and
Sadducees, that is, the conservatives and liberals. Both of
these groups—in other words, all of us—have a hidden gravity toward error and a way of adding and subtracting to the
biblical revelation which results in teaching for doctrine the
precepts of men.

(7) *Erroneous doctrine, however, does not in every case
indicate spiritual death or full allegiance to spiritual forces
inimical to the kingdom of God.* It is true that those who are
in vital contact with the real God must ultimately give allegiance to the real Christ, and this will express itself in doctrinal form (Rom. 10:9; 1 Cor. 12:3; 1 Jn. 4:2). But this may be
accompanied by great ignorance, error and inconsistency in
the vast periphery of related teaching, since the sanctification of the mind is just as variable among men as any other
area of Christian growth. Furthermore, every pastor has seen
Christians overloaded by the thrust of secular doctrine and
spiritually dislocated by the appeal of sin, so that the life
within them has become a hidden seed with little or no intellectual expression, which revives later when these blockages have been removed. This may in fact be the essential
story of the church in the twentieth century as it has struggled desperately to confront articulate neopaganism and
found itself so often overmastered by contrabiblical argument.

I doubt if any reader can embrace immediately every judgment on the surface of these statements; and, of course, there
are many underlying assumptions in them which are un-
mentioned but controversial. However, these theses do at-

tempt to show how orthodoxy is connected to spiritual reality, and why it is important as an instrument and sign of life, yet also limited in its ultimate role and significance. If the self-consciously orthodox can abandon their usual posture of intellectual self-righteousness and strike a more humble stance, admitting that doctrine is an implement of spirituality but not its ultimate goal, and if those alienated from orthodoxy can recognize the instrumental power of biblical doctrine to penetrate modern unbelief with incisive healing force, then live orthodoxy can lead both to the unity and purity of the coming church.

It is essential that conservative Christians hear this kind of critique and respond to it. The descendants of revivalism, Fundamentalism and the confessional traditions of Luther and Calvin are multiplying rapidly today. Without a balanced approach to biblical orthodoxy they will inevitably offer us unpleasant reruns of some of the worst pages of past history, with rigid separatism shattering the groups which stress doctrine and tradition, and sentimental and gullible enthusiasm diluting the strength of those who worship experience and innovation. If orthodoxy is to attain vitality—and stop frightening the rest of professing Christendom away from biblical thinking by producing such monuments as the American Bible Belt and South African Calvinism—orthodoxy must enlarge its task to include cleaning its own house along with detecting and denouncing heresy.

Considering the capacity of variant orthodoxies to divide the church, we might almost question how much doctrinal discernment God can safely entrust to the church. We do not give scalpels to angry children. To transplant an organ we must lower the body's threshold of discrimination until it can tolerate fusion with the tissues of another body. It often seems as if the only way to unite the fragmented body of Christ might be to depress the doctrinal sensitivity of the parts until they can heal together without destroying one another.

But this, of course, has been tried already, and it has failed. During much of the twentieth century, ecumenists have soft-pedaled the doctrinal purity of the church in order to attain its unity. But the body's tolerance can be increased only so far before we run the risk of fatal infection, which can lead to disintegration just as rapidly as the rejection syndrome. Mainstream churchpeople who have grown accustomed to assuming that there are no wolves in the fold, only some rather hoarse and disheveled sheep, had better listen more closely to some of the voices out there which are advocating the dismantling of a God-centered morality in exchange for an ethic revolving around human pleasure and social well-being, and presenting a theology with no place for God himself. The church of Christ ought not to be a forum for amplifying the best insights of secular humanism. Nor should it be a theological cafeteria in which both bread and arsenic can be ordered.

No, the unity and the purity of the church are interdependent and can only be obtained together. The catalyst essential for this attainment is live orthodoxy. This is Paul's thrust in the greatest biblical text on unity and orthodoxy, which still shines before us as a vision of the terminal grandeur of the church, for which all its past history seems like a disorderly rehearsal:

... building up the body of Christ, until we all attain to the unity of the faith and of the knowledge of the Son of God, to mature manhood, to the measure of the stature of the fulness of Christ; so that we may no longer be children, tossed to and fro and carried about with every wind of doctrine, by the cunning of men, by their craftiness in deceitful wiles. Rather, speaking the truth in love, we are to grow up in every way into him who is the head, into Christ, from whom the whole body, joined and knit together by every joint with which it is supplied, when each part is working properly, makes bodily growth and upbuilds itself in love. (Eph. 4:12-16)

UNITIVE
EVANGELICALISM

10

THE RELATIONSHIP BETWEEN CHURCH unity and revival has remained problematic ever since the disruptive revitalization of Christianity during the Reformation period. Church officials, in fact, have been suspicious of the schismatic potential within renewal movements since Montanism. More recent history seems initially to confirm the thesis that spiritual awakening inevitably produces new wine which bursts the skins of the old church order. In nearly every era of awakening, even if the central reforming movements do not themselves result in schism, they are surrounded by expanding rings of sectarianism which, on the surface, seem to emanate from the renewing impulse.

Thus in the Reformation era the magisterial Reformers, ejected by the church structure they had sought to restore, were themselves at odds with one another and with a wide spectrum of secessionary movements aiming at more radical reform, some of them variants of Protestant orthodoxy and other seemingly driven by another spirit.[1] The Puritan awakening, which had most of its energy within the established church system up to 1640, began to display the same pattern during the Revolutionary period: separation of orthodox Protestants into denominational segments according to differing polity or practice with an enlarging fringe of enthusiastic sectarians shading off into heterodoxy.[2]

The Great Awakening of the 1730s and 40s resulted in a Presbyterian schism in the Middle Colonies which lasted from 1741 until 1758 and broke up New England Congregationalism into the whole spectrum of existing denominations, adding new variations and isolated subgroups and congregations.[3] In the European phase of the First Awakening, the Wesleyans separated from Zinzendorf's Lutheran-Moravian Pietism through which John Wesley had come to understand justification. They separated from the evangelical Calvinism of Whitefield, one of their own original number, and were finally ejected from the English church they had set out to reform. Descendants of Zinzendorf's mission to revive and unite the denominations touched off separations in the Scandinavian state churches in the nineteenth century.

Revivalism in late nineteenth- and early twentieth-century America shattered many church structures. Evangelical forces often left the major denominational structures and collected in smaller, theologically homogeneous groups, or broke down into the ultimate atomic units, independent congregations.

Examining this record, it is easy to sympathize with the modern churchleader who looks upon Evangelical awakening as a divisive disease and wants to avoid it like the plague. This is a natural conclusion, but a dangerous one. At the opposite extreme, the occasional Evangelical who argues that separation from the impure structures actually leads to spiritual reawakening is on equally shaky ground. Separation, like some divorces, often produces a sense of release which seems constructive in the short run, but this is not renewal. Still there are obviously situations in which the separation of a revived segment of the church is either necessary for its continued survival or strategically advisable for some other reason, such as the efficient fulfillment of its vision. There are ambiguities here generated by the tension inherent in the traditional pairing of the concerns for peace and purity within the church. These ambiguities make it unlikely that simple generalizations about the relation of revival and separation, like those mentioned above, can be universally valid. If any guidelines can be attained in this difficult matter, they will have to emerge from serious historical and theological analysis.

It appears that the tension between peace and purity in church structures can only be held in a productive balance under very special conditions of spiritual health within the body of Christ. Unless the church is in a state of normative renewal, its disciplinary apparatus either works overtime, destroying its own tissues in an allergic reaction, or else it weakens into a permissive pluralism which harbors growths and organisms inimical to the body. Examples of both these extremes abound today, showing that the proper balance is hard to maintain.

Currently our denominations seem to break down into two categories: the smaller, conservative separatist bodies maintaining the pure church ideal with an antiseptic discipline so strong that it occasionally sterilizes their own creativity; and the large, historical descendants of earlier separations, now so indiscriminately inclusive that to Evangelicals they resemble mission fields. Evangelicals themselves, similarly, are divided into those who might be characterized as white corpuscles, members of separated churches committed to rigorous discipline, and red corpuscles, those who have tried to adapt themselves to the large, pluralistic bodies in order to feed and serve their memberships. In the 1920s and 30s tensions ran high between these two Evangelical subtypes. Since then, they and their descendants have learned to work together with somewhat less uneasiness in the various Evangelical parachurch organizations, which often seem to function more vigorously than either type of parent denomination taken by itself.

But does spiritual renewal always lead to the proper balance between peace and purity in the church? Today the stirrings of awakening among the Evangelical forces seem to have renewed this tension rather than relieving it. Among the emerging younger leadership, those who come from Fundamentalist backgrounds often tend to be red corpuscles, familiar with the unhealthy effects of excessive discipline and coveting the freedom and catholicity possible within the mainstream denominations. Converts from non-Evangelical church backgrounds, on the other hand, can often be hyperfundamentalist in their reaction to the failures and deformities of the inclusive churches which gave them their initial Christian nurture without ever exposing them to the heart of the gospel and challenging them to radical commitment to Christ.

These two groups of younger leaders tend to polarize against one another when they rub shoulders. There is a similar repolarization occurring among older Evangelicals of both types, who find it hard to control an urge to recruit the disaffected offspring of the opposing team to staff their denominations. How this heightening of tension can be the result of genuine renewal is a matter to be explored in the rest of this chapter, one thesis of which is that revival, like learning, is dangerous in small quantities.

Evidence of the renewed strain among Evangelicals over the question of separation is found in the increasing disaffection among some who have been working diligently within pluralistic denominations for years to effect reformation, but who are now reaching the end of their patience. A generalization frequently heard among these ministers is this: History proves that once a denomination becomes apostate, it never recovers its orthodoxy; therefore, the case is hopeless, and separation into a new denomination is clearly necessary.

Now this is a very problematic position. It begs several questions. It can equally well be argued that history proves that no separation ever resulted in a permanent reformation. The purified church inevitably develops again the old leaven of the Pharisees and Sadducees, and the result is another partially apostate body with a faithful remnant. The experience of Noah's family shows that even the most radical separation does not prevent the reappearance of corruption. Without the hope of recovery from apostasy we are trapped in a permanent state of spiritual entropy, a downgrade which no purification through separation ever cures.

The toil of all that be
Helps not the primal fault;
It rains into the sea,
And still the sea is salt.[4]

The thesis that no church ever recovers from apostasy is questionable also because it assumes that churches start in primal states of relative perfection before their irreversible decline begins. But it can be argued from the experience of the first generation of New Testament Christians that the foundations of churches and the beginnings of their apostasy are likely to occur almost simultaneously. If this is admitted, on the evidence of the Corinthian letters, Acts and Galatians, then it follows that some strategies of renewal within declining churches must be viable at least in some cases, or else all of our labors in creating and conserving church structures are useless from the start. It almost seems that in the Christian church, as in the human body, the processes of decay and regeneration, catabolism and metabolism, occur simultaneously from the point of birth onward.

The Unitive Thrust of Historic Evangelicalism

If we turn now to the history of the Evangelical movement, we can see many evidences that evangelicalism itself has from the beginning been designed as a regenerative force seeking to spread the leaven of the kingdom of God within the largest and most comprehensive church structures, rather than as a separatist movement aiming for a perfect church. As John McNeill has demonstrated in *Unitive Protestantism*, the magisterial Reformers were urgently concerned to preserve the largest possible bodies of professing Christians in the renewed church, and most of them made extraordinary efforts to try to bridge the denominational gulfs evolving between Protestants in different locales.

Luther himself in the early years of his reforming work was aiming, not at separation, but at the renewal of Western Catholicism. As late as 1520 he was still appealing "to the Pope better informed" and hoping that action from the head of the church system might heal the decay in its members. It is true that in that year he came to conclude that the apostasy of Rome was irremediable and that the Roman system was in fact the predicted expression of Antichrist in history—an eschatological assumption that was to haunt Protestant/Catholic relations for centuries—and that he later developed implacable hatred toward Zwinglian doctrine and the habits of sectarians. But the origins of modern Evangelicalism as a pan-denominational renewal movement can be traced back to his proposal in the Preface to the German Mass that the church be renewed not by separation but by the formation everywhere of *ecclesiolae in ecclesia*, little churches within the church.

Faced with a Lutheran constituency which behaved more like a pre-Christian "people movement" than a reformed church, Luther chose the difficult path of renewing the existing structure rather than the strategy of starting afresh adopted by the separatists of the Radical Reformation. When the early English Puritans sought for counsel on how to complete the partial reformation in the English church, Calvin and Bucer advised moderation, patience and tolerance toward the "many tolerable stupidities" in the church left over from Romanism.[5] It is clear that these men viewed their constituencies as partially Christianized bodies to be reached, renewed and shaped into the church of their ideal vision, and not as perfect Christian communities from which to measure decline in future centuries.

It is true that evangelical Anabaptists followed a different path and that their separatism preserved important values which might otherwise have vanished. But it is not among Anabaptists that the evangelical movement arises in the awakening movements of the seventeenth and eighteenth centuries, but rather in the mainstream flowing from the unitive Protestantism of the magisterial Reformers, which was transformationist in its strategy and ecumenist in its goal.

Among the sixteenth- and seventeenth-century Puritans there were from the beginning many powerful vectors toward separation and disunity which ultimately fractured the Puritan movement into separate sects during the Revolutionary period (1640-1662). However, we should not forget that by far the majority of English and American Puritans were conforming or nonseparating in approach, although the American innovations in polity and practice certainly tested the limits of conformity. As F. E. Stoeffler has pointed out, there was a gradual evolution of the main body of Puritanism away from the stress on precision in outward details of mores, practice and polity toward a general stress on inner spirituality.[6] It should also be remembered that although the Scotsman John Dury was considerably ahead of his time in the radical nature of his union proposals, he was still received with respect and attention by many of the leading Puritan leaders.[7]

After the scandal of the sectarian breakup of Puritanism between 1640 and 1662, it was not only latitudinarian churchmen who were seeking union on the basis of a lowest common denominator of doctrine, but also the major leader among the later Puritans, Richard Baxter. Baxter had an equal horror of heresy and schism. He labored for years to devise a basis for a comprehensive national church which would avoid sectarian division and yet permit a wide diversity of practice anchored to a base of radical orthodoxy. A great deal of his energy was spent in seeking a core of doctrine around which all English Christians could unite, according to the formula of Rupert Meldenius: "Unity in essentials, liberty in incidentals, and in all things charity."[8]

Baxter's concerns were picked up in America by Cotton Mather, whose vision of a revived church at the close of history involved the spiritual unification of Protestantism around the minimal core of doctrine essential to securing vital Christian piety. Mather compared the state of sectarian division with the church to warring tribes of bees, fighting one another because of differences in scent among the various hives. Just as the bees might be calmed and pacified by the sprinkling of a perfume which would make friend and enemy smell the same, Mather reasoned that an outpouring of the Holy Spirit which would create genuine godliness among Christians of differing minor persuasions might enable all of these to detect Christ in one another and attain unity.[9]

Unitive and transformationist concerns were even more clearly in evidence among the Pietists, the Lutheran counterpart to the Puritan revival. Although the early Pietists could project a fairly radical vision of a transformed and unified Christendom, as in J. V. Andreae's *Christianopolis*, they were generally more restrained and conservative than many Puritans, expressing their loyalty to the established church structure and calling simply for its renovation. While Spener and Francke were influenced by Puritanism and appreciative of many aspects of Reformed thought, they were cautious about any immediate hope for structural reunification among the fragments of Protestantism. Spener felt that this could only come after a general spiritual awakening in every sector of the church. But since "the hope of better times" was an essential dynamic in his faith and program, opponents were likely right in charging that Halle was concealing a "secret ecumenical theology."

But the main efforts of Spener and Francke were directed toward reviving the Lutheran Church through the spread of live orthodoxy, and through the stream of ministers emerging from Halle they made great headway toward the more immediate goal of conserving and transforming their own church structure.[10] In the background of their thinking, however, was undoubtedly the vision of the ultimate transformation of world culture through the impact of a revived and unified Christendom cherished by another great leader standing in a third stream paralleling the Puritans and Pietists, John Amos Comenius (1592-1670).[11]

One of the graduates of Halle was Count Ludwig von Zinzendorf, who took the transformationist vision of Spener and Francke beyond Lutheranism and sought to influence every sector of Christendom to bring about revival and spiritual unity. Herrnhut was ecumenist from the start, since it was composed not only of Moravian refugees but also of fragments from Reformed and Catholic backgrounds. Zinzendorf proceeded as if the experience of Herrnhut were a paradigm for the future of the whole church. His theological basis for renewal and union was remarkably brief; it embraced all as Christians who professed allegiance to the Lamb of God and "had experienced the death of Christ upon the heart." The transformationism implicit in his ecumenism was symbolized by the society he organized informally, the Order of the Mustard Seed.

Zinzendorf was not aiming at organizational unity and uniformity among Christians, however, since he believed that each denomination represented a *tropos paideia* (training ground), a unique cultural and traditional incarnation of the gospel with its own particular genius and expression of the Christian essence. He did not desire the dissolution of the *tropoi*, but only their binding together in fraternal charity, mutual respect, communication and communion within a sort of loose federation. He entertained the possibility that even a renewed and reformed Roman Catholicism might be a part of this structure. In this and other respects his vision moved far beyond the comprehension and agreement of the other leaders of the Great Awakening. But from our perspective he appears as one of the major architects of the interdenominational, pan-denominational renewal movement which today we call Evangelicalism.[12]

We have already seen that other leaders of the Great Awakening are more noted for their involvement in the disruption of the standing order than in its renewal. However, we must not overlook the fraternal respect which continued to persist between Wesley and Whitefield despite their doctrinal differences. The breadth of Whitefield's sympathies in his evangelistic work is particularly notable. The *Irenicum* of Gilbert Tennent and the confession and successful efforts toward reconciliation which accompanied it are perhaps more significant than the original disruption in the Presbyterian Church.[13] Edwards's later writings on revival uniformly attacked sectarian division and its causes. His *Humble Attempt to Promote Explicit Union in Prayer* was both an expression of the ecumenical vision of earlier leaders like Spener and Comenius, and an instrument of transforming and unifying international Protestantism.[14]

During the period of the Second Awakening, as we have mentioned, there were examples of continuing vitality among sectarian offshoots (particularly the contribution of Methodism in England and America) and examples also of the divisive impact revival often has. But the main centers of renewal in this era were movements of transformation within the largest and oldest denominations, linked together in an international fellowship of evangelicals cooperating in a broad range of missionary activities. Principal among these movements was the one which transmitted the Methodist impulse into the Anglican Church, and hence into the mainstream of English culture and society, through non-separating churchmen like John Newton, William Wilberforce, the Venns and Charles Simeon.[15]

In America the evangelical united front led by revived Presbyterians and Congregationalists was a parallel and related movement, although the New School Theology provoked a confessional backlash against ecumenism.[16] The explosive expansion of the Protestant missionary effort during this period both reflected and reinforced the transformationist/ecumenist impulses at the heart of the evangelical movement. The formation of the Evangelical Alliance in 1846 is simply one institutional expression among many of the spirit already informing and drawing together almost every fragment of Protestantism in the nineteenth century.

Turns in the Tide

There were other transforming and uniting forces at work by this time, of course, some of them antithetical to the evangelical impulse. On the extreme left, rationalism had made inroads both in Europe and America, creating its own atmosphere of transconfessional unity and enlightenment. The liberal stream descending from Schleiermacher in Europe also transformed and unified at least parts of all denominations. By the end of the nineteenth century one could not speak of a single ecumenical movement among the denominations; rather there were a number of parallel unitive movements competing for the control of the church.

Clearly, what was complicating the picture in the nineteenth century was the flourishing development of systematic secular humanism, which was either capturing the mind of the church (in the rationalist and liberal response) or driving it into traditional or parochial reactions. While some conservative responses, like Tractarianism, had at least a partially unitive direction, the predominant result was toward a neoconfessionalism producing a historical echo of the defensive sectarianism of the sixteenth and seventeenth centuries at their worst.

Some evangelicals continued to seek revival, but they were not unitive. Among them were the Campbellites, who used antisectarian principles to produce a new sect, and the Plymouth Brethren, who sought the renewal of the local congregation but renounced both the strategy of transformationism and the goal of transdenominational union. Like a new and very different breed of Herrnhuters, Darbyite (Plymouth Brethren) emissaries visited America in the mid-nineteenth century, preaching a new premillennial eschatology and the necessity of secession from the apostate institutional church. D. L. Moody's generation in the late nineteenth century accepted the first of these messages but rejected the second.

Facing an increasing secularization of the church's mind in the early twentieth century, however, American Evangelicals began more and more to be susceptible to the second Darbyite principle, since both the church and the surrounding culture seemed to be moving toward apostasy with increasing speed. As in the days of Baxter and Mather, Evangelicals sought to define a minimal core of doctrine around which Christians in all camps could rally. But many Fundamentalists, having affirmed this unity, proceeded to secede from all denominations into independent congregations, seeking a perfect freedom to follow the Bible and their consciences. Others followed the approach of confessionalist orthodoxy, seceding into "continuing churches" of one sort of another.

By the midtwentieth century many American evangelicals felt that the cause of interdenominational experiential orthodoxy was languishing under the conditions of isolation and disarray produced by this turn of events, and these began to move back to the original ideal of unitive evangelicalism, forming such institutions as the National Association of Evangelicals and the Evangelical Theological Society. The Evangelical coalition thus formed brought together two important yet distinct groups: (1) Neo-Evangelical forces like the Billy Graham Association and Fuller Seminary, which preserved the old intent to transform the major denominations, and (2) other Evangelicals more concerned to preserve confessional integrity and yet recognizing the Reformation imperative to acknowledge transconfessional unity with other orthodox Christians.

Increasingly, however, the core of concerns uniting this coalition reflected a limited and more narrowly defined version of the live, experiential orthodoxy of the era of Zinzendorf and Whitefield. These concerns were principally a high view of scriptural authority and evangelism with the goal of regenerate churches. By the mid-1970s both of these components were demonstrating increasing vigor, but were manifesting some strain over their differing ecclesiastical strategies, diverging terminology about scriptural authority, and the political polarization between conservative elders and the radicalized generation emerging from the 1960s.[17]

We might ask at this point what posture the Reformers would encourage given the denominational situation today —separatist perfectionism or the strategy of transformation? The Reformers in their own day counseled against Donatist separation from imperfect Protestant bodies. They themselves were really ejected from Rome because of the reforms they were advocating; they did not voluntarily separate themselves. Eventually, however, after the Council of Trent, they gave up hope of reconciliation with the Roman church, since its leaders did not at that point respond to their fundamental concerns for biblical authority and for the proclamation of the gospel of Christ without the corruption of Judaistic legalism.

What would the Reformers think of the theology prevailing in many of our larger denominations? In many, the way that individuals are saved has become a somewhat irrelevant issue (either because all are assumed to be elect or because a suprahistorical salvation has no meaning), and the basis of authority has become either autonomous reason informed by theological expertise or validation by the Holy Spirit of fragments of the biblical canon in the manner of the more extreme Anabaptist spiritualists. It is possible to argue that the Reformers would pronounce the secularized modern church as seriously in need of reformation as the Romanism of their day.

But it is also possible that the generations of Protestants following the Reformers gave up on Rome too quickly. After all, Rome has not been able to retain possession of the title *Antichrist* in our literature, not only because other candidates have emerged in history, but because it has shown a surprising stability of commitment to supernatural Christianity and even a susceptibility to modern movements of Evangelical renewal such as the Charismatic movement. The great seventeenth-century evangelical Georg Calixtus and Zinzendorf both entertained hope for the recovery of Rome. And thus the witness of history on the question of the reformability of decayed church structures is very ambiguous. Do the Scriptures themselves offer a clearer answer?

A Biblical Model of Apostasy and Recovery

It appears that the recovery of apostate bodies is not only a possibility according to biblical teaching but that it is in fact the central theme of the history of redemption. The families that fall away from the Abrahamic covenant line and fan out to form the gentile world are not lost in total or perpetual apostasy. Each of them is recovered at least in part through the Messianic seed, including the apostate covenant line, since God has shut up all in disobedience that he might show mercy on all. If the implications of Romans 11 are stretched a little, it would almost seem that apostasy is a prerequisite for recovery and that the proponents of every formal orthodoxy must be allowed to show their share in human nature by a period of backsliding and decay, so that every mouth may be stopped and God's mercy vindicated.

But along with the attribute of mercy, God's faithfulness is also displayed in the history of the Old Covenant. Neither Judah nor Israel is ever left without religious cultus by a secession of believing priests and prophets; these are always presented as gifts of God's continuing love to his covenant nation to restore it from apostasy. The northern and southern kingdoms were scattered in the exile, but in the apostolic age the remnant returned to Palestine is evangelized and the Diaspora became the primary missionary target in the Mediterranean world. The congregations gathered out of Judaism became a system for the dispersion of the gospel throughout the Roman Empire. It is almost as though the Diaspora were a rail system laid down for the delivery of the gospel in the New Testament era.

It is true that the institutional Judaism of apostolic times refused the gospel and ejected its followers. Nonetheless, this did not relieve subsequent generations of Christians from maintaining Paul's burden in Romans 10 and 11, and revisiting institutional Judaism with a credible witness to the gospel. The fact that the Christian church has dropped this burden is a testimony, not only to its own partial apostasy, but also to the evil effects of the separatist attitude.

It could be argued that in every age the message of the gospel should be brought ideally "to the Jew first," to every institutional body with roots in the Judeo-Christian lineage, no matter how great its current apostasy. Thus the ecclesiastical structures in any era would represent a rail system for the renewal of the interests and mission of God's kingdom. On this assumption we would expect to find God reviving the church close to the main trunks of its historical development, rather than in the twigs and branches leading off from these through separations. And we have found this true in history, although happily when God sends renewal he revives the twigs as well as the trunk and the major branches.

But there seems to be another dialectical tension here. Does not the Bible also state clearly that there are cases in which responsible separation is a necessity? Under the Old Covenant the Jews are commanded not only to abstain from involvement in the culture and politics of heathen nations under most circumstances, but involvement with apostate Israelites is condemned also, as in the case of Jehoshaphat's alliances with Ahab and Ahaziah (2 Chron. 18—20).

In the New Testament, are not the apostles commanded to gather churches out of Judaism, not to unite with it? This seems at first to be the thrust of the famous passage considered the *locus classicus* by advocates of separation:

> Do not be mismated with unbelievers. For what partnership have righteousness and iniquity? Or what fellowship has light with darkness? What accord has Christ with Belial? Or what has a believer in common with an unbeliever? What agreement has the temple of God with idols? For we are the temple of the living God; as God said, "I will live in them and move among them, and I will be their God, and they shall be my people. Therefore come out from them, and be separate from them, says the Lord. . . . " (2 Cor. 6:14-17)

If this passage applies to the belief and practice of Judaism, it is surely an ironic inversion of the Old Testament command for Israel to be separate from the Gentiles. The exact reference of the word *unbelievers* is however a little hard to discern from the context. The majority of commentators interpret the term *apistoi* as applying only to heathens and not to professing Christians.[18]

There are a number of other texts in the New Testament which counsel separation from those who are apparently inside the Christian fold, either because of moral delinquency of some kind (1 Cor. 5:11; 2 Thess. 3:6, 14) or because of false teaching (Rom. 16:17; Tit. 3:8-11). But in these instances the separation Paul enjoins has nothing to do with removal from church structures (either of the guilty party or of a righteous minority), but rather is a matter of shunning, of breaking off intimate fellowship with the offending party. Even in these cases Paul is not counseling absolute loss of contact with the person punished, since he commands fraternal exhortation in both moral and doctrinal cases of discipline (2 Cor. 2:6-7; 2 Tim. 2:24-26).

Paul's own example in facing the utterly destructive heresy of legalism is instructive. He neither institutes trials for heresy nor withdraws himself from communication with those who are teaching and believing error, but initiates and maintains the most urgent public dialog with the offenders within the arena of the church. In the only New Testament instance in which total separation from antichristian teachers is mentioned, the separation flows from the initiative of those who are apostate: "They went out from us, but they were not of us; for if they had been of us, they would have continued with us; but they went out, that it might be plain that they all are not of us" (1 Jn. 2:19).

There are certainly problems involved in moving directly from the situation in the first century church to the contemporary scene with its denominational systems and church judicatories. But it would appear that the New Testament strategy for combating error and delinquency within the church relies much more on vigorous and continued use of the weapons of truth than on either legal coercion or separation (2 Cor. 10:3-5).

Thus we conclude that revival and division are ultimately antithetical. Division within the church is not positively correlated with spiritual renewal either as cause or effect. And in fact the converse is certainly true: the hope of renewal in the church is intimately bound up with its unity.

This is certainly the thrust of Paul's great utterance on the interconnection of unity and optimum spiritual health in Ephesians 4:11-16, already cited as a kind of prophecy of ultimate renewal within the church. According to this passage the whole body of Christ and its component congregations cannot become mature and immune from the distorting influences of antichristian doctrinal currents in the surrounding culture until all its members are united in a fellowship which permits each organ to communicate its essential secretion to the body, speaking the truth in love.

The psalmist says, "Behold, how good and pleasant it is when brothers dwell in unity! It is like the precious oil upon the head, running down upon the beard, upon the beard of Aaron, running down on the collar of his robes!" (Ps. 133: 1-2). Spurgeon comments that this is a picture of the fullness of the Spirit descending upon Christians gathered in unity. We should add that the church cannot really fulfill its priestly function toward the surrounding world until it has this kind of anointing.

Dividing the church in the interest of renewing it is no more feasible than severing the parts of a body to improve its health. Even if the severed parts survive, they suffer loss, and they will never function properly until they are reunited in fellowship. Leaders who secede from imperfect denominations and denominations which eject imperfect leadership simply lose the values of the group they reject while they insure the unrestrained growth of its defects in a body of future converts.

Ministers who separate from impure churches alienate themselves, not only from the leadership structure they denounce, but also from the ongoing stream of lay people for which God intended them as gifts. These ministers should not be surprised to see repeated outpourings of the Spirit and fruitful reproduction of new leadership in the bodies they have left, because God is faithful to his covenant people in succeeding generations even if the present generation has gone whoring with false prophets. When the children of the most "liberal" churches are brought under the preaching of the central gospel, their response is often remarkably powerful both in depth and in numbers of converts, and the reason for this is the covenant faithfulness of God.

We have already seen that the predominant thrust of the evangelical movement has been unitive in accordance with these scriptural texts, although the orthodox confessional traditions which phase in and out of the stream of evangelical renewal have often been more insular. It might be argued that the evidence shows that evangelical awakenings are always divisive in effect whether or not they intend to be so. There is one sense in which this may be true. We have already noted that the flesh and the devil work inevitably to introduce impurities, exaggerations and counterfeits into every awakening. As a result, denominational bodies which are not sufficiently sensitive to the mixtures of grace and nature in the work may root up the wheat along with tares in their zeal for discipline and thus create schism.

The subjects of the revival, on the other hand, may be so immature in their understanding, and so aware of the contrast between the blazing world of Scripture to which they have just awakened and the ambiguous realities of the actual church, that they fall immediately into Donatist separatism. And this process is not helped by the inevitable presence of spiritual pride in new converts. They may also be moved by the presence of incidental theological elements in the revival which program it to be divisive, as in the case of the Puritan approach to scriptural teaching in matters of worship or polity, or the old Pentecostal teaching on the fullness of the Spirit. But these defects of spiritual adolescence which accompany every awakening are certainly no valid reason for the church to stay asleep.

When the actual historical circumstances surrounding the spread of evangelical renewal are closely investigated, frequently the schisms which occur are found to be basically unrelated to the awakening phenomenon. For example, they may be the result of underlying social causes, latent factors which the awakening process has for some reason failed to surmount, as H. Richard Niebuhr has demonstrated.[19] McNeill contends that most Protestant schisms have been the result of state interference in church affairs, particularly in the case of established churches with theocratic assumptions.[20] For every schism originating in the divisiveness of the awakening party, there must be several which result from the parent denomination's intemperate disciplinary rigor and indifference to the rights of conscience among other Christians.

Orthodox separatists within modern Evangelicalism may argue that they are continuing the unitive strain in evangelical history by their participation in Evangelical federations. At the same time they may assert that they are in line with the apostolic separation from Judaism and the Reformation separation from Romanism in their withdrawal from apostate broad churches and from the ecumenical movement in its twentieth-century form. This argument is plausible. But the apostolic and Reformation separations did not initiate in the parties separating but in the parent bodies which rejected them.

Postapostolic Catholicism and post-Reformation Protestantism are imperfect models for us to follow, because in most respects they shut themselves off from any continuing responsibility to revisit the apostate structures from which they separated, so that the recovery of later generations of Jews and Roman Catholics became almost impossible. It was not primarily separation of polity which generated the problem but the presence of latent prejudice and religious contempt. For centuries *Antichrist* was a code word among Protestants for Roman Catholicism. Even Edwards did not hope for the recovery of the Roman communion, for the later generations after the Reformers moved away from their careful recognition of a continuing stream of life hidden within Rome and came to view it as totally corrupt and unchangeably inimical to the kingdom of God.

It was a considerable shock to orthodox Lutheranism when Spener suggested that the term *Babylon* could also be appropriate to Protestants.[21] Spener assumed that the antichristian tendencies in Lutheranism were curable, but even he was relatively quiet about the possibility of a "hope of better times" for the papal Babylon. But modern Evangelicalism should not be locked into the assumption that apostasy is always terminal. Even when life and faith lapse very drastically in one generation of the church, we are responsible to pray for the recovery of the next generation and to present it with a clear proclamation of the gospel.

When Separation Is Necessary

Despite the desirability of remaining within seemingly apostate bodies to work toward their renewal, it must be recognized that separation is sometimes necessary and expedient. Not all Christians must labor for the recovery of broad-church denominations from inside those denominational structures. There are occasions when division is inevitable and even productive.

For example, there are obviously occasions when a group of Christians is forced to secede from a structure which violates its conscience or restrains its practice in essential areas. There is, of course, an obligation for the separating group to make sure the issue over which the schism occurs is one of ultimate importance. But this same responsibility is shared by the parent body whose disciplinary restraint has forced the separation.

Again, Paul's image of the church as a body implies that there are times when surgery must be done if that body is to remain healthy. Gangrenous limbs must be amputated if possible. What if the whole body were infected as in a case of terminal cancer? It is at least possible that the sound members should be transplanted into a healthy body if their own health is to remain uninfected and their powers to be put to some use.

But when does a church become terminally ill? To say that this occurs when a certain percentage of its leadership becomes apostate is to run the risk of Donatism and also to raise unanswerable questions concerning the discernment of spirits and the feasibility of constructing a calculus of evil. An alternate approach is to hold that a church is beyond hope when its doctrinal structures or its practice become subchristian or antichristian beyond a certain point. If that point could readily be determined through biblical guidance, this approach might hold water. But in fact the Scriptures simply give us accurate criteria concerning the apostasy of individuals, not groups, and even then it is not assumed that every apostasy is terminal.

In the laboratory of history we see evidences today of movements of renewal and recovery among many churches which are grossly defective doctrinally by Evangelical standards. Without even considering the mainline denominations, we could cite the Roman Catholic Church, the Coptic Church, some areas of Eastern Orthodoxy in America and parts of Quakerism (which is lacking both doctrinal standards and sacraments, but has produced a number of Evangelical leaders and one of the most impressive Christian social witnesses in history). Furthermore, some of the most vigorously evangelical churches, even among the mainline denominations, operate without articulated confessional standards by which apostasy can be measured.

Yet there remains a provisional validation for therapeutic separation that must be admitted on the scriptural basis of 2 Corinthians 6:14. As we have already said, this passage applies primarily to heathen and not to professing Christians, and the churchpeople from whom orthodox Evangelicals wish to separate are rarely "unbelievers" in the biblical sense of renouncing belief in Christ. Still the concept of a mismating, or an unequal yoking, which hinders the maximum working efficiency of the church by crippling some of its members, is a very valuable standard for assessing some situations which have arisen in the denominations.

If J. Gresham Machen and other teachers had not seceded from Princeton Seminary and initiated an alternate scholarly voice, the Evangelical movement in America in this century would have been considerably impoverished. The subsequent withdrawal of Orthodox Presbyterianism from the mother denomination constituted a disastrous loss of white corpuscles from the parent body. But it also saved the denomination from tearing itself apart in an allergic reaction, a spiritual equivalent of the disease called lupus. The isolated leukocytes went their way in less than optimal health, occasionally turning on one another in counterproductive attacks which showed that not all the fault was in the parent church. But their isolation did enable them to maintain a form of biblical orthodoxy with integrity of conscience, although not always with the balance and catholicity which continuing involvement with other leaders would provide. Their witness formed a plumb line for the rest of Evangelicalism, reminding it of the fallibility of modern innovations and holding before it an ideal of absolute fidelity to Scripture, even though this ideal was imperfectly attained. In many respects they lost contact with the real situation in the mainline denominations whose thrust they continued to challenge, and their prophetic witness to these denominations at times became uncharitable and parochial. But they did preserve their distinct approach, their *tropos paideia*, and they too are sprouting new leaves and bearing fruit in the midst of the present renewal.

It can even be argued that in the deepest sense such separatist movements do not really violate Ephesians 4:13-16 if they maintain a stance of openness defined, not in terms of monolithic structures of polity, but rather as a network of Christian hearts retaining fellowship and communication with one another. For the ecumenical ideal of the original evangelicals has been realized in this century both among Evangelicals (in the loose and informal federation of common interests which has grown up during the last thirty years) and among non-Evangelical churchpeople (in the more formalized World Council of Churches). Unfortunately

the network of communication between these two great
bodies is still very imperfect, while meaningful dialog between the separatist groups and the World Council is considerably less.

To put it in another way, one person's schismatic sect is
another's *tropos paideia*. Because of the relativity of discipline and polity structures, biblically considered, members
of separatist and inclusivist churches should not judge or
take offense at one another's particular mode of witness but
rather respect each other as followers of differing vocations
within the general task of building the kingdom. There are
really two different and equally reasonable approaches to
forming a denominational structure. One is to define as fully
as possible the system of truth in Scripture and gather a
group of Christians around this as a voluntary association of
witnesses to one strain of Christianity. The other is to seek
out the minimal circle of biblical truth which guarantees the
honor of God and the spiritual health of believers, and to
make this a rallying point for the largest possible number of
Christians, seeking to make the visible church approximate
the invisible as closely as possible.

In today's atmosphere of renewed appreciation for ethnic-
ity, when we have become bored with the indiscriminate
conformity of the melting pot and have grow to savor the distinctive flavor of a multitude of traditions preserved with
some integrity, we can acknowledge the positive function of
sectarian Christianity, up to a point. We can also understand
that the pluralist and inclusivist denominational structures
have an important place in building the kingdom, since perfectionist discipline is one of the main causes of schism and
indiscriminate weeding can destroy wheat along with tares.
Both the separatist and the inclusivist should respect one
another, keeping in mind that great buildings are sometimes
raised on rejected cornerstones.

Both of these ecclesiological postures require constant
attention and criticism, of course. They are makeshift cor-

rectives for the opposing errors of schism and indiscipline, which afflict the church in its imperfect historical existence. Each is slightly off balance and needs repeated tuning to keep its balance, so that it can avoid collapsing into parochial sectarianism or indiscriminate spiritual chaos.

The separatist needs to be reminded to maintain realistic contact with inclusivist denominations and federations and to seek federal (and where possible, organic) union with other Evangelical bodies. The fact that separatists often neglect these unitive procedures and even indulge in further separations is presumptive evidence that the original separation from the parent body was not fully principled but motivated by parochialism, hypercritical perfectionism or the source which Paul indicates as the root cause of schism, an exaggerated view of one's own tradition, party or personal leadership which puts any one or all of these ahead of the unity of the body of Christ.

The inclusivist needs to be warned to exercise discipline where this is necessary for the health of the church and advised to strive for sharp doctrinal clarity in the midst of twilight surroundings. Some inclusivists have remained in their denominations mainly because they have always been a little fuzzy in their doctrinal awareness. They can easily fall into a posture of downplaying doctrine altogether as a divisive factor and substituting experience.

The Delta Effect and Trends toward Reversal
In considering the inclusivist approach, what hope do we have today for the recovery of Evangelical influence in mainline denominations? To answer this question it is necessary to analyze the process by which that influence was originally lost.

In the middle of the nineteenth century, evangelical churchmen were in control of most American Protestant denominations, were sponsoring vigorous educational programs and were also directing powerful interdenominational enterprises such as the Y.M.C.A. By the 1930s, Fundamentalists were either outside the mainline structures or powerless minorities within them, the church-related schools were fast becoming secularized, and the "Y" was an instrument of ethical humanism. Today the observer walking around the American Zion and considering her ramparts sees an extensive fortress originally built by evangelicals, whose descendants are either camping outside or huddled in a few central hiding places, while nontheological mechanics control most of the buildings and battlements. How did this loss of ground come about? Is it a result of the general secularizing of Western culture in the last century, of the churches' falling away from their moorings or of weaknesses within the evangelical movement itself?

These three factors are related in a very complex causal structure in what electrical engineers call a feedback circuit. It is hard to seize upon one as predominant when each has powerfully affected the others. But it is my conviction that the root of decline may be in the evangelical movement itself, in accordance with the general biblical principle that the people of God prevail and prosper when they are in proper harmony with the will of God and lose control when they fail to obey. Evangelicals have preferred to consider themselves a believing remnant surviving in a tide of apostasy, which is an equally valid biblical paradigm but too facile an explanation for the remarkable losses we have suffered. It is also too easy to assign all the blame to the evangelical sector, however. The roots of the decline are located in a loss of power within the whole American church in the late nineteenth century.

Superficially the church appeared to be flourishing during the Gilded Age, but under the surface it was suffering profound decay like many other American institutions during this period. Confessional orthodoxy was cooling off and moving in the direction of a moonlit rationalism; revivalism had emptied revival of much of its content; and Christians concerned for social issues and uneasy with Moody's life-boat conception of mission were falling prey to Ritschl's humanistic redefinition of the gospel. Almost everyone was projecting a softened image of God, minimizing his holiness and maximizing his benevolence, although the Fundamentalist emphasis on the substitutionary atonement at least pointed toward the proper Christological solution of the tension between these attributes.

It was at this point that the storm of secularism which had been building since the Enlightenment struck the church broadside, intimidating it, dividing it, overpowering its voice and even reshaping its message in the minds of its younger leaders. D. L. Moody had been able to embrace and harness together productively orthodox zealots like R. A. Torrey and converts with liberal tendencies such as Henry Drummond,[22] but now these elements began to polarize and react against one another until alienation was complete.

Many Fundamentalists, persuaded that the end of history was near and that the institutional church was damaged beyond repair, withdrew their influence partially or totally from the denominational machinery. Those Fundamentalists who remained active within the denominations were knocked off balance. For some decades they went on the defensive and lost many of the qualities which had distinguished the original evangelicals: breadth of learning, theological depth, social concern and striving for ecumenical unity. The genetic pool of American Christianity was split in half: the "liberals" retained the characteristics just listed, but often lost the evangelical center of faith. The Fundamentalists retained the power and the message to do evangelism, but lost the breadth and wholeness of the evangelical tradition.

A few major evangelical leaders from the Moody era like John R. Mott and Robert E. Speer continued to exercise a creative influence within the churches, but increasingly the younger leadership was anti-Fundamentalist. Fundamentalists were failing to reproduce their leaders in sufficient numbers and failing to "breed true" in the leadership they did produce, which was mutating in a liberal direction. The leaders of the "liberal" wing of the church were frequently the children of Fundamentalists reacting against the deficiencies of their background. As the century went on, a coalition of liberals and mediating neo-orthodox leaders inherited the control of the major denominations, while Fundamentalism, deeply penetrated by the surrounding culture despite its protective shell of legalism, lost control of the mainline churches. If we want to learn why non-Evangelicals are running these churches today, we must take a hard look at early twentieth-century Fundamentalism.

At the present time the process of alienation and loss of Evangelical control of the major denominations has begun to reverse itself. The descendants of the Fundamentalist line have begun to reproduce themselves in increasing numbers. As we have seen, since World War 2 Evangelical scholars, evangelists and Christian workers have attempted to criticize and reform their own tradition as well as to point out the defects of liberals, and this has accompanied a marked and increasing change in the spiritual climate.

Since the 1960s a growing tide of young Evangelical leadership has begun to pour into Evangelical seminaries and also into denominational schools. Some of these are brand new converts reached not in their home churches but through campus ministries. Others are the children of a self-reforming Evangelicalism which is more consistently breeding true. In many instances the campus converts are "covenant children" from non-Evangelical churches which lacked the catalytic thrust of the redemptive challenge to repentance, faith and new life in Christ. The remarkable thing which is occurring is that the Evangelicalism which apparently cannot touch these men and women in their home churches is reaching them through campus missionaries and then thrusting them back into their home denominations via the seminaries to renew the leadership of the mainline churches.

Ministers and adminstrators within the mainline churches are puzzled, cautious and apprehensive. But most congregations are especially eager to hire young ministers with this kind of background. The result is that while most of the ecclesiastical scene in America looks like a parched lawn spiritually, from the Evangelical standpoint, the regions surrounding the Evangelical seminaries appear as enlarging green spots surrounding a sprinkler system.

It is interesting to speculate on what the rest of America might look like if Christian educational institutions projecting a renewed Evangelicalism were placed at regular intervals over the surface of the continent. And this is a possibility, because the Evangelical seminaries are not only turning out ministers, but are also producing good quantities of young intellectual leaders who will either have to create new institutions to work in or to enter and transform old ones. What happens to heterodoxy if orthodoxy, under the blessing of God, simply outreproduces it?

Of course, this new leadership could be diverted from the mainline churches either by resistance within the church leadership or by the growth of zeal for separation within its own ranks. Both these ways of miscarrying are distinct possibilities which will have to be watched carefully. But the mood within the rank and file of churchmembers is distinctly favorable to Evangelical expansion.

Here is the projection of futurologists Herman Kahn and B. Bruce-Biggs:

> Should the tone of the times become more conservative and more traditional, many of the clergy would follow.... Several current phenomena would tend to promote such a shift. Many of the laity are appalled and shocked at the turn their churches have taken. These people are not normally very well organized, and have been, in the past, easily manipulated by the more aggressive minorities who support new ideas. The religious conservatives have ex-

pressed their displeasure by not attending church or not contributing to it. Donations to many of the most "advanced" churches have dropped sharply. People have suggested that funds currently being used for "social action" be given to the poor. They have not felt that the Black Panthers, draft dodgers, and militants are proper objects of Christian charity, nor have they felt that Christianity is furthered by support for the Viet Cong, Al Fatah, the Grapepickers' Union, the Southern Christian Leadership Conference, or the Memphis garbage collectors. Those who have stopped giving have been roundly attacked by the liberal clergy as "racist," which they have not appreciated. Currently, many of the churches most active in the social area are having to lay off staff because of declining contributions. There is a noticeable softening of the radicalism and militancy of the clergy, and a glimmering of the idea that perhaps their primary duty is to tend to the spiritual needs of their congregations. This idea is likely to grow in strength during the 1970's, and may even become fashionable among the most forward-thinking young seminarians.[23]

There is a flavor of social quietism in this passage which will disturb many younger Evangelicals, but the sentiment is probably accurate. Popular pressure could move the whole church establishment in an evangelical direction, provided that the mood of lay people is perceived as grounded in real spiritual hunger and biblical concern, rather than being merely a conservative political/economic reaction. In the Evangelical newsletters springing up in many mainline denominations we have alternate voices which can raise the consciousness of lay people to needs within the denomination which are not visible to its leadership. Once the laity begin to be more fully informed, our task may be to moderate the popular urge for theological reform rather than to spur it on.

But there are encouraging signs that establishment leaders

may not have to be forced in an evangelical direction by lay
pressure. The repudiation in 1975 of a number of significant
modern heresies by a group of theologians at Hartford is one
straw in the wind.[24]

An even more hopeful sign was a response to the Thanksgiving Declaration of Evangelicals by the National Council of
Churches, providing a complementary confession from the
non-Evangelical wing of mainline Protestantism:

> We cannot separate our efforts to alleviate the distresses
> of human society from the urgency to proclaim the Gos-
> pel of Christ, which truly saves and frees persons to be-
> come what God created them to be.... Though some-
> times denounced as "radical," we have not been nearly as
> genuinely radical as the Gospel calls us to be.... We have
> not proclaimed the full truth of Christ, which brings a
> more profound diagnosis of the human condition, a farther-
> reaching cure, and the possibility of real healing and trans-
> formation of persons and communities.... So we seek a
> Christian discipleship that is no longer shy or diffident
> about proclaiming the complete Gospel of Christ, with
> both its personal and its social implications.[25]

When opposition parties within the church come to the point
of confessing their faults to one another, the renewal of the
church is either near at hand or already present.

Actually the theological centers of gravity in Evangelicalism and the mainline denominations are perhaps closer than
they have been since the early part of this century. The impact of secularism set conservatives and liberals swinging in
opposing arcs like the arm of a pendulum, reaching positions
which were initially widely opposed (Fundamentalism and
the old Liberalism), then somewhat closer (Evangelicalism
and right-wing neo-orthodoxy) and finally relatively close
(young Evangelicals and the establishment theologians mentioned in the preceding paragraph) as the arc of the pendulum diminished during this century.

Of course, the picture is complicated by the continuing

oscillations and divisions within these traditions themselves. On the non-Evangelical side, the ambiguous coupling
of left-wing neo-orthodoxy, like that of Tillich, with the unorthodox evangelicalism of Brunner has confused Evangelical onlookers. And the neoliberal evolution from Barthian-
ism to the secular theologians and proponents of the death
of God has convinced many that the drift has been irrevocably to the left, especially in light of denominational literature
and administrative utterences which reflect the neoliberal
movement among younger leaders. It is just possible, however, that administrative leaders have seen where neoliberalism is headed, have had enough of it and are moving back
toward an evangelical balance with some urgency.

William Hordern noted several years ago that the disintegration of neo-orthodoxy might make way in the major denominations for a centrist party including younger Evangelicals. Some establishment leaders favor such a development.
The river of American Christianity spread out at the turn of
this century into a delta of shallower, separate streams, diverging to the right and left (see Figure 2). But now the delta
effect seems to be yielding to a pattern of convergence as
these streams reunite to form a single river, which we may
hope be both broad and deep because of its union of complementary opposites.

The splits and reactions within the Evangelical consensus
are at the moment an ironic contrast to the growing convergence in American Protestantism as a whole. The Reformed
and Lutheran orthodoxies have gone their own insular way
with gritty integrity and dogged consistency. Neo-Funda-
mentalists on the extreme right have written off the Neo-
Evangelical center as a beast and false prophet rolled into
one. Currently older Neo-Evangelicals are more afraid of the
young Turks within their own movement than they are of any
external forces. There seems to be a law of inverse cohesion
among orthodox people, theologically analogous to the bio-
logical principle of territoriality: the closer two orthodox

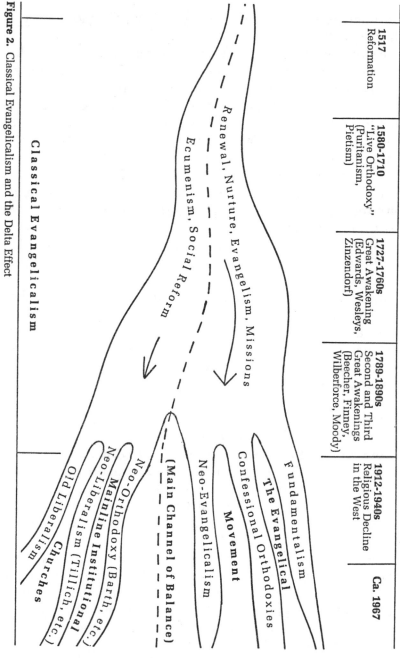

Figure 2. Classical Evangelicalism and the Delta Effect

Classical Evangelicalism

1517
Reformation

1580-1710
"Live Orthodoxy"
(Puritanism,
Pietism)

1727-1760s
Great Awakening
(Edwards, Wesleys,
Zinzendorf)

1789-1890s
Second and Third
Great Awakenings
(Beecher, Finney,
Wilberforce, Moody)

1912-1940s
Religious Decline
in the West

Ca. 1967

Renewal, Nurture, Evangelism, Missions

Ecumenism, Social Reform

Fundamentalism

The Evangelical

Confessional Orthodoxies

Movement

Neo-Evangelicalism

(Main Channel of Balance)

Neo-Orthodoxy (Barth, etc.)

Mainline Institutional

Neo-Liberalism (Tillich, etc.)

Old Liberalism

Churches

theologians get to one another's positions, the more reaction there is between them.

As the years go by, there is an increasing variety within Evangelicalism itself on the subject of Scripture with renewed haggling over the meaning of biblical authority and the terminology used to define it. This is not necessarily unhealthy. The authority of Scripture is as pivotal in its own way as the Christological formulations of the early church. It may not be an ultimate determinant of salvation, but it may have much to do with theological sanity, as the experiments of the last century seem to prove. Here, as in Christology, terminological minutiae may be important. But this interior search for perfection in defining the source of authority for theology must not be permitted either to sterilize or to divide the Evangelical forces, or to insulate them even further from dialog with the rest of the church.

Many discouraged Evangelicals are convinced that they have had as much communication with the liberal establishment as they need and have met only a brick wall of misunderstanding and opposition. But there may be a good deal of unconscious paranoia involved in this judgment, and there may not have been much real communication taking place.

Dialog and the Elijah Complex

There are various levels of intensity at which communication can occur. There is *concurrent proclamation*, in which both sides stand on different street corners and make their views known. This has been pursued for several decades now in popular theological journals, but unfortunately few members of one camp can stand to read the proclamations of the other with an open and sympathetic attitude. There is *reactive encounter*, in which members of differing parties rub up against one another on isolated issues, learn how appallingly different their approaches are and recoil from one another in horror. There is *confrontation*, in which parties square off against one another with an intense concern to fire their message at the opposing group like a bullet while demanding immediate capitulation, and with little listening sensitivity or mutual respect. Finally, there is *dialog*, in which two sides sit down with mutual respect and with some degree of that love which hopes and believes all things concerning one another. In this setting both sides seek to break through semantic and cultural barriers to achieve communication, not to lay manifestos upon one another, but to listen for whatever is of Christ in the concerns of the opposing voices.

How much dialog has there been? I do not feel we have discharged our responsibility toward one another until there has been quite a lot of it. Too often, however, Evangelicals have lacked patience and persistence to remain engaged in denominational machinery long enough to make an impression on it.

What can be done to insure the success of future dialog across theological lines? First, the negotiating leaders must be more theologically literate and less culturally/politically/economically motivated and polarized. Two kinds of persons are unsuited for dialog: those who are theologically untrained and insufficiently aware of the complexity of the issues being discussed, and those who cannot remain emotionally calm under the stress of differing opinions. It might be wise to use professional theologians along with other participants since sanctified learning does make a difference in the success both of comprehension and communication.

Second, the participants in dialog must accept their responsibility to love, respect and empathize with one another, and not draw back from this as if it were a dangerous heresy. All parties must be ready, at least provisionally, to learn something from Christ through one another and to recognize something of Christ in one another. Evangelicals must admit that many of the values present in the original evangelical movement are still preserved in non-Evangelical sectors of the church, sometimes more fully expressed there than among themselves. We must realize that our opponents are not always rejecting orthodoxy but only our handling of it. We must seek to help others to reach truth rather than passing sentence on those with imperfectly sanctified minds. We must grow to understand the historical forces which have distorted the faith of others and learn enough of the semantic and cultural roadblocks in their minds that we can speak in a tongue which will reach them. All must remember that there is plenty of historical evidence for the worst stereotypes the parties have of one another—and then forget the stereotypes and deal with present realities.

Third, Evangelicals should recognize that in seeking to reform and renew the church we are not fighting flesh and blood; we are hand-wrestling against principalities and powers. We are hampered by our own residual fallen nature as well as by that of our opponents. But beyond this we are facing a spiritual adversary whose interest is either to divide true Christians from one another or to unite them in professing falsehood. If we are not alert to this, we will spend our strength against fallible human beings like ourselves instead of confronting the real enemy, who seeks to color the reasoning of all parties and who constantly italicizes the stereotypes in the minds of believers.

Satan is also ready to depress us by offering his own estimate of the hopelessness of our case. I often tell my students that some of them feel I am overly optimistic about the recovery of the denominations, while many young Evangelical scholars feel I am too sanguine about the reformation of our own movement; but the devil is pessimistic about us all! A few recent setbacks among Evangelicals may not mean defeat but rather counterattack, something an army experiences when it is winning.

Paul sees clearly the work of Satan in church divisions:

And the Lord's servant must not be quarrelsome but kindly to every one, an apt teacher, forbearing, correcting his opponents with gentleness. God may perhaps grant that they will repent and come to know the truth, and they may escape from the snare of the devil, after being captured by him to do his will. (2 Tim. 2:24-26)

In Galatians 1:8-9 and other passages Paul presents an attitude toward heterodoxy which is harsher, and I believe that there are circumstances and times that call for such a stance. Our innate pride, however, especially the pride which can be an incidental effect of the possession of truth, makes it all too likely that we will turn every situation into a Galatians 1 affair and never get around to 2 Timothy 2. Paul's teaching does not imply that we should excuse the sin and error of those who have been struck with the paralyzing force of systematic antichristian thinking in our century until they can do little more than babble an echo of the world's wisdom with an occasional gesture toward the lordship of Christ. But what he says implies that we must handle them with patience and understanding, as fellow sinners who are inappropriate objects of the sentencing judgment of those who are cut from the same sinful cloth.

Both Evangelicals and non-Evangelicals have been reluctant to treat one another as fellow sinners, however, and have preferred to file one another. under the category of false prophet. We might call such a behavior pattern an Elijah complex.

The person who is alienated from Evangelicalism can very easily conclude that the movement is a stalking-horse for conservative politics and economic reaction, since even the new Evangelicalism has been socially quietistic while wealthy conservatives have paid the bills. It is natural for such a person to assume that Evangelicalism is offering American society a cheap fix with the opiate of the masses. An examination of the racial mores of the Bible Belt can lead him to the conclusion that Evangelicalism is offering cut-rate religion with cheap grace and minimal repentance, an agenda which certainly fits the classic profile of the false prophet.

The Evangelical Elijah, on the other hand, readily discerns

that many non-Evangelicals themselves have at best a ten-
uous hold on the redemptive message of grace, that they are
frequently doing very little but relaying the best (and occasionally the worst) thinking of the secular humanism which
surrounds us, and that the doctrine of God, and the person
and work of Christ are de-emphasized to the point of near
disappearance in their thinking. It is not hard to match up
this profile to the New Testament image of the antichristian
prophet.

Since both parties have shown signs of enculturation in
the past—Evangelicals in the late nineteenth-century individualism which Charles Reich calls Consciousness I, and
liberals in the social humanism which is Consciousness II—
it is easy for the parties to dismiss one another as antithetical
to the true interests of the kingdom of God.

Recent developments have helped convince both parties
that true prophecy exists at least in parts of the opposing sector. But Evangelicals especially need to face this question of
false prophecy squarely, because the separatist voices among
them are currently vigorous, plausible and positive in their
other contributions to the vitality of the movement. Evangelical *scholars* generally are quick to recognize the regeneracy and valid magisterium of persons outside their party,
since they have benefited so much from the research of other
scholars who give evidence of the creative direction of the
Holy Spirit, although they have not been formally identified
with the Evangelical movement. Often they have studied
under scholars who are outside Evangelicalism but who have
roots in it both in their background and their basic outlook.

Unfortunately most Evangelical *ministers* only come in
contact with non-Evangelical thinking under conditions of
reactive encounter. Much of their assessment of the gifts of
non-Evangelicals comes out of situations in which each
party is so acutely aware of the peculiarities of the other's
enculturation that its own response is polarized and exaggerated. If one addresses a congregation of bulls while

wearing a red suit, one is likely to conclude that dialog is use-less. Leaders who manage to project an image which has been purified from enculturation, who are courteous, charitable and free from intellectual self-righteousness, are likely to see a different side of the opposition. Ultimately both sides must come to recognize that they are dealing, not always with rag-ing wolves, but often only with confused and angry sheep.

Along with a strategy of *dialog,* then, some Evangelicals must adopt a posture of *involvement* in denominational structure which will bring them into contact with leaders in other theological traditions under conditions of shared responsibility for mission and ministry. If they can manage to exemplify "mere evangelicalism" in their contacts with other leadership, they are likely to find that there is an amaz-ing openness to their gifts and witness on the part of others, usually conjoined with considerable surprise at their wide divergence from the ugly Evangelical image.

They in turn are likely to have some edifying surprises. This will involve a considerable effort on the part of Evan-gelicals, who are often hopeless and passive within their denominations, devoted to their individual congregations but disengaged from the machinery of government between the churches. Often they justify this passivity by their dis-inclination to leave the world of ministry to persons in order to enter the realm of unfriendly bureaucratic machinery. But this may be an unrealistic dichotomy. Other ministers and administrators are also persons who need ministry, and the failure to see the hand of God and the interests of the kingdom in the business of judicatories may be due to prayer-lessness and spiritual myopia. Evangelicals should recog-nize that their own understanding of matters essential to Christian witness in the modern world needs to be aug-mented by the sensitivities of others who reflect other sectors of the wholeness of the original evangelical vision which was shattered by the estranging pressures of the twentieth century.

This presupposes some willingness on the part of the non-Evangelical proprietors who have inherited denominational control to permit, respect and even welcome Evangelical hands and voices in the direction of the church. In past years Evangelicals have been treated as the spiritual equivalent of cancer cells in the body of the church. In the course of the twentieth century they have been moved from a disciplining majority into an oppressed minority. As Tom Skinner has remarked, Evangelicals ought to be able to sympathize intuitively with the plight of the blacks because they themselves have been "niggerized," that is, ignored, repressed and treated as "the invisible man."

It is not surprising then that so many Evangelicals are consequently passive, hopeless and slow to enter into denominational enterprises, as well as being insecure and afflicted with a bad self-image. But if some are willing and able to accept a place in the leadership of the denominations, it must be given to them. Otherwise those who reject them will be in the ironic position of building the tombs of the prophets of the Reformation, Puritanism and the evangelical revivals while rejecting the most authentic modern spokespersons for their doctrinal positions. They must not be patronized and treated like strange mutations, extraterrestrial aliens, living fossils from some lost world, but welcomed as embodying part of the original genius of Protestantism.

At the present moment many of the mainline denominations are actively affording a larger role to responsible Evangelical leaders. During most of this century it has often seemed that "liberals" have often been the most illiberal and intolerant of churchpeople, perhaps because they have feared the division, interference, discipline and even retribution which might result from the increase of one kind of Evangelical. Now, however, visible gains in Evangelical leadership are occurring everywhere. This rising tide is most visible in some of the more traditionally conservative mainline churches such as the Southern Baptists or the Reformed

Church in America, but it is also beginning to percolate upward into more "liberal" churches.

Denominational colleges and seminaries are being re-
populated with Evangelical professors, and in some instances the central administrative leadership and policy are
Evangelical. The radio and television spokesman of one
mainline Reformed denomination is an Evangelical. Not
long ago, a large southern denomination, struggling with
severe polarization between liberals and conservatives,
chose an Evangelical as its secretary for evangelism, a rare
stroke of appropriate casting. The overt commitment of the
mainline churches to ecumenism and pluralism offers
leverage for Evangelicals who are positive, discreet, informed and constructive, and concerned to lend their talents
to give the major denominations theological and administrative balance.

It is just at this point, however, that Evangelicals of a
separatist persuasion will be most unsettled and dubious.
Is it possible for orthodox Christians to involve themselves
in denominations which have become so pluralistic that they
are virtually theological cafeterias, in which the member
congregations may choose any style of theology which suits
them? Isn't this sort of eclecticism the essence of the antichristian message Christianity has been fighting since the
appearance of Gnosticism? Doesn't this involve the total
abrogation of any principle of discipline within the church
order, which many Calvinists identify as one of the marks
of the church?

This is a crucial set of questions which must be effectively resolved if the recovery of the mainline denominations
is not to miscarry. The success of the resolution may depend
more on the spirituality of the Evangelical leadership promoting that recovery than on a set of guiding principles set
down in advance. Unitive efforts fail most often for want of
Christians who are sensitive to the Holy Spirit, rather than
for want of theology. But wrong principles can program dis-

unity, while right ones can promote unity. And so I offer at least a few tentative precepts.

Toward a Healthy Unity

First, effective discipline is indeed a mark of the church. It could almost be elevated to the position of one of the essential parameters of renewal reviewed in chapter three above, except that it is already latent there as a derivative of the community of believers. The pattern of Ephesians 4:1-16 requires that church leaders speak the truth in love to those who are harming or even destroying themselves and the body of Christ either by antichristian teaching or behavior. Matthew 18:15-18 (compare 18:5-9) states that erring members should ultimately be brought before the church. Unfortunately this passage does not tell us what to do if the majority of the church sides with the member in error. But it is clear there can be no real involvement in a church order without the assumption and exercise of the duty of rebuke, and, ultimately, of the last recourse of excommunication, the partial interruption of fellowship with errant individuals or groups.

But the critical matter to be kept in mind is that all discipline is designed to promote the health of the body, and, therefore, it must be restrained and governed by that ultimate goal. There are many cures which are worse than the diseases for which they are intended. Looking back at the secessions and excommunications of groups of Christians during the past five hundred years, who can say that the church would not have been healthier if it had proceeded with attitudes of patience and tolerance and by strategies of pluralism, inclusion and gradual education through mutual witness? The context of the disciplinary passage in Matthew 18 deals primarily with the need for restraint in our responses to the sins of others (vv. 21-35) and with the concern to seek and bring back the lost and straying (vv. 10-14). Church discipline which does not display these characteristics is more an allergic reaction between parts of the body than a constructive response to their need for care and protection.

Another matter which must be given careful consideration is the very problematic issue of defining the breadth of the circle of permissible doctrinal and behavioral variation within the church, which determines the point at which discipline must be brought to bear. Most of us are ready to accept Calvin's advice and put up with "tolerable stupidities"; our only question is the size and content of this category.

Many Evangelicals talk as if the Hodge-Warfield definition of the authority of Scripture were not only an item of belief necessary to salvation, but also an article of the creed by which the church stands or falls. Many younger Evangelicals would question whether a doctrinal circle which would rule out of the church's ministerium men like Emil Brunner, P. T. Forsyth or Helmut Thielicke is healthy for the church as a whole. Those who hold that it is had better follow their bent and peacefully secede to some smaller denomination attempting to give a pure witness to this tradition.

On issues such as unbelief in the deity of Christ and his bodily resurrection, however, it seems fairly evident that Evangelicals would have to take a clear disciplinary stance or risk violation of the gospel. If it proves impossible for Evangelicals to speak their minds and see the church responding in disciplinary action in matters like these, then the hope of denominational recovery without massive secession of Evangelicals is probably illusory. If the laity in the larger churches are kept alert to these issues, however, the church leadership, as their instruments, will probably be forced to respond in disciplinary actions which are in line with the biblical witness and traditional Christian doctrine and practice. The proper informing and activating of the laity, in fact, may be one factor in a renewed church which virtually eliminates discipline problems which were very difficult to resolve in the past. The education of the laity may be the fastest road to the re-education of the clergy.

What about transdenominational Evangelical renewal

within the ecumenical movement? We have noted above that there is already a functioning Evangelical ecumenical movement. The recognition of this fact is remarkably apparent in the recent admirable decision of the Presbyterian Church of America (the product of secessions from the Northern and Southern Presbyterian Churches) not to form its own Department of Missions, but rather to use the existing network of interdenominational Evangelical faith missions to disseminate its Reformed doctrinal position throughout the church.

We can certainly hope that other smaller churches concerned for the preservation of a doctrinal tradition will remain engaged within the Evangelical consensus even if this becomes increasingly pluralistic. We can also pray that separated churches having a similar basic stance will have a unitive conscience, and will move toward organic union with one another where this is practically possible and most helpful for their mission and the church at large.

There are three other related areas in which it is difficult to lay down general guidance in advance: union between individual mainline denominations; union between numbers of these, as in the Consultation on Church Union negotiations initiated by the Blake-Pike proposal; and involvement in the National and World Councils of Churches. Evangelicals are chronically resistive to all three of these for different reasons. Those in the more conservative of two merging denominations which are very close in tradition and polity usually see the merger, not as a possibility for enlarged witness, but rather as a ticket to doctrinal genocide. There is evidence in history which supports their fears, but somehow there is something suspicious about this defensive posture. What is being defended may not have much force with which to maintain and propagate its distinctive character.

The matter of C.O.C.U. is much more complex. Evangelicals may properly hesitate to embrace a merged church which they have not had a hand in designing. On the other hand, much of the Evangelical resistance to C.O.C.U. seems to spring from the defensive thinking just described and from a desire to hold on to the differentia of one's own denomination which may not be able to find satisfaction outside a separatist group. The architects of wider church union should make an effort to include in their number Evangelicals who have a unitive vision and who are not prepared to insist that the core of the united church be an elaborate systematic theology condensed on microfilm, like the creedal utterances of the Reformation.

The large federations of churches are genetically rooted in earlier evangelical unity movements but have had a very mixed character during the twentieth century. It is possible to maintain that the World Council of Churches represents the intertwining and attempted fusion of two separate ecumenical movements, one line descending from evangelical orthodoxy and later represented by the right-wing neo-orthodoxy of Faith and Order conferences, and the other springing from liberal and social gospel roots in the Life and Work conferences and continued by left-wing neo-orthodoxy, neoliberalism and secular theologies of one sort or another.

Currently the World Council seems to have become dominated by theological positions which define the church's mission almost wholly in terms of social liberation, and Evangelicals have fallen into a pattern of holding what are almost counterconferences on evangelism and mission. But at the latest of the Evangelical conferences, the Lausanne Congress of 1974, Latin-American Evangelicals injected a sharp reminder of the social dimension of biblical faith. Some Evangelicals have sensed an increasing burden to enter into closer continued dialog with the World Council in order to balance out in a similar manner the spectrum of its concerns and agenda. Others typically shrink back from this kind of involvement, fearing contamination and dilution of the faith with a foreign gospel derived from Marxism. Probably what is needed at this point is for a coalition composed of Evangelical theologians and conservative neo-orthodox thinkers to enter the arena of dialog in the WCC rather boldly and stay there until their concerns are recognized.

In recent years the World Council has been addressed both by Billy Graham and Leighton Ford, but such visits amount to encounter or confrontation and fall short of the kind of dialog which leads to mutual comprehension. Dialog would bring together a group of Christians who have thought very deeply about the biblical theology of mission with others who have deeply immersed themselves in the social and intellectual crises of our time, and out of this meeting of interests might come a new wholeness of vision.

Will the result of such dialog be a massive reconciliation and reunification of the divided stream of Christianity, like the tableau of Joseph and his brethren in Genesis 45? Or will it be the renewed polarization of the two streams with a small minority of conversions to one point of view or the other? Ultimately the question here is whether the two streams represent antithetical gospels or only complementary versions of the one gospel distorted by their alienation from one another. Since we are judging persons and not just ideas, it is hard to make a judgment until these two touchstones have rubbed up against one another.

Evangelicals who write off the World Council as an instrument of Antichrist should remember that the most embarrassing public relations problems for Christianity are created, not by socially concerned liberals, but by situations like that of South African Calvinist orthodoxy. It may be that Spener's opinion is correct and that ecumenical interrelationships are of little value until the constituent fragments of Christ's body are first revived.[26] On the other hand, it is possible that reunion may be the very instrument of revival or at least the precondition of the outpouring of a larger measure of life from the Holy Spirit. One is reminded of Ezekiel's vision of the valley of dried bones, in which the regathering of Israel precedes the inbreathing of life into the body (Ezek. 37:1-14).

It is interesting that the ecumenical movement which has dissolved so many quirks and prejudices of denominational tradition has used doctrinal indifferentism as the solvent. This weakness may have been essential to the reintegration of the church, like the lowered resistance induced by drugs in patients who are undergoing organ transplants so that their bodies will not attack and destroy the new organs which are being inserted. Live orthodoxy might have been a better solvent, but, as we have seen, human beings find it difficult to handle orthodoxy in a way that heals.

Is some kind of productive federal relationship possible between Evangelical Christianity and Roman Catholicism? It will still be difficult for many to entertain the idea of relations with the papal antichrist, as with the liberal antichrist of the WCC. It is true that the idolatrous and enculturated popular Catholicism of many regions is one of the most serious standing scandals in Christendom. On the other hand, the warfare between a fossil version of Protestant orthodoxy and that same Catholicism in northern Ireland is a scandal of equal proportions. The documents of Vatican II do not significantly erase the elements of Trent and Vatican I which Protestants must continue to regard as targets of reformation. However, the recognition they accord to the gifts and presence of the Holy Spirit among the separated brethren has opened the way for an amazing amount of interdenominational dialog at the grassroots level.

While it is hard to imagine the Vatican linking up with 475 Riverside Drive, let alone the National Association of Evangelicals, it is not fanciful to see local Catholic clergy engaging in more dialog and cooperation with local Evangelicals, if the latter can develop a unitive conscience as active as that of their liberal brethren. The most likely participants in forging a Catholic-Protestant unity are not administrators but Evangelicals grounded in (but not bound by) the Puritan tradition of live orthodoxy and Catholics with a discriminating knowledge of their own tradition of spiritual theology, along with Catholic Charismatics. Just such grassroots dialog and cooperation in home mission between young Evangelicals newly concerned for social ministry and liberals newly awakened to their need for spiritual anchorage and evangelistic potency may prove to be the growing edge of Protestant unification.

With the movement toward unity by-passing administrative centers and flourishing at the edge of the institutional church, it is tempting to think that institutional machinery is unimportant in renewal, a husk to be thrown out after organic spiritual unity is achieved. But this is too simplistic. There is also a need for the renewal of structures, because we should strive to preserve the fruits of the sacrificial labors of Christians in other generations where they have continuing relevance and usefulness. This principle of the conservation of structures is integral to transforming and recovering the denominational fragments of the body of Christ.

The institutional residues of Christendom often appear to be empty fossils left by previous life, shells that were once inhabited by growing organisms but are now inert and useless. But this is a mistaken image. The best analog is perhaps a southwestern desert landscape. All around us are *arroyos*, the empty gullies dug by floods from the spring rains, and the great river of institutional Christianity into which they lead is now an extensive mud flat with a thin ribbon of living water wandering through the center, almost hidden from view. But it requires only another spring for the gullies to fill again and the river to flow full to its banks, to make all things alive and even old things new. The psalmist sums up our desire: "Restore our fortunes, O LORD, like the watercourses in the Negeb! May those who sow in tears reap with shouts of joy!" (Ps. 126:4-5).

THE
EVANGELICAL
MUSE

11

WHEN I WAS FOURTEEN I BOUGHT my first record album, a 78 rpm recording of Rachmaninoff's *Second Piano Concerto* with Artur Rubinstein. For twenty years after that purchase, I never doubted that there was only one kind of significant musical culture: "serious music," a euphemism for "classical" compositions, which made it clear that all other kinds were frivolous. And so while the rest of society went through Crosby to Sinatra, and later through Elvis to the Beatles, I had periods of enthusiasm for Beethoven's slow movements (most of which I could manage on the piano), Debussy, Sibelius, Shostakovitch and Prokofiev, Aaron Copland and Roy Harris (while I was trying to write "American" style music), and finally a mature love for Bach, Mozart, Schubert, Brahms, Dvorak and Mahler, which is still there.

When I became an Evangelical Christian in my twenties

there were other reasons to continue this snobbery. Popular music was not only at a one-celled animal level of inspiration, it was "worldly" in its sentiments as well as in its "jungle rhythms." I heard attempts at "Christian rock-and-roll music" and shuddered. Schubert did get away with setting a section of the mass to a waltz, but sacred words and secular tunes just didn't go together.

As a Christian, however, I was praying for renewal in the church, and I assumed that spiritual awakening would mean an outpouring of Christian music as in the past. Now this music would have to be "serious," of course, but making use of the harmonic advances of this century, in the manner of Stravinsky's *Symphony of Psalms*, Britten's *War Requiem* or Poulenc's *Gloria*.

The only problem was that this kind of music, with roots in the past but an expanded harmonic vocabulary, was drying up in the 1950s and 60s; and most of what was left looked to me like a desert. Composers abandoned the old claims and ranged afield looking for virgin gold fields of musical novelty, and the kinds of things they came up with hurt my ears and didn't seem to fit Christian poetry. There was aleatory (chance-produced) music where composition was done with dice or the I-Ching sticks. On the other hand, there was "totally organized" serial music where little was left to chance (or inspiration), because the melody, harmony and sometimes even the rhythms of a piece were predetermined by the opening notes.

Now chance music (like "found" and junk art) seemed to imply that just about anything is beautiful. This relativized everything and contradicted my instinctive conviction that God has hidden beauty throughout creation like diamonds in clay, so that it must be intelligently mined. Serial music, on the other hand, had rules, but they were manmade, and they might contradict the God-made rules in the mathematics of the tonal system. Requiring that every other chord must be dissonant in order to defeat the listener's sense of tonality seemed, in a word, contrived. ("Why," said Pablo Casals to Arnold Schoenberg, "did you turn music over and show us its dark side?" "Ah," said Webern after hearing Schubert, "if we could only write like that today!")

Then there was postserial music, with its blops in the bass and bleeps in the treble separated by pregnant silences, and electronic music produced by technicians, *Augenmusik,* which looked great on paper but which sounded best as the soundtrack of science-fiction films. It seemed that "serious" music had crossed the line of despair into a wasteland of arcane lunacy, shortly to expire in a fit of self-inspired giggles.[1]

It was about this time that Leonard Bernstein came out with a good word for the Beatles, commending their sophisticated use of modal harmony. Simultaneously, the youth in my church came at us with a program comparing the new popular music at its more diabolical pole (the Doors, "Light My Fire") with its more significant productions (the Beatles, "She's Leaving Home," "Eleanor Rigby"). Now this, I thought, is something new: popular music using surrealist symbolism, string quartets and postimpressionist harmony. By the time I had seen *Help!* I was selectively hooked on the Beatles.

It suddenly seemed that though there was nothing new blooming in the orchid gardens of serious music, the fields were full of gorgeous popular wildflowers: Bob Dylan, Leonard Cohen and Joni Mitchell; Judy Collins, the fine artist who sang their songs with a pure clear voice; Simon and Garfunkel translating T. S. Eliot for the young; Burt Bacharach with his odd intervals and sprung rhythms; and so many others with surrealistic names that enumeration is impossible. I began listening to underground music on FM, and I found that even the top forty on AM had songs lovely enough to make one's beard stand on end—A. E. Housman's test for authentic beauty. (I realize that I am mixing schools and genres in a way which will freeze the blood of pop partisans, but I am through with musical snobbery forever.)

What was going on was readily apparent. While the serious musicians had gone off in the Sahara looking for utterly original gold fields, the popular composers were busy mining old claims, gathering baskets of precious leftovers uncovered by the musical exploration of the last three hundred years. Serious music was at the end of a blind alley, while popular music was enjoying its greatest renaissance since Haydn and Mozart wrote dance music. The action was in the pop scene. Some serious critics talked about "third stream music," mixing pop and serious, and predicted that new composers would be eclectics making patchwork quilts out of different stylistic fragments. The music of Bernstein, Gunther Schuller, George Rochberg and Michael Tippett seemed to confirm this.

There is no doubt that this efflorescence of culture has been used at times to push dubious products: drugs, sensuality, Eastern religion and revolution-for-the-hell-of-it. But what is obvious is that some forces (Marxism, for instance) are intelligently using the new culture for secular evangelism. Now why should the devil have all the best tunes? Perhaps the music produced by the present awakening will be a popular hymnology in which the allusive symbolism of the new lyrical style is harnessed to the Christian message.

Even non-Christians are writing such hymns now by some thrust of common grace: "Look down upon me, Jesus, you gotta help me make a stand, I can't make it any other way. . . . Come on, children, Jesus gonna heal you all. . . ." This may be God's prompting to show us how to communicate to the hunger of the new generation. The phenomenal popularity of *Godspell*, and even *Jesus Christ, Superstar* indicates the depth of that hunger and its responsiveness even to crumbs of evangelical truth when they are clothed in a sophisticated popular idiom.

I was at a concert given by Blood, Sweat and Tears one

summer, reflecting during the intermission on the vigorous brass and Hindemithean harmony of the group, when suddenly the little enclave of Christians I was with broke rather timidly into the verse of "To God Be the Glory." I confess that I shrank. Must we always face the contemporary world from behind the old brown hymnal? Wouldn't "Bridge Over Troubled Water" be a more effective statement, with perhaps some additional words?

For the sake of mission, at least some Christians are obligated to learn the musical language of the youth culture until it becomes their natural expressive medium. The younger generation are already producing this kind of art as an organic product of their Christian experience. Today, at the same time that secular popular musicians are repeating themselves or searching aimlessly for new modes of expression which move beyond the high-water mark of the last decade, Christian musicians are breaking new ground. It almost seems that the demonic muse of the 1960s has yielded to the Evangelical muse, the Spirit of Christ, in the 1970s. There are many artisans available who are gifted with the charism of Bezalel and Oholiab, "filled . . . with the Spirit of God, with ability and intelligence, with knowledge and all craftsmanship, to devise artistic designs" (Ex. 31:3-4).

Springs in a Dry Land

I know many young Christians, some of them not at all trained musically, who find themselves being "given" songs of such musical beauty and verbal subtlety that a very real kind of inspiration seems involved. Through this medium, in the coming decades, the gospel could penetrate with lightning speed to the ends of an earth much diminished by the communication explosion and opened up by the erosion of cultural walls. Christian music could play an important part in the greatest missionary impact of the Christian church in history.

The same fresh inspiration which is apparent in the musical gifts of younger Evangelicals is present also in other Christian artists working in literature, drama, film, graphic arts, architecture and dance. There is no shortage of gifted Christian artists to fill the media in America with a witness to the creative power latent in the gospel of Christ. If the rest of the church stands behind them with prayer and financial support, there is no reason why they should not erect new cultural monuments in this age to proclaim Christ with the same power resident in the great works of the cathedral builders, the religious painters, Bach and Handel, and Haydn and Mendelssohn.

In most cases, however, these artists receive even less support from Christians than the world has usually given to its Schuberts and its Mozarts. I know a young film maker, James Hodge, who is creating works with the depth and subtlety of Bergman; but he is working on a very small platform of financial backing, and experimental growth in cinema costs money.[2] Larry Norman, whose work is equivalent in quality to that of Dylan and the Beatles in the sixties, should be on Broadway and in television and films; but the strength does not seem to be there in the church as yet to vault him into those orbits. I know of other young musicians, such as James Ward and Ken Medema, who are creating works which fuse popular and serious elements to create works with the beauty and subtlety of classical lieder, but their candles burn under bushels of obscurity.

All this is plainly contrary to the will of Christ, who gave us these artists as gifts for the full expression of the gospel before the world. Jesus said, "Nothing is covered that will not be revealed, or hidden that will not be known. What I tell you in the dark, utter in the light; and what you hear whispered, proclaim upon the housetops" (Mt. 10:26-27). There are in the church today works of unspeakable beauty which are hidden in darkness, while the surface of the Christian world is flooded with tasteless songs and shallow anecdotal books. Francis Bacon remarked that it was the nature of heavy things to sink to the bottom of the stream of history while straw and stubble floats on top. This is true today in all forms of the church's utterance including its aesthetic witness. We are responsible to change this situation.

There are, however, a number of hindrances which are going to make it hard for us to do this. The first is a fact often noted by Christian musicians: the media, especially radio and television, are dominated by a power structure controlled by the flesh, the world and ultimately the devil. The media and the educational systems in many countries are deliberately used by ruling authorities to keep a steady stream of propaganda circulating among the minds of the people. In America and other capitalist nations, however, a more subtle control operates through the profit motive to spread non-Christian values and beliefs. Human beings are not always intentionally orchestrating this mixture of propaganda. It flows forth spontaneously from the carnal mind, searching for what will please the people and sell products, but the ultimate control which guides it is satanic.

Now the capitalist system in which this process operates is ultimately responsive to popular taste. If a large enough sector of the public adopts Christian values and makes those values known to advertisers, the media will begin to avoid material which is dissonant with Christianity and cater to Christian taste. But this will only occur if Christians rise up out of the almost total passivity toward shaping our culture which they have adopted throughout most of the century and make their values and desires known, requesting the work of Christian artists and others whose impact is positive and healthy, and resisting art and entertainment which is dehumanizing and socially corrosive, even through the use of the boycott if necessary. It will also be necessary to attack the system of kickbacks and payola, involving both money and drugs, which fuels the star-making system in many parts of the media. In some cases the only way to do that effectively may be to provide alternate channels of broadcasting which are free to present the best in Christian opinion and art.

But while the number of vital Christians seems to be increasing in the late 1970s at a pace which could soon give us the popular base for cultural reshaping, the most serious limits on our ability to achieve this goal are within the Christian movement itself. Those with money and power in Christian circles are usually middle-aged or older. They are often quite negative toward the forms of popular culture which could reach younger people in America and very satisfied with media presentations which appeal to the culture and taste of their age group. They are looking for the evangelistic equivalent of Lawrence Welk, and they cannot grasp the usefulness of having Christian Ingmar Bergmans and Bob Dylans. If the new Christian art which God is pouring out to help the church in its tasks of evangelism and nurture is to be lifted up in our society to do its work, mature Christians must come to recognize their enculturation and reach across the cultural barriers to give assistance to those working in the youth culture.

But there is a problem more serious than mere enculturation restraining fresh artistic expression in the church and its promotion toward visibility in society. This problem is the sterilization of art by ascetic moralism and oversimplified theology.

In the early years of my Christian life, as a converted intellectual drawing my spiritual nurture from the Evangelical world, I used to wonder why there were no Evangelical poets and novelists of major stature. Why did we have to turn to the Roman Catholic Church to find Graham Greene and Flannery O'Connor, Gerard Manley Hopkins and Robert Lowell? Among Protestants we had to go to Anglo-Catholicism to discover C. S. Lewis and Charles Williams, T. S. Eliot and W. H. Auden. I was convinced that Evangelical Protestantism had a strong hold on biblical truth and spiritual reality, and I was willing to tolerate the fact that it was an aesthetic desert because I was so thirsty for the experience of grace and wisdom which made it an oasis in the desert of the world. But I was troubled then by its relative barrenness in creative expression, and later by the lack of creativity in its theological life.

The Roots of a Barren Culture

Gradually through the study of history I was able to track down some of the causes for these problems. I found that Evangelicalism had its roots in Puritan and Pietist traditions which had fused the ascetic piety of the early church fathers with Protestant doctrine and which had also overreacted against the luxurious expression of Christian faith in symbolic liturgy, graphic art, music and architecture. As a result of these forces, the evangelical stream moved away from the sacramental vision of life in Catholic tradition, in which the created world is not only celebrated as good but recognized as a constant symbolic message about spiritual reality. Evangelicals moved almost in a Manichaean direction, toward a frame of mind in which the objects of sense and sight could drag us away from what was "spiritual."

To be sure, this ascetic tradition originated in Catholic Christianity and is still firmly planted there, so that G. K. Chesterton's attack on Puritanism is launched from a glass fortress.[3] But the double standard in Catholicism, which allows both for vocations of perfection employing ascetic rules and for the common life which is allowed to be somewhat sloppier morally and theologically, affords a freedom for creative growth which Protestant evangelicalism could not match because of its greater rigor of discipline. Evangelicals recognized only one standard which was supposed to be equally binding for clergy and laity, for the dedicated and the apathetic. The thrust of this still seems to be biblical. But the insistence on moral rigor can be deadening to culture, can make it like a barren soil soaked in chemical poisons, unless the moral sensibility of the church is very finely tuned. The church must discriminate only against real evil.

Otherwise, it can exert a sterilizing force similar to the restraints which Communist states have sometimes imposed on their artists.

This is the most serious factor limiting artistic creativity among Evangelicals today. The moral discriminator of the Evangelical community is so ill-tuned that it reacts against and casts out of the church nearly any creative expression which depicts life as freely as the Bible does. Evangelicals generally do not understand that what determines the edifying or corrosive power of a work of art is not the materials it uses and the actions it describes, but rather its moral outlook toward those materials and actions. We need to ponder the truth of the objection frequently made to many laws against pornography, that strict enforcement of such laws would suppress the Bible which rarely fails to call a spade a spade.

Consider one of Larry Norman's songs designed to reach the rock culture:

Gonorrhea on Valentine's Day
And you're still looking for the perfect lay
You think rock and roll will set you free
Honey, you'll be dead before you're thirty-three
Shootin' junk till you're half insane
A broken needle in your purple vein
Why don't you look into Jesus, He's got the answer.[4]

This is not great poetry, but it is an honest, realistic appeal to those caught in the lifestyle of the non-Christian youth culture, which vigorously addresses them in images which prove that the speaker has moved in their world and identifies with their needs. Any attempt to clean up the language or prettify the images would dismantle the ironic conjunction in the first line and emasculate the song's impact.

Christian audiences, producers and financial backers are going to have to learn to appreciate realism in Christian art or they will bind it in moralistic straitjackets which prevent its contact with the actual world, with non-Christian audiences and with young people of every sort, who will soon desert a gelded art to seek poetry and music which is free and real. The libretto for the film *Yellow Submarine*, which pictures a Victorianized England frozen into immobility by the Blue Meanies and released to bloom in life and creativity by the Beatles, describes a real weakness in culture which is inhibited by enforced moralism. If we do not set our own art free of moralistic overkill, we will lose our children again and again to the evangelizing force of non-Christian popular art.

The same warning needs to be sounded in connection with Evangelical scruples about musical languages. It is often assumed by Christians that any use of the idioms emerging from American jazz, blues and hard-rock music must be dishonoring to God because of the pagan origins of these forms in the American black and African cultures. This prejudice may involve covert racism, and it uses theological reasoning as weak as Tertullian's argument that the theater is a non-Christian form of art because it was first used in pagan worship ceremonies.

Other Christians feel that certain rhythms are inherently sexually suggestive, and some musical idioms so associated with the atmosphere of rock concerts and nightclubs that they are inappropriate media to express Christian truth. The first of these arguments seems to reflect a Victorian uneasiness about sexuality. The second overlooks the wide use of popular tunes for Christian purposes in earlier centuries, which made use of the very familiarity and congeniality of this music to overcome the sense of holy distance isolating the public from religion and to convince them that Christianity was part of the real world.

It is true that new converts out of the rock culture may have trouble for a lengthy period in associating their new life as Christians with the old context involving rock music. A conditioning process has been at work here which is difficult to overcome. There is also a natural tendency in any convert to throw over everything connected with pre-Christian existence in favor of a simplified and wholly Christianized world. But to fail to purify and refine the languages of non-Christian culture in order to reach those who speak them is to abdicate our responsibility both to evangelize and to subdue all of culture to the rule of Christ.

Beyond these moralistic obstacles to artistic expression, Evangelicals need to recover a theological creativity and a foundational world view deep enough to support viable art. When I was converted several decades ago the best medium for expressing popular Evangelical theology was probably the comic strip. This situation still prevails in some areas, although deepening and renewing penetration into Scripture is refreshing the sources of Evangelical theology. A two-dimensional theological outlook which divides the human population into the saved and the lost and identifies these categories with unmixed good and evil, without sensing the tragic ambiguity of indwelling sin and the mysterious movement of the Holy Spirit in common and special grace, cannot create a literature which rises above black-and-white caricatures of human experience. It has been spiritual theologians like Augustine and Luther who have made possible a realistic Christian literary vision, and a rebirth in spiritual theology among contemporary believers will inevitably have the same effect.

Since the Reformation burst forth within the Western church aided by the newly invented medium of the printed word, every evangelical awakening has made extensive use of all media available to advance the renewing work of the Spirit. Often the awakenings have also generated new artistic expression of the gospel, both in popular and serious forms of literature and music. For most of the present century, however, the church has made only marginal use of the new media of radio, television and film, and has given birth only to a small body of art which could be conveyed by these media.

Christian use of the new media up to now can generally be divided into the two categories of Evangelical ineptitude, providing what might best be described as biblical truth preserved in a glaze of corn syrup, and liberal skill, offering sophisticated presentations of material without much spiritual cutting edge. Neither camp has been able to master the art of drawing in the non-Christian listener or viewer before triggering the urge to switch channels. Now that God is raising up a growing body of Christian artists in music, literature and other forms related to film, television and radio, it is critically important that the church pull its resources together and lift up the best of its work before the observing world.

Among Evangelicals this will require a broadening of the current understanding of the nature of witnessing, missions and evangelism. Sharing the gospel is not accomplished only by mass evangelism and personal witness. It is also powerfully aided by the erection of cultural monuments in history like the work of Bach, which point as beacons to the cross, or more popular artistry like Christian rock music, which can make the gospel irresistably attractive to the masses. Evangelical lay people who have been trained to support missions and evangelism in a narrower definition of those terms must learn to promote a much broader range of witness by their giving.

The conversion of large numbers of people to vital Christianity in the present evangelical awakening will powerfully augment the financial base for funding Christian artists, both through the contributions of individuals and through the support of foundations created by the Evangelical publishing houses currently accumulating funds from Christian literature sold to the new converts. Christian rock music should fairly rapidly change from a financially dependent medium to an income-producing source, once it has been boosted into visibility beside its secular counterparts.

But Evangelical Christians will have to learn to think and

pray realistically about their responsibility in such traditionally "worldly" vocations as the entertainment world and
politics for any solid transformation to take place. The social
and cultural passivity of twentieth-century Evangelicalism,
the almost programmatic despair with regard to arresting
cultural decay, will have to be corrected through a reinvigor-
ation of the church's fighting spirit. And the depth of the
laity's financial stewardship will have to be increased. As
many younger voices have indicated, the automatic conformity with middle-class living standards common among
Evangelicals may have to be scaled back to a simpler lifestyle so that more money can be released for God's work.

The lay leaders in the Second Evangelical Awakening in
England and America were consumed with zeal for the social
and cultural expression of the gospel, and gave their time
and their money for the work of the kingdom without any
reservations. By the early 1900s a different pattern in American lay support took shape: wealthy lay people tithed their
incomes to the church but quietly steered its social and
political witness in directions which supported their interests. This pattern prevails today. Concern for the kingdom no
longer controls our giving; the church is simply a spoke on
the wheel of a wide variety of benevolent causes.

The reason for this shallow and manipulative support is
lack of depth in sanctification. American lay people are no
longer being challenged at the root of their concerns in the
process of evangelism and nurture. Consequently their ultimate concern is not the kingdom of God but the business of
business. It may require a retuning of the laity in all of the
dimensions of renewal before American Evangelicalism has
the controlling impact on our culture which it had in the
nineteenth century.

Toward a Renewed Culture
What kinds of programs in the church could reverse this
situation and revitalize Christian witness in the arts and the

media? First of all, churchpeople need to be alerted that God is giving these young artists to the church as instruments for ministry. They need to be introduced sympathetically to their work and rallied behind it in prayer. They need to be encouraged to support this work with their gifts, remembering that the Israelites brought a superabundance of resources and materials (including the jewels received from the Egyptians) to be reshaped into the furniture of the sanctuary by the artisty of Bezalel and Oholiab. Christian entrepreneurs are needed to set up performance networks among the churches for Christian music, drama and poetry. Colonies for the production of Christian art, music and literature should be subsidized, probably using the semicommunal lifestyle with which many younger Christians feel comfortable.

A deliberate effort must also be made to provide alternative radio and television programming aimed especially at large student population centers such as Boston and New York. Traditional Evangelical "family radio" programming will not reach the youth culture. What is needed is sophisticated Christian programming characterizing the whole output of a station, with a consistency of taste similar to that of the better underground rock stations. Foundation grants must be secured so that Christian poets and musicians can film one-hour specials for educational television. Ultimately a larger public demand for Christian art will build up in the culture at large, if this art can find its way around the satanic roadblocks in the present media situation to reach the public. The quality of much Christian rock music at the moment is palpably superior to its secular rivals, and young people will not fail to recognize that quality.

Do Christians have a responsibility to restrain the decadence of the media, as well as to promote the renewal of Christian art? This is a difficult and ambiguous question, as my remarks about Victorian censorship have already indicated. By ruling the cinema out of bounds, Evangelicals abdicated any position they might have had in shaping their expression during the 1930s, 40s and 50s, and it remained for Catholics and other Protestants to exert a pressure restraining cultural decay. The films of this period sometimes seem to have been helped by this pressure, moved toward depth and subtlety because they could not resort to crude sexuality, violence and other cheap forms of entertainment.

During the sixties and seventies the experience of greater freedom in cinema and television has produced some mature and intelligent art and a great deal of material in increasingly poor taste. The attack upon sexual and religious conventions begun in America by Lenny Bruce and pursued extensively in England has already led to a militant backlash among audiences. Unfortunately, television producers, forced to tone down violence in their programs in the late seventies, chose to escalate the content of sexually suggestive and anti-conventional material in their programs in order to hold their ratings. The more difficult solution of improving the taste and quality of their programming seems to have evaded their notice.

It is practically inevitable that the increasing population of Christians in America will join with feminists and other religious groups to protest the merchandizing of sex and boycott the advertisers who promote it. The campaign of Anita Bryant against the open expression of homosexuality among teachers is just one manifestation of a kind of super-saturation in the American conscience which is likely to crystallize in many other moralistic crusades, most of them repressive and destructive, if the arbiters of culture continue to pander to the lowest popular tastes. The question in the future will be not so much whether or not to restrain culture, but how to do so responsibly in order to reinforce art and quality rather than introducing a plastic moral conformity.

Violence and explicitly sexual behavior are not in themselves corrosive to our social and moral fabric when portrayed in films and television. The Bible contains both of these elements, as anyone knows who has read the Old Testament historical books or the Song of Solomon. The key factor in assessing the social and moral impact of sex and violence in the media is the moral and theological point of view underlying a particular presentation, and the reason these elements have been used. A relatively nonexplicit film which glorifies or idealizes extramarital sexuality can be as subversive to the consciences of young people as an X- or R-rated film. More explicit portrayals of the happiness of love within marriage might actually reinforce Christian standards and neutralize the residual asceticism in the church, which offends the world and makes Christians vulnerable to the devil's monopoly on sexuality.

A mayor of New York City once commented that no young lady was ever seduced by a book. That may be true, but it is probably equally true that literary, dramatic and musical portraits of extramarital sexuality have an impact in shaping or misshaping moral values, especially when this behavior is presented as not only exciting but also normal and acceptable. The current epidemic of early teen-age pregnancies indicates that one part of the youth subculture has become convinced that the loss of virginity is practically a rite of passage toward maturity and peer acceptance. If this culture pattern goes unresisted it could seriously weaken the fabric of the nation's marriages and family life. It is not surprising that Jesse Jackson, a leading black churchman concerned for the social and spiritual well-being of his people, has spoken out against explicit sex rock.

A fairly intelligent and responsible coalition of forces has already appeared to orchestrate popular opinion to shape television through pressure on advertisers, the organization known as Morality in Media. Christians should probably cooperate with groups like this while striving at all costs to keep them from censoring and destroying genuine art, no matter how unconventional in content. But the ultimate solution to cultural decay is not so much the repression of bad culture as the production of sound and healthy culture, which in a society salted with vital Christianity will readily crowd out the bad. Therefore, we should direct most of our energy not to the censorship of decadent culture, but to the production and support of healthy expressions of Christian and non-Christian art.

THE SPIRITUAL
ROOTS OF
CHRISTIAN
SOCIAL CONCERN

12

NOT ALL CHRISTIANS ARE HAPPY about the growth of Evangelical-ism in America during the 1970s. Many observers believe that this style of Christianity is inherently passive and con-servative socially because it is always motivated by "spir-itual" considerations (the search for meaning, inner emo-tional satisfaction), rather than by a realistic effort to meet the "real" problems in society. It is the pietism of the disin-herited, those who have been dislodged from past values by the psychological violence of future shock. It is therefore inherently self-centered and opposed to an outward-looking social altruism. Thus Tom Wolfe dismisses what he calls the "Third Great Awakening" as just a religious expression of the introversion of the seventies, which he labels "the dec-ade of me."[1]

The conclusion that spirituality and social concern are in-

versely related to one another is unfortunately rather easy to
justify from some of the evidence available today. People
who are "into Christian experience" may not be into anything else. One phase of the Jesus movement, echoed in some
Charismatic sectors, has exchanged the psychedelic power
of drugs for an ecstatic awareness of the Holy Spirit which
is apparently divorced from hard social realities. Among
many religious conservatives the concept of mission and
ministry to the world is narrowly restricted to verbal preaching of the gospel. Many seem to feel that *Evangelical* is a
noun derived from evangelism.

A recent private survey of conservative leaders in one
large denomination asked the question, "What changes
would you most like to see in our church?" A disturbing
percentage answered, "Give up social action and concentrate on evangelism." An even more unsettling set of surveys
seem to verify

> "the Marxian hypothesis" that church members who are
> deeply involved in the church reflect a sense of alienation
> from the world, a desire to escape from it through attach-
> ment to the church, a wish to have their church escape
> from the world with them, and hence a rejection of politi-
> cal activity by the church.

Another survey seems to show that "the more conservative
a Protestant group is, the less it tends to be concerned about
ethical values," and another indicates that

> those who place a high value on *salvation* are conserva-
> tive, anxious to maintain the *status quo*, and unsympathe-
> tic or indifferent to the plight of the black and the poor . . .
> having a self-centered preoccupation with saving [one's]
> own soul, an other-worldly orientation coupled with an
> indifference toward or even a tacit endorsement of a social
> system that would perpetuate social inequality and injus-
> tice.[2]

It is not surprising that some Evangelicals of the Reformed
tradition have attacked American Evangelicalism for its

"Pietism"[3] or that friendlier observers outside Evangelicalism have tried to defend a certain degree of social disengage-
ment as a natural concomitant of the search for meaning in
authentic religion.[4]

Since Carl Henry raised the issue of Evangelical neglect
for social concern in *The Uneasy Conscience of Modern
Fundamentalism* (1947), a considerable body of literature
has appeared which answers these critiques by documenting
the involvement of evangelicals in social reforms during the
past several centuries. In 1974 at Lausanne, the most recent
conciliar expression of the mind of Evangelicalism, Samuel
Escobar noted that a concern for the growth of social witness
among Evangelicals seemed to spring up all over the world
after the Berlin Conference on Evangelism in 1966.[5] David
Moberg has documented a number of ministries recently
created in the United States which endeavor to combine
social and spiritual renewal.[6] Gradually it has come to be
accepted almost as a truism among both "liberals" and "conservatives" that healthy Christianity should stress both personal renewal and social reformation.

Often, however, the social effects of past evangelical revivals are cited only to prove that what Evangelicals are
doing today (concentrating on the winning of individual
souls) is enough to produce significant change in society.
Many of the younger Evangelicals whom Moberg cites as
examples of social concern are almost moving toward a post-
Evangelical stance because they find little significant prophetic social criticism among religious conservatives and
very little financial support for initiatives which include
dimensions of social reform. From their perspective, both
"liberals" and "conservatives" have simply given lip service
to the rather costly demands of Christian social involvement.
The numerical growth of "born again" religion in what we
have described as a potential great awakening strikes them
as an almost blasphemous irony considering the depth of
unmet social need in America. For some the only solution

for this impasse seems to be the creation of a new religious movement consisting of dropouts from both the "liberal" and "conservative" establishments.

Are Evangelical Christians making adequate progress in the social application of their faith, or is the current growth in the number of those professing conversion just another ephemeral surge of piety produced by an atmosphere of crisis? In the remainder of this chapter, I shall attempt to answer this question with the help of history and Scripture. The theses I intend to prove are these: that authentic spiritual renewal inevitably results in social and cultural transformation; that no deep and lasting social change can be effected by Christians without a general spiritual awakening of the church; and that Evangelicals must stress more than evangelism and church growth if they are to duplicate the social triumphs of earlier periods in their own tradition.

Social Concern Prior to the Great Awakening
During the Reformation period, Protestantism was often too preoccupied with the tasks of self-preservation, consolidation and instruction to engage in any distinctive forms of social witness. However, the differing postures toward the relationship of church and state among the various strains of the Reformation have had continuing implications for Protestant social attitudes in later generations.

The Lutheran settlement, which depended heavily on the support of the landed aristocracy and actually placed the church to some degree under the supervision of the state, tended to encourage a separation of the spiritual and social realms and an uncritical submission of the church to secular policy. The almost theocratic flavor of Calvin's Geneva, on the other hand, embodied an effort to shape and discipline an ideal commonwealth which strongly reflected an Old Testament model, in which cultural mores, education and social relationships fall under the control and criticism of the clergy.[7] A different form of Christian society is represented in the separated communities of the Anabaptists, which sought to be models of the kingdom of heaven, somewhat like the medieval monasteries, although without their vows and restraints. They practiced corporate interdependence in a simple agrarian lifestyle and disengaged themselves from the moral compromises and use of force necessary for involvement in the state and the larger human community.

During the seventeenth century, when the Lutheran and Calvinist theologies of live orthodoxy were being forged, English and American Puritanism and German Pietism developed a stronger social witness. In breaking down monastery walls and endeavoring to make the whole parish into a community of mutual concern like the Old Testament tribal unit, the Puritans had added a stronger social dynamic to the medieval model, which had structured almsgiving to the poor and charity to other forms of need into its piety of works.

Puritan casuistry conceived of the individual's responsibility to society as an economy of radiating circles of concern, spreading out from the family's needs to embrace neighbors, countrymen and all mankind, with a slightly greater priority given to spiritual needs and to the needs of believers. Though the hierarchical concept of class structure was still taken for granted, and indeed carefully reinforced by religious sanctions, Puritanism had a certain implicit revolutionary dynamic due to its biblical stress on the excellence of the lowly, but this was restrained by another biblical vector enforcing respect for constituted authority.

The Protestant concept of vocation introduced a new egalitarian note against the older medieval attitude which ranked clerks above mechanics, insisting that careful fulfillment of a "low" vocation is as valid and praiseworthy as the same achievement in a calling of "higher status." While it was assumed on the authority of the Old Testament that normally the godly will prosper, there was no blanket endorsement of the wealthy as a class or capitalism as a system, but rather the emphasis was on restraint of usury and sinfully motivated economic endeavor. For this reason, the profit motive was universally condemned, competition was discouraged, a *via media* with respect to prosperity was endorsed as probably most healthy, and most forms of economic behavior were inherently suspect as either visionary or exploitative.

The result was a thoroughly social-minded ethical consciousness which was the polar opposite of rugged individualism. The governmental theory which resulted involved an approach to the relief of social need which endorsed "preventive charity" and the maintenance of public institutions such as colleges, hospitals, libraries and free schools.[8]

This, of course, was only in ministerial theory; how parishioners followed through on this ideal was, as always, another matter. But in New England Puritanism the community which developed from the first generation of founders actually was bound together with strong ties of mutual concern— Emery Battis characterizes Governor Winthrop's administration as a kind of welfare state which was less than acceptable to the prosperous merchant class already appearing in Boston. From this there developed a long tradition in New England of "public spirit" and social consciousness.[9]

Unfortunately, the conservatism of the Puritan mainstream with respect to class structure combined with its casuistic approach to the Bible to produce a toleration of the institution of slavery. William Perkins concluded from Paul's treatment of slavery that it might be considered ethically valid if carefully used and established by positive law in a country. However, he barely tolerated the practice, hedging it about with a number of imperatives concerning the duties of masters and preferring the use of hired servants.[10] Richard Baxter, in his *Christian Directory*, condemned the slave trade as "one of the worst kinds of Thievery in the World," but did not object to Christians owning slaves if they took pains to bring the gospel to them.[11]

During the Revolutionary period, English Puritanism produced a left wing which followed through on the movement's revolutionary dynamic more consistently than the mainstream. Oliver Cromwell's plans for English social welfare anticipated many aspects of nineteenth-century evangelical reform, as J. Wesley Bready has indicated.[12] More radically, the Levellers and Diggers attacked the English class structure and the enclosure of lands needed by the hungry poor. Gerrard Winstanley developed a remarkable anticipation of Marx's critique of the complicity between bad religion and oppressive regimes on the basis of a rather unorthodox religious naturalism.[13]

Unlike the university-trained leadership of mainline Puritanism, the leaders of the left wing emerged from the untrained poor. They were therefore less likely to be thoroughly orthodox, but more likely to challenge oppressive structures in English society. The most effective prophetic challenge within radical Puritanism emerged from the Quaker movement, which alone among the revolutionary sects took solid root in history.

George Fox, for example, called for governmental care for the poor based on systematic welfare rather than unregulated charity and for a leveling of the extremes of wealth and poverty in England. In 1671 he charged Quaker slaveholders in Barbados to care for their slaves both in soul and body and to release them after a stated number of years in service. Fox's concerns indicate a careful reading of the Old Testament combined with a heavy dependence on the inner illumination of the Holy Spirit and conscience, which, combined with his social origins and lack of conventional education, freed him from some of the inherited conservatism of mainstream Puritanism. Fortunately, Robert Barclay corrected many theological imbalances in Fox to produce a foundation for a continuing stream of evangelical Quakerism in which the revolutionary spiritual dynamic of the early movement was not entirely quenched by rising prosperity.[14]

While it might be expected that the Lutheran division between the two realms of state and church would inevitably produce a socially passive Christianity, this proved true only in confessional orthodoxy. The Lutheran counterpart of Puritan live orthodoxy, Pietism, generated an extremely vigorous social witness. Johann Arndt's *True Christianity* (1606-09), often caricatured as an epitome of world-fleeing mysticism, actually contains a strong social dynamic based on the command to love one's neighbors.[15]

J. V. Andreae, one of Arndt's friends, wrote a utopia called *Christianopolis* which offered an advanced set of suggestions for Christian social reform. Influenced perhaps by Calvin's work in Geneva, Andreae promoted associations for civic welfare, education and the support of impoverished students, and about government-directed relief for the poor and the sick.[16] In his *Pia Desideria* (1675), Philipp Jakob Spener challenged wealthy Christians to offer their goods for the welfare of the poor in order that begging might be eliminated. Elsewhere he worked out a careful scheme through which the church could care for several classes of poor people including non-Christians.[17]

At the end of the seventeenth century, Spener's pupil August Hermann Francke began his ministry at Halle by simultaneously feeding and catechizing orphans and the poor. During the course of several decades he transformed the town into a showcase of social and cultural reforms. The large cluster of buildings housing the institutions he began, including an orphanage, hospital, library and missionary center, are still preserved today as monuments to his labors. The local communist government has financed the care of his library because of its admiration for his social concern.

Erich Beyreuther maintains that Francke envisioned a systematic remedy for poverty and a narrowing of the gap between social classes as the result of the penetration of a revived Christianity. Beyreuther notes that at the end of the seventeenth century vital Christian humanism was joining with the beginnings of Enlightenment humanism to try to draft general plans for the reform of society and the alleviation of human misery. The Christian component of this movement differed from its secular counterpart only in insisting that the regeneration of individuals was an essential necessity in the renewal of society.[18]

We may note that most social progress since this period has come from these two sources, either independently or in combination. Non-Christian humanism has often assumed the main burden for social change whenever evangelical Christianity has dropped that burden. It is important to note that Francke's Lutheranism was thoroughly orthodox. He differed from confessional orthodoxy only in the spiritual dynamic inherent in his insistence on regeneration, which proves that the spiritual force of a movement is often more determinative of its social dynamism than the literal shape of its doctrines about church and state.

At the end of the seventeeth century in America, Cotton Mather was observing the expansion of spiritual and social renewal in Halle. Mather developed a revised Calvinist strategy for the reformation of society which would abandon the Puritan theocratic effort to force Christian ideals on the culture from the top down and would seek instead to transform society by the leaven of the gospel through the noncoercive witness of individuals and groups. Mather's approach was based on the assumption that God was about to pour out his Spirit upon the church to revive it before the premillennial return of Christ. This revival would lead to the full revelation of the essential beauty of the church, the missionary ingathering of "the fullness of the Gentiles" and consequent conversion of the Jews before the return of Christ.

Assuming the awakening of the church in such a revival, Mather proposed two basic strategies of social control to replace the coercion which had dominated the medieval period after Constantine and had been carried over into Calvinism: (1) a maximum effort of every Christian to exercise the rule of Christ in his or her vocation through benevolent acts, and (2) a combination of Christians in voluntary societies to advocate social and cultural reform. Mather's practical contributions to social reform in his own area included prophetic criticisms of the errors of both capital and labor in New England business life, the founding of a charity school for poor children and orphans and another for the education of Negroes (which was maintained for years solely at Mather's expense), the organization of his parish into cell groups caring both for the spiritual and bodily needs of churched and unchurched alike, and numerous acts of private charity given out of his own very slender means.

Mather's tendency to "meddle" in the reform of society generated irritation in the rising, religiously liberal merchant class in Boston. This partially accounts for the darkening of his image by later Unitarian historiography, whereas more recent scholarship has concluded with Carl Bridenbaugh that he was "without question the most public spirited colonial before Benjamin Franklin."[19] Mather's main importance for our purpose, however, is that he clearly states the strategy of posttheocratic social reformation which was followed in the greatest age of evangelical social action, the nineteenth century.[20]

Great Awakening Initiatives

Mather's Evangelical strategy prepared the way also for the Great Awakening in its American phase. While Edwards and the Tennents may seem at first glance to have been wholly preoccupied with retuning and applying Puritan live orthodoxy to produce spiritual renewal without giving much attention to social problems, Edwards's powerful attacks upon some of the intellectual and spiritual factors which would inhibit Protestant social concern after the Enlightenment should not be overlooked.

One of these factors was the ethical theory stated in Mandeville's *Fable of the Bees* (1723) that "private vices are public benefits" and that "every species of virtue is at bottom some form of gross selfishness." Mandeville's stand was widely reflected in the ethical theory of self-interest adopted by many British churchmen.[21] Edwards's ethical teaching is antithetical to the moral presuppositions of the economics of *laissez-faire* developed from the same kind of Enlightenment roots later in the eighteenth century. Edwards's ethics, which defined virtue as benevolence toward Being-in-general (primarily toward God and secondarily toward his creation) rather than as self-fulfillment, moved inevitably in a social direction. Samuel Hopkins, Edwards's pupil, further developed the notion of benevolence common to Mather and Edwards and worked out the social momentum implicit in the First Awakening by his explicit condemnation of slavery and slaveholding.

Alan Heimert has argued that while the main impact of the early Enlightenment in America in the beginnings of Unitarian liberalism was socially conservative in nature, the dynamism of Edwardsean evangelicalism was intrinsically revolutionary and democratic and helped lay the foundations for American social idealism.[22] Part of this dynamism was an effect of Edwards's shift of the prevailing eschatological strain in evangelical Protestantism toward postmillennialism, which continued dominant until the middle of the nineteenth century. While premillennialists like Mather had urged the reform of the church and society to anticipate the personal return of Christ and to bring about the conversion of the Jewish people which must precede the parousia, the postmillennial scheme even more vigorously demanded the reformation of society in order to help inaugurate the millennium.

On another level, Edwards responded to Charles Chauncy's critique of ecstatic introversion in the awakening by vigorously attacking pious emotionalism which did not

issue in public charity. He warns converts that in their practice of "external duties of devotion ... there [should] be a
proportionable care to abound in moral duties, such as acts
of righteousness, truth, meekness, forgiveness, and love
towards our neighbour."[23] He especially urges acts of social
charity as a means of both expressing and deepening God's
reviving work:

> If God's people in this land were once brought to abound
> in such deeds of love, as much as in praying, hearing, sing-
> ing, and religious meetings and conference, it would be a
> most blessed omen. Nothing would have a greater ten-
> dency to bring the God of love down from heaven to earth;
> so amiable would be the sight in the eyes of our loving and
> exalted Redeemer, that it would soon as it were fetch him
> down from his throne in heaven, to set up his tabernacle
> with men on the earth, and dwell with them.[24]

Edwards would be critical of both sides of the Evangelical/
social activist split in modern Protestantism:

> Some men shew a love to others as to their outward man,
> they are liberal of their worldly substance, and often give
> to the poor; but have no love to, or concern for the souls
> of men. Others pretend a great love to men's souls, that are
> not compassionate and charitable towards their bodies.
> The making a great show of love, pity, and distress for
> souls, costs 'em nothing; but in order to shew mercy to
> men's bodies, they must part with money out of their
> pockets. But a true Christian love to our brethren, extends
> both to their souls and bodies.[25]

It is significant that Edwards explicitly disarms several common arguments against the Christian support of welfare for
the poor. He maintains that we cannot deny help to the un-
deserving, since this would clash with God's gift of grace to
us and our consequent obligation to love even our enemies.
Nor can we fail to help the man whose indigence is due to
his own financial improvidence; this is not necessarily sin
but may be due to a want of economic sense which is as real

a handicap as blindness. Even if it is deliberate, it should be forgiven by fellow sinners. Even the man who is personally at fault and continues to be slothful after receiving help should continue to get it, for the sake of his family! Against the background of these rigorous deductions from the doctrines of grace, contemporary Evangelical conservatism sounds like an echo of non-Christian callousness.[26]

In the European phase of the First Awakening, Count Zinzendorf introduced a new dimension of social reality into the Pietism of Halle where he was trained. Like the Anabaptist communities, Herrnhut was a model of Christian social relationships, where private property was not abolished but all members were committed to care for the economic well-being of the community, placing their goods at one another's disposal on occasions of special need. This corporate concern for the social needs of the group was extended beyond each local Moravian community to encompass the needs of missionary outposts planted by Herrnhut so that the communities often took up collections for one another.

More than the Anabaptist settlements, Herrnhut turned its concerns outward to embrace the rest of the church and the world. It was organized around an urgent concern to revive professing Christendom and to reach the whole planet with the gospel. The pattern of foreign missionary effort established by the Herrnhuters included both the preaching of the Lamb and initiatives of social and cultural healing. They cared for the sick, established schools and provided for the aged, widows and orphans.[27] Thus the main thrust of Evangelical foreign missions, springing from the social concern of Halle and Herrnhut, has rarely lacked a social dimension even when the home missionary work of Evangelicals has been socially passive, as the case has often been during the twentieth century.

The phase of the Great Awakening most often connected with social reform by most English-speaking Christians is the Wesleyan revival, although the Wesleys and Whitefield derived much of their social momentum from the example of German Pietism. In addition to the standard Pietist concerns, however, John Wesley introduced several new emphases which were of critical significance.

In the most crucial of these, his attack upon slavery, Wesley had nevertheless been anticipated by another Christian group. The Quakers had studied their own members' part in the slave trade in 1743, and the publications of John Woolman and Anthony Benezet had raised the issue before the church's conscience.[28] Wesley read Benezet in 1772, and in 1774 his own Thoughts upon Slavery (1774) effectively established the Quaker interest in the abolition of slave trading and holding as a primary concern of English and American evangelicalism in the early nineteenth century.

Wesley again echoed the Quakers in his opposition to war, although he was not a doctrinaire pacifist. This concern was picked up by the evangelical peace societies in the next century. Similarly, Wesley led the way for later evangelicals in attacking the use of distilled spirits except for medical purposes, attempting to curb the problem of alcoholism among the poor, which was one of the major social evils attending the onset of the Industrial Revolution. In his concern to help prisoners Wesley for once anticipated the Quaker reformers led by Elizabeth Fry.

But one of the greatest contributions of the Wesleyan movement to evangelical social consciousness was simply the ingathering of large numbers of lower-class people into the church. Whitefield and the Wesleys were forced into the fields and streets by the closing of church pulpits. The result was the recapture for the church of great numbers of the alienated poor. The evangelical leadership of Methodism and other dissenting churches during the early nineteenth century reflected the pastoral concerns rising out of lower-class flocks. Thus it is no surprise that the British Labor movement in its beginnings was heavily leavened by the evangelical influence of leaders like Keir Hardy.

This championing of the poor man's viewpoint was utterly characteristic of John Wesley himself. J. Wesley Bready comments that

> Wesley supported fair prices, a living wage and honest, healthy employment for all.... Certain doctrinaire aspects of *laisser faire* ... would have made his blood boil; as for ... the Malthusian and Ricardian theories regarding food, disease, poverty, population and wages, he would have declared them diabolical.[29]

The Wesleyan movement set in motion the grassroots awakening which provided a broad popular base for the social achievements of the Second and Third Awakenings in England during the nineteenth century. But a critical factor in these awakenings was the penetration of live orthodoxy into the power centers of English life through the rise of evangelicalism in the Anglican Church. It is significant also that one of the main agents of Anglican renewal was the converted slave trader, John Newton, whose Eclectic Society functioned as an interdenominational alliance for evangelical reform in church and society.[30]

The strong antislavery impulse emanating from the Calvinist Newton blended with Wesley's concern and that of some Quakers to reinforce the parliamentary campaign against slavery led by William Wilberforce and other members of the Clapham parish church. The first parliamentary memorial dealing with slavery was introduced in 1783 by Quakers, and the committee of twelve organized in 1787 to pursue the battle in government was three-fourths Quaker in membership.[31] But the front line fighting was done by wealthy and titled members of the Clapham church who were knit together in a community as close and dynamically outgoing as Herrnhut.

Wilberforce had been concerned about the slave traffic even as a boy of fourteen, and after his conversion in 1785, the advice of Newton, Granville Sharp of Clapham and

Thomas Clarkson directed him to use his position in Parliament to destroy slavery. In 1787 he wrote in his diary, "God Almighty has set before me two great objects, the suppression of the slave trade and the reformation of manners."[32]

Ford Brown, Charles Foster and others have contended that much of the evangelical campaign for national righteousness in the decades that followed was a fearful effort to ameliorate the kind of abuses which brought about the French Revolution and even to subdue the lower classes. There is no doubt that these motives helped support the Clapham initiatives. But it is significant that Wilberforce defines the proposed reformation as a burden laid directly upon him by God two years before the Revolution and that antirevolutionary conservatives shaped the efforts of the Clapham group mostly by blocking and attacking its initiatives rather than by joining and supporting them.[33]

The campaign against slavery was a long and costly struggle for all concerned. Some of the leaders lost their health and their fortunes in the course of it. The opposition vilified "the Saints" as advocates of financial suicide for the British Empire; the attack on an institution which seemed so fundamental to the economic base of England appeared either as treason or insanity. Nevertheless, in 1807 the bill to abolish the slave trade was passed by a majority of 283 to 16 with an overwhelming acclamation for Wilberforce. In 1833 slaveowners in the British Empire were commanded to release their slaves in a year's time and compensated by a gift of twenty million pounds from the English treasury, an act which Lecky called "one of the three or four totally righteous acts of governments in history."[34]

One of the most important means used to attain this result was prayer. The Clapham leaders habitually spent three separate hours in prayer daily, and Christians all over England united in prayer on the eve of the critical debates. Other means used included ceaseless publicizing of the evils of slavery, the gathering of petitions from all over the country, and even the boycott of slave-produced goods. Although Wilberforce's inspired oratory helped reach and compel the conscience of Parliament, it is inconceivable that the work could have been accomplished without a broad base of popular sentiment supplied by conversions and awakening throughout the English churches.[35]

Second Awakening Initiatives

Alongside the labors of concerned individuals and parishes like Clapham, interdenominational voluntary societies contributed heavily to spiritual and social renewal in the Second Awakening in both England and America. C. C. Cole notes that the awakening in America proceeded through five developmental stages in which interdenominational evangelical voluntary societies spearheaded different levels of reformation: first, the missionary societies, which sought to stimulate the evangelistic progress of the church at home and abroad; second, the production of Christian literature both for evangelism and nurture, distributed through the Bible and tract societies; third, the societies promoting religion and education through Sunday Schools; fourth, societies for moral reformation; and fifth, societies for broadscale social reform on issues like temperance, peace and antislavery.[36]

Cole's list offers an intriguing logical morphology of the growth and maturing of revival, although the rise of individual societies does not always fall in his sequence. As Foster points out, the Americans often seem to have followed the lead of the English in the formation of societies. But there is also evidence that American leaders like Lyman Beecher developed concerns for specific issues of cultural and social reformation quite apart from English influence.[37]

The American reform movement evolved into an extensive interdenominational network of interlocking leadership which Gilbert Barnes has characterized as a "Benevolent Empire."[38] In the reform of mores it could on occasion appear to be moralistic or theocratic, as in the case of the sabbath and radical temperance movements. But there were social and humanitarian concerns motivating even these initiatives, though these concerns were more clearly visible in the societies for the poor, for prostitutes and for the abolition of slavery or the resettlement of blacks in Africa. The theological center of the Benevolent Empire was initially New School Presbyterianism. This, as George Marsden has shown was still predominantly Edwardsean in its theological cast, focused upon society by Hopkins's teaching on benevolence and given a striking urgency by Beecher's insistence that an unreformed nation could not fail to come under the judgment of God.[39]

As we shall see, the American evangelical enterprise had neither the balance nor the success of the English coalition. But in both cases a startling sociocultural transformation was visible by the mid-1800s. The sexual looseness and callousness toward injustice of the Regency period had been reversed by the evangelicals almost to the point of overreformation by the reign of Victoria. Alexis de Toqueville commented that "there is no country in the world where the Christian religion retains a greater influence over the souls of men than in America"[40] largely because its controlling agency in society was not enforced by government but by movements of spiritual renewal. Philip Schaff noted in 1854 that "there are in America probably more awakened souls and more individual self-sacrifice for religious purposes, proportionally, than in any other country in the world," attributing this also to the voluntary system and the impact of religious revivals.[41]

By the middle of the nineteenth century theological and spiritual shifts in evangelicalism were already visible which would lead to social passivity in twentieth-century Fundamentalism. Nevertheless, as Kathleen Heasman has shown, evangelicals during the latter half of the nineteenth century continued to demonstrate a strong and comprehensive concern over social issues, spurred on by the revolution of 1848 and challenged by the critique of Karl Marx. Many of the reforms of this period are simply further extensions of work begun by the Quakers, Halle, Wesley and those associated with Clapham and the Benevolent Empire.

In England the mantle of Wilberforce was picked up by Anthony Ashley, the seventh Earl of Shaftesbury, who spent his life and his rather slender means to continue the political campaign for social improvement in England. As many sources remark, Lord Shaftesbury's efforts against the oppression of the British working class were simply the logical extension of the Clapham battle against slavery. Shaftesbury worked with other evangelical political leaders such as Richard Oastler and Michael Sadler to limit the abuses of child labor in industry and the mines, and worked also to improve the care of the mentally ill and the housing of the poor.[42] His leadership was woven into many of the other evangelical reforming societies of this period, such as the "ragged schools" which extended the impetus of the Sunday-school movement begun by Robert Raikes in 1780.

The Pietist concern for orphans continued to be expressed in the work of George Mueller, Thomas John Barnardo and Charles Haddon Spurgeon. Concern for the religious and social welfare of young people moving into urban industrial centers led to the establishment of the Y.M.C.A. (1844) and Y.W.C.A. (1877) under evangelical leadership. Other societies continued to provide spiritual and social help for prostitutes, prisoners, the blind and the deaf (the pioneering work with these groups and such innovations as the use of Braille script were introduced by evangelicals), the crippled, the sick (the Red Cross was an expression of evangelicalism), the aged, and many vocational subgroups.

As Heasman comments, "By the mid-century it had become an accepted fact of evangelicalism that those who had experienced some spiritual renewal should straightway take part in the various efforts which were being made to help the less fortunate in the community."[43] Some of the most impor-

tant leaders in the social activities of the second half of the
century and many of the social workers were converts of the
midcentury revival of 1858-59. The visits of D. L. Moody to
England in 1873-75, 1881-84 and 1891 had a similar effect,
and there are strong indications that he recommended certain forms of social work to his adherents, particularly that
connected with young people.

On the continent the impetus of Lutheran Pietism continued to bear fruit in the work of the *Innere Mission,* a federation of voluntary charitable and educational institutions
founded by J. H. Wichern in 1848 and designed to bring
the gospel to the poor both in proclamation and demonstration.[44] In Holland one of the results of the Second and Third
Awakenings was the rise of evangelical Calvinism under
leaders like Willem Bilderdijk, Isaak da Costa and Groen van
Prinsterer. Parallels to the *Innere Mission* and the English
benevolent societies developed in this movement which
eventually produced the greatest evangelical theologian
after Edwards, Abraham Kuyper.

Kuyper shared the common evangelical concern to develop a nontheocratic way of shaping and influencing
society and culture which he felt could best be done by the
development of a Christian political party, the use of voluntary societies and the strengthening of the family. Kuyper
was concerned to listen carefully to the critique of social
abuses begun by the French Revolution and consolidated by
Marx and Engels, to provide Christian answers to the problems these leaders had uncovered and to motivate Christian involvement in all movements of social renewal which
bear the marks of God's common grace.[45]

American evangelicalism also continued to display social
concern after the middle of the nineteenth century. As Timothy Smith has shown, the reforming impetus of New School
Calvinists was continued by Finneyan and Wesleyan perfectionism, which insisted on moral integrity in those converted and worked also for the regeneration of society.[46] D. L.

Moody's role as President of the Y.M.C.A. and his activities in England carried over some of the momentum of the Benevolent Empire. Already, however, we can see the elements of a gradual transformation of the evangelical movement in the direction of social passivity. We can distinguish a number of separate shifts which brought about this transformation by the early twentieth century.

The Decline of Evangelical Social Concern

The first of these shifts was the partial disintegration of "the evangelical united front," the network of evangelical reforming societies in America. By the 1830s some American evangelicals were moving toward radical solutions which seemed logical but were not necessarily biblical, which other Christians termed "ultraist," such as the redefinition of temperance as total abstinence from all alcoholic beverages rather than moderation and the avoidance of distilled spirits. It is hard for us to appreciate today the impact which the controversy over Communion wine could have on biblical conservatives like Charles Hodge. But many denominational leaders began to think twice about the extraecclesiastical maneuvers of the reforming societies, and a resurgent confessionalism arose to counter the original evangelical impulse toward ecumenicity. Another factor in the breakup of the united front was fear of supradenominational control through the network of evangelical leadership, expressed in Calvin Colton's epithet "Protestant Jesuitism."[47] The breakup of Old and New School Presbyterianism at the 1838 General Assembly marked the beginning of a gradual dissolution of united evangelical social initiatives.[48]

A second shift, which was also divisive, was the emergence of diverging positions over the issue of slavery. While the English evangelicals had remained united in their opposition to this institution and had brought about a bloodless revolution in its abolition, American evangelicals began to divide on this issue in the 1820s into at least three groups: those who favored immediate abolition no matter what the cost, those who favored ultimate abolition but only after a vaguely defined period of preparation, and those who defended slavery on biblical and theological grounds. To cloud the issue further, an ultraist abolitionism with a thoroughly nonevangelical base appeared under the leadership of William Lloyd Garrison.

The formula which insists that the gospel should deal with "spiritual matters" and not meddle with political or social affairs, the familiar Fundamentalist argument for passive support of the status quo, emerged before the Civil War as a conservative evangelical defense of resistance toward or postponement of abolition. The seriousness of the break in evangelical ranks on this issue can hardly be overestimated. The results have included the necessity of fighting one of the bloodiest wars in history in order to accomplish what English churchmen did with prayer and argument, a persistent failure to deal with racism since the Civil War, and a retreat from all social applications of the gospel except a few relating to personal morality such as "temperance."

A third factor in the breakup of evangelical social concern was a monolithic shift in eschatology which occurred in the latter half of the nineteenth century. Up to this point premillennial, postmillennial and amillennial evangelicals had been united in working and praying toward spiritual, cultural and social renewal. Lord Shaftesbury, surely one of the most socially active evangelicals in the nineteenth century, adopted a premillennial faith akin to that of Cotton Mather. He intended his work to hasten the return of Christ, and he believed that this would not occur until the resettlement of the Jews in Palestine. But by the latter half of the century in America, Edwardsean postmillennialism was becoming secularized. While Edwards had believed that the millennium could not be brought in except through the rule of Christ through the outpouring of the Holy Spirit, the early proponents of the social gospel were keeping the momentum of the old concern for social transformation but substituting new doctrinal bases: the idea of progress, the perfectability of man, the immanence of God and the ubiquity of the grace of Christ.

With the onslaught of post-Darwinian secularism, evangelicals reacted against this secularized version of the revivalist hope and moved toward an eschatology which explained more clearly the spiritual degeneration they saw instead of progress. D. L. Moody, who was converted to Darbyite Dispensationalism and transmitted it into the warp and woof of Fundamentalism, summed up this reaction rather graphically:

> The word of God nowhere tells me to watch and wait for the coming of the millennium, but for the coming of the Lord. I don't find any place where God says the world is to grow better and better, and that Christ is to have a spiritual reign on earth of a thousand years. I find that the earth is to grow worse and worse and that at length there is going to be a separation (of the saved from the unsaved).[49]

Henry Ward Beecher reported, "He [Moody] thinks it is no use to attempt to work for this world. In his opinion it is blasted—a wreck bound to sink—and the only thing that is worth doing is to get as many of the crew off as you can, and let her go."[50] While Moody and converts like F. B. Meyer were much more socially involved than this phraseology implies, the whole momentum of Dispensational theology moved toward a form of premillennialism which was evangelistically active but socially passive. This outlook expected the world to become increasingly corrupt and conceived of the church's main duty as witnessing to the justifying work of Christ, not making disciples whose growth in sanctification could change the world. The result was an outlook which accurately predicted the apostasy of Western Christendom in the twentieth century but which may also have helped produce it.

A variety of other events and forces developed along with

these factors to drive twentieth-century Evangelicalism away from the original stance of social engagement. From the Moody era onward evangelicals were receiving much of their support from wealthy Christian lay people who were adherents of *laissez-faire* capitalism and ministering to converts who were rising economically. The few wealthy Christians who identified with the socially conscious political liberalism which Charles Reich has called Consciousness II tended to identify religiously with theological Liberalism. Wealthy evangelicals, on the other hand, gravitated toward the rugged individualist viewpoint which Reich calls Consciousness I. This harmonized well with the socially passive Christianity developed by Moody's successors.

As Paul Henry has pointed out, American evangelicals were unconsciously incorporating into their social outlook some questionable features of "the American dream": a self-centered individualism derived from Locke's Enlightenment outlook and a negative view of the state similar to that of Hobbes.[51] Gradually a political double enculturation of the church appeared. Evangelicals became the Republican Party at prayer, and Liberals, the religious expression of Democratic ideals. Evangelical families who had stood with Lincoln against slavery became loyal to his party no matter what coalition of interests it might represent at a given moment in history.

In the early twentieth century there was increasing polarization between evangelicals and social gospelers like Walter Rauschenbusch who could not find a theological rationale for their deepest heart concerns in Moody's concept of mission. The last balanced expression in America of the classical evangelical twofold thrust of individual regeneration and social transformation was probably the Men and Religion Forward Movement of 1912.[52] The year 1912 also saw the publication of *The Fundamentals*, edited by A. C. Dixon, who during his first pastorate had become thoroughly disillusioned with the limited effects of social ministry and became committed to the priority of evangelism.

During the years of World War 1 the Fundamentalists and the social Liberals seem to have moved apart and hardened into polar opposition. It is possible that the failure of the experiment with Prohibition, a belated result of the Evangelical Temperance Crusade, disillusioned Evangelicals with social reform as much as it disillusioned America with Evangelicals. While the social gospelers, on the basis of an inadequate theology, were trying to deal responsibly with the Marxist challenge toward the elimination of structural social evil, the Fundamentalists were trying to preserve their theology in Bible schools where the post-Darwinian world could not overwhelm them. They had little time for integrating the new sciences of economics and sociology with their biblical understanding. The Fundamentalist controversy of the 1920s somehow ended by identifying evangelism with one side and social action with the other, and desperately estranging the two.

David Moberg has suggested that this polarization is not so much the effect of two different gospels opposing one another as it is the result of a specialization, in which priestly (or pastoral or evangelistic) talent accumulated in one sector of the church while prophetic (or diaconal) gifts concentrated in another sector.[53] We have already suggested that this kind of breakup occurred at the beginning of this century, in which the broad river of classical evangelicalism divided into two main branches with a variety of subordinate expressions (see Figure 2, p. 321). The result is comparable to the Mississippi delta: a deep and powerful river has been divided into a number of smaller, weaker, shallow streams running out into history. The genetic pool of classical evangelicalism has been so broken up that no part of the American church today accurately reflects the movement as it originated.

By the middle of this century, however, the Evangelical reform movement was refocusing on the importance of social concern. The neglect of social responsibility was one of the key confessions in Carl Henry's *The Uneasy Conscience of Modern Fundamentalism* (1947).[54] In the 1950s and 60s the growing body of renewed Evangelicalism seemed to draw back uncertainly from commitment in this area. On the one hand, Billy Graham's evangelistic strategy condemned racism and increasingly spoke of concern for the poor. On the other hand, mainstream or "establishment" Evangelicalism remained identified with politically conservative approaches and kept a low profile during the struggles over civil rights and Vietnam. But Evangelical offspring growing up during the sixties and many of the youth converts of the seventies were socially awakened by the protest movements and the darkening image of the future in the nuclear age, and they were capable of reawakening their elders.[55]

New streams of social concern began to emerge among these "young Evangelicals,"[56] some identified with the Calvinist approach of the *Reformed Journal*, others with a renewed Anabaptist approach and some with premillennialist Arminianism. In 1973 a representative group among these issued the Chicago Declaration, a detailed confession of Evangelical neglect of social concern.[57] At Lausanne, in 1974, a powerful impact was made by Latin-American representatives who unveiled an Evangelical form of liberation theology seeking to deal realistically with the terrible extremes of wealth and poverty existing in the Third World, the disparity between American prosperity and mass starvation elsewhere, and the tendency of multinational corporations to reinforce these patterns out of a blind concern for profits.[58] More recently, World Vision, an important Evangelical ministry, has begun to channel American funds abroad to relieve hunger through a variety of programs, and a remarkable Christian coalition including Evangelical leadership, Bread for the World, has begun to lobby for the creation of an American grain reserve to feed the world in the likely event of world famine.

Despite these evidences of renewed social concern, however, the enlarging bulk of Evangelicalism still seems remarkably inert in the social dimension. The organization growing out of the Chicago Declaration, Evangelicals for Social Action, struggled for survival in its early years, the victim of internal disputes and repeated rejection by establishment Evangelicals. There is an immense dissonance between the scope of the Evangelical awakening in America described by the media and the continued prevalence of crime, racism and poverty. It is no wonder that many young Evangelicals are as skeptical about the supposed revival as "liberals."

What is going on here? Is the present awakening going to lead automatically to social renewal, eventually, or will it be necessary to make changes and inject new additives if this is to occur? In the rest of this chapter I shall examine the implications for Evangelical social witness of the dynamics of spiritual life displayed in Scripture and history.

Primary Renewal Elements and Social Concern

It is a clear lesson of history that there can be no effective social witness without a revived church. The misfiring of the social witness of liberal leaders in the latter half of this century has not always been because they were echoing humanist counsels and dubious strategies. Often they have been recommending valid goals to an unevangelized and unrevived laity.

In the Clapham era the church was producing a different kind of lay person, people who were spending three hours daily for the work of the kingdom and giving much of their income toward its building. Lord Shaftesbury commented, "No man, depend upon it, can persist from the beginning of his life to the end of it in a course of generosity ... unless he is drawing from the fountain of Our Lord Himself."[59] When his son asked him how he could manage so many reforming initiatives at once, he answered, "By hearty prayer

to Almighty God before I begin, by entering into it with faith
and zeal, and by making my end to be His glory and the good
of mankind."[60]

It was through the support of wealthy lay people like the
Tappan brothers, who were socially radical because they
were spiritually energized through commitment to the kingdom of God, that slavery was finally abolished in the United
States.[61] Charles Finney felt that part of the difficulty in
achieving abolition in America was that this crusade was
running ahead of the evangelizing of the nation, whereas
abolition should be made "an appendage of a general revival
of religion."[62]

On the other hand, it is an equally clear lesson of history
that evangelism alone, particularly with a shallow understanding of repentance, is not enough to bring about social
reformation. Born-again racists and totally individualistic
pietists are so numerous still that it is obvious that a powerful application of all the dynamics summarized in Figure 1
(p. 75) is essential for social renewal, including solid, mind-
transforming instruction based on adequate biblical integration of economics and sociology.

So the remedy for lack of social concern among Christians
is not less spirituality but a complete and balanced piety
which recovers the dynamics present in classical evangelicalism. The preconditions of renewal listed in Figure 1 are
especially important here, particularly the understanding of
the depth of sin. The Old Testament prophets habitually
called for a threefold repentance on the part of God's people:
the rejection of idolatry or false religion; the renunciation
of adultery, drunkenness and other personal sins; and a
renewal of caring for the poor and needy, forsaking indifference, fighting oppression and seeking justice.

In this century the Evangelical sector has specialized in
theological and personal repentance and the "liberal" sector
has specialized in social repentance. This division of labor
has not worked very well. It is time for a united church to call

the American people to *comprehensive repentance* on the basis of a doctrine of sin which accurately defines the sins of doctrinal apostasy, personal iniquity and tolerating or abetting social injustice. Evangelism and nurture must call for repentance in this comprehensive framework, spotlighting corporate patterns of sin like racism which are so common they are almost invisible and showing that Christians cannot be "righteous" in an individual sense without fighting the elements of injustice and unrighteousness present in the corporate structures in which they are involved.

Non-Evangelical critics seem to assume that the preoccupation with individual spiritual growth leads to an introverted "pietism" which inevitably dampens social concern. This can certainly happen; F. E. Stoeffler delineates one strain of early Pietism which degenerated into precisely this sort of religiosity and emotional pulse taking.[63] Many Evangelical audiences today lose interest rapidly in preaching which deals responsibly with problems in society but fails to home in immediately on "spiritual" issues in their lives. Others are so tied up in programs of spiritual self-improvement that they have no time to care about anything but the throbbing self-concern at the center of their consciousness.

But these forms of fleshly spirituality are precisely those which a real experience of spiritual deliverance breaks up. A clear understanding and appropriation of the primary elements of spiritual dynamics settles personal problems and sets the individual Christian free from self-concern to care for others and for society. It clears the way for the Holy Spirit to fill the horizon of consciousness with love for God and mankind and causes self-concern to dwindle to a small, steady awareness of self-affirmation grounded on the love of God.

Once Christians have worked into their deepest consciousness habitual responses of faith to the truths of cleansing from guilt through justification, of freedom from sin through sanctification and of the ready availability of fellowship with the Holy Spirit, there is no need to spend time and energy constructing the elaborate ladders of devotional machinery previously considered necessary to remain in contact with God. Radical faith in Christ frees the Christian from spiritual self-concern to give attention to God and others, and to think and pray about the reformation of structures.

In this connection the fourth primary element takes on a new significance which is much broader than individual defensive spiritual warfare. Not only can we expect to carry on offensive warfare which takes ground away from Satan in the exorcism of persons, we can also undertake, when we have liberty from God to do so, the exorcism of structures occupied by demonic forces—not only fallen structures in the church in the process of reformation and revival, but also fallen structures in society which are instruments of injustice.

Harvey Cox has suggested the possibility of structural exorcism, and many other writers closer to the Evangelical mainstream have echoed him.[64] In much of this literature, however, there is a significant tendency to adopt without question Bultmann's demythologizing approach. Paul's references to superhuman powers in history are explained as pictures of "forces, spheres, and patterns of our lives which present themselves to us as possible objects of idolatry,"[65] including moral codes, technological activity, educational patterns, sexual pursuits, racial and ethnic allegiances, economic and governmental structures.

It is important to recognize that we do experience spiritual resistance to the kingdom of God in the form of human idolatry focused on these suprapersonal or nonpersonal forces. But it is also important to insist that the strength of this resistance comes from *personalities* behind these forces who are clinging to them, manipulating them and holding them rigidly in place as false absolutes. Ideologies and structures are easy to straighten out in the abstract. But when they are instruments of fallen human personalities, the corporate flesh which the Bible speaks of as "the world," and demonic agents, they can be extremely intractable.

For this reason it is important to recognize that in most of the passages cited in which Paul deals with "the powers" (for example, Rom. 8:38-9; Eph. 2:1-3; 6:10-20) he is talking not only about fallen structures but also about demonic agents controlling those structures through manipulation of fallen human beings. This is the point of Paul's comment that "we are not fighting flesh and blood." We are up against fallen angels, and therefore we must not expect to succeed unless we take upon us "the whole armor of Christ."

Structural exorcism is therefore real spiritual warfare which requires more than theorizing, demonstrating, legislating, making pronouncements and other conventional modes of social action. It may require all of these. But it also requires comprehensive spiritual renewal through the strength available in Christ. And especially it requires the exercise of prayer.

Failure to understand Paul clearly on this matter can result in underestimation of the strength required to confront fallen personalities, human and angelic, behind the crooked structures which men have built. It can also lead us to remain passive and uninvolved with the reform of structures because we confuse them with the principalities and powers which Christ condemned and defeated at the cross. "The church does not attack the powers," says one writer, "this Christ has done. The church concentrates upon not being seduced by them. By her existence she demonstrates that their rebellion has been vanquished."[66]

Sometimes this is all the church can do. She has all she can manage at times exorcizing her own structures! But if she is healthy, growing and in a normal state of revival, eventually she is able to exert a transforming influence on whole cultures and societies. This is an undeniable part of her essential witness within history. Christians should not draw back

from involvement in structures and programs which are temporarily "occupied" by the world, the flesh and the devil because they are afraid of compromising by joining "the
powers." There are no structures wholly free from such occu-
pation even in the smallest sect or commune. Boarding a
pirated ship in order to drive off the pirates sometimes suc-
ceeds, sometimes not; but it is never automatic complicity in
crime.

Mission and Social Concern

This brings us to the first secondary element of renewal, engagement in mission, which is today surrounded by a cluster of theological problems. Some concepts of mission totally
rule out social action; others subordinate it to evangelism or
make it an indirect result of preaching the gospel; still others
almost make it an exhaustive definition of the church's role
in the world. Neo-Anabaptist theologies of mission today
limit the church's social role to the modeling of an ideal
social community which must separate itself from the rest of
society in order to keep its integrity. Evangelical social thinkers in the Reformed sector, in contrast, believe that the
church can have a transforming impact on society and culture which in some measure reflects the kingdom of God.

The classical evangelical position has been that of holistic
witness to the gospel including evangelistic preaching
directed toward the redemption of individuals conjoined to
works of love and prophetic social action. The church should
neither withdraw from involvement in the structures of
society nor try to dominate them in the Constantinian fashion, but should operate as a transforming agent both in
changing hearts and changing structures.[67] The countercultural strategy of Anabaptism can help in this process by
erecting on hills its cities which cannot be hid (Mt. 5:14),
its models of pure community. It virtually has to adopt this
strategy when it espouses doctrinaire pacifism, because it insists on laying down the sword of power which govern-

ments (and Christians in government) are responsible to bear. But it should exercise respect for other Christians whose concepts of mission lead them into the heart of ambiguous structures, recognizing that Jesus compares the kingdom of God to leaven which transforms a loaf of bread.

Quite evidently the Anabaptist and Reformed models of social action can have exactly the same corrective influence on one another that we see in the separatist and ecumenist models of the church. The Anabaptists can warn the Reformed against selling out to a corrupt establishment, and the Reformed can warn the Anabaptists to avoid accusatory despair. Neither strategy can accomplish much without a general spiritual awakening. Once such an awakening is present, both can effect change, the one at the center of a society and the other at the grassroots level.

Even some premillennial and Barthian streams which are skeptical about establishing utopias within history can go along with such a holistic approach. George Eldon Ladd's masterful statement of premillennial faith recognizes that the kingdom of God is at least partially realized within history, and Philippe Maury's *Politics and Evangelism* recognizes that real works of social transformation can sometimes serve as pointers toward the ultimate and transcendent kingdom.[68]

What strategies of social transformation should Christians follow? Many believers conclude from reading the New Testament that the shortest route to social change is changing hearts through preaching the gospel and making disciples through "spiritual" instruction, so that our main duty to the poor is to preach the gospel to them. I believe this conclusion is natural but wrong, for reasons which can be clearly identified both in Scripture and history.

First, the Old Testament shows that whenever professing believers become so dominant in a society that they can influence its structures, they are responsible to help establish justice. John Howard Yoder is correct in stating that the messianic King is never presented in Scripture as the ruler over a realm of shadows, a never-never land outside history. He is the Son of David who is to bring in the Year of Jubilee (the redistribution of wealth so that the poor recover their possessions), who is finally going to establish justice for the poor and who is going to liberate the oppressed by casting down their oppressors and raising up the humble to leadership.[69]

In the New Testament, Jesus comes bringing not only forgiveness to the faithful but healing for the sick, bread for the hungry, sight for the blind and hearing for the deaf. We might be inclined to spiritualize all of these matters, but we have seen Christians within history bringing them to literal fulfillment! We would do better to broaden their meaning to include the healing of sick societies.

The Christians in Acts practiced "Pentecostal economics," not by abolishing private property but by putting all their goods at the disposal of one another and the kingdom. Paul engineered redistribution of wealth among the churches. If we had only Matthew 25:31-46 and the letter of James, we would have to conclude that the New Testament is as uncompromisingly earthy and literal as the Old in its demands for social justice. It calls for sacrifices which are not payable only in spiritual and emotional currency. They cost money and effort as well as love.[70]

We see then that Christians are responsible to carry out a holistic ministry which cares for people's bodies as well as their souls and which seeks to change structures as well as hearts. Under some circumstances it is strategically impossible to effect radical social change without first building up a body of believers to leaven a society with their influence. This is the lesson of Paul's reticence about slavery, which the Holy Spirit will always call to mind in situations which demand this approach. In other circumstances it is not only possible to bring about social healing at the same time the gospel is preached, but it is even a necessary demonstration validating that preaching. Under these conditions love and the Spirit's leading will dictate the particular strategies to be followed.[71] But it is never the case that we have a first priority to see that a man's soul is saved, and then, if our funds hold out, to do something for him socially and materially. Our responsibility is to respond to him in love on every level, within the bounds of what is possible and practicable.

Our survey of history has shown us several viable strategies for lasting social change which have influenced men to bless the church and believe its message. The formation of voluntary societies dealing with individual social issues (such as hunger) is one strategy. The responsible activity of Christian lay people in business and government is another. There is a power latent in our laity which could prove to be social dynamite if Christians would widen the scope of their spiritual concern from fishing for individual souls within their vocational fishponds to include the Christianizing of business and government. The difficulties here must not be underestimated. But the Clapham tradition shows that nations and business ventures, and not just individuals, can be born again, at least for moments within history, when the conscience of an awakened and enlarged church captures the conscience even of nonbelievers and leads every knee to bow to Christ.

We do not believe it necessary or advisable to dismantle capitalism totally in order to bring about such moments, as poisonous as *unprincipled* free enterprise can be. Proper concern for society and the will of God are simply the obverse side of a *genuinely* enlightened self-interest. Christians who assume predominant leadership in businesses can model an economic lifestyle which is not just ethically righteous. They can direct company policy not simply to grasp at the largest margin of profit but to hold profit in balance with the interests of employees, consumers, the environment and the whole body of society for which the business is a service, from God's perspective. Leaders in government can seek not just to serve the economic interests of their constituencies or this nation but can hold these interests in balance with the well-being of the whole human community.

I recognize that this vision may strain belief. It requires an ethical revolution within the church based on a spiritual revolution where concern to establish the kingdom of God takes priority over striving for success in the system as it is. I recognize that Reinhold Niebuhr has said that individuals can be moral but groups cannot, but I doubt that Niebuhr was aware of Clapham and the force of God's grace demonstrated in past spiritual awakenings.[72]

When Lord Shaftesbury was twenty-four, he wrote in his diary:

> I have a great mind to found a policy upon the Bible; in public observing the strictest justice, and not only cold justice, but active benevolence. That is good toward individuals: is it so toward nations? ... Generosity in private affairs is strength to the giver with little hazard; in empires it confers the discreditable charge of imprudence with great danger, through the increased force of the rival nation, and no gratitude. But justice—raw justice—is the Shekinah of governments.[73]

We have seen what Shaftesbury went on to achieve practically, and we have seen the admiration his policy commanded.

Should a contemporary strategy of mission include the church's responsibility, not only to seek justice, but also to shape cultural values according to Christian mores, which Wilberforce called "the reformation of manners"? This is a delicate question. History seems to connect the transformation of mores with vital Christianity, sometimes as part of the cause of spiritual awakening and sometimes as part of the result.

A skeptical critic of the Second Awakening admits that the evangelical movement in one generation changed the sexual looseness of Regency England into the modesty of the

Victorian era: "A classic illustration is furnished by Walter Scott's story of his grandmother who toward the end of her life found herself blushing as she read in privacy a novel of Aphra Behn that she could remember having read aloud in mixed company when she was a girl."[74]

In the twentieth century, however, as Evangelicals have generally refrained from fighting back against a series of sexual revolutions (and many at times have welcomed the increase of corruption as hastening the Lord's return), we see little correlation between increasing numbers of conversions and the mores of society at large. The evidence indicates that when Christians are quiet and passive about either mores or issues of social justice transformation does not occur. The implicit power to shape culture latent in a general awakening almost needs political organization if Christians are to function as "the salt of the earth" to inhibit cultural decay.

On the other hand, history also shows that theocratic imposition of Christian values often backfires, as in Puritan New England and Prohibition. But Constantinian abuses in the past need not warn us away from shaping culture in the future. They can serve as guides to help us avoid wrong issues and strategies. The Victorian moral reversal and the Communist societies today which are the last puritan societies on earth indicate that non-Christians recognize dimly that antichristian morals are socially corrosive and lead to decadence. And there are moments in history when the guilt and anger building up in the recognition of this fact can be mobilized by Christians to reform a culture.

The present strong unrest in our society over crime, drugs, political corruption, abortion and the sexual revolution indicate the growth of a reservoir of hatred, zeal and disgust toward the decay in our society. This reservoir can be tapped by Christian voluntary societies, such as Morality in Media, putting economic pressure on the main sources of cultural decay. I am not calling for censorship in the media. I am simply calling attention to the fact that in an economic democracy like America advertisers will not knowingly risk offending any large group by supporting what that group regards as blasphemous or morally offensive. American capitalism guarantees that our culture will reform itself if the Christian mind is made known to business. Our main problem today is not the difficulty of reformation but the danger of plunging into Victorian imbalance or some form of fascism. But the lessons of history can keep us from overshooting our goal.

Should Christians favor the use of legislation to insure social justice? During much of the Civil Rights struggle Evangelicals dismissed this approach on the premise that the law cannot change hearts and produce love. They forgot that for the Reformers one of the three uses of the law was to restrain sin and produce a relative degree of justice. On the other hand, another function of law is to stir up sin and make it more violent in its expression, as Romans 7:7-11 indicates. Therefore a raw confrontation of law and corporate sin can sometimes be counterproductive (as perhaps in the busing controversy) unless legal pressure is reinforced by a general awakening of the churches. But the efforts of modern humanists to enforce justice by means of law demand Christian approval and support. Where they are inadequately balanced, it is often because humanists have had to take arms against evils which Christians were tolerating or even producing.

Prayer, Community and Social Concern

Most American Christians would probably assume that prayer, the second of the secondary elements of renewal, has little to do with social action. This is because most of those who are praying are not praying about social issues, and most of those who are active in social issues are not praying very much. No wonder little social or cultural impact is made either by "liberals" or Evangelicals! We have already noted that the Clapham lay leaders spent three hours daily in prayer. It is obvious that simply to fill up this amount of time they must have expanded their scope of intercession to include social and cultural issues in the nation and the world.

If modern Evangelical lay people pray at all about their vocational world, they pray almost exclusively about their own responsibilities and the conversion of their associates, seldom about the moral shape of the corporation they work for. No wonder American business is a jungle! Local congregations pray about their members, programs, budgets and evangelistic outreach. How often do they pray about the social needs of their community or the nation? American Evangelicalism in this century has organized prayer support only for evangelistic ventures. In contrast, the leaders of the Second Awakening made cultural and social renewal the focus of "concerts of prayer" at which information could be disseminated and concern aroused.[75]

Evangelicals whose vision has broadened sufficiently that they can begin to sense their responsibility for social involvement are often baffled by the size and number of the problems they face. Where can I help in changing the situation, they ask; what can I do? The shape of the warfare to establish the kingdom of God is such a subtle and invisible thing, and subject to such change from day to day, that it can only be discerned by continuous identification with the mind of Christ in prayer. The best advice for both ministers and laity is to read the daily paper while thinking biblically in dependence on the Spirit, turning the information gained into prayer.

Once the Spirit has begun to lead individuals and groups out in attack upon specific problems, every initiative must be surrounded by and completed by prayer. Our intercession must be extensive enough to sweep regularly across the whole scene displayed by the news media like the revolving scanner on a radar scope, discovering the presence of obstacles to the progress of the kingdom of God. Then we must face these mountains as Jesus told us to and command them in prayer to move into the sea. The prophets speak of the strongholds of satanic power as mountains which oppose the progress of God's kingdom and encourage us to clear those mountains from the King's highway by prayer: "Fear not, you worm Jacob, ... Behold, I will make of you a threshing sledge, new, sharp, and having teeth; you shall thresh the mountains and crush them, and you shall make the hills like chaff" (Is. 41:14-15).

Social injustice and cultural evil are deeply rooted in the exaltation of bad leadership. This leadership clings to power and will not be dislodged unless the hand of God is moved by prayer to cast the mighty from their thrones and exalt the humble, the righteous leaders who are crowded into corners under the oppression of the strong. The seventh-century B.C. prophet Jeremiah, whose very name means either "God tears down" or "God builds up," was given a commission to exercise those functions in prayer: "See, I have set you this day over nations and over kingdoms, to pluck up and to break down, to destroy and to overthrow, to build and to plant" (Jer. 1:10).

The same commission is now exercised by the risen Lord as he intercedes at the right hand of his Father and by all Christians as the Spirit sweeps us into the stream of that intercession. We have the right of declaring war in prayer against every leader on earth who violates the will of God by oppressing the poor, denying civil rights and deforming society. Wherever we see satanic power structures planted in American culture, it is our responsibility to take arms against them in prayer, "for the weapons of our warfare are not worldly but have divine power to destroy strongholds" (2 Cor. 10:4).

It should already be obvious that the dynamic of community is essential for Christian transformation of society. On the local level Christians must model the kingdom they wish to see established on a wider scale. In the larger picture initiatives of social transformation will have an impact only as strong as the unity of Christian opinion behind them. We have seen that the strength of the Second Awakening in America was weakened by disunity in the 1830s, and we have seen the amazing power of British Christianity in the early nineteenth century because the evangelical consensus held together. One of the first places prayer should be focused in the church today is on the disunity of Evangelicalism and the rest of the church around it. Where this is the result of misunderstanding and unconscious misrepresentation, the satanic forces responsible must be exorcized from persons and structures. Since American Christians are the center of the greatest economic empire in the world, bound together and sometimes suffering from the errors of the multinational corporations, it is especially important for us to be in close touch with Christians in other parts of the world who represent the interests of the poor and the oppressed. The concerted prayer and action of Christians throughout the world community is essential for the inbreaking of the messianic rule, in whatever measure that is possible in history.

In all these efforts Evangelicals should unite with all other professing Christians wherever possible and also with non-believing persons of good will. The Clapham leaders joined forces with Unitarians and agnostics in their social initiatives. Similarly, Abraham Kuyper advocated a policy of cobelligerancy which endorsed Christian involvement in movements bearing the marks of common grace. David Moberg comments that Evangelicals typically wake up to the existence of a social problem ten years after "liberals" have begun to deal with it, study it for several years and then come to the same conclusions as the "liberals" on a better theological basis.[76] If this is so, closer cooperation at the outset of a study in the church might be of help to both sectors. Evangelicals who fear that too much contact with non-Evangelicals will lead to compromise and contamination are cer-

tainly wrong in the case of social concern; in most cases it
leads to conversion in the other direction, since non-Evangelical believers are often receptive to Evangelical convictions when they find their own concerns shared by Evangelicals.

Disenculturation, Theological Integration
and Social Concern

The implications of the dynamic of disenculturation for this
subject are probably clear to the reader by now. In order for
American Christians to present a united front on social initiatives, non-Evangelical Christians must break free of their
enculturation in non-Christian humanist liberalism (Consciousness II), and Evangelicals must be released from their
bonding with the secular American dream of rugged individualism (Consciousness I). Only through this twofold disenculturation can the streams separated through the delta
effect become again a river of life in American society.
American Christianity as a whole must transcend its insular and parochial identification with the myth of the American empire and become able to view the kingdom of God
through the eyes of Second and Third World Christians. And
Christians in all these diverse cultures must become able to
learn from one another while also sharing the insights gained
from their unique perspective, submitting to one another at
times, asserting their gifts to lead at others.

Another essential ingredient in this process of reunion
must be the dynamic of theological integration. Part of the
breakup of the evangelical united front in the nineteenth
century and the transfer of social initiative to secular humanism in the twentieth was the failure of evangelicals to integrate biblically the disciplines of sociology and economics
after Marx. We should candidly admit that most of the evangelical social action which has been reviewed in this chapter
involved surface remedies for conditions produced by bad
economic and social structures, and not with the radical

causes for those conditions. Whether or not the church can ever really do surgery on the roots of injustice, we are responsible to understand those roots.

Once we have some consensus here, it may well be possible to direct a concerted effort against the preconditions of injustice which is at least as effective as the attack upon surface problems waged during the Second Awakening. Evangelical theologians must recognize that the Bible does deal with practical matters like bringing freedom to captives (the exodus) and redistributing unequally accumulated wealth (the sabbatical and Jubilee legislation). The freeing of slaves was the fundamental theme underlying all nineteenth-century evangelical social initiatives, and Evangelicals today should put themselves unequivocally behind a purified biblical theology of liberation.

What is the role of Marxism, capitalism and mediating economic systems in Christian social thought and action? At the very least Evangelicals must recognize that Marxism is a heresy derived from Christian ethical impulses which offers a Christian goal—"to each according to his need, from each according to his capacity"—which can only be achieved through the Christian regeneration of society. Evangelicals should emulate Roman Catholics and other Protestants who have set up dialog with Marxist leaders who are beginning to be disillusioned with the ability of their system to deliver what it promises. Latin-American Evangelicals have announced their freedom to use *diagnostic insights* from Marx which shed light on their situation without endorsing Marxist *remedies* which spring from antichristian roots. Revolution, in most cases, is an operation with too many dangers of subsequent infection, a cure which is worse than the disease.[77]

At the moment the world is largely divided between two great interrelated empires. One of these empires is at least in some areas a showcase of human freedom, where democracy is rooted in Christianity. The other empire is trying to be a showcase of material justice where poverty and hunger are abolished out of humanist idealism. As Jean-Claude Revel has suggested in *Without Marx or Jesus*, the Third World is not eager to buy justice without liberty, the Russian Revolution without the American Revolution, unless it has no other alternatives.[78] America and the West have the opportunity now to build a model society which embodies both liberty and justice; Revel to the contrary, however, that building can only be done with Jesus. The political pressure of that model combined with full-scale spiritual warfare by an awakened world church could have the potential for fulfilling the great dream expressed by Alexander Solzhenitsyn in his Nobel Prize speech: that the world would no longer have two hearts, one beating to the pulse of freedom and the other in the rhythm of ideological slavery.

If even a small measure of this vision is to be accomplished through the consolidation and maturing of the present awakening, Evangelicals will have to give social initiatives the same time and concern they have concentrated on evangelism in meetings like Lausanne. Lausanne itself has pointed in that direction.

A natural place to begin rebuilding the evangelical united front on social issues is an already existing organization, Evangelicals for Social Action, which has recently reconstituted itself with a central board of about fifty members representing different centers in the Evangelical sector of the church. This could function as a public, carefully representative current version of the social leadership active in the Second Awakening. The function of this board is to meet annually for a time of prayer, discussion and mutual consciousness-raising, evaluating already existing social and cultural initiatives and charting the need for new ones.

If the board of ESA can be broad enough to include some Evangelicals with unimpeachable credentials also involved in the National and World Councils of Churches, and others in the Lausanne Continuation Committee, this could lead to church-wide coordinated initiatives on selected problems like world hunger. This organization currently plans to sponsor conferences to educate and coordinate the Evangelical sector, with task forces designed to awaken Christians in crucial vocations to their social responsibilities. It seeks to maintain connections with socially-concerned Evangelicals in other countries and to serve as a resource pool for future meetings of the Evangelical world community like Lausanne.

Until recently the membership of Evangelicals for Social Action has been discouraged and disunified. Some of its younger troops are still learning to combine the spiritual dynamics essential to evangelical awakening with the deep concerns which are driving them toward social witness. They have caucused together for political reasons, but they have done little praying and sharing together and have experienced little complementary repentance and sanctification. Consequently, they have been sitting ducks for the divisive tactics of Satan. But if a whole generation of young Evangelicals can mature in their spirituality, and if older Evangelical leaders can expand their vision, we have the potential for a new level of evangelical impact within the church and on society.

The goal of this kind of organization is not the creation of a bureaucratic superchurch which will try to change conditions by legislative fiat in the old liberal model which Reich calls Consciousness II. The projected coalition is not a cadre of Protestant Jesuits but a network for exchanging information and raising the church's consciousness. Shaftesbury's greatest contribution was not his political authority but his willingness to investigate social abuses and bring information about them to an awakened church which could then mobilize action both in Parliament and at the grass-roots level. We dare not risk the creation of a Babel or an antichrist. But we simply want to stimulate concern and reform at the level of independent local communities and to do this through the exchange of accurate information through the capillary network of Evangelical media.

I believe that something like this unifying program is not just an interesting option for the church, but a necessity. Evangelicals cannot recover their own wholeness and vitality, or prevent the loss of their own offspring to humanism or liberalism until they recover their social dynamic. Christians concerned for social action, both Evangelical and non-Evangelical, cannot reach their goals without general spiritual renewal. The general awakening of the church to its full maturity within history will not occur without the conjunction of piety and justice in its laity and its leadership:

> Is not this the fast that I choose: to loose the bonds of wickedness, to undo the thongs of the yoke, to let the oppressed go free, and to break every yoke? Is it not to share your bread with the hungry, and bring the homeless poor into your house; when you see the naked, to cover him, and not to hide yourself from your own flesh? Then shall your light break forth like the dawn, and your healing shall spring up speedily; your righteousness shall go before you, the glory of the LORD shall be your rear guard. Then you shall call, and the LORD will answer; you shall cry, and he will say, Here I am.
>
> If you take away from the midst of you the yoke, the pointing of the finger, and speaking wickedness, if you pour yourself out for the hungry and satisfy the desire of the afflicted, then shall your light rise in the darkness and your gloom be as the noonday. And the LORD will guide you continually, and satisfy your desire with good things, and make your bones strong; and you shall be like a watered garden, like a spring of water, whose waters fail not. And your ancient ruins shall be rebuilt; you shall raise up the foundations of many generations; you shall be called the repairer of the breach, the restorer of streets to dwell in. (Is. 58:6-12)

PROSPECTS
FOR
RENEWAL

13

AT THE HEIGHT OF THE SECOND EVANGELICAL Awakening in America, six years before he was to write his caustic attack on "Protestant Jesuitry," Calvin Colton, in a book on American awakenings, expressed a remarkable optimism about the future:

> It was a general historical truth in the days of our Saviour, and seems to be so yet, "that strait is the gate and narrow is the way that leadeth unto life, *and few there be that find it.*" ... But this will not be true in the days of the Millennium. It was a general historical truth in the apostolic age ... that the public opinion of the world was against Christianity. But it is not so now. ... And some, not a few, go so far as to imagine, that the darkest time the church has ever seen, is just about to come. Now it is a pity that Christians, who have enough, in any case, to care for, should "borrow

trouble"—that they should waste their anxieties on false deductions. For every item of care, that is bestowed unnecessarily, is so much waste; . . . it fills a mind which ought to be occupied in doing positive good. . . . It is unnecessary to write another book, or make another argument, or preach another sermon, to establish the supremacy of Christianity in the respect of mankind. That work is done, and done for ever. . . . Christians now have only to take advantage of that impression—of that state of society, which God in his providence has induced, in the progress of 1800 years . . . to plant their feet upon this ground, start from this point, and, by one united and vigorous onset, march directly to the conquest of the world, in the use of the simple and naked weapons of evangelical truth.[1]

Colton was expecting "a *perpetual* revival of religion—a revival without a consequent decline—an outpouring of the Spirit not to be withdrawn, or relaxed, so as to bring in all of the same and of every community and every nation, and to support all in a steadily progressive course of sanctification."[2] Viewing the world from our current perspective, we can be excused for smiling. Colton did not know what was about to hit him, and the pessimists he chides were exactly on target.

Colton's optimism is an expression of a theological trend in America which began with Jonathan Edwards. Edwards speaks more warily, with great respect for the strength of Enlightenment rivals of Christianity, but with an encouragement, like Colton's, which was born in the warmth of the awakening experience:

Now the world, by their learning and wisdom, do not know God; and they seem to wander in darkness, are miserably deluded, stumble and fall in matters of religion, as in midnight darkness. Trusting to their learning, they grope in the day-time as at night. . . . They scorn to submit their reason to divine revelation, to believe any thing that is above their comprehension. . . . But yet, when God has sufficiently shown men the insufficiency of human wisdom and learning for the purposes of religion, and when the appointed time comes for that glorious outpouring of the Spirit of God, when he will himself by his own immediate influence enlighten men's minds; then may we hope that God will make use of the great increase of learning as a handmaid to religion, as a means of the glorious advancement of the kingdom of his Son. . . . And there is no doubt to be made of it, that God in his providence has of late given the world the art of printing, and such a great increase of learning, to prepare for what he designs to accomplish for his church in the approaching days of its prosperity.[3]

Edwards foresees a union of nations and races as a result of a great missionary movement with America as its base, with the rising of strong Christian movements in what we now call the Third World:

Then all countries and nations, even those which are now most ignorant, shall be full of light and knowledge. . . . It may be hoped, that then many of the Negroes and Indians will be divines, and that excellent books will be published in Africa, in Ethiopia, in Tartary, and other now the most barbarous countries. . . .

There shall then be universal peace and a good understanding among the nations of the world. . . . Then shall all the world be united in one amiable society. . . . A communication shall then be upheld between all parts of the world to that end; and the art of navigation, which is now applied so much to favor men's covetousness and pride . . . shall then be consecrated to God, and applied to holy uses. . . . All the world shall then be as one church, one orderly, regular, beautiful society.[4]

These passages evoke a peculiar combination of emotions in Christians at the end of the twentieth century. On the one hand, we admire the ideal and we are grateful for the parts of Edwards's vision which have so far come to pass. On the other hand, the persistence until now of so much depravity, false religion and sub-Christian humanism produces a powerful sense of irony. Edwards, of course, would probably not be shaken if he could share our perspective. He did not expect the millennial state to be won without more periods of counterattack, and he did not expect a revived world without an antecedently revived church.

But our sense of irony is not easily disarmed. The vigorous optimism of classical evangelicalism does not harmonize well with our experience. Many readers of this book may have turned away before reaching this chapter simply because they are not used to imagining that the church, let alone the world, might be moving away from apostasy and toward revival. Others may be profoundly uneasy about the previous chapter because it assumes our responsibility to work for better conditions in the world. This is not in tune with many Evangelical instruments today. There are not many Evangelical theologians of hope.

Most Evangelicals, without realizing it, agree with the Enlightenment doctrine of religious entropy—that the vigor of Christianity is running down as history proceeds. Many agree with the secular critics who call this a post-Christian era. There is a mood among older Christians of "Après moi, le déluge." Many premillennialists are exchanging their hopes for a rapture before the final tribulation for grim preparations for hardship and persecution. At Lausanne, Malcolm Muggeridge spoke of living through an apocalypse. Billy Graham enumerated a rising tide of what look like terminal dangers—droughts, floods, famines, inflation, conversions to the occult and preparations for nuclear war. "Most of us hold the view of Scripture that teaches that as we approach the end of history things will get worse—that our Lord predicted in Matthew 24, false prophets, earthquakes, famines, wars, betrayals, moral permissiveness, persecution, apostasy, would precede his return."[5] Fortunately (and characteristically) this expectation does not dampen Graham's evangelistic zeal or his labors for revival: "But I believe as we approach the latter days and the coming of the Lord, it could be a time also of great revival. . . . James seems to associate the 'latter rains' with the return of Christ."[6] This is a modern expression of the premillennial revivalism of Cotton Mather.

Among many premillennialists, however, conviction that the end is near is liable to dampen their zeal for a program of social initiatives and to constrict their vision of the full scope of spiritual renewal toward which we should work. David Wilkerson's *Vision* is a Charismatic version of the predominant future expectation of most American Evangelicals. Wilkerson warns of economic crises in the West, labor pains in nature, an increasing flood of pornography and the rise of a persecution madness in the West which will lead to harassment of Evangelicals and the ejection of Charismatic Christians from the Roman Catholic Church. He warns that the ecumenical movement will revive from the dead, with Rome at its head, and form a monolithic world superchurch which will ordain homosexual ministers and permit séances and nude dancing in the churches. Wilkerson, like Graham, also expects great revival in a separated church of true believers ejected from the ecumenical superchurch and in great awakenings behind the Iron Curtain. But healing of the division in the church and united efforts toward reformation, revival and social renewal are foreign to his vision.[7]

What shall we say to this? Does premillennial eschatology inevitably discourage the program of renewal laid down in this book? If so, its work among present-day Evangelicals will be drastically curtailed! But I do not believe this is the case. In order to get a clear perspective on this problem, we need again to review the history of the Evangelical movement, this time focusing on the interplay of eschatological convictions in its development.

Church Fortunes and Church Expectations
The early fathers of the church, with the exception of the

Alexandrians and a handful of the Apostolic Fathers, were chiliasts, that is, they believed in a literal thousand-year reign of glory for the saints on earth preceding the eternal state.[8] Justin Martyr, Tertullian and Irenaeus were premillennialists; they believed that before the chiliad, the thou sand-year reign, Christ would return bodily to rule with the saints. This conception of the end of earthly history agrees with the Jewish intertestamental apocalyptic literature in the centuries before Christ. It was reinforced by the status of the church as a persecuted minority in the first several centuries of its existence; the end seemed always near, and the church was looking for an apocalyptic deliverance from its trials.

Instead of this, however, the leaven of Christianity penetrated the Roman Empire until at length it became politically possible, and perhaps necessary, for its rulers to be Christians. With the advent of Constantine premillennialism was increasingly eclipsed. This was in part due to the Montanist scandal, a rising current of antijudaism and the appearance of an ascetic movement which judged literal chiliasm to be carnal in its expectations of an earthly paradise. But it was also a function of the church's changed position in society. The end no longer seemed so near, and the church was on top of the situation.[9]

The pivotal theological expression of this change in outlook was Augustine's adoption of an amillennial conception of history, which interpreted the thousand-year reign of the saints mentioned in Revelation 20 as a symbolic portrayal of the church's militant expansion during the whole process of its earthly history. Augustine concluded that the binding of Satan mentioned in this passage—"that he should deceive the nations no more, till the thousand years were ended"— was effected by the death and resurrection of Christ, and that it signified the potential lifting of the veil from the minds of the elect in all nations, making possible an effective missionary outreach of the now established church to the ends of the earth. The devil was not so restricted that he could not counterattack the saints, but his occupying army was inevitably bound to recede before the army of the saints, overcoming "by the blood of the Lamb and by the word of their testimony."

The church would grow and flourish until the end of history, surrounded still by the unbelieving multitudes typified by the nations Gog and Magog. Then Satan would be loosed, the church would suffer awful persecution for three years under Antichrist, and Christ would return to rescue the church. Augustine's eschatology was in some respects a rather casual stab at solving the problems of eschatology—some interpreters have even called him a postmillennialist, although he seemed unsure whether or not the rule of the church is to last a thousand years—but his outlook came to dominate medieval eschatology and helped to nerve the church for its great missionary outreach during the Middle Ages.[10]

The Reformation era seems to carry over Augustine's amillennial position, although its eschatological references are extremely terse. The creeds of this period condemn chiliasm as heretical. Luther came to identify the papacy as the antichrist and predicted its final downfall in 1520 and again in 1545. Calvin interpreted the Isaianic prophecies of the flourishing of Israel as referring to the Christian church and seemed to hope for the same expansion of Reformation faith which Augustine predicated for Catholicism. Calvin's mentor, Martin Bucer, developed the younger theologian's amillennialism by making one important change. Bucer believed on the basis of Romans 11:11-32 that a large-scale conversion of the Jewish nation to Christianity would occur in history following the successful reformation of the church and the entrance into it of "the fullness of the Gentiles." All this, he believed, must necessarily precede the bodily return of Christ.

In this significant shift Bucer established an evangelical theology of hope for the church, the Jews and the nations, which came to dominate classical evangelicalism until the middle of the nineteenth century. Among the English Puritans only Richard Baxter held to what might be called "neutral amillennialism": that the church's fortunes would oscillate with rather indeterminate progress until the end of history. Most other Puritans believed in what I shall call "positive amillennialism," in which the church has laid out for it a definite plan of reformation, renewal and expansion among the nations until a worldwide church of such beauty and spirituality is created that Jewish onlookers are made jealous and come to believe in their Messiah in great numbers.[11] This "hope of better times" was adopted by William Perkins, Richard Sibbes, John Owen, John Dury, John Eliot, and the Pietists Philipp Jakob Spener and J.A. Bengel.

On the other hand, J. A. Alsted and Joseph Mede, in the early seventeenth century, diverged from the Augustinian view to teach a very moderate chiliasm which was not quite premillennial since it did not postulate the bodily return of Christ before the thousand-year reign of physically resurrected saints on earth.[12] Isaac Newton and the Mathers followed a more consistent premillennial scheme adapted from Mede. A second stream departing from the amillennial position was the postmillennial outlook, which seems to have been inaugurated by Daniel Whitby in 1703 and which influenced Philip Doddridge and Jonathan Edwards. The remarkable thing about this spectrum of millennial views is that all positions were used to support efforts at revival and social reform, since even the premillennialists believed that an outpouring of the Spirit and the conversion of large numbers of Jews and Gentiles would precede the millennium. They also believed that a witness of social healing would hasten this ingathering and the return of Christ.[13]

Jonathan Edwards believed that a fully awakened church would inaugurate a literal thousand-year period of unparalleled blessing on earth, ruled not by the bodily presence of Christ but by an unprecedented fullness of the Holy Spirit among believers. As in Augustine's scheme a body of unbelievers would still surround the church throughout this period, and at its close the unbound Satan would energize Antichrist, God and Magog, and finally be vanquished by the bodily return of Christ. Most American evangelicals through the Finney era seem to have followed Edwards's postmillennial scheme in an undogmatic way.

In Europe the mixture of positive amillennialism, postmillennialism and revivalist premillennialism continued among evangelicals. Sometimes the positions are almost indistinguishable, but they all concur in "the hope of better times for the church" through the middle of the nineteenth century. As J. A. de Jong has pointed out in a helpful thesis, this generalized "millennial optimism" coincided with the greatest missionary expansion of the church yet seen on earth.[14] Isaac Watts's "Jesus Shall Reign," a paraphrase of Psalm 72, expressed in 1719 the positive amillennial hope for the outreach of world mission. Fifteen years later Watts wrote a preface to Edwards's *Narrative of the Surprising Work of God* suggesting that the Northampton revival might be the overture to "the church's happy state."

In 1748 Edwards published *An Humble Attempt to Promote an Explicit Agreement and Visible Union of God's People through the World, in Extraordinary Prayer, for the Revival of Religion and the Advancement of Christ's Kingdom on Earth, Pursuant to Scripture Promises and Prophecies, Concerning the Last Time.* This work and Edwards's edition of Brainerd's *Diary* virtually energized the missionary labors of the late eighteenth and early nineteenth centuries. The "hope of better times" and especially the eager longing for the conversion of the Jews was at the heart of the missionary concern in men like William Carey, Henry Martyn, Andrew Fuller and Charles Simeon.[15] Despite their differences (and occasional vagueness) in eschatological detail, classical Evangelicals were united by the vision of a positive goal summarized in a verse they quote again and again: "For

the earth will be filled with the knowledge of the glory of the
LORD, as the waters cover the sea" (Hab. 2:14).

The Rise of Passive Premillennialism

In a very remarkable way the premillennial position came to
dominate the evangelical movement during the latter part of
the nineteenth century. Much of the reason for this probably
lies in D. L. Moody's turning away from the postmillennial
optimism which had captured the American evangelical
stream to embrace the Dispensational premillennialism of
John Nelson Darby. Darby's doctrine explained the post-
Darwinian world in a way that Edwards's did not. It taught
that society and the church were going to fall away from biblical Christianity in a great apostasy and that those who believed in the gospel would be raptured out of the world before this apostasy climaxed in a period of great tribulation.
Once again, as in the first two centuries of the church's existence, premillennialism made sense out of an experience
which would otherwise be quite discouraging.

We have already seen that in Moody's era premillennialism did not undercut zeal for revival, world mission and
even many forms of social action. Lord Shaftesbury was an
ardent premillennialist, and yet he was driven by a sense of
responsibility for needs on this side of the millennium:
"When I feel old age creeping upon me and know that I must
soon die—I hope it is not wrong to say it—I cannot bear to
leave this world with all the misery in it."[16]

Not all Americans abandoned the postmillennial view
during this period. Among theologians who maintained the
position were the Hodges, Shedd, Strong and Warfield. But
in the early twentieth century nearly all American Christians
—even those who were neutral amillennialists following
Kuyper, Bavinck and Geerhardus Vos, and even those with
no millennial position at all—were gradually soaked to the
bone by a growing, prevailing pessimism about the future. In
the course of this century practically all American Evangel-

icals, except for maverick postmillennialists like Loraine Boettner and J. Marcellus Kik, have concluded that the old medieval jeremiad is correct: *hora novissima, tempora pessima*—the later it gets in history, the worse the times will be. It is hard to deny that this conviction often dampened zeal for reform and revival, especially in the area of social renewal. But the form of premillennialism which is at the root of this mood is very different from the faith which drove the Mathers and now energizes Billy Graham. It should be called *passive premillennialism*, in distinction from *active premillennialism*. And it must also be admitted that there are many passive amillennialists around!

This short survey shows that in the history of evangelical-ism *doctrinal structure* is often less determinative of the shape and vigor of the church's mission than *spiritual vitality*. Again we have to say that a living dog is better than a dead lion. This is true not only in nurture and evangelism but in reform and renewal. When the tide of the Spirit is flowing strongly in a sector of the church, that sector becomes like a healthy organism which neutralizes every poison in its system and uses constructively every source of strength. When the Spirit withdraws, even strengths become weaknesses, and weaknesses become poisonously destructive. There is a profound difference between Edwardsean post-millennialism and the optimism about progress and human nature characteristic of much liberal social activism, although the social gospel is a descendant of Edwards's view. And there is a visionary outreach in Abraham Kuyper and the Dooyeweerdian movement which contrasts strongly with the dogged persistence in most neutral amillennialists.

Insights from History

As we examine the shifting balance of eschatologies during the history of the evangelical movement, we can draw several general conclusions.

First, the main eschatological consensus in the church

tends to vary according to the apparent success or defeat of the Christian enterprise. Periods of embattlement or recession favor premillennial teaching in which the church is dramatically delivered from its difficulties by the bodily return of Christ. Periods of widespread awakening encourage the hope that the church will continue to prevail and consolidate its position through the spiritual reign of Christ brought about by the outpouring of the Holy Spirit.

Second, each eschatological position, pragmatically considered, can be of help in encouraging the church in its warfare and its mission. Premillennialism explains the apparent growth of evil in the world and nerves the church to stand firm under persecution. Postmillennialism can energize the church to rise up out of social passivity and work to transform a whole culture so that God's kingdom may come on earth as it is in heaven. Amillennialism can equip the church to keep steady under good conditions or evil, constantly holding forth the word of God and pressing for the maximum expansion of the gospel without being discouraged at setbacks.

Third, each eschatological position can be misused to throw the church off course in its mission and conflict. Premillennialists can adopt a bomb-shelter mentality which withdraws from social and cultural engagement and simply waits for the end to come, passively tolerating or even welcoming the spread of evil because it hastens the return of Christ. Postmillennialists can seriously underestimate the strength of the opposing forces, call for advance when retreat and consolidation are in order, and fail to confront the world realistically when they are infiltrated by myths of progress and human goodness. Then, too, they can lose their awareness that only through the spiritual rule of Christ can evil be restrained. Amillennialists can become routine functionaries who pay no more attention to the prevailing of the kingdom than they do to the state of the weather, doggedly serving up dead orthodoxy week after week and plodding along with little concern for success or victory.

Here, as in the general panorama of the history of evangelical theologies, whether a particular viewpoint is a stimulant or a depressant in the church's life seems to depend more upon the relative spiritual vitality of Christians than upon the precise doctrinal shape or even the biblical strength of the position. When the church is gripped by the central core of live orthodoxy and infused with the power of the Holy Spirit, beliefs which might become depressants are somehow restrained and inoperative, and beliefs which can serve as stimulants are reinforced. When the church is moving away from "the power of godliness" toward formalism, even the most biblical conceptual scheme can become an instrument of death.

We cannot, however, go so far as to say that relative doctrinal strength is wholly irrelevant in eschatology or in any other province of belief. Other things being equal, a biblical "living lion" is much stronger in directing the church's mission than any number of "living dogs." We must also insist that there is one factor of belief which almost always tends to disturb the practical usefulness of any eschatology: the notion that we can be certain now where we are on the eschatological time line. This is especially true if we assume we are near the end of the line, as so many have in past history, and are certain that "the church's happy state" or the return of Christ are sure within the next decade.

The Dangers of Eschatological Speculation
On one occasion Christ chided the Pharisees and the Saducees because they were unable to "interpret the signs of the times" (Mt. 16:3) and recognize that the Messiah had come. In his most extensive teaching on the end of history, however, he warns the disciples not to come prematurely to the conclusion that the end is near:

You will hear of wars and rumors of wars; see that you are not alarmed; for this must take place, but the end is not yet. For nation will rise against nation, and kingdom against

kingdom, and there will be famines and earthquakes in
various places: all this is but the beginning of the birth-
pangs. (Mt. 24:6-8)

It is clear that he does speak of worsening conditions at the
time of the end:

Then they will deliver you up to tribulation, and put you to
death; and you will be hated by all nations for my name's
sake. And then many will fall away, and betray one another, and hate one another. And many false prophets will
arise and lead many astray. And because wickedness is
multiplied, most men's love will grow cold. (Mt. 24:9-12)

It is interesting that even postmillennialists like Edwards
find a place for the period of tribulation with the rise of Antichrist at the close of the millennium.

Again, in the parable of the fig tree, Jesus observes that just
as we know the summer is near when we see the leaves
emerge, we may have a general awareness that the end is
near. But then he goes on to add that we should "watch
therefore, for you do not know on what day your Lord is coming. . . . For the Son of man is coming at an hour you do not
expect" (Mt. 24:42, 44).

The apostles also warn against the premature conclusion
that the end has come and the church's business is nearly
finished. Paul cautions the Thessalonian Christians that the
end will not arrive until an unprecedented falling away from
the faith occurs, together with the rise of an especially
powerful and deceptive antichrist, supported by "pretended
signs and wonders," who will be vanquished by the bodily
return of Christ (2 Thess. 2:1-10). Peter indicates that the time
scale of the Lord's return is hard to determine, since "one
day is as a thousand years, and a thousand years as one day"
(2 Pet. 3:8). While the apostles speak of the spread of evil and
false prophets in "the last days," it is clear that "the last
days" is a phrase which encompasses all time from the resurrection of Christ until the day of his return, since Paul and
John point to the appearance of antichrists and moral degen-

eration in their own era in connection with this phrase (2 Tim. 3:1-9; 1 Jn. 2:18-19).

The problem in fixing upon any given moment as the climax of the growth of evil and the prelude to the return of Christ is that history contains many expansions of evil accompanying periods of religious decline and even paralleling religious awakenings, such as the coincidence of the Great Awakening and the Enlightenment. As fallen mankind "comes of age" and the City of Man more and more consistently expresses the rebellion against God which is its inner essence, each "falling away" becomes a more strident crescendo of evil. It is a constant temptation for the church to fix upon one of these as the last and worst apostasy. But yeilding to that temptation has produced many false alarms.

Another factor which cautions us against the assumption that the late twentieth century is the climax of evil which presages the end of history is that the Scripture so clearly insists that the kingdom of God is also growing and enlarging throughout history along with the City of Man. In Matthew 24 Jesus observes significantly that the end of history cannot come until "this gospel of the kingdom will be preached throughout the whole world, as a testimony to all nations" (Mt. 24:14). The parable of the leaven (Mt. 13:33) implies that the progress of the gospel within history is to involve at least some measure of gradual permeation and transformation of humanity by the gospel until all of the meal is leavened, that is, until every nation has heard the gospel. In the same context Jesus compares the kingdom to a mustard seed, one of the smallest of seeds: "But when it has grown it is the greatest of shrubs and becomes a tree, so that the birds of the air come and make nests in its branches" (Mt. 13:32).

The growth of the kingdom of God to a position of commanding eminence is portrayed in the Old Testament under the image of the rising of the mountain of the Lord:

It shall come to pass in the latter days that the mountain of the house of the LORD shall be established as the highest of the mountains, and shall be raised above the hills; and all the nations shall flow to it, and many peoples shall come, and say: "Come, let us go up to the mountain of the LORD, to the house of the God of Jacob; that he may teach us his ways and that we may walk in his paths." For out of Zion shall go forth the law, and the word of the LORD from Jerusalem. He shall judge between the nations, and shall decide for many peoples; and they shall beat their swords into plowshares, and their spears into pruning hooks; nation shall not lift up sword against nation, neither shall they learn war any more. (Is. 2:2-4)

It is clear that ultimately the "feast of fat things" (Is. 25:6) on this mountain is an emblem of the eternal state. But Isaiah's words describe God s truth going out to reach and gather in the nations, which implies that the growth of this mountain is also substantially within ordinary history. This is the thrust of one of the greatest of messianic prophecies:

For to us a child is born, to us a son is given; and the government will be upon his shoulder, and his name will be called "Wonderful Counselor, Mighty God, Everlasting Father, Prince of Peace." Of the increase of his government and of peace there will be no end, upon the throne of David, and over his kingdom, to establish it, and to uphold it with justice and with righteousness from this time forth and for evermore. The zeal of the LORD of hosts will do this. (Is. 9:6-7)

This implies that whatever the rise of Antichrist and the final apostasy may mean, they are part of the process of the growth of Christ's rule and not a peculiar terminal exception to it.

Enlightenment Humanism and the Revival of Paganism

In the last several decades it has been suggested by some observers both within and outside the church that the late twentieth century is a "post-Christian era." Technology and the world view of atheistic, materialistic humanism are supposed to have laid the ghosts of all religions once and for all.

This is a restatement of Herbert Spencer's thesis that civilization inevitably moves through an infant stage of superstition to a stage of organized religion and from this to a third stage in which belief is superseded by science and understanding. In the last decade many antitechnological writers have rejected the notion of a postreligious world and called for a rebirth of spirituality, and the counterculture has actually produced such a rebirth in the spread of oriental mysticism and occult paganism.[17] This is of little help to our argument, since this upsurge of religiosity can so easily be interpreted as a despairing reversion to earlier stages in Spencer's scheme of development, a reaction against temporary problems in the unfolding of the scientific era.

But Peter Gay has shown that Enlightenment humanism is not a linear successor to religion in the development of history but only a revival of the antireligious materialism born in the Gold and Silver Ages of Greek and Roman paganism. The idea of a closed material universe entirely controlled by natural laws originates in the pre-Socratic philosopher Democritus. This idea was developed into an outlook not far removed from modern atheism by Epicurus and the poet Lucretius. Lucretius's effort in De rerum natura is to inform mankind of the laws which govern sky and earth in order to free them from the fear of death and the manipulation of priestcraft and to make them independent of superstition. Vergil's tribute to Lucretius sums up his theme: "Happy the man who can know the causes of things, and has trampled underfoot all fears, inexorable fate, and the clamor of greedy hell."[18]

This enlightened paganism lay dormant in classical literature during the Middle Ages, like the germ of some ancient plague in a tomb. In the Renaissance the tomb was opened and there was a resurgence of many forms of paganism, somewhat restrained in Northern Europe by Christian humanism and later by the Reformation. In the seventeenth and eighteenth centuries the ubiquity of classical learning was a seed bed for the rebirth of paganism, especially in countries like France where a weakened form of Christianity was linked to an oppressive social system.

Gay shows that deistic and atheistic motifs from the classics possessed the minds of the young leaders of the Enlightenment with a very powerful spiritual force, effecting what can only be described as conversions—away from Christianity.[19] The neopaganism thus revived created among a small group near the summit of society a counterculture including a spectrum of many forms of antichristianity somewhat more widespread today: skepticism and agnosticism, materialistic atheism, sensualism and even witchcraft, which was a throwback to lower forms of paganism.

From Gay's analysis we can draw several important conclusions. First, the high paganism of Lucretius was not simply a depressant against the fear of God; it was also a trenchant critique of bad religion which included many insights into the scientific outlook of the future. This means that it could serve as midwife to the release of modern science and technology from the restraints of superstition, and also that it could spread rapidly when opposed by weak Christianity.

Second, Spencer's theory of linear historical "progress" toward a post-Christian era is erroneous. The germs of modern alternatives to Christianity were already present in pagan culture before Christ, and thus the pattern of history is really that of a mutual growth of two belief systems side by side: Christianity and the conglomerate of antichristian doctrines we call paganism. To put it another way, world history includes two great religious communities, the City of God and the City of Man; both disclose a pattern of cyclical decline and revival!

Third, this variable pattern seems partially determined by the fortunes of combat between the two Cities, and partially not. The Second Great Awakening retarded the outworking of the Enlightenment in England and America, while the depression of Western Christianity during the twentieth century permitted a flourishing growth of materialistic humanism in Western society. Still, it is hard to say whether a fully revived Christianity would dampen and subdue neopaganism (this would be Edwards's postmillennial expectation) or goad it into new forms of virulence (according to some premillennial or amillennial outlooks).

The best conceptual image of the two Cities is perhaps that of the Cold War era among the superpowers, in which East and West underwent independent cycles of growth and decline, sometimes at one another's expense and sometimes not. But in no case can it be said that we have arrived at an era where paganism will hold a position of revival in the West until the end of history while Christianity continues to remain unrevived. In other parts of the world the balance of revival and decline between the two Cities is quite different. And in the world as a whole, despite the religious depression still present in parts of the West, the prevalence of vital Christianity is probably at an all-time high. There seems to be no reason why a revived and purified Christianity could not form an alliance with those elements of scientific humanism which through God's common grace promote the attainment of mankind's full maturity and produce new demonstrations within history of the power of the gospel to preserve and transform cultures.

Futurology and Eschatology

The analysis above only follows if we are really unable to chart our present position on the time line of eschatology. And there are many Western Christians today who claim that it is unavoidably obvious that we are near the final tribulation, in part because the problems of environmental pollution, expanding population, famine and the constant threat of thermonuclear war seem to show that the game is nearly up for fallen humanity. Even some secular futurologists adopt this posture. Robert Heilbroner's *Inquiry into the*

Human Prospect (1974) shows the liberal humanist mind at the end of its tether, losing faith in reason and social engineering in the face of the persistence of racism and industrial disorder. Heilbroner recognizes that technological solutions cannot touch the real essence of our problem, which he recognizes as a radical flaw in human nature which disposes it toward the worship of totalitarian leaders and fanatical nationalism.

Heilbroner sees no way into the future which does not involve the restraint of economic growth and the subordination of individual freedom to societal control. He has no reason to be especially hopeful that human beings will voluntarily make these adjustments without catastrophic accompaniments:

> At this final stage of our inquiry, with the full spectacle of the human prospect before us, the spirit quails and the will falters. We find ourselves pressed to the very limit of our personal capacities, not alone in summoning up the courage to look squarely at the dimensions of the impending predicament, but in finding words that can offer some plausible relief in a situation so bleak. There is now nowhere to turn other than to those private beliefs and disbeliefs that guide each of us through life. . . .[20]

There are two possible responses to Christians who conclude from this kind of analysis that the close of history is near. First, there are alternative views among futurologists. Herman Kahn, for example, actually argues that a continuation of "business as usual" will raise the living standards of the Third, Fourth and Fifth Worlds, thereby limiting population increase. He believes that energy and raw materials are still available for continual growth while we are in transition to superior sources of power and more intelligent handling of industrial resources. Kahn holds that the food and pollution problems are solvable with current technology, and that apart from the dangers of thermonuclear war and some unforeseen catastrophe related to technology the future of mankind is secure for the next several centuries, even if man goes on being as selfish and sensate as ever.[21]

On a more idealistic level, R. Buckminster Fuller believes that the world is like an egg which contains the nutrients a chick needs until the time of hatching. The benevolent wisdom of God has provided us with fossil fuels which are running out just as the need arises to switch to nonpolluting energy sources, which are plentiful. Fuller believes that Malthusian anxiety (which he believes is unrealistic) has driven men into self-defeating patterns of selfish acquisition, but that technological ephemeralization ("doing more and more with less and less") can lead us into an era of universal affluence if we can only learn to trust that the world works the way God made it and cooperate with one another in learning how to operate it.[22]

Obviously both of these approaches are not taking full account of the Fall and the radical corruption of human nature. Kahn assumes that selfishness and materialism are "normal" and that society functions acceptibly when these are unrestrained. We would more readily assume that death and disintegration is the result of unchecked sin on a corporate as well as an individual level. Fuller assumes a deistic universe in which human beings can easily be re-educated to trust God and manage the world according to his operating manual. But it is extremely significant that both Heilbroner and Fuller, unlike Kahn, believe that our current situation is one of such crisis that it is forcing mankind to recognize the need for radical spiritual transformation.

It is at least conceivable, and not at all contrary to sound theology and the biblical data, that we could be at a stage much before the end of history in which a forced recognition of the limits of human nature, like the crisis period of individual adolescence, is leading world civilization toward great people-movements which will sweep non-Western nations into the same intimate acquaintance with Christianity that the West has alternately enjoyed or suffered since

Constantine while restoring the faith of the West itself.

Calvin Colton expected this to happen if America could continue in its course of revival until it became a showcase of pure biblical Christianity, illuminating the world like the city set on a hill or the candle elevated and freed from its enclosing cover.[23] And Edwards, of course, expected it also:

> But yet, when God has sufficiently shown men the insufficiency of human wisdom and learning for the purposes of religion, and when the appointed time comes for that glorious outpouring of the Spirit of God, when he will himself by his own immediate influence enlighten men's minds; then may we hope that God will make use of the great increase of learning as a handmaid to religion, as a means of the glorious advancement of the kingdom of his son.[24]

Edwards posits a divine agency, overlooked by Fuller and Heilbroner, which solves the problem of indwelling sin they also ignore: the grace of God applied by the Spirit of Christ, transforming many members of society and powerfully restraining sin in others. This could only take place, of course, as the result of an unprecedented outpouring of the Holy Spirit reforming and revitalizing the church and turning the hearts of many in the surrounding world to respond to the gospel. But we have seen such reformation and revival happen many times in the past under warning circumstances as grave as those today. Futurologists like Heilbroner do not take into their consideration historical examples of society's power to change its habits in times when the church is revived, as in the Second Evangelical Awakening, and thus their pessimism about human nature is not balanced by a realistic optimism about grace.

A New Era of Missionary Expansion?

I am not following Edwards and Colton into their postmillennial vision. I am disposed to think that this position leads too readily to unwarranted optimism and hopes for the achievement of a permanent plateau of revival. Positive amillennialism and active premillennialism lead to more realistic assessments of the church's situation in a world which is "in the power of the evil one" (1 Jn. 5:19). I am simply suggesting that what has happened already on a wide scale in the relationship between Christianity and Western culture could happen also throughout the entire world if a purified and disenculturated form of Christianity were widely displayed among the nations. And I am suggesting that there is no valid reason to believe that we are too near the close of history for this to happen.

As a church historian I am automatically rather cautious about the assumption that these are literally the last days. There is no depressed era in Christian history which has not felt itself to be on the verge of Christ's return. And depressed eras have a way of turning into Christian resurgences that regain lost ground and move beyond it to embrace a larger area with purer expressions of the gospel. One scenario for the future envisions a misdirected technology, the god that failed, combining with religious decay to destroy humanity. Another postulates a revived and reformed Christianity regaining a degree of dominion over the conscience of the Western world, with technology harnessed to solve at least partially the ecological, population and hunger problems of the underdeveloped countries, while these countries are simultaneously experiencing powerful Christian growth.

Actually there are some indications that we are entering the greatest period of opportunity for the spread of the gospel which the world has ever seen. The world Evangelical community is organizing for mission now with a technological skill which is unprecedented. The number of available missionary fraternal workers is growing daily. The information and transportation explosions and the evolution of two great trade empires, the Communist and capitalist worlds, have contracted the planet, if not to a single village, at least to several towns which are in close touch with one another. During the 1960s this world community fostered the

transfer of drugs, music and mysticism from the East to
America. It is possible that now the tide is beginning to run
the other way.

Western nations which have concluded that the United
States is the last bulwark of strength against the encroaching
Communist world are watching America with increasing
interest, feeling somehow closer to it after the public display
of its fallibility in Watergate but curious also about the rising tide of vital Christianity in this country. At least in the
initial years of his presidency they were delighted in Jimmy
Carter, who was in effect their president also, combining a
stress on regenerate Christianity with a concern for social
justice in a way we have not seen since Wilberforce and
Shaftesbury.

If America were to follow this kind of leadership and to be
"born again" for a generation as England was "born again"
during the Second Awakening; if America were to become a
showcase of justice as well as liberty; if Christian opinion
were visibly to compel the sharing of America's resources to
feed and train the whole human community; if the network
of multinational corporations were tamed and brought into
service as a rail service for the gospel, as the Clapham leaders
tamed the British empire and used it for world mission; then
"the Great Century" of missionary expansion, the nineteenth, would in all likelihood yield to an even greater successor.

Let us remember that Jesus Christ is not to return again
physically until the gospel has first been preached to all nations. It might be objected that this has already happened.
But this objection strikes a shocking dissonance in the mind
with a developed historical consciousness. Christianity has
saturated the Western world for a thousand years; even the
calendars and the economic patterns of Western nations bear
constant witness to the lordship of Christ. What comparable witness has been born in the Islamic world, among the
Chinese and the many other hundreds of millions who live

only in the meager starlight of gospel witness? Is preaching of the good news to the nations limited to flying over once or twice in a gospel blimp and dropping tracts? Or may we not expect what the psalmist implies when he compares God's redemptive truth to the sun: "Its rising is from the end of the heavens, and its circuit to the end of them; and there is nothing hid from its heat" (Ps. 19:6)? I am not insisting that every nation must experience the degree of cultural infusion which Christianity has attained in the West. But it seems that the millions of Muslims and Chinese should gain something more than a brief glimpse of a flare shot off over another country.

There is another dissonance which rings in the mind of a historian confronting the notion that the mission of the church might be near its end with the last years of this century. Has the meaning of the gospel ever yet been adequately embodied in a widespread movement of the church, displaying for any sustained period the fullness of life available in Christ? Has the church ever been publicly revealed as the glorious bride of Christ, without spot or wrinkle, holy and without blemish? Our study of awakening movements only turns up what appear to be rehearsals for some final revelation of the full splendor of God's kingdom, intimations of its dimensions which I have tried to spell out in this book, which probably still fall far short of the vision of what God intends to work out within history. It is hard to believe that God will not grant the church some greater experience of wholeness and vitality than has yet appeared in the stumbling record of her history, in order, as Ezekiel says, that Israel and the nations may know that he is the Lord.

In the areas of the world in which the power of the gospel is still opening up and growing, in Africa and Eastern Asia, it must seem that the world is still in a pre-Christian era, in the dawning of the church age. Until recently Western observers have naturally but parochially assumed that the obvious downgrade toward secularism in the West was a sure sign of terminal apostasy. They have not considered the hypothesis that the downgrade is the natural result of an un-revived church which fails to salt the culture. Now that the numerical impact of the church, at least, is growing, many observers still point to the prevalence of more and more blatant forms of evil, such as the neopagan renaissance of witchcraft, as a sign of the end.

Most forms of serious witchcraft appear to be a reversion from the "high" paganism of secular materialism to the low paganism reflected in the forms of idolatry condemned in the Bible, the worship of a male, horned God (Baal) and his female counterpart (Ashtoreth). After a long period in which it became a rather subtle task in the West to apply the biblical condemnations of idolatry, the Scriptures are once again speaking more bluntly than we might have imagined to the habits of the great mass of humanity. But this may simply indicate that we are moving from an era of weak Christianity, in which our worst opponent has been irreligion, into an era of reformed and revived Christianity, in which our most serious opposition will come from counterfeit religions. Satan can fight a corrupt church with the option of no church at all, but when the church is strong, he must offer religious options.

Or perhaps the rise of neopagan religion in the West is simply a momentary backflow from the tidal interconnections which are being established as the world is more and more securely bound together in one community of interest and information. As we saw earlier, history may be considered as a series of stages in which one territory is substantially conquered for Christ; a contraction follows as the war is opened within a wider radius; and then a renewed Christian assault sweeps outward to widen the diameter of the reign of Christ. Phenomenologically, a revival of the opposing forces, the powers of darkness, seems to occur in three situations: first, when the Christian forces are spiritually at a low ebb themselves (as in eighteenth-century France); sec-

ond, when they are relatively strong, but a new and wider
mission front has opened up (the normalization of New
England's "national monastery" by the immigration of non-
Puritans in the late seventeenth and early eighteenth centuries); or third, when a renewed Christian offensive is
simply being met by a counterattack from the other side (the
midnineteenth century). Thus a revival of paganism is not
necessarily a sign of Christian weakness. It may simply be a
signal that our troops are on the move and that a wider field
is opening.

To use another metaphor, Christianity is like a fire which
periodically develops a vigorous blaze but is each time
covered with increasing quantities of green wood which
must dry out before they can be ignited. We may be near the
point in history when virtually all of the available wood on
the planet is about to be put on the fire. The outcome of this
situation could be terminal apostasy and great tribulation, or
it could be terminal awakening of the church and a new era
embracing the splendor of a purified Christian movement
confronted by new countermovements of opposition.

Eschatology and a Theology of History
All of the traditional eschatological positions can be harmonized with the model of the church's missionary movement presented here, which considers it as an army of liberation progressively freeing and clearing territory from demonic control in a pulsating series of advances and temporary fallbacks. Graphing the church's fortunes in history as
an ascending sine curve, we can see that amillennial, premillennial and postmillennial positions all are consistent
with a theology of history grounded on the assumption that
the church will continue to experience massive general
awakenings right up to the end of its career in history, when
Christ will return to deliver it from the last and greatest
counterattack of the powers of darkness.

When Jews are told that Jesus is the Messiah, it is common

for them to look around them with a wry smile and reply that nothing seems to have changed. It may not be legitimate for Christians to evade this objection by saying that the messianic kingdom is a "spiritual" entity only visible to "spiritual" eyes. Jewish people are looking for spiritual splendor and for justice; seldom do they find them in or around the Christian church.

Paul, echoing Isaiah and Deuteronomy, says, "God gave them [the Jews] a spirit of stupor, eyes that should not see and ears that should not hear" (Rom. 11:8), but he also asks, "have they stumbled so as to fall? By no means! But through their trespass salvation has come to the Gentiles, so as to make Israel jealous" (Rom. 11:11). Ultimately this situation will be changed, as Paul intimates in verses 12, 15 and 23, and finally states plainly: "I want you to understand this mystery, brethren: a hardening has come upon part of Israel, until the full number of the Gentiles come in, and so all Israel will be saved. . . . For the gifts and the call of God are irrevocable" (Rom. 11:25-26, 29). Evidently the maturing of the gentile church which accepts the Messiah will eventually be so palpably real that it will move the Jews to jealousy and draw them to recognize their king.

Paul's strategy to reach his kinsmen was thus to bring the fullness of Christ to the Gentiles: "Inasmuch then as I am an apostle to the Gentiles, I magnify my ministry in order to make my fellow Jews jealous, and thus save some of them" (Rom. 11:13-14). Now we must ask ourselves with some seriousness whether the state of most congregations of Christians presently on earth is vital and beautiful enough to make their Jewish neighbors jealous. A greater fullness both of numbers and of life must lie still in the future for the gentile church if large numbers of Jews are to be saved by the stirrings of divine jealousy.

Therefore I am compelled to agree with the theology of hope springing from Bucer and Bullinger which aimed at the recovery of the Jews through the reviving of the gentile

churches and which fired evangelical zeal for three centuries
both for the renewal of the church and for its spread among
all nations. We must resume these tasks with even greater
zeal and with equal balance. And we must agree with the
new theologians of hope who say, like Edwards and Wesley
and the leaders of the Second Awakening, that the good news
is more than "pie in the sky when you die," that it includes
a significant demonstration of the righteousness of the kingdom here on earth.

The central theme of the biblical drama of redemption is
the recovery of apostate peoples through the mercy of God.
The early chapters of Genesis trace the falling away from
knowledge of the true God of the various tribes of the Gentiles, while the covenant line which will flower in Israel
is held steady in the sphere of his grace. Israel is designed to
be an instrument for the recovery of believing multitudes out
of the gentile lines. When it fails in perceiving and fulfilling this task and in living out the righteousness of God as
an example to the nations, it is first scattered in the exile,
then regathered in part to set the stage for the appearance of
the individual in whom are summed up all the tasks and
promises given to Israel, the Branch, the Messiah. When
Israel again refuses the task of recovering the Gentiles
through rejecting the Messiah, the task of recovering both
Gentiles and apostate Jews, in an ironic inversion, is handed
on to a people of God largely composed of gentile believers.

We have seen in history that the church, "the Israel of
God," has failed almost as grievously as Israel under the Old
Covenant in living out God's righteousness. Though it has
reached many of the Gentiles and led them into a form of godliness, it has only rarely displayed that measure of spiritual
power which would offer compelling proof that Jesus is the
Messiah. It remains for gentile churches to lay hold of the
principles and the reality of fullness of life in Christ and to
demonstrate the reality of his reign within history among
his people. It remains for multitudes of messianic Jews to

join with gentile Christians while preserving intact those aspects of Jewish culture which form a perfect setting for the jewel of the gospel.

> For the gifts and the call of God are irrevocable. Just as you were once disobedient to God but now have received mercy because of their disobedience, so they have now been disobedient in order that by the mercy shown to you they also may receive mercy. For God has consigned all men to disobedience, that he may have mercy upon all. (Rom. 11:29-32)

Renewal and the Hopes of Israel

Is the national resettling of Israel significant in this picture of terminal renewal? Perhaps. Some Jewish Christians believe that more Jews have recognized their Messiah since the Six Day War than ever before in history. Israel as a nation is still hostile or indifferent to Christianity, but perhaps the wind has not yet breathed upon the valley where the dry bones have been reassembled (Ezek. 37:1-14). Certainly the persistence of the Jewish people as a distinct ethnic body throughout history, herded together by wolves of persecution and rejection, is no accident. It seems intended to draw the world's attention. We can only speculate what might be the effect upon the world if a broad-scale awakening in the gentile church was accompanied by large numbers of conversions among the Jews.

But what happens within the borders of Palestinian geography is not the main focus of the biblical promises concerning Israel. As the Puritans would say, these may be fulfilled either in the letter or in the better. What seems unavoidably clear in Romans 11 and its background in Old Testament prophecy is that the appearance, spread and reviving of the gentile church is all in order to recover the Israelite Diaspora, whose massive return to its rejected Messiah may be the climax of the greatest spiritual awakening in history.

While many exegetes interpret the Old Testament prophecies of the recovery of scattered Israel as already accomplished in the return of a small remnant of Jews to Palestine
during the intertestamental period, many others question
whether the full meaning of these promises has yet been fulfilled. Jeremiah states that the recovery of scattered Israel is
as vital an event in salvation history as the exodus:

> Therefore, behold, the days are coming, says the LORD,
> when it shall no longer be said, "As the LORD lives who
> brought up the people of Israel out of the land of Egypt,"
> but "As the LORD lives who brought up the people of Israel
> out of the north country and out of all the countries where
> he had driven them." For I will bring them back to their
> own land which I gave to their fathers.
>
> Behold, I am sending for many fishers, says the LORD,
> and they shall catch them; and afterwards I will send for
> many hunters, and they shall hunt them from every moun-
> tain and every hill, and out of the clefts of the rocks. (Jer
> 16:14-16)

The fishers of men described by Jeremiah are identified by
Zephaniah as believing Gentiles who offer believing Jews as
wave offerings to God (Zeph. 3:9-10). The missionary expansion of the gentile church seems clearly foreshadowed in
these passages. Isaiah and Zechariah hold out the same hope
of the recovery of an Israel renewed in faith (Is. 60:4, 10;
Zech. 10:6-12).

The recovery of Israel is virtually a second exodus, a new
declaration among the watching nations that the God of
Israel is alive and active, as Ezekiel says:

> And I will set my glory among the nations; and all the na-
> tions shall see my judgment which I have executed, and
> my hand which I have laid on them. The house of Israel
> shall know that I am the LORD their God, from that day for-
> ward. And the nations shall know that the house of Israel
> went into captivity for their iniquity.... Then they shall
> know that I am the LORD their GOD because I sent them into

exile among the nations, and then gathered them into their own land. I will leave none of them remaining among the nations any more; and I will not hide my face any more from them, when I pour out my Spirit upon the house of Israel, says the Lord GOD. (Ezek. 39:21-23; 28-29)

Nothing in the intertestamental period or the course of church history up to this point has presented a return of the Israelite people to spiritual and temporal prosperity equal to the terms in these prophecies, especially the extensive treatment of Israel's recovery in Ezekiel 36—48. Some elements in the prophets' vision of Israel's restoration may have been fulfilled before the time of Christ. However, the larger promises of spiritual restoration loom up like a great range of distant mountains beyond the few foothills already reached in history.

At present, it may well be that the ruined and partially apostate Christian churches of the Western world stand almost on a level with the Jewish people in their need of redemption and recovery of the heart of the Christian message. Ezekiel strongly connects Israel's renewal with the heart of the New Covenant:

And the nations will know that I am the LORD, says the Lord GOD, when through you I vindicate my holiness before their eyes. For I will take you from the nations, and gather you from all the countries, and bring you into your own land. I will sprinkle clean water upon you, and you shall be clean from all your uncleannesses, and from all your idols I will cleanse you. A new heart I will give you, and a new spirit I will put within you; and I will take out of your flesh the heart of stone and give you a heart of flesh. And I will put my spirit within you, and cause you to walk in my statutes and be careful to observe my ordinances. You shall dwell in the land which I gave to your fathers; and you shall be my people, and I will be your God. (Ezek. 36:23-27; compare 11:16-20)

Throughout the prophets God makes it clear that he is seeking for a people who will combine awareness that a supreme sacrifice is needed to put away their guilt with a deep intention to lead transformed lives. The same duality lies behind this search that is reflected in the balancing of law and sacrifices in the Old Testament, justification and sanctification in the New Testament, evangelism and social action in the church's history. God rejects the sacrifice which covers sin if it is not conjoined to the sacrifice which transforms the life. "For I desire steadfast love and not sacrifice, the knowledge of God, rather than burnt offerings" (Hos. 6:6; compare Is. 1:11-18 and Mic. 6:6-8).

God declares his intention of providing among the nations a priesthood which will offer the sacrifice of righteousness through the one great sacrifice of the priest and king who is the Messiah:

> The messenger of the covenant in whom you delight, behold, he is coming, says the LORD of hosts. But who can endure the day of his coming, and who can stand when he appears?
>
> For he is like a refiner's fire and like fullers' soap; he will sit as a refiner and purifier of silver, and he will purify the sons of Levi and refine them like gold and silver, till they present right offerings to the LORD. Then the offering of Judah and Jerusalem will be pleasing to the LORD as in the days of old and as in former years. (Mal. 3:1-4)

The priests who will ultimately offer this sacrifice are neither Levites nor parish ministers. They are a whole people of God who present their bodies "as a living sacrifice, holy and acceptable to God," which is their spiritual worship or service; they are not conformed to this world but are being transformed by the renewal of their minds, so that they may test what is the will of God, which is good and acceptable and perfect (Rom. 12:1-2). As they come to the living cornerstone of Ezekiel's second temple, who was "rejected by men but in God's sight chosen and precious," they are like living stones themselves "built into a spiritual house, to be a holy priesthood, to offer spiritual sacrifices acceptable to God through Jesus Christ"; and they serve among the nations as "a chosen race, a royal priesthood, a holy nation, God's own people," declaring the wonderful deeds of him who called them out of darkness into his marvelous light (1 Pet. 2:4-5, 9).

As Joseph, Daniel and other Jewish leaders sought the welfare of the nations where they were held captive, and as Jonah called Ninevah to repentance, so the priesthood of messianic believers must call the nations to repentance and general submission to the rule of Christ, warning that the nation that will not serve him shall perish (Is. 60:12). As the Levites stood among all Israel to declare God's truth and model his worship, so the new Israel of God, which is composed of believing Gentiles and Messianic Jews both filled with all the fullness of Christ, must stand to minister among all nations in a position of commanding eminence.

Paul promises that "all Israel shall be saved; as it is written, 'The Deliverer will come from Zion, he will banish ungodliness from Jacob; and this will be my covenant with them when I take away their sins' " (Rom. 11:26-27). We cannot tell how much of the righteousness of the kingdom will be established within ordinary history, but it is our responsibility to pray and work that that kingdom will be established on earth as it is and will be in heaven. As we look through history toward the great mountain of the Lord, we cannot wholly distinguish its foothills from its ultimate fulfillment where there is no longer day and night, revival and decline, but only perpetual light in the face of the Lamb of God. We can only know that we are required to move toward that mountain with every grace and energy that the outpoured Spirit can provide.

> On this mountain the LORD of hosts will make for all peoples a feast of fat things, a feast of wine on the lees, of fat things full of marrow, of wine on the lees well refined. And he will destroy on this mountain the covering that is cast over all peoples, the veil that is spread over all nations. He

will swallow up death for ever, and the Lord GOD will wipe away tears from all faces, and the reproach of his people he will take away from all the earth; for the LORD has spoken.

It will be said on that day, "Lo, this is our God; we have waited for him, that he might save us. This is the LORD; we have waited for him; let us be glad and rejoice in his salvation. (Is. 25:6-9)

Notes

Preface
[1]For examples of the literature of Catholic spiritual theology, see Louis Bouyer, et al., eds., *History of Christian Spirituality* (London: Burns & Oates, 1963-69); Pierre Pourrat, *Christian Spirituality* (Westminster, Md.: Newman Press, 1953-55). No comparable body of literature written from a Protestant perspective yet exists, apart from some works devoted to forms of Catholic and Protestant mysticism.

[2]Philipp Jakob Spener, *Pia Desideria*, trans. and ed. Theodore G. Tappert (Philadelphia: Fortress Press, 1964).

[3]For material in Edwards especially pertinent to this book, see C. C. Goen, ed., *The Great Awakening* (New Haven: Yale Univ. Press, 1972).

[4]Martin Luther, *Table Talk*, in *Luther's Works*, ed. Jaroslav Pelikan (Philadelphia: Fortress Press, 1967), LIV, 340.

[5]A. W. Boehm, "Preface" to Johann Arndt's *True Christianity*, 2nd ed., rev. (London: D. Brown & J. Downing, 1720), p. xxii.

[6]Ibid., pp. v-vi.

[7]Ibid., p. viii.

[8]Ibid., p. xiv.

[9]Benedict of Nursia, *The Rule of Saint Benedict*, trans. and ed. Owen Chadwick (Philadelphia: Westminster Press, 1948), p. 293.

[10]Kenneth Scott Latourette and other historians have detected movements of genuine renewal within Catholicism parallel to the major Protestant awakenings ever since the Reformation and accompanying Counter Reformation. Similarly, the current Evangelical resurgence is paralleled by the rise of Catholic pentecostalism. The doctrinal and causal questions raised by this observation need close investigation and are beyond the scope of this work. The detection of a common spiritual impulse behind these movements is not meant to minimize the problem of their doctrinal distance from Evangelical Protestantism on crucial issues such as justification by faith, the sole authority of Scripture and the denial of an ecclesiastical hierarchy which bestows the charismata by virtue of apostolic succession. For a more extensive indication of my approach, see my "A Call to Historic Roots and Continuity," in *The Orthodox Evangelicals*, ed. Robert Webber and Donald G. Bloesch (Nashville: Thomas Nelson, 1978).

Chapter 1
[1]This chapter omits reference to many currents within twentieth-century church life which can also be understood as vectors toward renewal, including elements within the ecumenical movement, some varieties of neo-orthodoxy and the biblical theology movement, the liturgical renewal, and the theology of the laity. The scope of this chapter has necessarily been contracted to focus on the stream of Evangelical Protestantism which has been my nurturing environment. For

a contrasting definition of the stream of renewal in this century, see William G. McLoughlin, *Revivals, Awakenings, and Reform* (Chicago: Univ. of Chicago Press, 1978).

[2]Marlin Van Elderen, "The 'Jesus Freaks,' " *The Reformed Journal*, 22, No. 6 (May/June, 1971), 16-20.

[3]"The Jesus Movement," *Time Magazine*, 96 (Aug. 3, 1970), 31-32.

[4]For example, the Conferences on Reformed Piety sponsored during 1975-76 in the seminaries of the United Presbyterian Church.

[5]Dean M. Kelley, *Why Conservative Churches Are Growing* (New York: Harper and Row, 1972).

[6]David S. Schuller, et al., *Readiness for Ministry: Volume 1, Criteria* (Vandalia, Ohio: Association of Theological Schools in the U.S. and Canada, 1975).

[7]Ernst Benz, "Pietist and Puritan Sources of Early Protestant World Missions," *Church History*, 20 (1951), 28-55.

[8]James Mackinnon, "Humanism in Relation to the Reformation," *The Origins of the Reformation* (London: Longmans and Green and Co., 1939); Johan Huizinga, *Erasmus and the Age of Reformation* (New York: Harper & Bros., 1957).

[9]Margaret Mann Phillips, *Erasmus and the Northern Renaissance* (London: Hodder and Stoughton, 1949).

[10]See Richard F. Lovelace, *The American Pietism of Cotton Mather: Origins of American Evangelicalism* (Grand Rapids: Eerdmans, 1979); Jonathan Edwards, *A Faithful Narrative of the Surprising Work of God*, in Goen, *The Great Awakening*, pp. 22-23, 153-56.

[11]See Arthur James Lewis, *Zinzendorf the Ecumenical Pioneer* (Philadelphia: Westminster Press, 1962).

[12]Edwards, *Faithful Narrative*, pp. 160-71.

[13]See Archibald Alexander, *The Log College* (London: Banner of Truth Trust, 1968); Leonard J. Trinterud, *The Forming of an American Tradition* (Philadelphia: Westminster Press, 1949).

[14]Alan Heimert and Perry Miller, eds., "Introduction," *The Great Awakening* (Indianapolis: Bobbs-Merrill Co., Inc., 1967).

[15]Jonathan Edwards, *The History of Redemption*, in *The Works of Jonathan Edwards*, rev. and ed. Edward Hickman, (London: Banner of Truth Trust, 1974 [1834], I; and *An Humble Attempt to Promote Explicit Agreement and Visible Union of God's People in Extraordinary Prayer for the Revival of Religion and the Advancement of Christ's Kingdom on Earth*, in *Jonathan Edwards: Apocalyptic Writings*, ed. Stephen J. Stein (New Haven: Yale Univ. Press, 1977).

[16]Edwards, *Thoughts on the Revival in New England*, in Goen, *The Great Awakening*, pp. 410-13, 494-95.

[17]Edwards, *Thoughts on the Revival*, pp. 527-28; see also *Religious Affections*, ed. John E. Smith (New Haven: Yale Univ. Press, 1959), pp. 383-461.

[18]Cotton Mather, *Diary*, (New York: F. Ungar Publishing Co., 1957), II, 443-44.

[19]Edwards, *History of Redemption*, pp. 604-6.

[20]Secondary studies which document the sense of lagging spiritual initiative at the end of the eighteenth century and the recovery of momentum in the Second Awakening include Charles Roy Keller, *The Second Great Awakening in Connecticut* (Hamden, Conn.: Archon Books, 1968); Leonard Elliott-Binns, *The Early English Evangelicals* (London: Lutterworth Press, 1955); and Ford K. Brown, *Fathers of the Victorians* (Cambridge: Cambridge Univ. Press, 1961).

[21]For accounts of the frontier revivals, see Charles Albert Johnson, *The Frontier Camp Meeting* (Dallas: S.M.U. Press, 1955); Catherine Caroline Cleveland, *The Great Revival in the West* (Chicago: Univ. of Chicago Press, 1916); and Peter Cartwright, *Autobiography* (Nashville: Abingdon Press, 1956).

[22]Keller, *The Second Awakening in Connecticut.*

[23]Perhaps the best of a number of books analyzing the reforming activities of American evangelicals in the Second Awakening is George M. Marsden's *The Evangelical Mind and the New School Presbyterian Experience* (New Haven: Yale Univ. Press, 1970). A number of others are listed in the notes to chapter twelve.

[24]For a survey of the Second Awakening in England, see Elliott-Binns, *The Early English Evangelicals*, and E. M. Howse, *Saints in Politics* (Toronto: Univ. of Toronto Press, 1952).

[25]J. Edwin Orr, *Evangelical Awakenings in the South Seas* (Minneapolis: Bethany Fellowship, Inc., 1976); *Evangelical Awakenings in Southern Asia* (Minneapolis: Bethany Fellowship, Inc., 1975); *Evangelical Awakenings in Eastern Asia* (Minneapolis: Bethany Fellowship, Inc., 1975); *Evangelical Awakenings in Africa* (Minneapolis: Bethany Fellowship, Inc., 1975); *Campus Aflame* (Glendale: Regal Books, 1972); *The Eager Feet: Evangelical Awakenings,1790-1830* (Chicago: Moody Press, 1975); *The Fervent Prayer: The World Wide Impact of the Great Awakening of 1858* (Chicago: Moody Press, 1974); *The Flaming Tongue: Evangelical Awakenings, 1900—*, 2nd ed., rev. (Chicago: Moody Press, 1975).

[26]*Religion in America 1977-78*, The Gallup Opinion Index, Report No. 145 (Princeton: American Institute of Public Opinion), p. 43.

[27]Edwards, *History of Redemption*, p. 601.

[28]Arthur Wilford Nagler, *Pietism and Methodism* (Nashville: Publishing House M. E. Church South, 1918), p. 41; Lewis, *Zinzendorf.*

Chapter 2

[1]Jehoshaphat, 2 Chron. 17:1-19; Hezekiah, 2 Kings 18:1-8; Josiah, 2 Kings 22.

[2]See also Hos. 6:1-2; Hab. 3:2; Ps. 80:3 and Jer. 31:18.

[3]Wallace Stevens, "Esthetique du Mal," in *Transport to Summer* (New York: Alfred A. Knopf, 1951).

[4]See Mt. 4:1-11 (Lk. 4:1-13); 8:28-34 (Mk. 5:1-20); 9:32-34; 12:22-29; 15:22-28 (Mk. 7:24-30); 17:14-21 (Mk. 9:14-29; Lk. 9:37-42); Mk. 1:

23-28; 34; Lk. 8:2; 10:17-20; Jn. 8:43-44; 12:31; 13:2; 14:30 and 16:11.

Chapter 3

[1]John Calvin, *Institutes of the Christian Religion,* I:1.

[2]See Ernest Gordon Rupp, *The Righteousness of God* (London: Hodder and Stoughton, 1953).

[3]See Philip S. Watson, *Let God Be God* (Philadelphia: Fortress Press, 1947).

[4]Richard K. Curtis, *They Called Him Mr. Moody* (Garden City, N.Y.: Doubleday, 1962), pp. 127-28, 133-35.

[5]On the liberal side, the theologies of Albrecht Ritschl and Adolf von Harnack are the main exemplars of this trend, and their influence has weakened the doctrine of God in many non-Evangelical quarters throughout the twentieth century. While many enclaves of Fundamentalist Christianity have preserved a harsher image of God, Bernard Weisberger notes a sentimentalizing reaction to this imbalance among Evangelicals in the late nineteenth century. See *They Gathered at the River* (Boston: Little, Brown and Co., 1958), pp. 171-73.

[6]Jonathan Edwards, "Sinners in The Hands of an Angry God," in *Works,* II, 9.

[7]The shift toward Pelagianism in American Evangelicalism is seen most clearly in the theologies of Nathanael W. Taylor and the great evangelist Charles G. Finney.

[8]See also Rom. 10:17; Ps. 19:7-14 and 119:130.

[9]Søren Kierkegaard, *Attack upon Christendom,* trans. Walter Lowrie (Boston: Beacon Press, 1956), p. 108.

[10]See Jn. 7:7; 8:23; 12:31; 14:16-17, 22, 27; 15:18-19; 16:33; 17:9; 18:36; 1 Cor. 1:20-21; Eph. 6:12; Jas. 4:4; 1 Jn. 2:15-17.

[11]See Ezra 9:5-15; Neh. 1:4-11; Dan. 9:3-19.

Chapter 4

[1]Anselm, *Cur Deus Homo,* in *Anselm of Canterbury: Works,* trans. and ed. Jasper Hopkins and Herbert Richardson (New York: Edwin Mellen Press, 1976), III.

[2]H. Shelton Smith, ed., *Horace Bushnell: Twelve Selections* (New York: Oxford Univ. Press, 1965), pp. 310-12.

[3]Ibid., pp. 196-98.

[4]See, for example, Rom. 5:1-11 and Col. 2:10-15.

[5]Gal. 2:16; 3:1-14; cf. Rom. 3:19-28.

[6]Dietrich Bonhoeffer, *The Cost of Discipleship,* trans. R. H. Fuller (New York: Macmillan, 1959).

[7]John Owen, *Of the Mortification of Sin in Believers,* in *Works,* VII, ed. Thomas Russell (London: Richard Baynes, 1823), p. 350.

[8]See, for example, Handley C. G. Moule, *The Epistle of St. Paul to the Romans* (New York: A. C. Armstrong and Son, 1902), pp. 161-69; Andrew Murray, *Abide in Christ* (New York: Fleming H. Revell, n.d.) pp. 36-44; *Holy in Christ* (New York: Fleming H. Revell, n.d.),

pp. 158-66.
[9]John of the Cross, The Dark Night of the Soul, in The Complete Works of St. John of the Cross, trans. and ed. E. Allison Peers (Westminster, Md.: Newman Press, 1964). For a fascinating Protestant counterpart of The Dark Night of the Soul, see Thomas Goodwin, A Child of Light Walking in Darkness, in Works, III (Edinburgh: James Nichol, 1861).
[10]Richard Sibbes, A Fountain Sealed, in Complete Works, ed. A. B. Grosart, (Edinburgh: James Nichol, 1863), V; Thomas Goodwin, The Work of The Holy Ghost in Our Salvation, in Works, VI (Edinburgh: James Nichol, 1863); John Owen, The Holy Spirit (Grand Rapids: Kregel, 1954) and Communion with God The Father, Son, and Holy Ghost, in Works, X (1824).
[11]Nils Bloch-Hoell, The Pentecostal Movement (London: Allen and Unwin, 1964); Walter J. Hollenweger, The Pentecostals (London: SCM Press, 1972); John Thomas Nichol, Pentecostalism (New York: Harper and Row, 1966); Vinson Synan, The Holiness-Pentecostal Movement in the United States (Grand Rapids: Eerdmans, 1971); Vinson Synan, ed., Aspects of Pentecostal Origins (Plainfield, N.J.: Logos International, 1975).
[12]Charles Simeon, The Offices of The Holy Spirit (New York: Swords, Stanford, 1832).
[13]See Arnold Bittlinger, Gifts and Graces, trans. Herbert Klassen (Grand Rapids: Eerdmans, 1968).
[14]Ernest Wallace Bacon, Spurgeon: Heir of the Puritans (Grand Rapids: Eerdmans, 1968), pp. 154-56.
[15]See Rom. 6:3-5; 1 Cor. 12:13; Gal. 3:27; Col. 2:12. See also Gordon D. Fee, "Hermeneutics and Historical Precedent—A Major Problem in Pentecostal Hermeneutics," in Perspectives on the New Pentecostalism, ed. Russell P. Spittler (Grand Rapids: Baker Book House, 1976).
[16]Gustav Aulen, Christus Victor, trans. A. G. Hebert (London: S.P.C.K., 1950).
[17]See, for example, Don Basham, Deliver Us from Evil (Washington Depot, Conn.: Chosen Books, 1972); Pat Brooks, Out! In the Name of Jesus (Carol Stream, Ill.: Creation House, 1972); John Richards, But Deliver Us from Evil (London: Dartman, Longman and Todd, 1974).
[18]Ignatius Loyola, The Spiritual Exercises, trans. Louis J. Puhl, S. J. (Westminster, Md.: Newman Press, 1951), pp. 141-50.
[19]John Downame, The Christian's Warfare ... (London, 1604); Thomas Brooks, Precious Remedies against Satan's Devices (London: Banner of Truth Trust, 1968); William Gurnall, The Christian in Complete Armor (London: Banner of Truth Trust, 1974).
[20]John Bunyan, Grace Abounding to the Chief of Sinners in Complete Works (Philadelphia: Bradley, Garretson and Co. 1872), George Whitefield, Journals (London: Banner of Truth Trust, 1960), pp. 52-58.
[21]Evan Roberts and Jessie Penn-Lewis, War on the Saints (New York: T. E. Lowe, 1973).
[22]John L. Nevius, Demon Possession and Allied Themes (Chicago: Flem-

ing H. Revell, 1894).

[23]Hal Lindsey, *Satan Is Alive and Well on Planet Earth* (Grand Rapids: Zondervan, 1972); Martin I. Bubeck, *The Adversary* (Chicago: Moody Press, 1975); John C. Hagee, *Invasion of Demons* (Old Tappan, N.J.: Fleming H. Revell, 1973); Donald R. Jacobs, *Demons* (Scottdale, Pa.: Herald Press, 1972); Kurt E. Koch, *Occult Bondage and Deliverance* (Grand Rapids: Kregel, 1971); Merrill F. Unger, *What Demons Can Do to Saints* (Chicago: Moody Press, 1977).

[24]C. S. Lewis, *The Screwtape Letters* (New York: Macmillan Co., 1943).

[25]For the classic account of this problem, see Bunyan, *Grace Abounding*, pp. 40-45.

[26]Kierkegaard, *Attack upon Christendom*, p. 111.

Chapter 5

[1]Ronald M. Enroth, Edward E. Erickson, Jr., and C. Breckinridge Peters, *The Jesus People* (Grand Rapids: Eerdmans, 1972), pp. 21-54.

[2]See Perry Miller, "Declension in a Bible Commonwealth," *Proceedings of the American Antiquarian Society*, LI (1941).

[3]Edmund S. Morgan, *The Puritan Family* (New York: Harper and Row, 1966), pp. 168-86.

[4]Ralph Winter, *The Twenty-Five Incredible Years, 1945 to 1969* (South Pasadena, Calif.: William Carey Library, 1970).

[5]Jonathan Edwards, *An Humble Attempt to Promote Explicit Agreement and Visible Union of God's People in Extraordinary Prayer*, in *Jonathan Edwards: Apocalyptic Writings*.

[6]J. Edwin Orr, *The Second Evangelical Awakening in America* (London: Marshall, 1952) and *The Flaming Tongue*.

[7]See Charles G. Finney, *Lectures on Revivals of Religion* (Cambridge: Harvard Univ. Press, 1960), pp. 9-23.

[8]Thomas Goodwin, *The Return of Prayers*, in *Works*, III.

[9]Cotton Mather, *Grata Brevitas* (Boston, 1712), p. 14.

[10]Pourrat, *Christian Spirituality*, III, 23-48.

[11]J. Howard Kauffman, *Anabaptists Four Centuries Later* (Scottdale, Pa.: Herald Press, 1975), p. 80.

[12]F. Ernest Stoeffler, *The Rise of Evangelical Pietism* (Leiden: Brill, 1965), p. 19; J. T. McNeill, *A History of the Cure of Souls* (London: SCM Press, 1951), p. 180.

[13]Spener, *Pia Desideria*, pp. 87-92.

[14]Lewis, *Zinzendorf*, pp. 47-77.

[15]Pierre Teilhard de Chardin, *The Future of Man*, trans. Norman Denny (New York: Harper and Row, 1964), p. 105.

[16]Ibid., pp. 105-6.

[17]See Peter Brown, *Augustine of Hippo* (Berkeley: Univ. of California Press, 1967); Elmore Harris Harbison, *The Christian Scholar in the Age of the Reformation* (New York: Scribner, 1956).

[18]See Josef Pieper, *Scholasticism*, trans. Richard and Clara Winston (London: Faber and Faber, 1960).

[19]See Mackinnon, *The Origins of the Reformation.*

[20]Walter J. Ong, *Ramus: Method, and the Decay of Dialogue* (Cambridge: Harvard Univ. Press, 1958).

[21]See Matthew Spinka, *John Amos Comenius: That Incomparable Moravian* (Chicago: Univ. of Chicago Press, 1943).

[22]Perry Miller, *Jonathan Edwards* (New York: Meridian Books, Inc., 1959 [1949]).

[23]See William Haller, *The Rise of Puritanism* (New York: Harper, 1957, [1938]); Stoeffler, *The Rise of Evangelical Pietism.*

[24]See Peter Gay, *The Rise of Modern Paganism,* Vol. I of *The Enlightenment: An Interpretation* (New York: Alfred A. Knopf, 1967, [1966]).

[25]See Charles Cuningham, *Timothy Dwight 1752-1817: A Biography* (New York: Macmillan, 1942); Hugh A. E. Hopkins, *Charles Simeon of Cambridge* (London: Hodder and Stoughton, 1977).

[26]C. S. Lewis, "The Funeral of a Great Myth," in *Christian Reflections* (Grand Rapids: Eerdmans, 1967).

[27]I have in mind here the conservative neo-orthodox theologians, especially Karl Barth, Emil Brunner and Dietrich Bonhoeffer.

[28]*The Epistle to Diognetus,* in *Documents Illustrative of the History of the Church,* ed. B. J. Kidd (London: Macmillan & Co., 1920), I.

[29]Karl Adam, *The Spirit of Catholicism,* trans. Justin McCann (London: Sheed and Ward, 1952).

[30]Tertullian, "The Apparel of Women," and "The Chaplet," in *Tertullian: Disciplinary, Moral and Ascetical Works* (New York: Fathers of the Church, Inc., 1959).

[31]See H. B. Workman, *The Evolution of the Monastic Ideal* (Boston: Beacon Press, 1962 [1913]).

[32]Augustine, *The City of God,* trans. William M. Green (Cambridge: Harvard Univ. Press, 1963), II, 337-51, 375-91.

[33]See Karl Holl, *The Cultural Significance of the Reformation,* trans. Karl and Barbara Hertz and John H. Lichtblau (New York: Meridian Books, 1959).

Chapter 6

[1]Alvin Toffler, *Future Shock* (New York: Random House, 1970).

[2]Søren Kierkegaard, *The Sickness unto Death,* trans. Walter Lowrie (Princeton: Princeton Univ. Press, 1946).

[3]P. T. Forsyth, *Christian Perfection* (New York: Dodd, Mead and Co., 1899), p. 9.

[4]Ibid., pp. 7-8.

[5]Quoted in Erich Beyreuther, *August Hermann Francke, 1663-1727, Zeuge des lebendigen Gottes,* 2te Aufl. (Marburg: Francke-Buchhandlung, 1961), p. 51.

[6]Richard Baxter, *The Reformed Pastor,* ed. Hugh Martin (London: SCM Press, 1956).

[7]Michael Harper, *A New Way of Living* (Plainfield, N.J.: Logos International, 1973).

Chapter 7

[1]Thomas Merton, *The Seven Storey Mountain* (New York: Harcourt, 1948).

[2]The group mentioned here is an interdenominational fellowship associated with a renewal center named Peniel in Luzerne, New York.

[3]Quoted by Cotton Mather, *Manuductio ad Ministerium* (Boston, 1726), p. 60.

[4]For a lengthier analysis of the loading of conversion, see chapter three of my *The American Pietism of Cotton Mather*.

[5]Lyman Beecher, *Autobiography*, ed. Barbara M. Cross (Cambridge: Harvard Univ. Press, 1961), I, 30.

[6]Charles G. Finney, *Memoirs* (New York: A. S. Barnes and Co., 1876), pp. 20-23.

[7]For example, Reuben Archer Torrey, *The Baptism with the Holy Spirit* (New York: Fleming H. Revell, 1897); *The Holy Spirit* (New York: Fleming H. Revell, 1927).

[8]Owen, *Of the Mortification of Sin in Believers*, p. 350.

Chapter 8

[1]Samuel M. Jackson, ed., *New Schaff-Herzog Encyclopedia of Religious Knowledge* (New York: Funk and Wagnalls, 1909), IV, 149.

[2]See Geoffrey F. Nuttall, *The Holy Spirit in Puritan Faith and Experience* (Oxford: Basil Blackwell, 1947).

[3]Ronald Knox, *Enthusiasm* (Oxford: Clarendon, 1950). Knox denies this intent (p. 8), but this seems a fair summary of his case. For a good review of the use of the word *enthusiasm*, see pp. 1-8.

[4]Ibid., pp. 1-4.

[5]Ibid., p. 580.

[6]Charles Chauncy, *Seasonable Thoughts on the State of Religion in New England* (Boston: Rogers and Fowle, 1743).

[7]Edwards, *Thoughts on the Revival*, p. 417.

[8]John of the Cross, *The Dark Night of the Soul*, pp. 332-49.

[9]Edwards, *Thoughts on the Revival*, p. 414.

[10]Ibid., p. 416.

[11]Ibid., p. 418.

[12]Ibid., p. 421.

[13]Ibid., pp. 421-22.

[14]Ibid., p. 422.

[15]Ibid., p. 424.

[16]Ibid., p. 431.

[17]Ibid., p. 423.

[18]Cotton Mather, *The Tryed Professor* (Boston, 1719), p. 43.

[19]Edwards, *Religious Affections*, pp. 197-239, 383-461, *Thoughts on the Revival*, pp. 466-71.

[20]Edwards, *Thoughts on the Revival*, pp. 96-102, 119-21, and *Original Sin*, ed. Clyde A. Holbrook (New Haven: Yale Univ. Press, 1970), pp. 223-36; C. Conrad Cherry, *The Theology of Jonathan Edwards* (New

York: Anchor Books, 1966), pp. 12-18.

[21]See 1 Tim. 4:6; 2 Tim. 1:13; Tit. 1:9, 13; 2:1, 2 and 8.

[22]Jonathan Edwards, *Images or Shadows of Divine Things*, ed. Perry Miller (New Haven: Yale Univ. Press, 1948).

[23]For a critical but revealing analysis of post-Finneyan revivalism, see William G. McLoughlin, *Modern Revivalism* (New York: Ronald Press Co., 1959).

[24]Edwards, *Thoughts on the Revival*, pp. 244, 344, 385, and *Religious Affections*, p. 86.

[25]See Dan. 10:13, 20; Zech. 3:1,2.

[26]Edwards, *A Faithful Narrative*, pp. 205-11.

[27]Ibid., p. 162.

[28]Edwards, *Thoughts on the Revival*, p. 410.

[29]Ibid., p. 495.

[30]Ibid., p. 494.

[31]See Mt. 24:24-26; 1 Tim. 4:13; 1 Jn. 2:18; 4:1.

[32]See Leon Festinger, et al., *When Prophecy Fails* (New York: Harper and Row, 1964).

[33]See George Huntston Williams, *The Radical Reformation* (Philadelphia: Westminster Press, 1962), pp. 38-58, 351-86, 477-85, 815-32.

[34]Nuttall, *The Holy Spirit in Puritan Faith and Experience*, pp. 34-47.

[35]Edwards, *Thoughts on the Revival*, pp. 438-39.

[36]Edwards, *Thoughts on the Revival*, pp. 436-37.

[37]Ibid., p. 434.

[38]Ibid., pp. 437-38.

Chapter 9

[1]Emil Brunner, *The Divine-Human Encounter* (Philadelphia: Westminster Press, 1943), pp. 31, 112, 153-54.

[2]Ibid., pp. 39-40.

[3]Bonhoeffer, *The Cost of Discipleship*, pp. 35-47.

[4]Stoeffler, *The Rise of Evangelical Pietism*, p. 134.

[5]Beecher, *Autobiography*, p. 68.

[6]Ibid.

[7]Ibid.

[8]Brunner, *Divine-Human Encounter*, pp. 29-30.

[9]See Jn. 3:20-21; 7:17; Rom. 1:19-23; 1 Tim. 6:3-4; 2 Tim. 2:23-26; 3: 6-8; 4:3-4; Tit. 3:9-11.

Chapter 10

[1]See Williams, *The Radical Reformation*.

[2]Nuttall, *The Holy Spirit in Puritan Faith and Experience*.

[3]See C. C. Goen, *Revivalism and Separatism in New England, 1740-1800* (New Haven: Yale Univ. Press, 1963).

[4]A. E. Housman, *The Collected Poems of A. E. Housman* (New York: Henry Holt and Co., 1940), p. 166.

[5]John T. McNeill, *Unitive Protestantism*, rev. ed. (Richmond: John

Knox Press, 1964).

[6]Stoeffler, The Rise of Evangelical Pietism, pp. 78-99.

[7]See J. M. Batten, John Dury, Advocate of Christian Reunion (Chicago: Univ. of Chicago Press, 1944).

[8]For more information on Baxter, see Alfred H. Wood, Church Unity without Uniformity (London: Epworth Press, 1963).

[9]Cotton Mather, The Stone Cut Out of The Mountain (Boston, 1716), p. 6.

[10]See Stoeffler, The Rise of Evangelical Pietism and German Pietism During the Eighteenth Century (Leiden: Brill, 1973).

[11]See Spinka, John Amos Comenius.

[12]See Lewis, Zinzendorf.

[13]Gilbert Tennent, "Irenicum Ecclesiasticum," in The Great Awakening, ed. Alan Heimert and Perry Miller (Indianapolis: Bobbs-Merrill Co., 1967), pp. 365-75.

[14]Edwards, An Humble Attempt.

[15]See Howse, Saints in Politics.

[16]See Charles I. Foster, An Errand of Mercy (Chapel Hill, N.C.: Univ. of North Carolina Press, 1960); and Marsden, The Evangelical Mind and the New School Presbyterian Experience.

[17]See Carl Henry, Evangelicals in Search of Identity (Waco, Tex.: Word Books, 1976).

[18]See, for example, John Calvin, Commentary on the Epistles ... to the Corinthians (Edinburgh: Calvin Translation Society, 1849), pp. 257-58; Charles Hodge, An Exposition of the Second Epistle to the Corinthians (Philadelphia: Presbyterian Board of Publication, 1859), pp. 165-69; F. F. Bruce, First and Second Corinthians (London: Oliphants, 1971), pp. 214-15; William Barclay, The Letters to the Corinthians (Philadelphia: Westminster Press, 1975), pp. 220-23; Philip Edgecumbe Hughes, Commentary on the Second Epistle to the Corinthians (Grand Rapids: Eerdmans, 1962), pp. 244-48; Alfred Plummer, A Critical and Exegetical Commentary on the Second Epistle of Saint Paul to the Corinthians (New York: Scribner, 1915), pp. 206-7; R. V. G. Tasker, The Second Epistle of Paul to the Corinthians (Grand Rapids: Eerdmans), p. 98.

[19]H. Richard Niebuhr, The Social Sources of Denominationalism (New York: Henry Holt and Co., 1929).

[20]McNeill, Unitive Protestantism, pp. 260-65.

[21]Spener, Pia Desideria, pp. 68-75.

[22]Curtis, They Called Him Mr. Moody, pp. 323-27.

[23]Herman Kahn and B. Bruce-Briggs, Things to Come: Thinking about the Seventies and Eighties (New York: Macmillan Co., 1972), pp. 100-1.

[24]Peter L. Berger, et al., "The Hartford Declaration," Theology Today, 32 (April, 1975), 94-97.

[25]"A Response to Declaration of Evangelical Social Concern," Post American, 4, No. 3 (March, 1975), 27.

[26]Nagler, *Pietism and Methodism*, p. 41.

Chapter 11
[1]While accepting Francis Schaeffer's general contention that twentieth-century art forms increasingly express the spiritual bankruptcy of secularized culture, I am hesitant to follow him in some of his attempts to discern corruption in the stream of modern music (see *Escape from Reason* [Downers Grove, Ill.: InterVarsity Press, 1968], p. 44; *The God Who Is There* [Downers Grove, Ill.: InterVarsity Press, 1968], pp. 37-80). I must also admit recognizing genius in many works of Schoenberg, Berg, Webern and some who have followed the third Viennese school. At this juncture in history, however, it looks as though the effort to discard tonality altogether has led to a dead end. The established classics of twentieth-century music are mostly those which retain tonality but expand harmonic language, and the way to the future now seems likely to involve an eclectic revisiting of the past, related to the basic harmonic instincts of folk music but making regular excursions beyond this.
[2]Hodge, of Hamilton, Massachusetts, has made one award-winning film, *The Interlude*, based on a parable of Kierkegaard, but has had difficulty raising capital for further works.
[3]See Maisie Ward, *Gilbert Keith Chesterton* (London: Sheed and Ward. 1944), p. 512.
[4]Larry Norman, "Why Don't You Look into Jesus," from the album *Only Visiting This Planet* (Hollywood, Calif.: Solid Rock Records).

Chapter 12
[1]Tom Wolfe, *Mauve Gloves and Madmen, Clutter and Vine* (New York: Farrar, Straus & Giroux, 1976).
[2]David Moberg, *The Great Reversal* (Philadelphia: Lippincott, 1972), p. 53.
[3]Ibid., pp. 56-57. Recently George Gallup's opinion index, *Religion in America 1977-78*, has appeared to vindicate Evangelicals by data which imply that they have the strongest commitment to the application of Christianity in society within any sector of American Christianity. We can be thankful that this momentum still remains from the Evangelical activism of the nineteenth century. We must question, however, whether it is expressed in a way which is wholly relevant to twentieth-century concerns for justice.
[4]Kelley, *Why Conservative Churches Are Growing*, pp. 146, 149-50, 162.
[5]Samuel Escobar, "Evangelism and Man's Search for Freedom, Justice and Fulfillment," in J. D. Douglas, ed., *Let The Earth Hear His Voice* (Minneapolis: World Wide Publications, 1975), pp. 303-26
[6]Moberg, *The Great Reversal*, pp. 166-73.
[7]John T. McNeill, *The History and Character of Calvinism* (New York: Oxford Univ. Press, 1954), pp. 166-67, 190-96.

[8]C. H. and K. George, The Protestant Mind of the English Reformation (Princeton: Princeton Univ. Press, 1961), pp. 83-85, 89-90, 104, 131-39, 156-58, 162-69.

[9]Emery Battis, Saints and Sectaries (Chapel Hill, N.C.: Univ. of North Carolina Press, 1962), pp. 103, 117.

[10]C. H. and K. George, The Protestant Mind, pp. 300-2.

[11]Richard Baxter, A Christian Directory, in Practical Works, (London: George Virtue, 1845), I, 640-64.

[12]J. Wesley Bready, England, Before and After Wesley (London: Hodder and Stoughton, 1938).

[13]Gerrard Winstanley, Works, ed. George H. Sabine (New York: Russell & Russell, 1965 [1941]); Lewis Henry Berens, The Digger Movement in the Days of the Commonwealth (London: Holland & Merlin, 1961).

[14]Auguste Jorns, The Quakers As Pioneers in Social Work, trans. Thomas Kite Brown, Jr., (Port Washington, N.Y.: Kennikat Press, 1969), pp. 57-58, 197-98.

[15]See Arndt, True Christianity, trans. A. W. Boehm (London: 1712), I, 154-206; and Erich Beyreuther, August Hermann Francke und die Anfange der Ökumenischen Bewegung (Hamburg: Herbert Reich Evang. Verlag, 1957), pp. 26, 36-37; August Hermann Francke, 1663-1727, Zeuge des lebendigen Gottes, 2te Aufl. (Marburg: Francke-Buchhandlung, 1961), p. 147.

[16]J. V. Andreae, Christianopolis, trans. and ed. F. E. Held (New York, 1916), pp. 242-43, 272-75.

[17]Beyreuther, August Hermann Francke und die Anfange, pp. 39-40; Klaus Deppermann, Der Hallesche Pietismus und der preussische Staat unter Friedrich III (Göttingen: Vandenhoeck & Ruprecht, 1961), pp. 51-55.

[18]Beyreuther, August Hermann Francke und die Anfange, pp. 30-31, 50.

[19]Carl Bridenbaugh, Cities in the Wilderness (New York: Alfred A. Knopf, 1938), pp. 233-34, 252.

[20]For further documentation of this thesis, see my The American Pietism of Cotton Mather.

[21]Bready, England, Before and After Wesley, p. 40.

[22]Alan Heimert, Religion and the American Mind (Cambridge: Harvard Univ. Press, 1966).

[23]Edwards, Thoughts on the Revival, p. 522.

[24]Ibid., p. 527.

[25]Edwards, Religious Affections, p. 369.

[26]Jonathan Edwards, "Christian Charity," in Works, (New York: Burt Franklin, 1968), V, 420-22, 426-27.

[27]Lewis, Zinzendorf, pp. 93-94.

[28]Jorns, The Quakers As Pioneers, pp. 206-7.

[29]Bready, England, Before and After Wesley, pp. 248-50; see also pp. 225-52, 316.

[30]Howse, Saints in Politics, pp. 73-76.

[31]Jorns, The Quakers As Pioneers, pp. 209-14.

[32]Howse, *Saints in Politics*, p. 32, see also pp. 10-12.

[33]See Brown, *Fathers of the Victorians*.

[34]Howse, *Saints in Politics*, p. 137.

[35]Earle E. Cairns, *Saints and Society* (Chicago: Moody, 1960), p. 60.

[36]C. C. Cole, *The Social Ideas of the Northern Evangelists* (New York: Octagon Books, 1966), p. 102; see also Foster, *An Errand of Mercy*, pp. 275-80, where the various societies are itemized.

[37]See Beecher, *Autobiography*.

[38]Gilbert Barnes, *The Antislavery Impulse, 1830-1844* (Gloucester, Mass.: P. Smith, 1973).

[39]Marsden, *The Evangelical Mind and the New School Presbyterian Experience*, pp. 7-23, 31-39.

[40]Alexis de Toqueville, *Democracy in America*, 2 Vols. (New York: Vintage Books, 1945), I, 314.

[41]Philip Schaff, *America* (New York: Scribner, 1854), pp. 94, 118.

[42]See J. Wesley Bready, *Lord Shaftesbury and Social-Industrial Progress* (London: G. Allen & Unwin Ltd., 1926); Georgina Battiscombe, *Shaftesbury: The Great Reformer, 1801-1885* (Boston: Houghton Mifflin, 1975).

[43]Kathleen Heasman, *Evangelicals in Action* (London: Geoffrey Bles, 1962), pp. 286-87.

[44]Kenneth Scott Latourette, *Christianity in a Revolutionary Age* (New York: Harper, 1958-62), II, 102-6.

[45]Ibid., pp. 239-49; see Abraham Kuyper, *Christianity and the Class Struggle*, trans. Dirk Jellema (Grand Rapids: Piet Hein, 1950).

[46]Timothy L. Smith, *Revivalism and Social Reform in Mid-Nineteenth Century America* (New York: Abingdon, 1957).

[47]Calvin Colton, *Protestant Jesuitism* (New York: Harper & Bros., 1836)

[48]Foster, *An Errand of Mercy*, p. 273; Marsden, *The Evangelical Mind*, pp. 71-75.

[49]Quoted in Curtis, *They Called Him Mr. Moody*, p. 266.

[50]E. J. Goodspeed, *A Full History of the Wonderful Career of Moody and Sankey in Great Britain and America* (New York: Henry S. Goodspeed, 1876), pp. 234-35.

[51]Paul Henry, *Politics for Evangelicals* (Valley Forge, Pa.: Judson Press, 1974), pp. 29-48.

[52]While the Men and Religion Forward Movement has often been treated as an outgrowth of the social gospel, Gary Smith has shown (in a paper so far unpublished) that this crusade was supported and led by moderate Evangelicals working together with more liberal Christians.

[53]Moberg, *The Great Reversal*, p. 36.

[54]Carl Henry, *The Uneasy Conscience of Modern Fundamentalism* (Grand Rapids: Eerdmans, 1947).

[55]Compare Henry's *Aspects of Christian Social Ethics* (Grand Rapids: Eerdmans, 1964), which is predominately a conservative critique of non-Evangelical strategies of social reform, with *A Plea for Evangelical Demonstration* (Grand Rapids: Baker Book House, 1971).

[56]Richard Quebedeaux, The Young Evangelicals (New York: Harper and Row, 1974).

[57]Ronald J. Sider, ed., The Chicago Declaration (Carol Stream, Ill.: Creation House, 1974).

[58]J. D. Douglas, ed., Let the Earth Hear His Voice, pp. 116-46, 271-72, 303-26, 675-97, 1251-66.

[59]Florence M. G. Higham, Lord Shaftesbury: A Portrait (London: SCM Press, 1945), p. 32.

[60]Ibid., p. 87.

[61]See Rebecca J. Winter, The Night Cometh (South Pasadena, Calif.: William Carey Library, 1977); Bertram Wyatt-Brown, Lewis Tappan and the Evangelical War against Slavery (Cleveland: Press of Case Western Reserve University, 1969).

[62]Cole, The Social Ideas, p. 208.

[63]Stoeffler, The Rise of Evangelical Pietism, pp. 212-17.

[64]Harvey Cox, The Secular City (New York: Macmillan, 1975), pp. 149-63; Vernon C. Grounds, Evangelicalism and Social Responsibility (Scottdale, Pa.: Herald, 1969), p. 99; see Richard J. Mouw, Political Evangelism (Grand Rapids: Eerdmans, 1974), pp. 15-18; Richard J. Mouw, Politics and the Biblical Drama (Grand Rapids: Eerdmans, 1975), pp. 85-116; John Howard Yoder, The Politics of Jesus (Grand Rapids: Eerdmans, 1972), pp. 136-52; Jim Wallis, Agenda for Biblical People (New York: Harper and Row, 1976), pp. 63-77.

[65]Mouw, Politics and the Biblical Drama, p. 89.

[66]Yoder, Politics of Jesus, p. 153.

[67]See H. Richard Niebuhr, Christ and Culture (New York: Harper, 1951).

[68]George Eldon Ladd, The Presence of the Future (Grand Rapids: Eerdmans, 1974); Philippe Maury, Politics and Evangelism, trans. Marguerite Wieser (Garden City, N.Y.: Doubleday, 1960).

[69]For an analysis of the biblical material supporting this judgment, see Yoder, Politics of Jesus, pp. 26-63.

[70]See Ronald J. Sider, Rich Christians in an Age of Hunger (Downers Grove, Ill.: InterVarsity Press, 1977).

[71]For an interesting spectrum of scenarios for Christian social action matched to differing political environments, see Samuel Escobar's analysis in Douglas, ed., Let the Earth Hear His Voice, pp. 313-14.

[72]See Reinhold Niebuhr, Moral Man and Immoral Society (New York: Scribner, 1932).

[73]Bready, Lord Shaftesbury, pp. 21-22.

[74]Brown, Fathers of the Victorians, p. 41.

[75]Foster, An Errand of Mercy, p. 62.

[76]Moberg, The Great Reversal, p. 40.

[77]See Vernon C. Grounds, Revolution and the Christian Faith (Philadelphia: Lippincott, 1971); George Orwell, Animal Farm (New York: Harcourt, Brace and Co., 1946).

[78]Jean-Claude Revel, Without Marx or Jesus, trans. J. F. Bornard (New York: Dell Pub. Co., 1972).

Chapter 13
[1]Calvin Colton, *History and Character of American Revivals of Religion*, 2nd ed. (London: Frederick Westley and A. H. Davis, 1838), pp. 141-43.
[2]Ibid., pp. 195-96.
[3]Edwards, *The History of Redemption*, in *Works* (New York: Burt Franklin, 1968), V, 226-27.
[4]Ibid., p. 251, 253.
[5]J. D. Douglas, ed., *Let the Earth Hear His Voice* (Minneapolis: World Wide Publications, 1975), pp. 23-44.
[6]Ibid., p. 1466.
[7]David Wilkerson, *The Vision* (Benwood, W. Va.: Pyramid Press, 1974)
[8]Besides Clement of Alexandria and Origen, early church leaders who were not chiliasts include Clement of Rome, Ignatius, Polycarp and the author of the *Epistle to Diognetus*. See D. H. Kromminga, *The Millennium in the Church* (Grand Rapids: Eerdmans, 1945), pp. 41-52.
[9]Ibid., pp. 102-13.
[10]Ibid., pp. 114-24.
[11]See Iain Murray, *The Puritan Hope* (London: Banner of Truth Trust, 1971), and J. A. de Jong, *As the Waters Cover the Sea: Millennial Expectations in the Rise of Anglo-American Missions 1640-1810* (Kampen: Kok, 1970).
[12]Peter Toon, *Puritans, The Millennium and the Future of Israel* (Cambridge: J. Clarke, 1970).
[13]For a study of an activistic premillennialist who expected renewal and expansion of the church as a prelude to the conversion of the Jews and the return of Christ, see my *The American Pietism of Cotton Mather*.
[14]See de Jong, *As the Waters Cover the Sea*.
[15]Murray, *The Puritan Hope*, pp. 150-55.
[16]Georgina Battiscombe, *Shaftesbury: The Great Reformer* (Boston: Houghton-Mifflin, 1975), p. 287.
[17]See my "The Occult Revival in Historical Context," in *Demon Possession*, ed. John Warwick Montgomery (Minneapolis: Bethany Fellowship, 1975), pp. 65-90.
[18]Vergil, *Georgics*, II, as quoted in Gay, *The Rise of Modern Paganism*, p. 99; see further pp. 100-2, 45-55.
[19]Gay, *The Rise of Modern Paganism*.
[20]Robert Heilbroner, *An Enquiry into the Human Prospect* (New York: Norton, 1974), pp. 136-37.
[21]Kahn and Bruce-Briggs, *Things to Come: Thinking about the Seventies and Eighties*. Herman Kahn, William Brown and Leon Martel, *The Next Two Hundred Years* (New York: Morrow, 1976).
[22]R. Buckminster Fuller, *Operating Manual for Spaceship Earth* (New York: Pocket Books, 1969); *Utopia or Oblivion* (London: Allen Lane, 1970).
[23]Colton, *Revivals of Religion*, pp. 164-67.
[24]Edwards, *History of Redemption*, pp. 226-27.

Index

Chapter headings and subheadings have not been included in the index. To locate a discussion of a particular subject, always consult the table of contents as well as the index.